The book series 'Contributions to Finance and Accounting' features the latest research from research areas like financial management, investment, capital markets, financial institutions, FinTech and financial innovation, accounting methods and standards, reporting, and corporate governance, among others. Books published in this series are primarily monographs and edited volumes that present new research results, both theoretical and empirical, on a clearly defined topic. All books are published in print and digital formats and disseminated globally.

This book series is indexed in Scopus.

Claudia-Diana Sabău-Popa
Editor

Artificial Intelligence in Finance, Accounting and Business Administration

Applications and Challenges in the Romanian and Hungarian Context

Springer

Editor
Claudia-Diana Sabău-Popa
University of Oradea, Faculty of Economic Sciences
Oradea, Romania

ISSN 2730-6038 ISSN 2730-6046 (electronic)
Contributions to Finance and Accounting
ISBN 978-3-032-22736-2 ISBN 978-3-032-22737-9 (eBook)
https://doi.org/10.1007/978-3-032-22737-9

This Springer imprint is published by the registered company Springer Nature Switzerland AG
The registered company address is: Gewerbestrasse 11, 6330 Cham, Switzerland

Preface

Artificial intelligence has emerged as a transformative force reshaping economies, industries, and societies across the globe. The integration of AI technologies into finance, accounting, and business administration represents not merely a technological advancement, but a fundamental reimagining of how organizations create value, make decisions, and compete in an increasingly digital world. This book explores this transformation through the lens of two neighbouring Central European nations—Romania and Hungary—whose experiences offer valuable insights for policymakers, academics, practitioners, and students navigating the AI revolution.

This book has been developed and funded within the project titled *Exchange of Experience for research and usage of Artificial Intelligence' Advanced Techniques in finance, accounting and business administration in Bihor-Hajdu Bihar Region*, code ROHU00120, financing contract number 37950/19.02.2025 and acronyms E2U-AI. This project was funded under the Interreg VI-A Romania-Hungary Programme, the period of implementation is from 19.02.2025 to 18.02.26. The two project partners involved in implementing project activities are: University of Oradea (Romania)—as partnership leader and University of Debrecen (Hungary)- as project partner. The E2U-AI project was conceived with a clear purpose: to foster cross-border institutional collaboration and knowledge exchange on advanced artificial intelligence techniques within the Bihor–Hajdú-Bihar Euroregion.

Team experts of the project from University of Oradea, Faculty of Economic Sciences and from University of Debrecen, Faculty of Economics and Business and lecturers of the training courses in AI applied in finance, accounting and business administration, each of whom were authors or coauthors of a chapter, are involved in the elaboration of this book.

The structure of this book reflects a comprehensive approach to understanding AI's role in contemporary economies. It begins by establishing the state of the art in AI applications across finance, accounting, and business administration in both countries. It then examines the broader digital economy landscape, governmental initiatives, and labor market responses to technological change. Subsequent sections present concrete case studies of AI implementation in companies, public sector pilot projects, and successful fintech startups. The final chapters address research perspectives, human capital development, and future directions for regional collaboration.

This volume is designed as a valuable resource for various audiences: master's and doctoral students who want to know and understand advanced artificial intelligence techniques applied in finance, accounting, and business administration; researchers and academics exploring the intersection of technology, economics, and organizational change; business professionals and executives evaluating artificial intelligence adoption strategies; decision-makers and government agencies designing digital transformation initiatives.

The findings and perspectives presented here reflect genuine cross-border collaboration and the commitment of both universities to advancing knowledge in service of economic and social progress. We hope this book contributes meaningfully to the ongoing global conversation about how artificial intelligence can be harnessed responsibly, ethically, and effectively to create value for organizations and society.

Oradea, Romania

Full professor Claudia-Diana Sabău-Popa
Dean of Faculty of Economic Sciences, University of Oradea, Manager of the project ROHU00120, Acronym E2U-AI

Contents

Contributors

Péter Bajnai Faculty of Economics and Business, University of Debrecen, Debrecen, Hungary

Olimpia Iuliana Ban Faculty of Economic Sciences, University of Oradea, Oradea, Romania

Alexandra-Maria Bele Faculty of Economic Sciences, University of Oradea, Oradea, Romania

Corneliu Cristian Benţe Faculty of Economic Sciences, University of Oradea, Oradea, Romania

Victoria Bogdan Faculty of Economic Sciences, University of Oradea, Oradea, Romania

Elena Aurelia Botezat Faculty of Economic Sciences, University of Oradea, Oradea, Romania

Dorin Cristian Coita Faculty of Economic Sciences, University of Oradea, Oradea, Romania

Alexandru Constăngioara Faculty of Economic Sciences, University of Oradea, Oradea, Romania

Liviu-Adrian Cotfas Bucharest University of Economic Studies, Bucharest, Romania

Camelia Delcea Bucharest University of Economic Studies, Bucharest, Romania

Anca Otilia Dodescu Faculty of Economic Sciences, University of Oradea, Oradea, Romania

Laurenţiu Droj Faculty of Economic Sciences, University of Oradea, Oradea, Romania

István Füzesi Faculty of Economics and Business, University of Debrecen, Debrecen, Hungary

Dóra Gazdag-Kerezsi Faculty of Economics and Business, University of Debrecen, Debrecen, Hungary

Dana-Simona Gherai Faculty of Economic Sciences, University of Oradea, Oradea, Romania

Anita Kiss Faculty of Economics and Business, University of Debrecen, Debrecen, Hungary

Peter Lengyel Faculty of Economics and Business, University of Debrecen, Debrecen, Hungary

Codruţa Mare Faculty of Economics and Business Administration, Babeş-Bolyai University, Cluj Napoca, Romania

Diana Elisabeta Matica Faculty of Economic Sciences, University of Oradea, Oradea, Romania

Diana Claudia Perţicaş Faculty of Economic Sciences, University of Oradea, Oradea, Romania

Dorina-Nicoleta Popa Faculty of Economic Sciences, University of Oradea, Oradea, Romania

Luminiţa Rus Faculty of Economic Sciences, University of Oradea, Oradea, Romania

Claudia-Diana Sabău-Popa Faculty of Economic Sciences, University of Oradea, Oradea, Romania

Carmen Mihaela Scorţe Faculty of Economic Sciences, University of Oradea, Oradea, Romania

Monica Ariana Sim Faculty of Economic Sciences, University of Oradea, Oradea, Romania

János Szenderák Faculty of Economics and Business, University of Debrecen, Debrecen, Hungary

Gergő Tömöri Faculty of Economics and Business, University of Debrecen, Debrecen, Hungary

List of Figures

State of the Art of Artificial Intelligence Application in Finance, Accounting and Business Administration in Romania and Hungary

The Current State of the Digital Economy in Romania and Hungary

Governmental Initiatives and EU-Funded Projects

The Romanian Labour Market and Its Response to Digital Transformation

AI in Data Visualisation

AI in Data Analysis: A STATA Guide

Artificial Intelligence for Enhanced Integrated Reporting in Romania

A Successful Romanian AI-Based FinTech Startup

Regional Collaboration: AI Initiatives in Central and Eastern Europe

List of Tables

State of the Art of Artificial Intelligence Application in Finance, Accounting and Business Administration in Romania and Hungary

Camelia Delcea, Liviu-Adrian Cotfas, and Claudia-Diana Sabău-Popa

Abstract Recent advances in artificial intelligence (AI) have permeated economics, particularly finance, accounting, and business administration, enabling automation through predictive algorithms, robotic processes, and large language models. This chapter examines the state of the art in AI applications within these domains in Romania and Hungary—two rapidly digitizing Central and Eastern European economies with distinct institutional capacities. We used bibliometric analysis of a articles Clarivate Analytics Web of Science Core Collection, complemented by topic modelling via Latent Dirichlet Allocation (LDA) and BERTopic. The review highlights finance-focused areas (risk management, predictive modelling, customer innovation), cautious AI integration in accounting, and diverse business administration applications (economic development, digital transformation). Despite modest publication volume, methodological sophistication has grown significantly.

1 Introduction

The advances made in the latest period in the field of artificial intelligence (AI) have been further translated into various research areas, including economics, and the fields of finance, accounting, and business administration have not been left behind.

As a result of the rapid diffusion of AI technologies, which has been made through various transmission channels such as the predictive algorithms provided, the robotic automation processes or the rise of the large language models, new opportunities for automation have been created, with effects in risk management and strategic planning. Considering the European Union, where the digital transformation has been

C. Delcea · L.-A. Cotfas
Bucharest University of Economic Studies, Bucharest, Romania

C.-D. Sabău-Popa (✉)
Faculty of Economic Sciences, University of Oradea, Oradea, Romania
e-mail: dpopa@uoradea.ro

C. Sabău-Popa (ed.), *Artificial Intelligence in Finance, Accounting and Business Administration*, Contributions to Finance and Accounting,
https://doi.org/10.1007/978-3-032-22737-9_1

made across all the member states, it has been observed that the national adoption patterns remain uneven.

As two dynamically evolving economies in Central and Eastern Europe, Romania and Hungary have been characterised by a rapid digitalisation, even though institutional capacities and innovation ecosystems have been different in the two-mentioned countries.

In this context, the present chapter aims to shed some light on the state of the art of AI applications in finance, accounting, and business administration in Romania and Hungary. Based on a bibliometric analysis approach, doubled by a topic analysis, the chapter aims to map the main research directions, collaboration networks, and emerging trends identified in the papers selected from the Clarivate Analytics Web of Science Core Collection regarding the use of AI in applications developed in the two mentioned countries.

Furthermore, by identifying basic, motor, niche, and emerging themes, the chapter highlights the intellectual structure of this research field and its evolution over the considered period, with the purpose of providing relevant insights to policy-makers, educators, and practitioners aiming to strengthen digital competitiveness in the region.

The chapter is structured as follows: an overview of the selected research is provided in Sect. 2, Thematic analysis through the use of bibliometric tools is discussed in Sect. 3, 4 and 5, while Sect. 6 is dedicated to topic analysis through the use of Latent Dirichlet Allocation (LDA) and BERTopic. A review of the most relevant works is put forward in Sect. 4. The paper ends with concluding remarks.

2 Overview of the Selected Research

The dataset extracted by following the steps highlighted in the previous section is analysed in this section in terms of authors, sources and citations, providing an overview of the dataset.

The characteristics of the dataset are discussed in Tables 1–4. The mentioned tables offer the values extracted for various indicators that provide a better understanding of the papers included in the dataset.

The timespan for the selected papers is 2007–2024, while the number of sources in which the papers have been published is 18. Please consider the data in Table 1. Given the fact that the dataset is made by 22 papers, the number of sources indicates a dissipative choice for the sources, being expected that in most of the cases each paper is published in a different journal, with only a few papers being published in the same journal.

Based on the data provided in Table 1 an annual growth rate of 13.01% can be noticed, which is a promising value given the growth rate of similar economic fields. The value of the indicator average years from publication is 3.55, showing that most of the papers have been published in the recent years, highlighting once more the development of this research field and continuous growth.

Table 1 Main information about the data

Indicator	Value
Timespan	2007:2024
Sources (Journals, Books, etc.)	18
Documents	22
Annual growth rate (%)	13.01
Average years from publication	3.55
Average citations per documents	4.909
References	1214

Table 2 Document contents

Indicator	Value
Keywords Plus (ID)	54
Author's Keywords (DE)	96

Table 3 Authors

Indicator	Value
Authors	67
Authors of single-authored documents	4

The average citations per document are quite high, namely 4.909, given the short period of time since the papers' publication.

The number of references used in the 22 papers included in the dataset is 1214, which gives approximately 55.18 references per paper.

In terms of keywords, as reported in Table 2, a number of 96 authors' keywords have been extracted, which will be further used in the word analyses and thematic maps provided in this chapter.

Furthermore, 54 Keywords Plus have been extracted for the 22 papers included in the dataset. It should be mentioned that the Keywords Plus (ISI WOS) are a particular category of keywords, extracted by the Clarivate Analytics Web of Science database based on the most used words in the titles of the papers cited by the papers included in the dataset. Even this type of keyword will be further used in the analyses conducted on the extracted dataset.

Regarding the authors of the papers included in the dataset, a number of 67 authors have been identified, with only 4 authors writing single-authored papers, as presented in Table 3.

Table 4 provides information related to the author's collaboration network. It can be observed that there are 5 documents of single author, while the number of co-authors per document is 3.09, which is in line with the expectations given the specificity of the field. It is known that papers in the economic area tend to have fewer authors per paper than other domains, such as medicine.

Table 4 Authors collaboration

Indicator	Value
Single-authored documents	5
Co-Authors per Documents	3.09
International co-authorship (%)	0

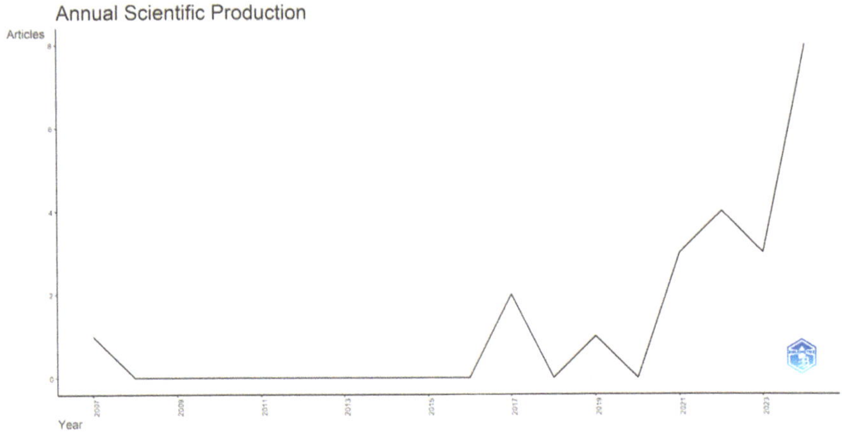

Fig. 1 Annual scientific production evolution

Different from the results encountered in other bibliometric analyses (Sandu et al. 2025; Cişmaşu et al. 2025; Tsilika 2023), the international co-authorship is 0% in this case, suggesting that the authors have preferred to conduct the research by collaborating with other researchers from the same country rather than from a different country. This situation is to some extent explainable through the specificity of the selected domain, which focuses on studies in finance, accounting and business administration in two particular countries, as mentioned before, namely Romania and Hungary.

Figure 1 provides information with regard to the annual scientific production. As observed from the values recorded for the Average years from publication indicator, it is expected that the papers included in the dataset to be mostly published in the years close to the end of the analysis period, namely year 2024.

In terms of article citations, the evolution of the average article citations per year is highlighted in Fig. 2. As observed, there is a boom in citations starting with 2019 which might be due to the increasement in publication in the years following the COVID-19 pandemic, but can be, in the same time, due to the advancement made in the AI area and the inclusion of these advancements into various fields, such as, in our case, the field of finance, accounting and business administration.

Regarding the sources, Fig. 3 provides an overview of the outlets. The journals *Sustainability* and *Electronics* contribute the largest share of articles (three).

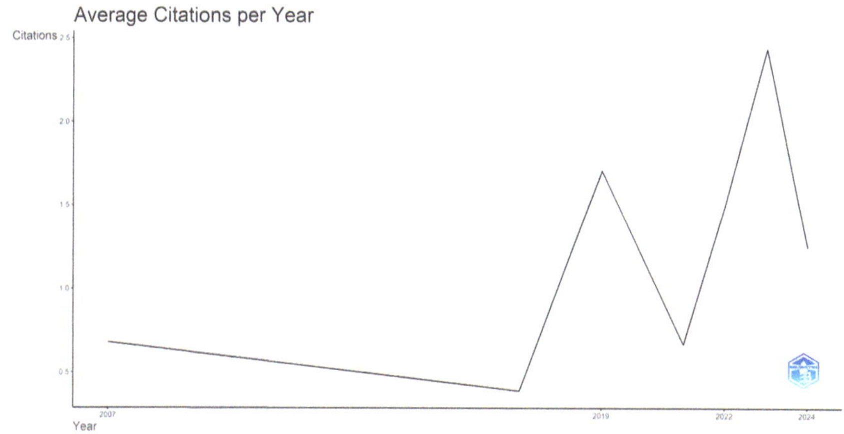

Fig. 2 Annual average article citations per year evolution

Several journals contribute one article each, showcasing the wide disciplinary dispersion of AI-related scholarship. These include *Amfiteatru economic, Brain—broad research in artificial intelligence and neuroscience, Central European business review, Electronics, Information, International journal of sociology and social policy, International journal of strategic property management, Journal of East European management studies, Market—Trziste, Public finance quarterly—Hungary, Romanian journal of economic forecasting, Romanian statistical review, Studies in informatics and control, Sustainability, TalTech journal of European studies, Telecom, Transfer—European review of labour and research*, and *Transformations in business & economics.*

Fig. 3 Journals

The journals' productivity is further assessed through the Bradford's Law (Onyancha and Ocholla 2022). According to this law, a picture of the journals' productivity is presented by arranging them in descending order by the number of published articles and citations, and separating them into 3 zones. According to this principle, a limited number of journals account for a relatively large proportion of the total publications, while the majority of journals contribute only a few articles each. As a result, the most influential and frequently cited journals are identified as core sources and grouped within Zone 1. This categorisation enables researchers to concentrate their efforts on these key outlets when conducting comprehensive literature reviews.

For the extracted dataset, Fig. 4. Depicts the results of the Bradford's Law. As expected, in the core sources area are the journals with the highest number of papers, namely *Electronics* and *Sustainability*, as well as some journals in the remainder list (the ones that are alphabetically listed at the top of the list of journals which have published only one paper).

H-index indicator is further provided. This index is a measure of the number of papers published in a journal that has been cited H times each (Woeginger 2008). Figure 5 provides the results for the considered dataset. As it can be observed, there are only two journals with a H-index greater than 1, namely *Sustainability* and *Electronics*, both of them with a H-index of 2. The small values recorded in this case can be due to the reduced number of papers included in the dataset, as well as the reduced number of years between the papers' publication and the time of this analysis.

As for the journals' growth, the analysis has been conducted for the two most prominent journals by number of published papers and H-index, namely *Sustainability* and *Electronics*. As observed from Fig. 6, the papers included in the dataset have been published in these journals after 2022, with a visible increase in the recent years.

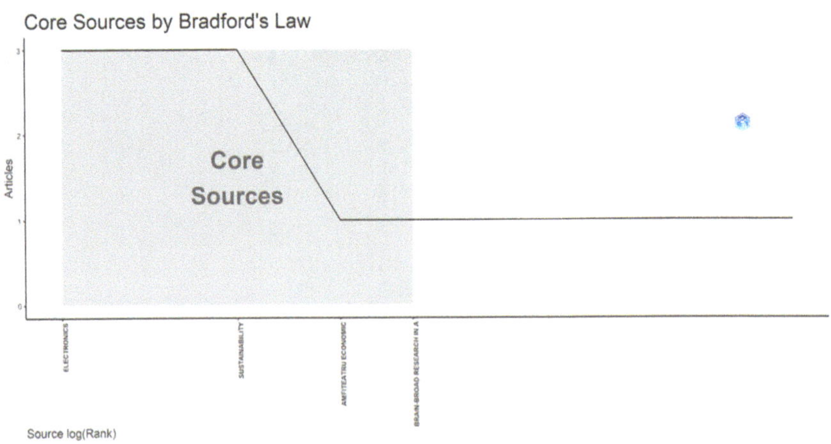

Fig. 4 Bradford's law on source clustering

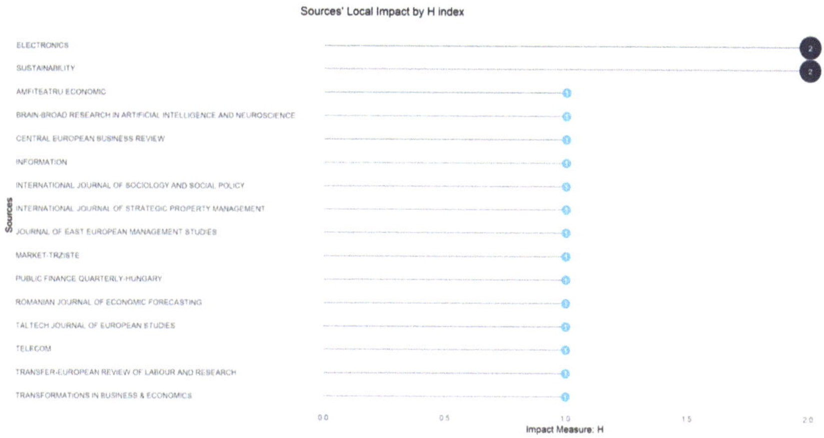

Fig. 5 Journals' impact based on H-index

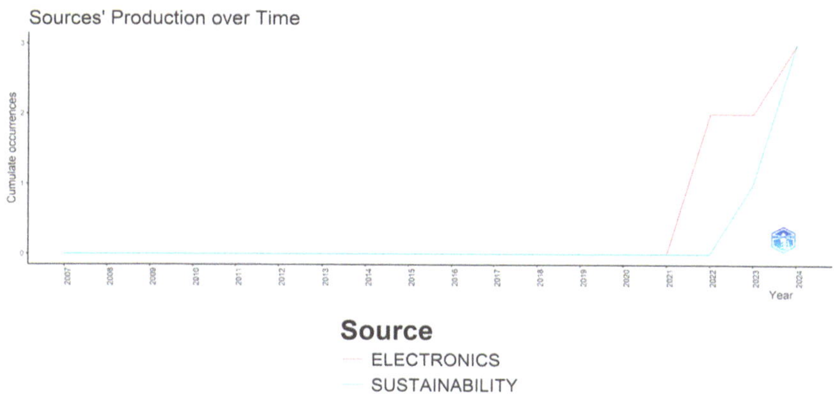

Fig. 6 Journals' growth (cumulative) based on the number of papers

In terms of the most prominent authors as resulting from the number of citations, all the authors except for Varzaru A. have had a number of one paper, while the mentioned author has written two papers included in the extracted dataset.

As for the most relevant affiliations, which resulted from the number of papers published and included in the dataset, the results highlighted in Fig. 7 have been obtained. In Fig. 7 only the affiliations with more than two contributions have been listed, the remainder of the affiliations (not listed in the figure) have only contributed with a paper to the body of work.

The worldwide visualisation map in Fig. 8 provides contributions from each country. As it can be observed, due to the restrained area of research, the contributions have mainly been from countries such as Romania—with 16 outlets, Hungary—4 outlets, and Denmark and Russia—each of them with 1 outlet.

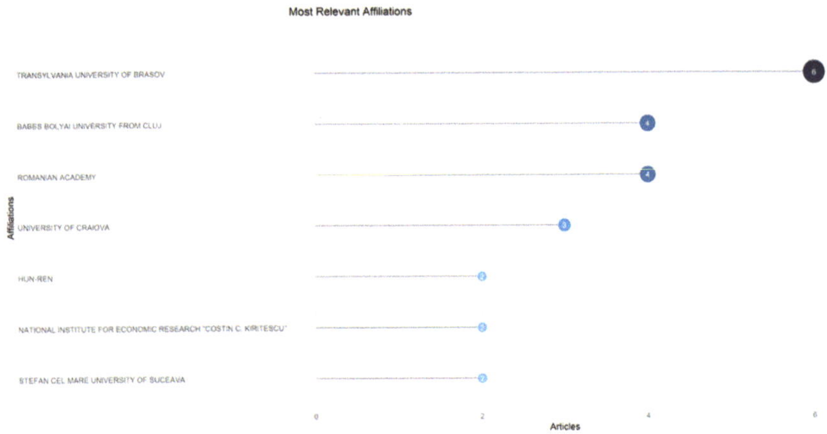

Fig. 7 Most relevant affiliations

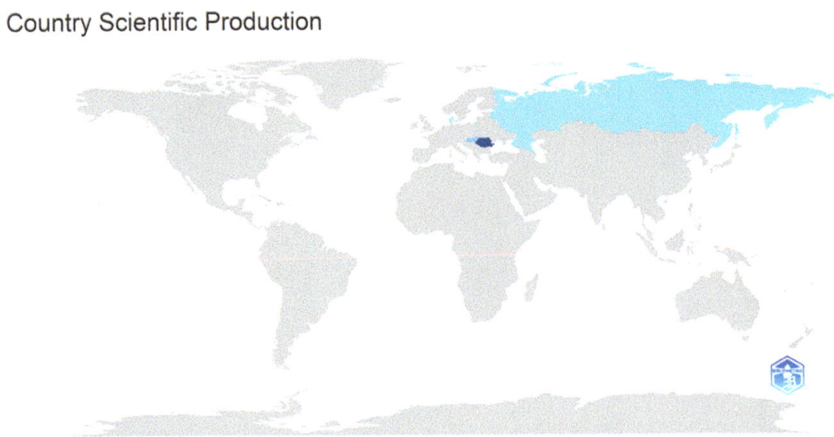

Fig. 8 Scientific production based on country

In terms of most cited countries, Romania leads the top with 79 citations, followed by Hungary with 21 citations, as depicted in Fig. 9.

Considering the extracted documents, in the following, an analysis of the most used words has been performed.

First, the most used keywords in the authors' keywords have been extracted. As presented in Table 5, it can be observed that the most frequent word is "artificial intelligence" with 14 occurrences, followed by "Hungary" with 3 occurrences, "machine learning" with 3 occurrences, while the remainder of the words have had only 2 occurrences.

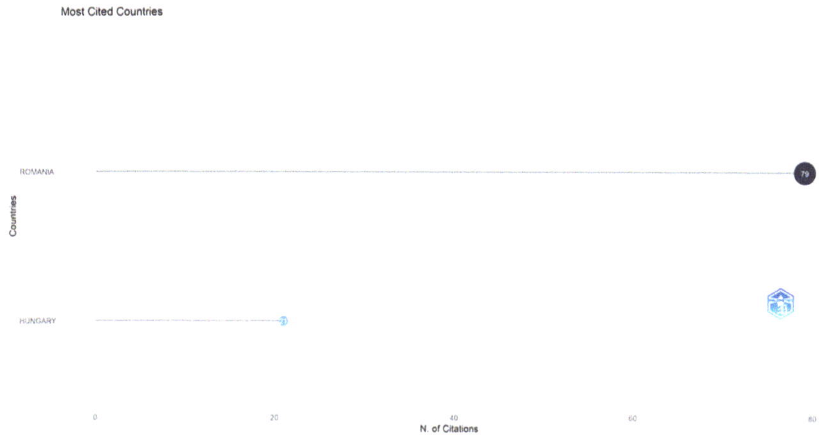

Fig. 9 Citations based on countries

Table 5 Most frequent words in authors' keywords

Words	Occurrences
artificial intelligence	14
Hungary	3
machine learning	3
chatbots	2
digital technologies	2
e-commerce	2
technology acceptance	2

The most frequent unigrams in titles are depicted in Table 6. Even in this case, among the most used unigrams it can be observed that one can encounter the "artificial", "intelligence", "ai" words, along with "Romania" and other specific keywords related to the area of research, such as "banking", "market", "accounting", "impact", and "models".

In terms of bigrams in titles and abstracts, the information in Table 7 has been retrieved. While for the titles, only the "artificial intelligence" bigram outstands the other extracted bigrams, having an occurrence of 5 times, in the case of the bigrams in the abstracts, various bigrams have been extracted.

Even in the case of the abstracts, the "artificial intelligence" bigram stands out, having the highest number of occurrences, followed by other bigrams which shape the selected research field: "managerial accounting" and "smart technologies"—each one of them with 7 occurrences, "digital technologies" and "project management"—each one of them with 6 occurrences, "intelligence ai" and "machine learning"—each one of them with 5 occurrences, and the remainder of the bigrams with 4 occurrences "acceptance model", "accounting profession", "customer satisfaction".

Table 6 Most frequent unigrams in titles

Words	Occurrences
artificial	8
intelligence	5
banking	4
Market	4
Romania	4
accounting	3
AI	3
Impact	3
Models	3

Table 7 Top 10 most frequent bigrams in abstracts and titles

Bigrams in abstracts	Occurrences	Bigrams in titles	Occurrences
artificial intelligence	23	artificial intelligence	5
managerial accounting	7	accounting profession	1
smart technologies	7	adoption behavior	1
digital technologies	6	ai development	1
project management	6	ai impact	1
intelligence ai	5	ai solutions	1
machine learning	5	artificial intelligence-based	1
acceptance model	4	artificial neural	1
accounting profession	4	artificial systems	1
customer satisfaction	4	banking chatbot	1

Furthermore, the Keywords Plus option offered by the Clarivate Analytics Web of Science Collection platform to extract the most used keywords from the titles of the cited papers has been used and the data in Table 8 has been obtained.

Thus, it can be observed that even in the case of the references used in the selected papers, the most used keyword is "artificial intelligence" with 4 occurrences. Also, the keyword "model" is also present in the list with an equal number of occurrences as "artificial intelligence". The remainder of the keywords are listed in Table 8.

A summary of the top-50 words in Keywords Plus, authors' keywords, titles and abstracts is depicted in Fig. 10.

Figure 11 provides an overall view on the most frequent keywords, no matter the provenience of these keywords, namely from abstracts, titles, and authors' keywords. As expected, the central keyword is "artificial intelligence", part of the largest cluster depicted in red in the figure.

In order to better understand the co-occurrence network provided in Fig. 11, the additional information offered by Biblioshiny, such as the cluster, betweenness centrality value, closeness centrality value and PageRank have been used.

Table 8 Most frequent Keywords Plus

Words	Occurrences
artificial-intelligence	4
model	4
technologies	3
analytics	2
big data	2
digitization	2
impact	2
networks	2
prediction	2
technology acceptance model	2

From the analysis, it has been noticed that 4 clusters have been determined, one of them characterised by AI and digitalisation (cluster 1, in red), modelling and adoption (cluster 2, in blue), an analytics/data-driven cluster (cluster 3, in green), and a digital transformation cluster (cluster 4, in purple).

Furthermore, the heatmap in Fig. 12 reveals a single dominant cluster, made by several conceptual zones.

The first zone that can be observed is a core high-density zone (center–top left) dominated by "artificial intelligence", "artificial-intelligence", "technologies", and "digital transformation", followed by a zone characterized by adjacent concepts, positioned in the middle-right side of the map, characterized by words such as "digitization," "digital technologies," "big data," "analytics," "communication".

The third zone, located in the upper region of the heatmap, is dedicated to applied and managerial contexts, characterised by words such as "e-commerce," "chatbots," "impact," "Hungary".

Lastly, the fourth zone, located in the lower region of the map, refers to methodological and conceptual aspects, being characterised by words such as "model," "machine learning," "prediction," "technology acceptance".

Going further with the analysis and considering the values reported for the betweenness centrality, it can be observed that "artificial intelligence" (with a value of 35) acts as the main connector linking the other separate research themes. Another keyword, "model" (with a value of 1), also serves a minor bridging role between the applied and technical clusters.

The highest closeness values (0.5 or 1.0) with respect to the Closeness centrality indicator belong to "model," "machine learning," "technology acceptance," "analytics," "big data," and "digital transformation," showing these are highly integrated concepts within their clusters.

Lastly, in terms of PageRank, it has been noticed that "artificial intelligence" (0.238) dominates the field, with a value reported for this indicator that exceeds all the other values. Additionally, "digital transformation" and "digitisation" (≈0.056) are secondary anchors.

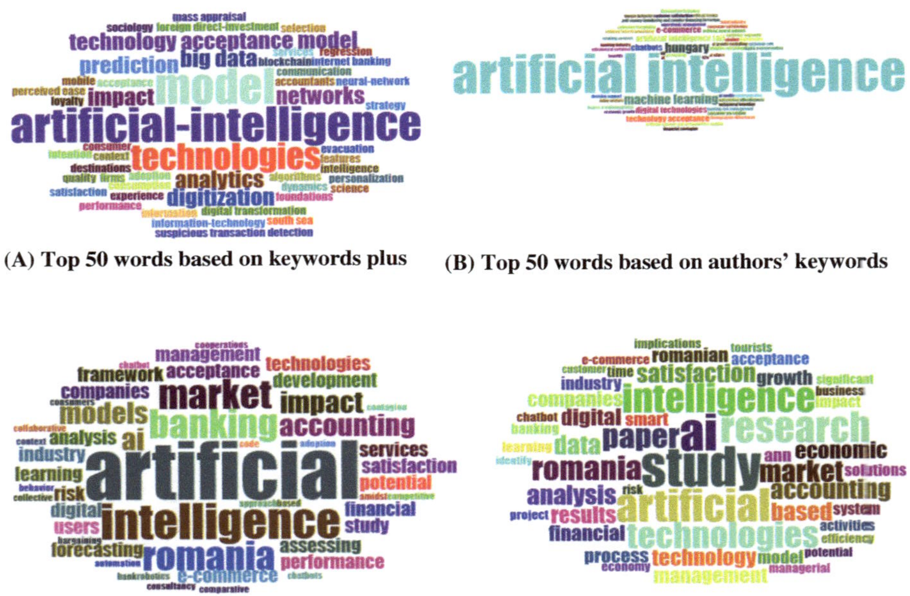

(A) Top 50 words based on keywords plus

(B) Top 50 words based on authors' keywords

(C) Top 50 words based on title

(D) Top 50 words based on abstract

Fig. 10 Top-50 words based on keywords plus (**a**), authors' keywords (**b**), title (**c**), abstract (**d**)

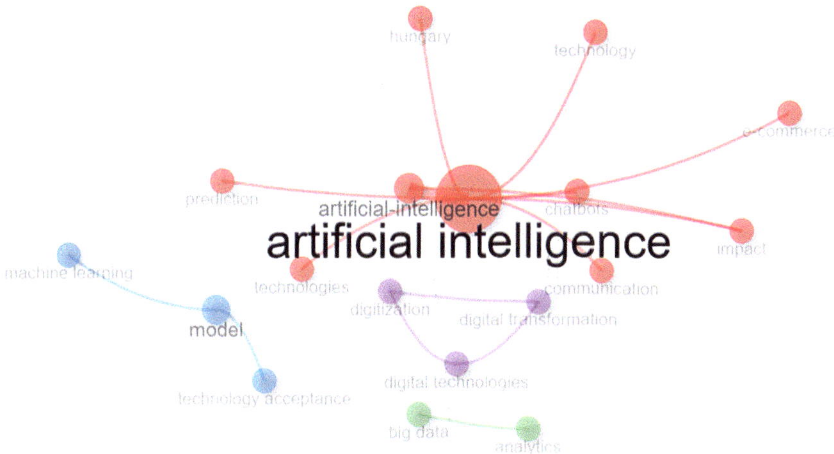

Fig. 11 Co-occurrence network based on all keywords

Table 9 groups into thematic clusters the information gathered through the analysis of the values extracted for betweenness centrality value, closeness centrality value and PageRank, providing an overview of the keywords in each cluster, the central node, while highlighting the role of the cluster and a possible interpretation of the studies included here.

Based on the information in Table 9, it can be stated that Cluster #1 refers to a core theme, represented by *Artificial Intelligence and digital communication,* Cluster #2 is focused on *Modelling and adoption*, Cluster #3 is dedicated to *Data analytics*, while Cluster #4 refers to *Digital transformation and technologies.*

3 Collaboration Networks Characteristics

Clarivate Analytics' Web of Science Core Collection database, also known as Web of Science (2025) has been used for the extraction of the dataset for the bibliometric analysis and topics discovery. The choice for this database has been grounded on other research conducted in the field, such as, but not limited to cybernetics (Cibu et al. 2023), agent-based modelling (Domenteanu et al. 2025a), agent-based modelling in transportation (Domenteanu et al. 2023), urban decision-making (Sandu et al. 2024), hernia surgery (Carhuallanqui-Ciocca et al. 2023), sarcopenia (Koca 2023), machine learning and big data (López Belmonte et al. 2020), twitter-related studies (Yu and Muñoz-Justicia 2020), transportation research journals research (Modak et al. 2019), digital era governance (Ravšelj et al. 2022), electric vehicles (Domenteanu et al. 2025b), smart cities (Dobre et al. 2025), neutrosophic theory mapping (Delcea et al. 2023), grey systems theory mapping (Sandu et al. 2025). Even more, the choice for the use of this database has been supported by Valente et al. (2022) who have underlined

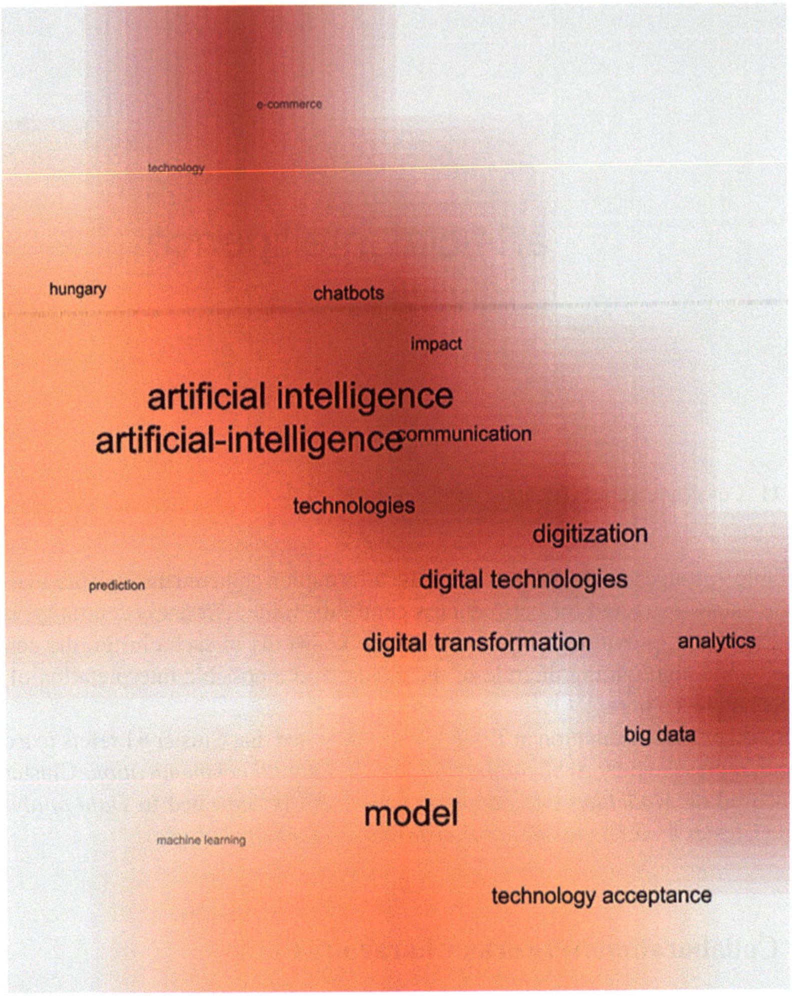

Fig. 12 Heatmap for the co-occurrence network based on all keywords

the platform's robust query engine and the possibility offered by the platform to download the papers' metadata in a single document, which can be easily processed by well-known bibliometric tools (such as Biblioshiny, VOSviewer, etc.).

Furthermore, as access to the mentioned database is made upon paid subscription. As a result, different subscriptions give various access to the indexes offered by the platform. As a result, as Liu (2019) suggested, it is necessary that when extracting the data from this platform, one to list the indexes offered by the used subscription.

Table 9 Thematic clusters interpretation in co-occurrence analysis

Cluster	Keywords	Interpretation	Central node	Role
Cluster #1	artificial intelligence, artificial-intelligence, Hungary, technologies, chatbots, communication, e-commerce, impact, technology, prediction	Captures the *applied and regional dimension* of AI research, especially in business communication, e-commerce, and national case studies	*Artificial intelligence*—the global connector of the entire map	*Basic theme*—broad, transversal, and foundational
Cluster #2	model, machine learning, technology acceptance	Reflects the *technical and behavioural modelling* strand of research—works using AI/ML models or Technology Acceptance Models (TAM/TOE frameworks)	*Model*—links quantitative modelling to adoption and learning	*Motor theme*—methodologically strong and influential in shaping future work
Cluster #3	analytics, big data	A compact, emerging cluster emphasising *data-driven intelligence* and the role of big data analytics in AI-based decision-making	-	*Niche or emerging theme*—specialised and technologically focused
Cluster #4	digital technologies, digital transformation, digitisation	This theme consolidates the *strategic and organisational perspective* of digitalisation in business contexts	-	*Motor theme*—tightly connected and conceptually mature, often co-occurring with AI in strategic management and organisational innovation papers

In our case, the access has been to all the 10 indexes offered by the platform, as follows:

- Science Citation Index Expanded (SCIE): 1900–present.
- Social Sciences Citation Index (SSCI): 1975–present.
- Arts & Humanities Citation Index (A&HCI): 1975–present.

- Emerging Sources Citation Index (ESCI): 2005–present.
- Conference Proceedings Citation Index-Science (CPCI-S): 1990–present.
- Conference Proceedings Citation Index-Social Sciences and Humanities (CPCI-SSH): 1990–present.
- Book Citation Index-Science (BKCI-S): 2010–present
- Book Citation Index-Social Sciences and Humanities (BKCI-SSH): 2010–present.
- Current Chemical Reactions (CCR-Expanded): 2010–present.
- Index Chemicus (IC): 2010–present.

In order to extract the dataset, the steps provided in Table 10 have been followed, which is further summarised in Fig. 13 (Page et al. 2020).

The first exploration step regards the use of the selected keywords for extracting the dataset. As the current research is focused on the use of AI in the studies regarding Romania and Hungary, the queries associated with this step have been conducted by using "artificial_intelligence", "Romania", and "Hungary" keywords. The "_" has been used in the search to ensure the resulting results contain both words "artificial" and "intelligence" as a group and not as individual keywords. As a result of step 1, 256 papers have been retrieved from the database.

The second exploration step has been dedicated to limiting the papers included in the dataset to those written in English. This choice has been made in accordance with other studies from the field (Politzer-Ahles et al. 2020; Ji and Bouillon 2021). After applying this limitation, the dataset has been reduced to 253 papers.

Document type has been limited to "article" in the third step of data extraction. This action was needed in order to ensure the comparability between outlets (Donner 2017; Smail et al. 2023). It should be mentioned that the selected database retains in the article-type section only research considered relevant, this not being limited to articles published in journals (WoS: Document Types). As a result of applying this limitation, the dataset has been further reduced to 168 papers.

The period for which the papers have been extracted has been further considered. As the extraction steps were conducted in October 2025 and the year 2025 was still ongoing at the moment of papers' extraction, the search has been limited to the papers published in 2024. Thus, the dataset has been reduced to 121 papers.

As besides the keywords used for papers' extraction, namely AI, Romania and Hungary, the purpose of the paper was to map the knowledge regarding the papers in the finance, accounting and business administration, a further analysis has been performed through which the titles and abstracts of the papers have been read and only the papers in the three mentioned research areas have been kept in the analysis. This action has reduced the dataset to 22 papers.

In terms of analysis, a series of indicators will be reported in the following section in connection with the extracted dataset in order to better shape the state of the art in this research field. Additionally, the review of the most cited papers is conducted, highlighting the papers that have caught the attention of researchers in this field. Furthermore, the thematic map analysis conducted through the use of Bibliometrix

Table 10 Data assortment steps

Exploration steps	Questions on Web of Science	Description	Query	Query number	Count
1	Title / Abstract / Author Keywords	Contains artificial intelligence as keyword	"artificial_intelligence (Title) OR artificial_ intelligence (Abstract) OR artificial_ intelligence (Author Keywords)"	#1	259,345
		Contains Romania as keyword	Romania (Title) OR Romania (Abstract) OR Romania (Author Keywords)	#2	51,819
		Contains Hungary as keyword	Hungary (Title) OR Hungary (Abstract) OR Hungary (Author Keywords)	#3	44,448
		Contains either Romania or Hungary as keywords	#2 OR #3	#4	93,368
		Contains artificial intelligence and one of the Romania or Hungary keywords	#1 AND #4	#5	256
2	Language	Limited to papers written in English	(#5) AND LA = (English)	#6	253
3	Document Type	Limit to article	(#6) AND DT = (Article)	#7	168
4	Year published	Exclude 2025	(#7) NOT PY = (2025)	#8	121
5	Selecting the papers in specific fields	Limit to papers in finance, accounting and business administration	Manually selected papers	#9	22

(Aria and Cuccurullo 2017) will be put in connection with the results obtained through topic analysis.

Regarding the topic analysis, it should be mentioned that both LDA and BERTopic have been conducted.

LDA is a generative probabilistic model widely employed for topic modelling in natural language processing (NLP), being used to uncover hidden topics within a given corpus of documents (Delcea et al. 2024; Întorsureanu et al. 2025). In order to perform LDA, term normalisation was needed as the analysis treats words such as "artificial intelligence" and "AI" as separate entities. Even more, domain-specific stop words, such as the ones used as filters during the paper selection process, have

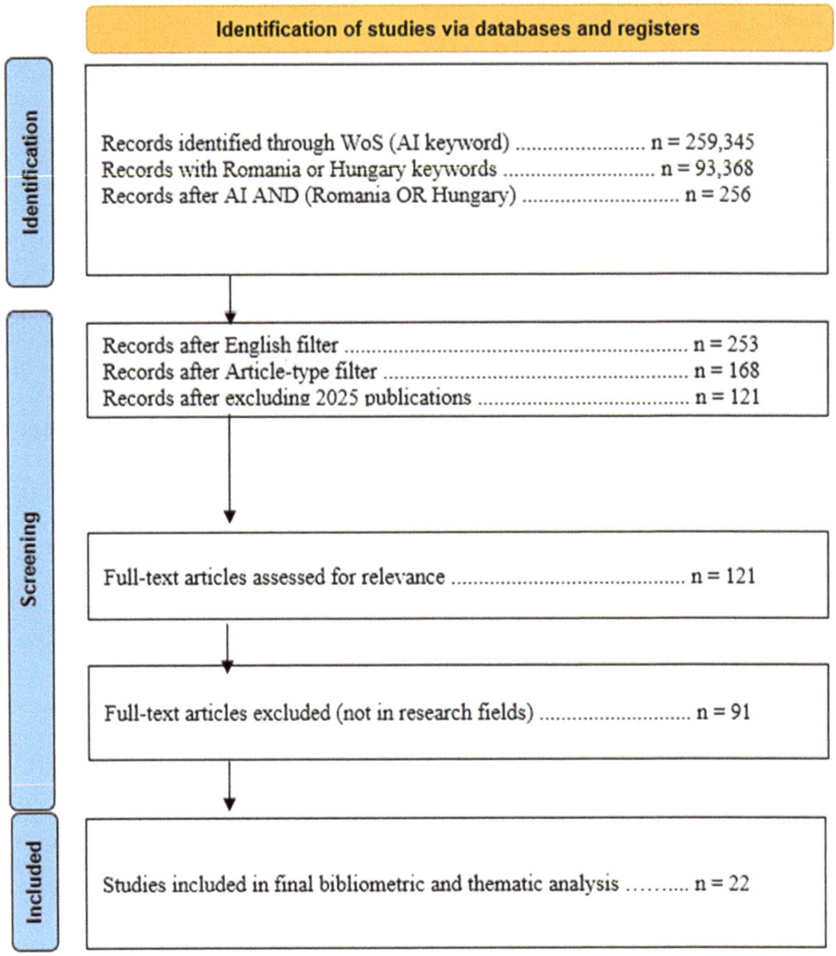

Fig. 13 Studies identification

also been removed. In order to optimise the results provided by LDA, a grid search procedure was conducted to identify the most suitable values for the *alpha* and *eta* parameters (Řehůřek and Sojka 2010).

On the other hand, BERTopic provides competitive results when compared to the given benchmarks (Grootendorst 2022). This approach generates coherent topic representations through a class-based adaptation of the TF–IDF. Even in this case, for reaching a better topic detection accuracy, the text data were pre-processed by converting all content to lowercase and removing punctuation. Additionally, the *minimum cluster size* and *minimum samples* parameters of the HDBSCAN clustering algorithm have been fine-tuned for obtaining a better balance between the topics' relevance and their interpretability (Cotfas et al. 2025).

4 Review of the Selected Research

The top 10 most cited papers are depicted in Fig. 14. As observed from the figure, the citations of the papers range between 5 and 13. In terms of citations per year, the top-10 most cited papers range between 0.67 to 4.50. The paper with the highest value for the total citations per year belongs to Ionescu et al. (2023) and discusses the residual contagion in Romania's banking market for mortgage loans. Overall, given the reduced time between the publication of the paper and the number of citations, the recorded values can be considered high.

In terms of the normalised total citations indicator (NTC), it can be observed that the top-10 most cited papers range between 0.68 and 3.60. It should be mentioned that the NTC indicator is a special type of indicator which is highly dependent on the papers included in the dataset and measures how many times a paper has received more citations than the average citations received by the papers published in the same year as this paper and included in the dataset. Even in this case, the highest value, namely 3.60, has been retrieved by the paper written by Ionescu et al. (2023), highlighting the fact that the paper has received a high attention from the research community.

In the following, the extracted dataset has been divided between the three considered research areas, namely application in finance, accounting and business Administration in Romania and Hungary, and a review of the works has been provided.

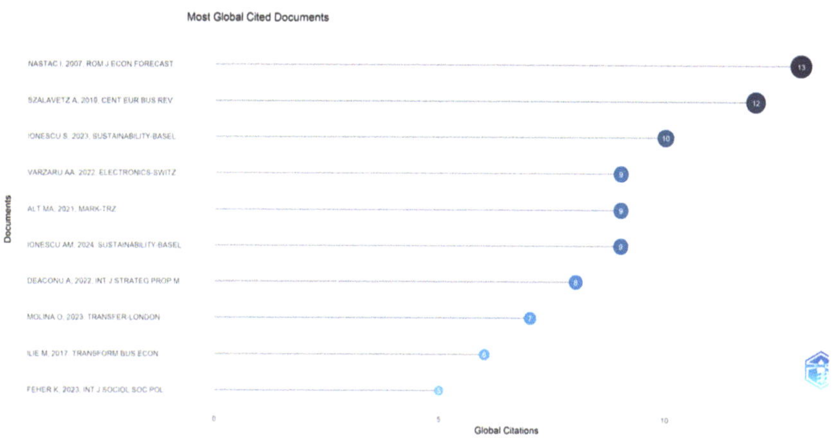

Fig. 14 Top-10 most cited works

4.1 AI Applications in Finance

The papers addressing issues related to the financial sector in Romania and Hungary demonstrate an increasingly diversified integration of artificial intelligence, including research focusing on banking operations, risk management, forecasting, and financial decision support.

Considering the papers included in the dataset, it has been observed that nine of them can be associated with the research in the finance area, in which elements related to AI are used for increasing the predictive accuracy, operational resilience, and regulatory compliance in the case of the applications discussed in the research.

First, it can be observed that there are several studies that have a focus on banking supervision and risk management, which can be put in connection with a growing interest in the regulatory actions in the region.

The paper authored by Prisznyak (2022) discusses how supervised and unsupervised learning algorithms can support anti–money laundering (AML) processes in Hungary. In the research paper, the author underlines the role of hybrid models in combining classification and anomaly detection, while also discussing institutional challenges in aligning AI deployment with the Financial Action Task Force (FATF) recommendations. Another work from the extracted dataset comes to further complement this research by presenting a conceptual exploration of AI-based tools such as Value at Risk (VaR) and volatility estimation models (Treapăt and Gheorghiu 2017). The authors are positioning the AI tools as essential instruments for improved capital allocation and performance measurement in Romanian financial institutions.

Another research direction identified in the papers associated with finance is represented by the papers exploring forecasting and predictive modelling through the use of tools such as machine learning and neural networks. Thus, some papers propose architectures capable of adapting to dynamic market data in the case of Romania (Belciug et al. 2021; Nastac et al. 2007), while others focus on using AI to visualise and analyse the determinants of foreign direct investment in Hungary, bridging econometric analysis and data-driven modelling (Singh 2021).

In the area of credit and real estate, the work conducted by Deaconu et al. (2022) focuses on comparing the artificial neural networks (ANN) with generalised linear models for estimating the apartment prices in Cluj-Napoca. According to the results of the research, the authors concluded that the ANN models are superior in terms of predictive performance and stability (Deaconu et al. 2022). Furthermore, the paper authored by Ionescu et al. (2023) in the area of residual financial contagion in Romania's banking market for mortgage loans features the use of an agent-based model (ABM) for studying the systemic risk propagation. The results of the study underline the fact that interbank connectivity can amplify contagion effects.

Another notable contribution, provided by Alt and Ibolya (2021), extends financial AI research toward customer interaction and service innovation. The authors are using clustering and technology acceptance modelling for segmenting the Romanian banking customers according to their openness to chatbot technologies. Thus, the research is being positioned at the intersection of behavioural finance and digital adoption.

Finally, the work conducted by Ilie et al. (2017) in the area of customer satisfaction in the context of the use of ANN employs feed-forward neural networks to model customer satisfaction determinants in the Romanian banking sector. The research findings reinforce the capacity of AI to capture non-linear relationships between service attributes and client perceptions, offering data-driven tools for improving customer experience management.

Considering all the above-mentioned studies, it can be observed that the main research areas can be identified regarding the AI adoption in finance within Romania and Hungary:

- Risk management and regulatory compliance;
- Predictive modelling for financial forecasting and valuation;
- Customer-centric innovation.

Thus, the extracted papers demonstrate a clear regional capacity for integrating AI methods into the financial domain. Having this background, more systematic, cross-sectoral studies that align with EU-level regulatory and ethical frameworks can be put forward in future research.

4.2 AI Applications in Accounting

Research addressing the application of artificial intelligence in accounting within Romania and Hungary represents the smallest corpus of papers within the extracted dataset.

Considering the works included here, the paper authored by Varzaru (2022a) distinguishes itself from the remainder of the papers as it puts an emphasis on the ethical implications, technology adoption, and digital transformation. The author examines how ethical factors, among which one can mention autonomy, responsibility, and trust, affect accountants' perceptions of AI usefulness and efficiency. The research is based on a structural equation modelling approach used on data from Romanian practitioners and concludes that while AI enhances performance and decision-making, it also introduces new ethical challenges that must be managed through responsible design and governance.

Another work from the dataset in the area of accounting has been conducted by Anton et al. (2024), which aims to explore the role of AI-powered virtual assistants in improving sustainability and financial communication practices. Considering a large number of accounting and consultancy firms, namely 11,000, the research demonstrates that chatbot implementation supports transparency, accuracy, and stakeholder engagement in integrated reporting. The authors show that this situation mainly occurs in the case of companies with higher liquidity and digital maturity.

Finally, the research conducted by Fulop et al. (2024) is dedicated to investigating the adoption dynamics of digital and AI technologies through a Technology

Acceptance Model (TAM) integrated with the Technology–Organisation–Environment (TOE) framework. The results of the research underline the fact that Romanian accountants are at an early stage of digital transition compared to EU peers, with organisational readiness and perceived usefulness as key determinants of adoption.

Thus, based on the above-discussed papers, it can be stated that a transformative but cautious integration of AI in Romanian accounting can be observed in the selected papers, with a high potential for expansion in future studies.

4.3 AI Applications in Business Administration

The application of artificial intelligence in **business administration** within Romania and Hungary reflects a multifaceted approach, which combines themes related to economic growth, organisational transformation, digitalisation, and consumer interaction. The papers associated with this area constitute the largest number of papers included in the extracted dataset.

Considering the paper authored by Kiritescu et al. (2024) underpins AI's potential as a driver of national economic development. According to the authors, this potential can be uncovered through the innovative activities of small and medium-sized enterprises. On the other hand, in the case of Hungary, Szalavetz (2019) discusses the entrepreneurial ecosystem of AI start-ups, underlying the fact that the innovation can strengthen local economic upgrading and technological sovereignty within global dependencies.

At the organisational level, the work conducted by Molina et al. (2023) investigates labour relations and algorithmic management. The authors are comparing institutional responses across various European countries, including Hungary, to the challenges of AI regulation and employee participation.

With regard to the rapid digital transition of the retail sector, a series of research addresses the transformative impact of digitalisation in specific business sectors in the case of Romania (Nistor and Zadobrischi 2024; Ardelean and Ionescu 2024).

Various hospitality and tourism applications are examined in the papers authored by Makivic et al. (2024) for the case of Hungary and Ionescu and Sarbu (2024) in the case of Romania. Both studies demonstrate how AI-driven personalisation and smart technologies enhance customer experience and operational efficiency.

Furthermore, the implications of AI for industrial innovation and sustainability are discussed in the research paper authored by Gavrus et al. (2024). The authors provide evidence related to the diffusion of digital technologies that supports competitiveness even among small and micro firms.

In terms of strategic and managerial dimensions of AI in business, the work conducted by Feher and Veres (2023) identify trust, ethics, and cross-sector collaboration as key for sustainable AI adoption in Hungary. Additionally, in the paper written by Varzaru (2022b), the TAM is applied in project-based organisations, highlighting the fact that innovation, customisation, and perceived efficiency drive digital transformation in management practices.

Thus, considering the papers included in this area from the dataset, it can be noticed that the AI adoption in business administration across Romania and Hungary is characterised by dynamicity, while being sensitive to the context and exhibiting a sectoral diversity.

5 Basic, Motor, Niche and Emerging Themes

In this section, the themes approached in the papers included in the dataset are uncovered by using the thematic map analysis provided by Biblioshiny.

First, this analysis has been conducted by considering only the unigrams in the titles of the papers. The themes reported as a result of the analysis are presented in Fig. 15.

In terms of motor themes, two main research directions can be remarked, referring to AI applications in accounting and banking, which combine digital technologies, performance analysis, and risk management.

The basic themes focus on AI and e-commerce, highlighting the transformative role played by AI in the business area. The niche themes focus on satisfaction and services, while the emerging themes have as central point issues related to market development, local industry adoption, and user acceptance.

Additionally, the network of the terms included in the construction of the thematic map in Fig. 15, is provided in Fig. 17. In this figure, each node represents an unigram,

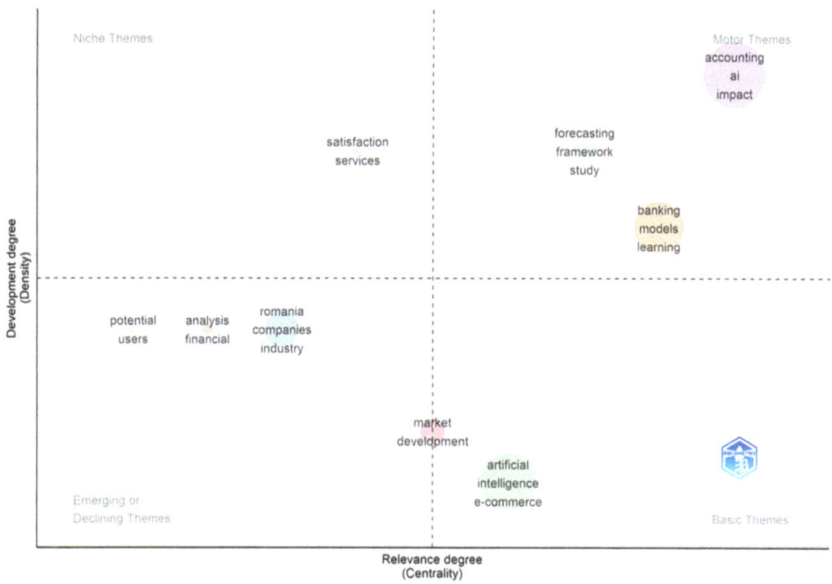

Fig. 15 Thematic map based on unigrams in titles

while the size of a node reflects its frequency. The distance between nodes and thickness of edges show semantic proximity, namely shows how often two terms co-occur in the same titles. The colour-code is the same as in the previous figure and represents thematic communities, namely groups of words that frequently appear together and form coherent research topics.

As a result of the representation in Fig. 16, it can be stated that six major clusters emerge, which are further discussed in Table 11.

Moving further with the analysis, a thematic map based on the bigrams in abstracts has been created. Due to the large corpus of words in abstracts compared to the titles, the thematic map created in this case is more populated than in the previous case. Figure 17 depicts the results obtained.

In this case, the motor themes quadrant is the most populated, representing the core zone of the analysis, positioned in the upper right quadrant. In this quadrant, it can be observed that the core cluster (depicted in blue in Fig. 17) is characterised by the

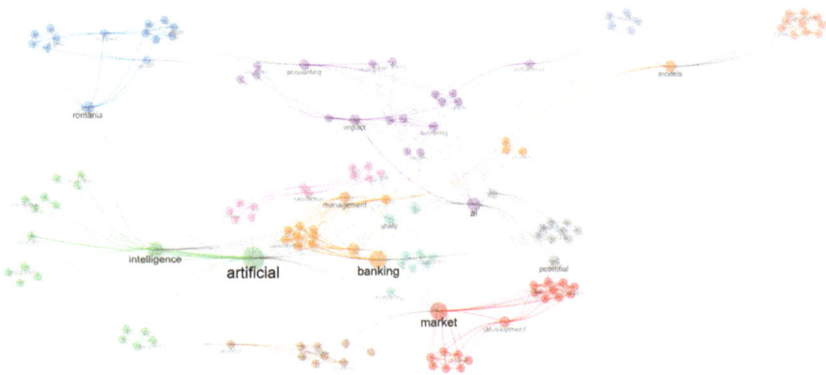

Fig. 16 Network in thematic map based on unigrams in titles

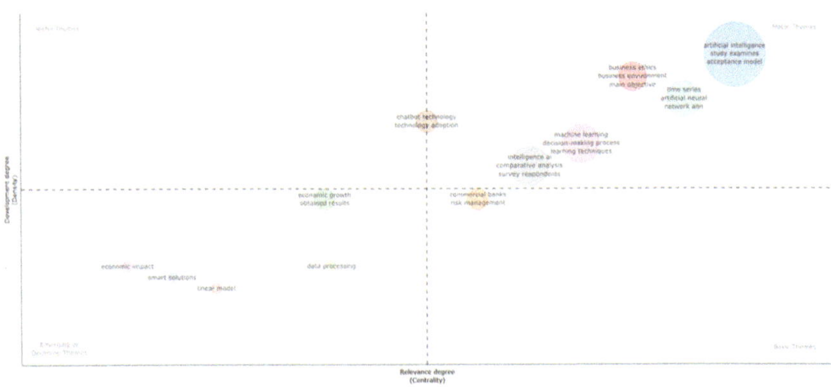

Fig. 17 Thematic map based on bigrams in abstracts

Table 11 Major clusters interpretation in thematic map on titles analysis

Cluster	Core nodes	Interpretation	Focus
Green	artificial, intelligence, automation, e-commerce, consumers, economic	AI is conceptually tied to digitalisation, automation, and online markets	*AI and digital business*
Purple	accounting, impact, assessing, performance, instruments, ethical	Studies examining AI's role in accounting, performance measurement, and ethical or managerial implications	*Accounting and impact assessment*
Orange	banking, management, satisfaction, bankrobotics, risk, study	AI applications in the banking sector, focusing on risk prevention, management systems, and customer satisfaction modelling	*Banking, management, and risk*
Blue	Romania, companies, industry, chatbots, degree	Highlights Romanian contexts (e.g., case studies on accounting firms or industry-level adoption)	*Romania and industry*
Red	market, development, potential, users	Focus on economic growth, market dynamics, and adoption potential of AI technologies	*Market development and its potential*
Brown/ Grey	models, financial, analysis, approach, inflow, forecasting	Groups technical studies that apply AI and machine learning models for forecasting, valuation, and financial analytics	*Analytical and modelling approaches*

following bigrams: "artificial intelligence", "study examines", "acceptance model". Considering the remainder of the clusters included in the motor themes quadrant, it can be mentioned that they focus on research on AI adoption frameworks (Technology Acceptance Model, TAM) with empirical analyses of AI use in finance, accounting, and management, further supported by the bigrams in the area of quantitative and predictive modelling referring to artificial neural networks and time series.

For the basic themes quadrant located in the lower right side of the figure, a series of key clusters can be observed, such as: *machine learning, decision-making process, learning techniques, business environment.* It can be observed that these themes are linking I's technical side to decision support and organisational applications. Furthermore, the occurrence of the "risk management" bigram suggests that AI tools are becoming standard instruments in financial analysis and business strategy.

Moreover, the nice themes located in the upper left quadrant include clusters such as *chatbot technology, technology adoption.* The works included here are expected to be specialised in empirical studies, most of them in accounting, consultancy, and customer communication.

The emerging or declining quadrant located in the lower left side of the thematic map comprises clusters focusing on *economic impact, smart solutions, linear model, and data processing.*

6 Topics Discovery Through LDA and BERTopic

In this section, topic discovery is conducted through the use of LDA and BERTopic by respecting the information provided in the materials and methods section.

First, through the LDA analysis, a number of 4 topics have been identified as depicted in Fig. 18. In this figure, the intertopic distance map can be observed on the left-side of the figure, having the purpose of highlighting the spatial distribution of topics and to what extent the topics are distinct or overlap, while the top 30 most relevant terms per topic are listed on the right side of the map, showing the vocabulary defining each theme.

As observed in Fig. 18, the identified topics do not overlap, reflecting the fact that the dataset captures several well-defined areas of research within the field of artificial intelligence applications in finance, accounting, and business administration. Furthermore, the relative size of each circle reflects its marginal topic distribution, showing that Topic 1 represents the largest share of the corpus, followed by Topics 2, 3, and 4.

Regarding the most salient words, terms such as *growth, industry, risk, machine learning, economic, mechanism, and technology acceptance* are observed among the extracted keywords, which highlight the centrality of the themes related to economic performance, industrial transformation, predictive modelling, and adoption mechanisms.

LDA Topic 1, depicted in Fig. 19, retrieves the highest number of the extracted tokens, respectively 34.5% and it is composed of terms such as *phase, growth, time, industry, determinant, risk, efficiency, mechanism, economic, degree, crisis, technology acceptance,* which can be put in connection with the studies featuring AI

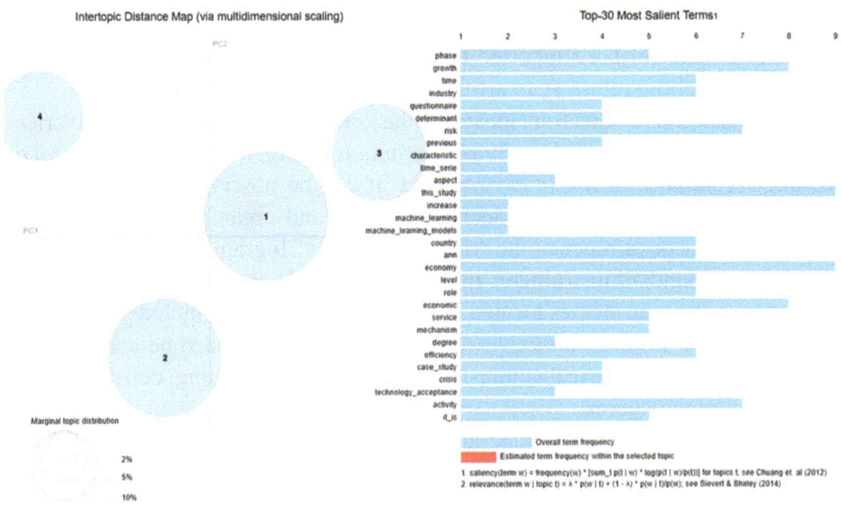

Fig. 18 LDA results

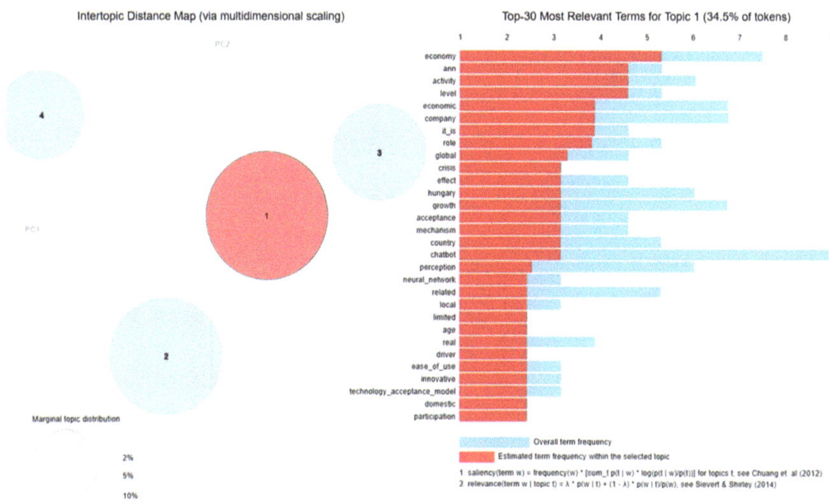

Fig. 19 LDA Topic 1

and economic development, focusing on growth determinants, industry transformation, and risk-efficiency trade-offs. Furthermore, the co-occurrence of terms such as *economic*, *growth*, and *phase* suggests macro-level analyses, which can be connected with AI's role in national or sectoral performance.

With a percentage of 29.1% of tokens, the LDA Topic 2 depicted in Fig. 20 features a series of top-terms such as *chatbot, business, questionnaire, accounting, communication, adoption, efficiency, case study, trust, satisfaction, responsibility, implementation_of_AI, digital, industry, region.* Given this prevalence of terms, the topic is expected to capture empirical studies that investigate AI adoption in organisational and service settings, especially in accounting, consultancy, and tourism.

Also, the LDA Topic 2 features a series of tokens that refer to the human–machine interaction and ethical or user acceptance dimensions, such as *chatbot*, *trust*, *responsibility*, and *satisfaction.* Additionally, it is expected that the studies associated with this topic to have a survey-based research design, given the occurrence of terms such as *questionnaire* and *case study.*

LDA Topic 3 gravitates around technical and financial studies, with a particular focus on machine learning models used in finance, forecasting, and investment decision-making. As noticed from Fig. 21, the most salient words comprise the following terms: *machine learning, models, growth, determinant, market, company, financial, investment, business, benefit, management, expansion, region, impact.*

Furthermore, the research included in LDA Topic 3 is expected to have an applied nature marked by the occurrence of the *market*, *financial*, and *investment* terms. Measures or economic metrics are expected to be employed in these studies as a result of the occurrence of *growth* and *determinant* terms. This topic retains 19.7% of tokens, making it the third-largest extracted topic.

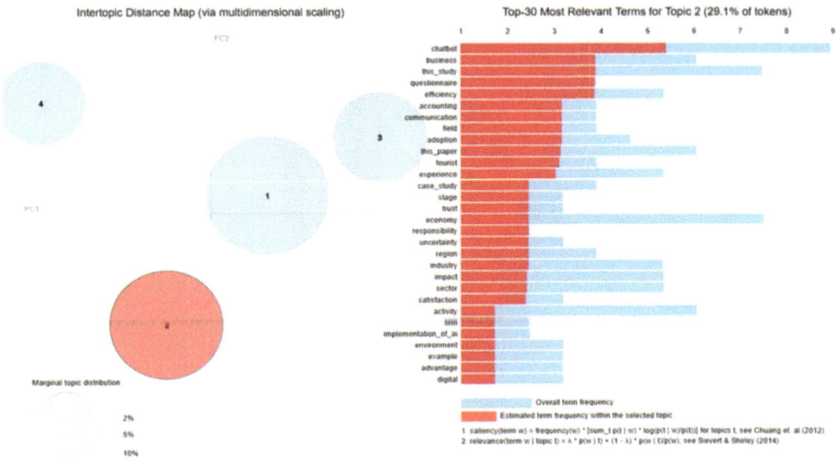

Fig. 20 LDA Topic 2

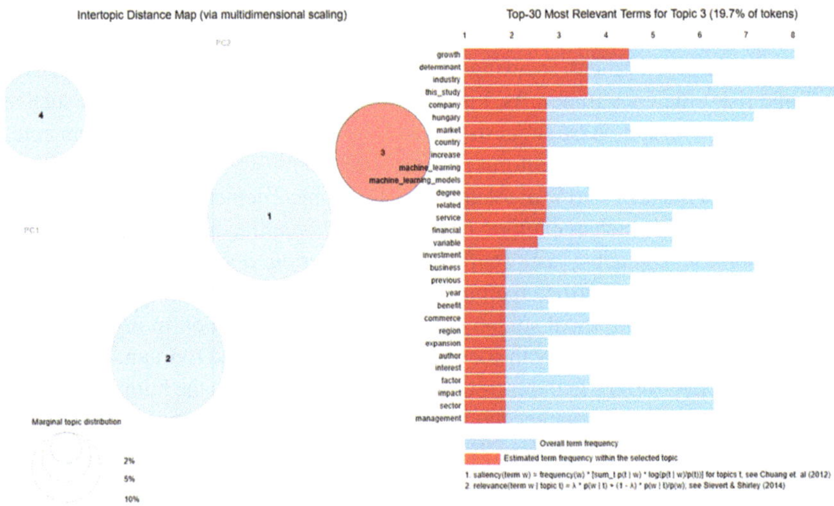

Fig. 21 LDA Topic 3

Lastly, LDA Topic 4, which gathers 16.7% of tokens, features a series of key terms such as *risk, time_serie, perception, economic, ai_based, technology acceptance, mechanism, prediction, project, organisation, case study, learning, and financial data.* Considering these terms, it is expected that the topic to bridge risk management and predictive analytics, which are usually encountered within papers providing technology acceptance or behavioural models. Moreover, the occurrence of t*ime series* and *financial data* terms connects the AI to predictive risk modelling. Quantitative analyses are also expected in the studies from this area, which is highlighted by

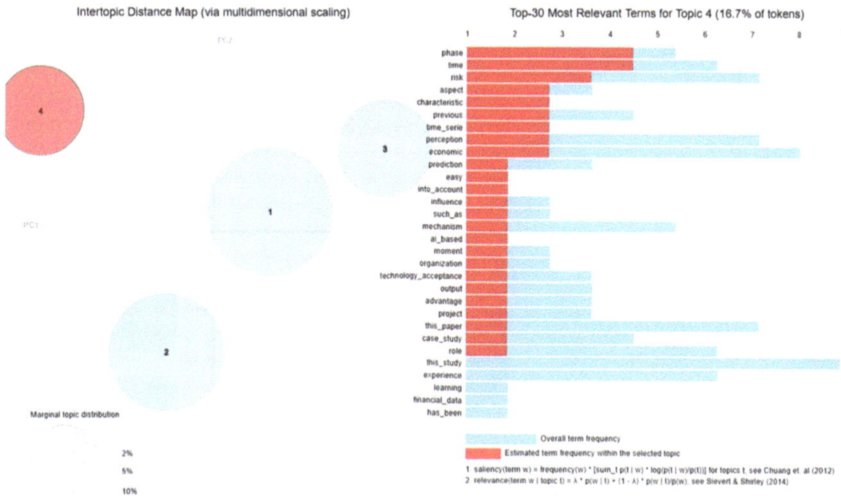

Fig. 22 LDA Topic 4

the presence of the keywords such as co-occurrence of *ai_based*, *organisation*, and *perception.*

Given the structure of the 4 LDA topics discussed above, it can be summarized that the focus of the topics is as follows: LDA Topic 1: *AI-driven economic transformation and technology adoption*, LDA Topic 2: *Organisational adoption, communication, and ethical implications of AI*, LDA Topic 3: *Machine learning models for financial and market analysis*, and LDA Topic 4: *AI-based risk assessment and organisational learning* (Fig. 22).

Next, BERTopic analysis has been used for the identification of semantically cohesive clusters of documents using transformer-based embeddings. Two major clusters are identified through BERTopic, noted with Topic 0 and Topic 1 in Fig. 23, where the top-5 most salient words in each topic are depicted.

BERTopic 0 is defined by a series of keywords such as *ann*, *artificial*, *time*, *risk*, *banking*, *financial*, *training*, *contagion*, *FDI*, and *price*, which highlight a focus of the works included in this topic on the application of artificial neural networks (ANNs) and other machine learning methods to financial modelling, risk assessment, and contagion analysis. Additionally, as the terms such as *time* and *price* are included in the top words associated with this topic, it is expected that the topic to also include time-series data and predictive modelling for financial forecasting and investment decision-making, offering a quantitative and analytical dimension of AI research in the financial sector through modelling approaches.

BERTopic 2 is characterised by terms such as *AI*, *technologies*, *intelligence*, *accounting*, *research*, *companies*, and *digital,* which might suggest that the research associated with this topic features the adoption and integration of AI technologies in accounting and business contexts, as well as their impact on organisational digital

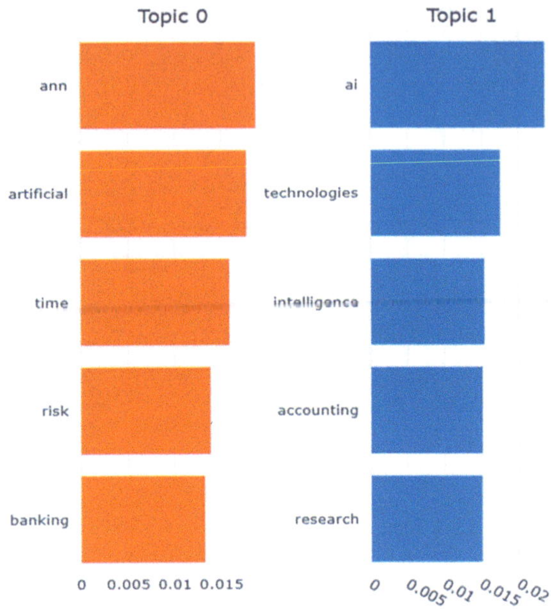

Fig. 23 BERTopic results

transformation. Even more, the occurrence of the *artificial intelligence* and *technology* terms can be put in connection *with* the presence of studies dealing with managerial, ethical, and acceptance aspects of AI implementation in firms.

Based on the above observations, it can be mentioned that BERTopic 1 is dedicated to *Artificial Neural Networks and Financial Risk Modelling*, while BERTopic 2 is related to *Artificial Intelligence Adoption and Digital Transformation in Accounting*.

Considering the results obtained through LDA and BERTopic analysis, it can be noticed that LDA provides a broad probabilistic overview of AI-related themes, while BERTopic produces more semantically cohesive clusters, which emphasise two main research directions, namely technical-financial modelling and organisational adoption of AI technologies.

7 Concluding Remarks

The advancements made in the area of AI in finance, accounting and business administration in the case of Romania and Hungary are discussed in the chapter.

By using specific tools, such as bibliometric analysis, topic modelling and review, the papers extracted from the Clarivate Analytics Web of Science Collection have been analysed.

Even though the volume of publications remains modest, as observed from the final dataset retained in the analysis, the thematic diversity and methodological sophistication have increased significantly over the last decade.

Considering the results of the thematic map, a well-structured research landscape is noticeable, dominated by motor themes such as AI adoption, digital transformation, and machine learning applications, alongside basic themes like technology acceptance, data analytics, and risk management. Furthermore, niche and emerging themes, such as those dealing with chatbots, smart technologies, and user satisfaction, illustrate the field's expansion toward specialised, sectoral applications.

The LDA topic analysis identified four topics, which ranged from AI-driven economic transformation and organisational adoption to machine learning in financial modelling and AI-based risk assessment. As a result of this analysis, it can be stated that it is observed a balance between technical and managerial orientations in the considered studies.

Additionally, the BERTopic analysis results confirmed and restrained the patterns observed through the LDA analysis, by identifying only two distinct clusters: one centred on data-driven financial modelling, and the other on AI-enabled organisational innovation in accounting and business administration.

Based on the conducted review, it has been observed that in the area of finance, the research is mainly focusing on three areas such as risk management and regulatory compliance, predictive modelling for financial forecasting and valuation, and customer-centric innovation. The accounting area, even though restrained, has been characterised by research that focuses on transformative but cautious integration of AI, but showing a potential for development in further studies. Lastly, for the business administration area, the studies have had various focuses, ranging from AI and economic development, AI in work and organisational dynamics, AI and digital transformation of business sectors, and AI and digital project management.

The research suffers from limitations which are mostly due to the extraction of the analysed dataset. By changing any of the elements considered in the data extraction process, such as the database, the language of the papers, the type of papers, the period of analysis, the obtained dataset might have been different. Furthermore, as the final selection of the papers has been made upon a subjective approach, it is possible that the final version of the dataset might have been different if stricter or less strict criteria had been applied.

The future studies could consider expanding upon elements restrained in this research, by considering various types of papers or more databases for the dataset extraction.

References

Alt M-A, Ibolya V (2021) Identifying relevant segments of potential banking chatbot users based on technology adoption behavior. Mark-Trž 33:165–183. https://doi.org/10.22598/mt/2021.33.2.165

Anton CE, Ciobanu E, Brătucu G, Bucs L (2024) Using chatbots to enhance integrated reporting: insights from accounting and consultancy companies from Romania. Electronics 13:4801. https://doi.org/10.3390/electronics13234801

Ardelean A, Ionescu I-M (2024) The Romanian consumer's perspective on the integration of artificial intelligence in e-commerce. J Natl Inst Stat 4.
Aria M, Cuccurullo C (2017) Bibliometrix: an R-tool for comprehensive science mapping analysis. J Informetr 11:959–975. https://doi.org/10.1016/j.joi.2017.08.007
Belciug S, Sănditã A, Costin H, Bejinariu S-I, Matei PG (2021) Competitive/collaborative statistical learning framework for forecasting intraday stock market prices: a case study. Stud Inform Control 30:43–54. https://doi.org/10.24846/v30i2y202104
Carhuallanqui-Ciocca EI, Echevarría-Quispe JY, Hernández-Vásquez A, Díaz-Ruiz R, Azañedo D (2023) Bibliometric analysis of the scientific production on inguinal hernia surgery in the Web of Science. Front. Surg. 10:1138805. https://doi.org/10.3389/fsurg.2023.1138805
Cibu B, Delcea C, Domenteanu A, Dumitrescu G (2023) Mapping the evolution of cybernetics: a bibliometric perspective. Computers 12. https://doi.org/10.3390/computers12110237
Cişmaşu I-D, Cibu BR, Cotfas L-A, Delcea C (2025) The persistence puzzle: bibliometric insights into dropout in MOOCs. Sustainability 17:2952. https://doi.org/10.3390/su17072952
Cotfas L-A, Sandu A, Delcea C, Diaconu P, Frăsineanu C, Stănescu A (2025) From transformers to ChatGPT: an analysis of large language models research. IEEE Access 13:146889–146931. https://doi.org/10.1109/ACCESS.2025.3600739
Deaconu A, Buiga A, Tothăzan H (2022) Real estate valuation models performance in price prediction. Int J Strateg Prop Manag 26:86–105. https://doi.org/10.3846/ijspm.2022.15962
Delcea C, Domenteanu A, Ioanăş C, Vargas VM, Ciucu-Durnoi AN (2023) Quantifying neutrosophic research: a bibliometric study. Axioms 12:1083. https://doi.org/10.3390/axioms12121083
Delcea C, Oprea S-V, Dima AM, Domenteanu A, Bara A, Cotfas L-A (2024) Energy communities: Insights from scientific publications. Oeconomia Copernic 15:1101–1155. https://doi.org/10.24136/oc.3137
Dobre F, Sandu A, Tătaru G-C, Cotfas L-A (2025) A decade of studies in smart cities and urban planning through big data analytics. Systems 13:780. https://doi.org/10.3390/systems13090780
Domenteanu A, Cibu B, Delcea C, Cotfas L-A (2025a) The world of agent-based modeling: a bibliometric and analytical exploration. Complexity 2025:2636704. https://doi.org/10.1155/cplx/2636704
Domenteanu A, Cotfas L-A, Diaconu P, Tudor G-A, Delcea C (2025b) AI on wheels: bibliometric approach to mapping of research on machine learning and deep learning in electric vehicles. Electronics 14:378. https://doi.org/10.3390/electronics14020378
Domenteanu A, Delcea C, Chirita N, Ioanăş C (2023) From data to insights: a bibliometric assessment of agent-based modeling applications in transportation. Appl Sci 13. https://doi.org/10.3390/app132312693
Donner P (2017) Document type assignment accuracy in the journal citation index data of Web of Science. Scientometrics 113:219–236. https://doi.org/10.1007/s11192-017-2483-y
Feher K, Veres Z (2023) Trends, risks and potential cooperations in the AI development market: expectations of the Hungarian investors and developers in an international context. Int J Sociol Soc Policy 43:107–125. https://doi.org/10.1108/IJSSP-08-2021-0205
Fülöp MT, Ionescu CA, Măgdaş N, Topor DI, Breaz TO (2024) Acceptance of digital instruments in the accounting profession. J East Eur Manag Stud 29:283–313. https://doi.org/10.5771/0949-6181-2024-2-283
Gavrus C, Petre IM, Pârv L (2024) Industry 4.0—premise for sustainability: implementation degree in manufacturing companies from Romania. Sustainability 16:807. https://doi.org/10.3390/su16020807
Grootendorst M (2022) BERTopic: neural topic modeling with a class-based TF-IDF procedure. https://arxiv.org/abs/2203.05794. https://doi.org/10.48550/ARXIV.2203.05794
Ilie M, Moraru A-D, Ghita-Mitrescu S (2017) The hierarchical determination of customer satisfaction with banking services using an artificial neural network. Transform Bus Econ 16:401
Întorsureanu I, Oprea S-V, Bâra A, Vespan D (2025) Generative AI in education: perspectives through an academic lens. Electronics 14:1053. https://doi.org/10.3390/electronics14051053

Ionescu Ș, Chiriță N, Nica I, Delcea C (2023) An analysis of residual financial contagion in Romania's banking market for mortgage loans. Sustainability 15:12037. https://doi.org/10.3390/su151512037

Ionescu A-M, Sârbu FA (2024) Exploring the impact of smart technologies on the tourism industry. Sustainability 16:3318. https://doi.org/10.3390/su16083318

Ji M, Bouillon P (2021) Predicting the linguistic accessibility of Chinese health translations: machine learning algorithm development. JMIR Med Inform 9:e30588. https://doi.org/10.2196/30588

Kiritescu C, Ioan-Franc V, Gaf-Deac II (2024) "Costin C Kiritescu" National Institute for Economic Research—Romanian Academy, Bucharest, Romania: Participation of Artificial Intelligence in Economic Growth in Romania. Amfiteatru Econ 26:944. https://doi.org/10.24818/EA/2024/67/944

Koca TT (2023) Bibliometric analysis of "sarcopenia" in Web of Science. Egypt Rheumatol Rehabil 50:26. https://doi.org/10.1186/s43166-023-00194-w

Liu W (2019) The data source of this study is Web of Science Core Collection? Not enough. Scientometrics 121:1815–1824. https://doi.org/10.1007/s11192-019-03238-1

López Belmonte J, Segura-Robles A, Moreno-Guerrero A-J, Parra-González ME (2020) Machine learning and big data in the impact literature. A bibliometric review with scientific mapping in Web of Science. Symmetry 12:495. https://doi.org/10.3390/sym12040495

Makivić R, Vukolić D, Veljović S, Bolesnikov M, Dávid LD, Ivanišević A, Silić M, Gajić T (2024) AI impact on hotel guest satisfaction via tailor-made services: a case study of Serbia and Hungary. Information 15:700. https://doi.org/10.3390/info15110700

Modak NM, Merigó JM, Weber R, Manzor F, Ortúzar JDD (2019) Fifty years of transportation research journals: a bibliometric overview. Transp Res Part Policy Pract 120:188–223. https://doi.org/10.1016/j.tra.2018.11.015

Molina O, Butollo F, Makó C, Godino A, Holtgrewe U, Illsoe A, Junte S, Larsen TP, Illésy M, Pap J, Wotschack P (2023) It takes two to code: a comparative analysis of collective bargaining and artificial intelligence. Transf Eur Rev Labour Res 29:87–104. https://doi.org/10.1177/10242589231156515

Nastac I, Dobrescu, E., Pelinescu, E (200) Neuro-adaptative model for financial forecasting. Romanian J Econ Forecast 8.

Nistor A, Zadobrischi E (2024) The scale-up of e-commerce in Romania generated by the pandemic, automation, and artificial intelligence. Telecom 5:680–705. https://doi.org/10.3390/telecom5030034

Onyancha OB, Ocholla DN (2022) Dispersion of ICT-related subject terms in information and knowledge management publications: A Bradford analysis. Humanit Soc Sci Commun 9:176. https://doi.org/10.1057/s41599-022-01189-2

Page MJ, McKenzie JE, Bossuyt PM, Boutron I, Hoffmann TC, Mulrow CD, Shamseer L, Tetzlaff JM, Akl EA, Brennan SE, Chou R, Glanville J, Grimshaw JM, Hróbjartsson A, Lalu MM, Li T, Loder EW, Mayo-Wilson E, McDonald S, McGuinness LA, Stewart LA, Thomas J, Tricco AC, Welch VA, Whiting P, Moher D (2021) The PRISMA 2020 statement: an updated guideline for reporting systematic reviews. BMJ n71. https://doi.org/10.1136/bmj.n71

Politzer-Ahles S, Girolamo T, Ghali S (2020) Preliminary evidence of linguistic bias in academic reviewing. J Engl Acad Purp 47:100895. https://doi.org/10.1016/j.jeap.2020.100895

Prisznyák A (2022) Bankrobotics: artificial intelligence and machine learning powered banking risk management: prevention of money laundering and terrorist financing. Pénzügyi Szle. Public Finance Q 67:288–303. https://doi.org/10.35551/PFQ_2022_2_8

Ravšelj D, Umek L, Todorovski L, Aristovnik A (2022) A review of digital era governance research in the first two decades: a bibliometric study. Future Internet 14. https://doi.org/10.3390/fi14050126

Řehůřek R, Sojka P (2010) Software framework for topic modelling with large corpora. https://doi.org/10.13140/2.1.2393.1847

Sandu A, Diaconu P, Delcea C, Domenteanu A (2025) Emphasizing grey systems contribution to decision-making field under uncertainty: a global bibliometric exploration. Mathematics 13:1278. https://doi.org/10.3390/math13081278

Sandu A, Cotfas L-A, Stanescu A, Delcea C (2024) Guiding urban decision-making: a study on recommender systems in smart cities. Electronics 13. https://doi.org/10.3390/electronics13112151

Singh D (2021) Interpretable machine-learning approach in estimating FDI inflow: visualization of ML models with LIME and H2O. TalTech J Eur Stud 11:133–152. https://doi.org/10.2478/bjes-2021-0009

Smail B, Aliane H, Abdeldjalil O (2023) Using an explicit query and a topic model for scientific article recommendation. Educ Inf Technol 28:15657–15670. https://doi.org/10.1007/s10639-023-11817-2

Szalavetz A (2019) Artificial intelligence-based development strategy in dependent market economies—any room amidst big power rivalry? Cent Eur Bus Rev 8:40–54. https://doi.org/10.18267/j.cebr.219

Treapăt L-M, Gheorghiu A (2017) Artificial systems and models for risk covering operations. BRAIN Broad Res Artif Intell Neurosci 8:59–72

Tsilika K (2023) Exploring the contributions to mathematical economics: a bibliometric analysis using Bibliometrix and VOSviewer. Mathematics 11:4703. https://doi.org/10.3390/math11224703

Valente A, Holanda M, Mariano AM, Furuta R, Da Silva D (2022) Analysis of academic databases for literature review in the computer science education field. In: 2022 IEEE Frontiers in Education Conference (FIE). IEEE, Uppsala, Sweden, pp 1–7. https://doi.org/10.1109/FIE56618.2022.9962393

Vărzaru AA (2022a) Assessing the impact of AI solutions' ethical issues on performance in managerial accounting. Electronics 11:2221. https://doi.org/10.3390/electronics11142221

Vărzaru AA (2022b) An empirical framework for assessing the digital technologies users' acceptance in project management. Electronics 11:3872. https://doi.org/10.3390/electronics11233872

Web of Science Advanced search—all databases. https://www.webofscience.com/wos/alldb/advanced-search. Last accessed 27 May 2025

Woeginger GJ (2008) An axiomatic characterization of the Hirsch-index. Math Soc Sci 56:224–232. https://doi.org/10.1016/j.mathsocsci.2008.03.001

WoS: Document Types. https://webofscience.help.clarivate.com/en-us/Content/document-types.html. Last accessed 3 Dec 2023

Yu J, Muñoz-Justicia J (2020) A bibliometric overview of twitter-related studies indexed in Web of Science. Future Internet 12:91. https://doi.org/10.3390/fi12050091

Artificial Intelligence and the Digital Economy in Romania and Hungary

The Current State of the Digital Economy in Romania and Hungary

Claudia-Diana Sabău-Popa, Alexandra-Maria Bele, and Monica Ariana Sim

Abstract Digital economy in Europe is an integral part of the information environment, shaped in accordance with the needs of the real sector of the economy and the requirements of society, which change under the influence of technological innovations. Its key components are found under the aegis of sustainable development, digital technologies, and artificial intelligence, considering their interdependence, as well as their continuity with previously developed conceptual frameworks. The chapter analyses the current state of digitalization in the EU and emphasizes the assessment of the level, dynamics and development trends of technological innovations in Romania and Hungary. In order to clearly understand the purpose of this study, the importance of the essence of the digital economy and the stage of its development is demonstrated by using the Digital Economy and Society Index (DESI) indicator.

1 Introduction

The European Union has laid the foundations in recent years for a long-term vision to address a globally competitive single market and to serve as a cornerstone of global competitiveness. Given the current and emerging global challenges, in particular in terms of technology, security and sustainability, which cut across all relevant policy areas, new commitments are needed from both Member States and the EU institutions.

The key issue is the need to create a business environment that is conducive to investment, innovation and entrepreneurship. In other words, European markets

C.-D. Sabău-Popa (✉) · A.-M. Bele · M. A. Sim
Faculty of Economic Sciences, University of Oradea, Oradea, Romania
e-mail: dpopa@uoradea.ro

A.-M. Bele
e-mail: alexandra.bele@didactic.uoradea.ro; alexandra.bele95@gmail.com

M. A. Sim
e-mail: msim@uoradea.ro

C. Sabău-Popa (ed.), *Artificial Intelligence in Finance, Accounting and Business Administration*, Contributions to Finance and Accounting,
https://doi.org/10.1007/978-3-032-22737-9_2

are encouraged to operate, regardless of their business model, to expand and be sufficiently sustainable on global markets, in a digital environment that ensures a global level playing field.

Digitalisation is a driver of sustainable and integrated economic development. The importance of digitalisation is horizontal and should therefore permeate all policies. Digital transformation can significantly reduce administrative burdens and improve the framework conditions for business investments. New, forward-looking digital regulations are a prerequisite for a well-functioning single market that promotes innovation.

2 Literature Review

One of the most frequently discussed contemporary issues is the need for digital transformation. Most researchers are convinced of the importance of digitalisation both at the level of institutions as well as at the level of regions and countries. Among the most relevant positive effects of the extensive use of information and communication technologies (ICT) are: increased labour productivity, cost reduction, increased competitiveness and increased capitalisation (Vărzaru and Bocean 2024). In addition, a series of researches emphasises the fact that digitalisation leads to the emergence of new management methods (Mihu et al. 2023).

The European Union announced the launch of the Digital Single Market Strategy in 2015 (EU for Digital 2024), as part of the Europe 2020 project, which aims to transform the European Union into "the most dynamic and competitive knowledge-based economy" by 2020 (Birch and Mykhnenko 2014). In fact, since the beginning of this period, it can be said that the EU has come to understand the need to take systemic measures to stimulate the digital transformation.

Digital technologies and digital business models have been identified as key factors of the EU's competitiveness. In addition, the need to improve the regulatory framework to attract investment in the IT sector is increasingly emphasised (European Parliament 2025b).

The European Commission has set objectives such as simplifying access for consumers and businesses to the use of digital goods and services across the European Union and creating the most favourable conditions for the intensive development of digital networks and innovative services (Marcus 2024).

In 2019, the European Commission (EC) started to consistently implement measures aimed at furthering the digital transformation of society. These measures were reflected in the EC's 6 main priorities for the period 2019–2024, including "A Europe fit for the digital age" (Hernández Quirós et al. 2023). It was noted that the implementation of this priority should be based on three main principles: "Technology at the service of people", "A clear and competitive digital economy", "An open, democratic and sustainable society". In other words, we are talking about the fact that digitalisation is based not only on technological transformation, but also on sustainable transformation as part of the SDG approach (Castro et al. 2021). Traditional goods and services have gradually begun to be replaced by "virtual practices" that reduce both energy consumption and carbon emissions (Guaita Martínez et al., 2022).

Later in 2020, the European Commission (2025a) published a series of documents that should define this EU digital development strategy for the next five years. Among them, it is worth noting the aspects related to artificial intelligence, the European Data Strategy and the Digital Strategy (European Commission 2020). The following year, the EC presented a new digitalisation strategy until 2030—the Digital Decade (Hernández de Rojas et al. 2024).

The 2030 Digital Compass is an integral part of the European Green Deal and has as its primary objective transparency through the digital change of SMEs in Europe. Thus, through the new industrial strategy, we have a double transition that involves both the transformation of traditional business strategies into green strategies and more sustainable production at the level of all industrial structures (Chatzistamoulou 2023).

3 Digital Economy and Society Index—Structure and Components

The digitalisation of the economy is one of the main pillars of the Europe 2020 strategy, which sets out the economic growth objectives of the European Union (approved in May 2015). It includes 16 specific initiatives launched by the Commission in January 2017 and discussed in the European Parliament and the Council of the EU (Boikova et al. 2021).

The main objective of digitalisation is to improve the use of the potential of information and communication technologies to promote innovation, support economic development and stimulate scientific and technological progress in general, and, ultimately, to promote the formation of "smart", sustainable and inclusive growth of the region's economy. At the same time, the development of ICT infrastructure has multiple benefits. In addition to increasing employability and jobs, we can also talk about a new era of the digital industry with a significant and positive impact on economic growth (Pradhan et al. 2021).

According to a study by Sturgeon (2021), a functioning digital market can make a significant contribution to economic development. However, like any dynamic process, digitalisation creates certain conditions that require a person to possess a number of skills for coordinating high-quality interaction, for example, the ability to work with information and communication technologies, to use new opportunities in the digital space for professional and personal needs.

The Digital Economy and Society Index is particularly valuable for assessing the level of digitalisation. Which is a composite measure examining the digital performance of Europe. DESI was first calculated in 2014, using statistical data from 2013, developed by the European Commission to provide an evidence-based contribution to the assessment of digital development in the EU as a whole (Zdražil and Kraftová 2022).

DESI (Digital Economy and Society Index) measures the degree of digitalisation in the economy and society. It is a composite index that summarises relevant digitalisation indicators in Europe as a whole and in each Member State (Başol and Yalçın 2021). It is structured in four chapters:

1. Connectivity—Fixed broadband, mobile broadband and prices
2. Human capital—Internet use, basic and specialised digital skills
3. Digital technology adoption—Digitalisation of business and e-commerce
4. Digital public services—E-government and e-health (Başol and Yalçın 2021)

4 Romania's and Hungary's Performance in DESI

The main dimensions considered for the analysis of the current state of the digital economy in Romania include a comparison between the average indicators of the EU-27 Member States, Romania and Hungary. The comparisons are made with 4 dimensions developed by DESI: connectivity, digital human capital, technology integration in business, and digital public services.

Connectivity involves the implementation of broadband infrastructure and its quality. In this sense, we analysed the indicator "Broadband internet coverage by speed" for the EU27, Romania and Hungary average from 2015 to 2024. As a unit of measurement, the indicator is measured in Percentage of households, and the defining element selected in our analysis is more than 100 megabits per second (Mbps). As can be seen in the Fig. 1, the trend is an upward one, both at the EU level and at the level of the two countries.

A constant increase can be noted, with a notable jump in the period 2018–2021. The country with the best broadband internet coverage by speed with more than 100 megabits per second is Romania, which reached a maximum of 96.4% in 2024, surpassing Hungary which recorded 95.3% and the EU average of 91.1%.

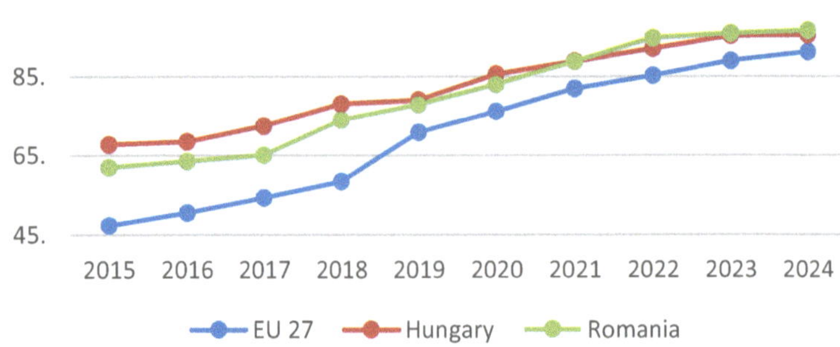

Fig. 1 Broadband internet coverage by speed for the EU27, Romania and Hungary. *Source* Own elaboration based on data collected from Eurostat

Digital human capital analyses the diversity of activities carried out by citizens on the internet. Our analysis follows the evolution of the Individuals' level of digital skills indicator at the EU, Hungary and Romania average level for the years 2021 and 2023. Thus, Individuals with basic or above basic information and data literacy skills show an upward trend in the analysed period. Hungary exceeds the EU average percentages by registering 85.15% in 2021 and 88.96% in 2023. The relatively low overall level of digital literacy among Romanians is explained by the low values of the indicators, more precisely by 65.73% in 2021 and 71.56% in 2023 (Fig. 2).

The integration of technology into business is essential for the digitalisation of businesses and the development of the online sales channel. In this sense, we analysed the indicator "Artificial intelligence by NACE" at the level of all activities carried out. Size classes in the number of persons employed are 10 h more for enterprises that use at least one of the AI technologies in the period 2023–2024 for the EU, Hungary and Romania. Although a significant increase can be observed from one year to another at the EU level, with almost 5 percent, the situation in the 2 countries is below average. If Hungary reaches almost half of the EU average, Romania has very low percentages of 1.51% in 2023, respectively 3.07% in 2025 (Fig. 3).

Digital public services involve the digitalisation of services in the public system with an emphasis on government services. Thus, our analysis focuses on the indicator E-government activities of individuals via websites of public authorities (last 12 months) in the period 2022–2024. Although the trend is an upward one, without major fluctuations, significant differences are noted between the analysed elements (Fig. 4).

If Hungary is above the EU average throughout the analysed period, reaching a maximum of 79.44% in 2024, Romania is well below the average level. The maximum reached is 25.28% in 2024.

Regarding the IT workforce, we analysed, based on Eurostat data, Employed ICT specialists in the period 2015–2024 for the EU 27, Hungary and Romania.

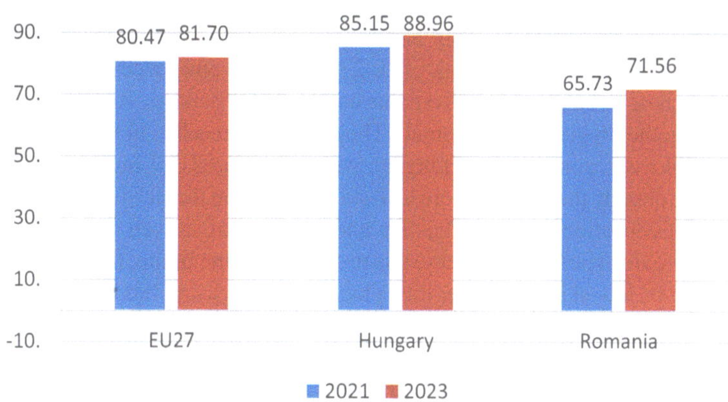

Fig. 2 The evolution of the Individuals' level of digital skills indicator at the EU27 level, Hungary and Romania. *Source* Own elaboration based on data collected from Eurostat

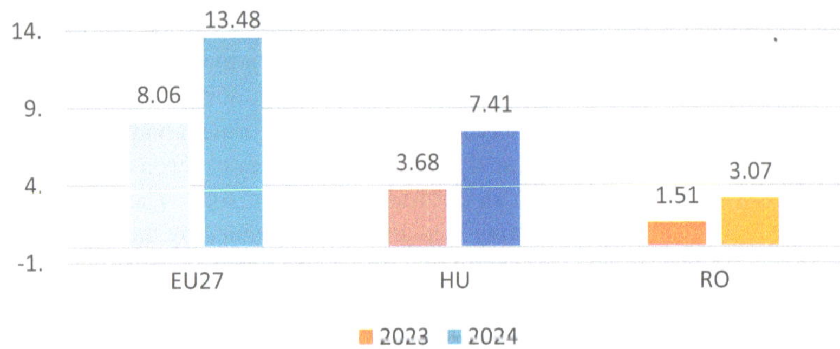

Fig. 3 The evolution of artificial intelligence by NACE indicator at the EU 27 level, Hungary and Romania. *Source* Own elaboration based on data collected from Eurostat

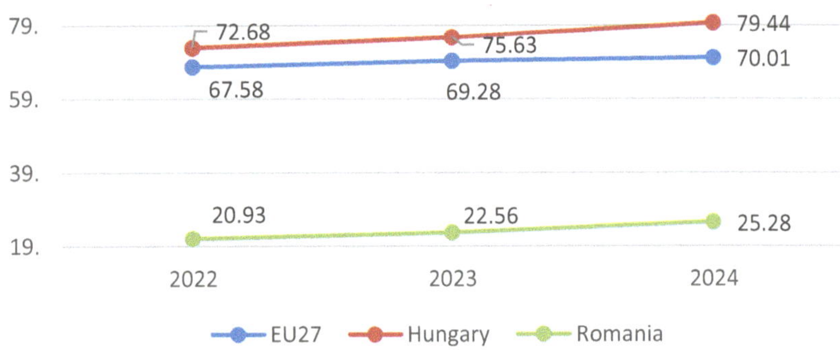

Fig. 4 The evolution of digital public services at the EU 27 level, Hungary and Romania. *Source* Own elaboration based on data collected from Eurostat

Currently, the IT personnel market has become even more dynamic and competitive. At the EU level, companies have generally adapted to the new realities, changing their approaches to hiring, training and managing IT personnel. These trends are continuing to grow, reaching a peak of 10,273.6 million employees (Fig. 5).

The deficit of IT employees in Romania and Hungary persists. Although the trend is increasing, the progress is quite small. The maximum reached in Romania is 221.6 million employees, compared to Hungary, which reached 211.1 million employees.

There are already three times more low-skilled adults in the EU than jobs requiring low levels of education, but digitalisation and automation, as well as ongoing structural changes, are expected to increase this proportion in the future, further worsening the situation of low-skilled people, thus placing an increasing burden on social and health systems. Hungary has significant reserves of resources in terms of the workforce, but it is largely made up of adults with low qualifications or who need retraining or continuous training. Therefore, in addition to new labour market expectations, it is important to find innovative approaches and tools that can successfully engage these

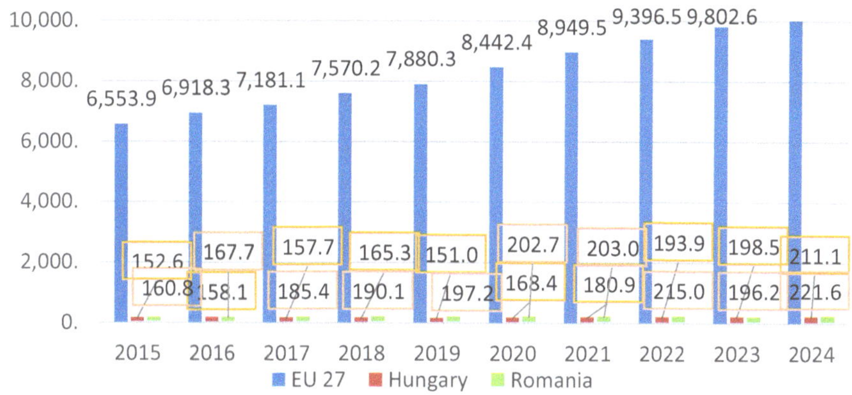

Fig. 5 Employed ICT specialists from 2015 to 2024 for the EU 27, Hungary and Romania. *Source* Own elaboration based on data collected from Eurostat

people in skills development, where they can benefit from appropriate development (Budai 2022).

Last but not least, we analysed the digitalization of activity in SMEs through the indicator Internet purchases by individuals who have made a last online purchase, in the 12 months. Thus, in the period 2020–2024, an upward trend can be observed, with a balanced growth, without major fluctuations in the three elements analysed (Fig. 6).

Hungary exceeds the EU level with a maximum of 74.18% in 2024, with almost 3 percentage points more. A notable but significant difference is Romania, which started in 2020 at 37.86% and reached a maximum of 56.12%.

The assessment of the level of digital skills is based on information about the actions carried out by Individuals with basic or above basic overall digital skills,

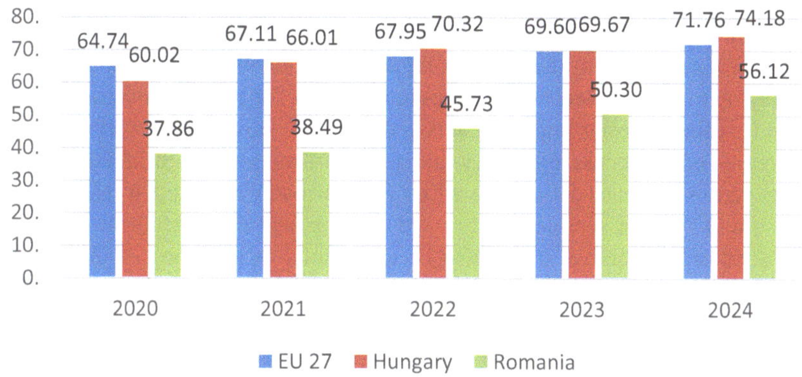

Fig. 6 Internet purchases by individuals who have made a last online purchase in the 12 months in the EU 27, Hungary and Romania. *Source* Own elaboration based on data collected from Eurostat

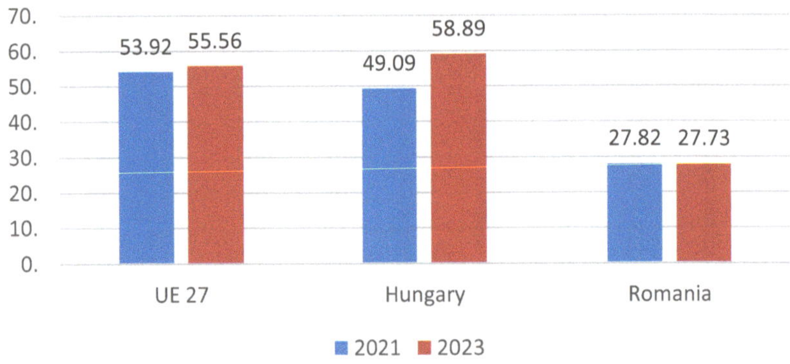

Fig. 7 Individuals who have basic or above basic overall digital skills. *Source* Own elaboration based on data collected from Eurostat

regardless of age. The data were collected annually from Eurostat for 2021 and 2023, respectively (Fig. 7).

Thus, the EU average in 2021 was 56.92% of the population with basic or above basic overall digital skills, with a slight increase in 2023 to 55.56%. As for Hungary, if in 2021 the percentage approached the EU average, in 2023 the level increases significantly and ends up exceeding it. As for Romania, the situation is much more worrying. If in 2021, we were halfway to the EU average with 27.82% of the population with basic or above basic overall digital skills, in 2023, we decreased by a few hundredths.

5 Romania's Progress in E-Government

E-Government is, in its general sense, the use by Government of computer applications and other information technologies, based on the Internet, combined with processes that implement these technologies, to improve access to and delivery of information to Government and services to the public, or to other government agencies and entities. It brings improvements to the way the Government works that result in increased effectiveness, efficiency and quality of services (Păceşilă 2007).

E-government can be defined in various ways. Broadly speaking, it can be defined as the use of ICT for service delivery and development of government operations. From another perspective, it can also be understood as a method of using digital technologies to improve the openness, transparency, efficiency and quality of services provided by government officials. In addition, e-government can be defined as a system for the more efficient operation of government agencies and provision of high-quality services to citizens and businesses using ICT (Twizeyimana and Andersson 2019).

Romania, together with all EU Member States, has declared its commitment at the highest level for the digital transformation of the state, for the recovery, prosperity, security, competitiveness and well-being of society. The European Digital Decade policy programme 2030, established by Decision (EU) 2022/24811, guides the digital transformation of all EU Member States on four main lines of action, with concrete and measurable targets and objectives, namely: digital public services, digital skills, digital transformation of enterprises, as well as secure and sustainable infrastructures (Ministry of Research, Innovation and Digitalisation 2024).

Romania is expected to see an increase in the digitalisation of public services for citizens of up to 62.7% in 2024, compared to 52.2% in 2023, but the country remains below the EU average of 82.3%. Also, the average digitalisation of public services for companies is 55.1% in 2024, up from 50% in 2023, according to the European Commission (2025b, c).

The report mentions major projects announced or already implemented by Romanian institutions, which should transform the way public services are delivered. However, they will require an adequate degree of development and maintenance over time, and the public entities carrying out these projects should receive the necessary resources, such as financial, project management and ICT specialists (Ciubotă 2025).

Romania is today facing the challenge of moving from an e-Government approach—focused on the use of ICT to promote efficiency in the public sector—to a Digital Governance, that is, the use of digital technologies that transform the way the public sector operates and the services offered to citizens, so as to accelerate the effort to promote well-being, prosperity and democracy. A comprehensive and coherent approach to digital transformation in the public sector can contribute to rethinking existing public institutions and promoting a more open, participatory and inclusive Romanian society (Ministry of Research, Innovation and Digitalisation 2024).

However, efforts to digitise the Romanian public sector are ongoing, with initiatives such as RO e-Transport—the electronic system implemented by ANAF to monitor the transport of goods with high tax risk or Ro e-Sigiliu—an integral part of Ro eTransport (National Agency for Tax Administration 2025). The national electronic invoicing system (RO e-Factura) has made significant progress with the implementation of the system, aiming to expand digitalisation, invoicing, fiscal transparency and efficiency in B2C and B2B controls.

ANAF has strengthened the infrastructure necessary for the implementation of DAC 7 in Romania with the development of the procedure and created an effective reporting mechanism to increase transparency and combat tax evasion generated by digital platform operators. These projects are part of the data and information sources that will feed the Big Data platform with their own information. (National Agency for Fiscal Administration 2025).

According to (Ministry of Research, Innovation and Digitalization 2024) the major reforms and investments aimed at the digital transformation of public services that were initiated within the national recovery and resilience plan in 2022, in line with the "Strategic Framework for the Adoption and Use of Innovative Technologies in

Public Administration 2021–2027", continue to be implemented and will contribute to the achievement of the EU's digital transformation objectives.

The latest reports for DESI, as noted by the authors Fernández-Portillo et al. (2020), show us that the lowest value at the European level is attributed to technological integration, because European companies cannot currently compete on the global market in terms of investments in information technology.

6 The State of Digitalization in Hungary

According to research by (Budai 2022) a 1% increase in digital literacy would mean a 0.123% increase in GDP, which, in the case of Hungary, could lead to a GDP surplus of 34.7 billion forints per year. Since the bulk of the Hungarian employment structure is made up of unskilled, routine and low-skilled workers, a significant development of digital competence would dramatically improve social mobility, as this is where the greatest opportunity for advancement lies.

Given that the digital economy is estimated to directly and indirectly provide employment opportunities for over 20% of employees, the proportion of companies facing a shortage of workers in digital jobs is increasing. The digitalization of jobs is happening faster than the formation of the digital workforce. Technological changes (robotization, automation, artificial intelligence) are radically transforming the labor market and the expected skill areas. According to a report by (PwC 2019), 900,000 jobs in Hungary could be affected by technological changes in the next 15 years.

In the EU, 54% of people aged 16–74 have at least basic digital skills, according to a 2021 survey. In Hungary, less than half (49%) of the population aged 16–74 have at least basic digital skills. 42% of people without digital skills are unemployed (https://www.ksh.hu/?lang=en).

In recent years, Hungary's performance has been improving at a similar pace to the EU average. However, Hungary was still in the category of low-performing countries (Cseh 2020). However, the deterioration of overall performance does not necessarily mean that the direction of development is wrong (Fig. 8).

In 2021, each of the public administration organizations had its own website. In parallel with the continuous expansion of the information available on the websites of public offices and public institutions and the range of issues that can be managed electronically, the rate of public use is also increasing (https://www.ksh.hu/stadat_files/ikt/en/ikt0021.html).

Two-thirds of Hungarians aged 16–74 downloaded and submitted a form online to a public office or institution for private purposes in 2021. In 2010, only 24% of the Hungarian population downloaded and 17% submitted completed forms online (https://www.ksh.hu/stadat_files/ikt/en/ikt0020.html) (Fig. 9).

Regarding the proportion of services available on the websites of public administration, defence and compulsory social insurance institutions in Hungary, the trend is increasing, with an upward risk, without major fluctuations (Fig. 10).

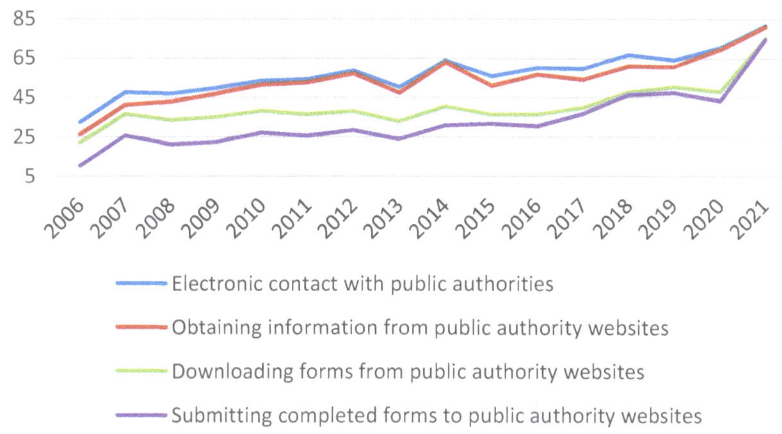

Fig. 8 Use of e-government portals by e-administration levels in Hungary. *Source* Own elaboration based on data collected from https://www.ksh.hu/informacio-kommunikacio

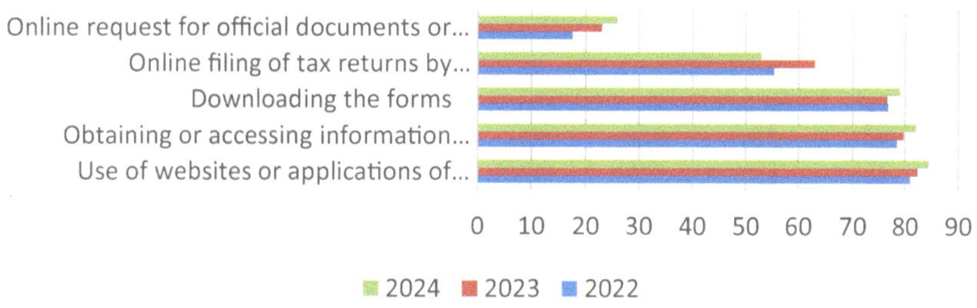

Fig. 9 Use of electronic services offered by public authorities. *Source* Own elaboration based on data collected from https://www.ksh.hu/informacio-kommunikacio

The peak was reached in 2023 by the category of local news related to the community with 91.1%, while the lowest percentage was also reached in 2023 by the chat service with 2.9%. Overall, the second category in terms of availability is given by customer service information, namely the category of organizational information with contact details.

Figure 11 on the use of information and communication tools in public administration, defence and compulsory social insurance in Hungary shows a constant trend for some categories of tools such as computer, internet or email.

Websites started from a percentage of 58% in 2011 and reached 100% in 2023. Intranet had a constant but modest rise from 17.3% in 2009 to 30% in 2023. As for social media tools, they started from a percentage of 35.5% in 2015 and reached 78.6% in 2023.

The rapid development of information and communication technologies determines the direction of development and transformation of society and economy. E-government is a significant tool in achieving sustainable development goals. This

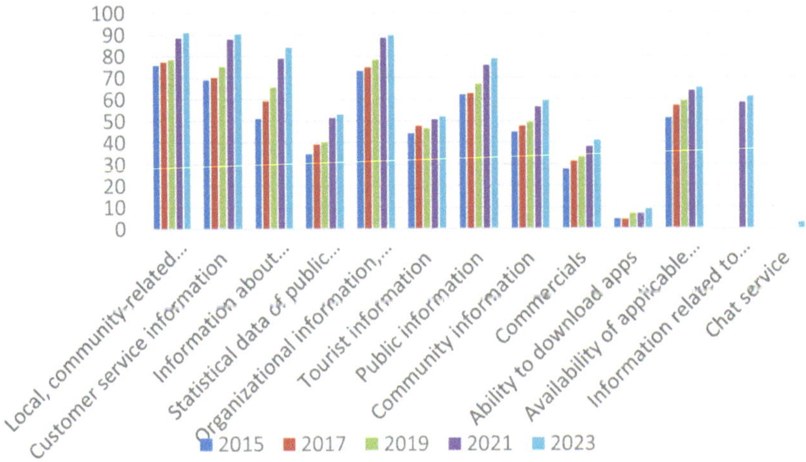

Fig. 10 Proportion of services available on the websites of public administration, defence and compulsory social insurance institutions [%]. *Source* Own elaboration based on data collected from https://www.ksh.hu/informacio-kommunikacio

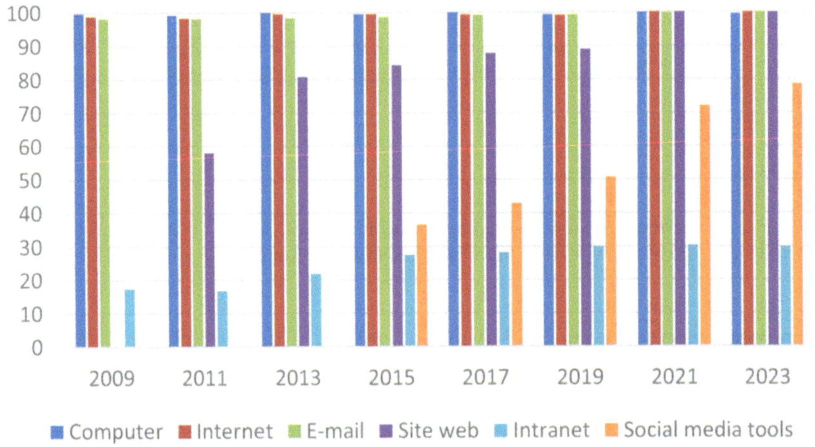

Fig. 11 Use of information and communication tools in public administration, defence and compulsory social security [%]. *Source* Own elaboration based on data collected from https://www.ksh.hu/informacio-kommunikacio

aspect is very well highlighted by the situation of the digital economy in Hungary. Most indicators show us a significant and steady growth, which in some situations exceeds the EU average.

7 Conclusions

The global trend towards digital business transformation is growing daily. This is driven by the constant changes in the economic climate and an extremely competitive environment. Meeting customer expectations, attracting and retaining them across all sectors and segments, is becoming increasingly difficult year by year. Therefore, companies need to be flexible and highly efficient—and digital transformation is a fundamental tool in achieving this goal.

The digital transformation in recent years in the European Union allows us to note the presence of a significant evolution. Thus, if the first digital strategy, "Digital Single Market", focused mainly on creating a single regulatory area that would fix the relevant sphere of the economy, the latest strategy developed to date "Digital Decade", is based on clearly measurable objectives by 2030, which are fully consistent with the principles of setting SMART objectives.

The digital transformation strategy is in a direct interdependent relationship with the content of the Sustainable Development Goals (SDGs). In this context, we observe a clear hierarchy of strategies, in which digital transformation ensures the achievement of the objectives set at a global level.

Summarising the study of the characteristics of the development of the digital economy, we can conclude that, in general, a trend of rapid spread of modern technologies is developing throughout the world.

The last decade marks an important stage in the digital transformation of Romania. Technology continues to transform various aspects of the lives of citizens and companies, creating new opportunities for growth and development. Key sectors—from industry and agriculture to education and health—continue to actively implement digital solutions, making Romania more competitive internationally.

In Hungary, a favorable trend can be observed in the use of services that represent higher levels of e-government development. The downloading of forms and their electronic submission by the public is continuously increasing in Hungary, looking back over a longer period of time. According to the data provided, the EU average exceeded the Hungarian level in all but two years analyzed from 2010 to 2020. However, according to the details provided by Központi Statistizkaia Hivatal (KSH) (https://www.ksh.hu/stadat_files/ikt/en/ikt0020.html) in 2021, the domestic indicator significantly exceeded the average of the EU27 Member States in terms of the proportion of people obtaining information from the websites of public institutions (72%) and those downloading forms (67%).

Turning to specific sectors and processes within Romania, digitalisation can help streamline interactions between government agencies and society, making them more transparent and efficient by developing e-government and digital services for citizens. It can facilitate the creation of new jobs by developing innovative startups and companies. It can improve the quality of social services and access to them for a wider segment of the population by introducing digital technologies in the fields of health, education and social services.

However, challenges remain for Romania on the path to full digitalisation, such as ensuring cybersecurity, developing infrastructure and training qualified personnel. The government and the business environment must continue to collaborate to overcome these obstacles and create conditions for sustainable economic and societal growth in the digital world.

References

Agenția Națională de Administrare Fiscală (2025, August 21) Raport de activitate semestrul I 2025. ANAF. https://static.anaf.ro/static/10/Anaf/Informatii_R/18.08.2025%20-%20Raport%20de%20activitateANAF_2025S1_V7.pdf

Başol O, Yalçın EC (2021) How does the Digital Economy and Society Index (DESI) affect labour market indicators in EU countries? Hum Syst Manag 40(4):503–512. https://doi.org/10.3233/HSM-200904

Birch K, Mykhnenko V (2014) Lisbonizing versus financializing Europe? The Lisbon agenda and the (un)making of the European knowledge-based economy. Eviron Plann C Gov Policy 32(1):108–128. https://doi.org/10.1068/c1246r

Boikova T, Zeverte-Rivza S, Rivza P, Rivza B (2021) The determinants and effects of competitiveness: the role of digitalisation the European economies. Sustainability 13(21):11689. https://doi.org/10.3390/su132111689

Budai BB (2022) A digitális kompetencia növekvő szerepe [The growing role of digital literacy]. Pro Publico Bono—Magyar Közigazgatás 30(2):30–59. https://real.mtak.hu/146942/1/02_budai_30-59_PPB_2022_2.pdf

Castro GDR, Martín-Fórtiz SJ, Yánez-Valdés R (2021) Unleashing the convergence amid digitalisation and sustainable development goals. J Clean Prod 289:125710. https://doi.org/10.1016/j.jclepro.2020.122204

Chatzistamoulou N (2023) Is digital transformation the Deus ex Machina towards sustainability transition of the European SMEs? Ecol Econ 206:107739. https://doi.org/10.1016/j.ecolecon.2023.107739

Ciubotă D (2025, Iunie 20) Raport: Digitalizarea serviciilor publice crește în România, dar este cu circa 20% sub media Uniunii Europene. Economedia. https://economedia.ro/raport-digitalizarea-serviciilor-publice-creste-in-romania-dar-este-cu-circa-20-sub-media-uniunii-europene.html

Cseh G (2020) A digitális gazdaság és társadalom fejlettségét mérő mutató—Magyarország európai uniós teljesítménye a digitalizált világban. Miskolci Jogi Szemle, 15(1)(special edition):51–60

EU for Digital (2024) EU digital strategy. Retrieved from EU for Digital: https://eufordigital.eu/ro/discover-eu/eu-digital-strategy/

European Commission (2020) Shaping Europe's digital future (Communication). Publications Office of the European Union. https://ec.europa.eu/info/sites/info/files/communication-shaping-europes-digital-future-feb2020_en_4.pdf

European Commission (2025a) 2030 digital compass: your digital decade. Futurium. Retrieved from https://futurium.ec.europa.eu/ro/digital-compass

European Commission (2025b) Europe's digital decade: digital targets for 2030. Retrieved from https://commission.europa.eu/strategy-and-policy/priorities-2019-2024/europe-fit-digital-age/europes-digital-decade-digital-targets-2030_en

European Commission. (2025c). Romania 2025 digital decade country report. Shaping Europe's digital future. https://digital-strategy.ec.europa.eu/en/factpages/romania-2025-digital-decade-country-report#:~:text=According%20to%20the%20special%20Eurobarometer,fake%20news%20and%20disinformation%20online

European Parliament (2025a) 5G action plan [Legislative Train]. Retrieved from https://www.europarl.europa.eu/legislative-train/theme-a-europe-fit-for-the-digital-age/file-5g-action-plan
European Parliament (2025b) Report on European technological sovereignty and digital infrastructure* (Report A-10-2025-0107/2025). Report. European Parliament, Committee on Industry, Research and Energy, Rapporteur: Sarah Knafo. Adopted 11 June 2025. Available at: https://www.europarl.europa.eu/doceo/document/A-10-2025-0107_EN.html. Accessed 4 Aug 2025.
Fernández-Portillo A, Almodóvar-González M, Hernández-Mogollón R (2020) Impact of ICT development on economic growth: a study of OECD European Union countries. Technol Soc 63:101420. https://doi.org/10.1016/j.techsoc.2020.101420
Guaita Martínez JM, Puertas R, Martín Martín JM, Ribeiro-Soriano D (2022) Digitalization, innovation and environmental policies aimed at achieving sustainable production. Sustainable Production and Consumption 32:92–100. https://doi.org/10.1016/j.spc.2022.03.035
Hernández de Rojas F, Pita PR, Pérez Martínez JE (2024) Assessing the European association between digitalisation and innovation. Telecommun Policy 48(7):Article 102810. https://doi.org/10.1016/j.telpol.2024.102810
Hernández Quirós L, Smith RS, Schade S (2023) Landscaping the monitoring of interoperability and digital transformation: Streamlining the monitoring of digital policies in the European Commission (EUR 31564 EN, JRC 133628). Publications Office of the European Union. https://doi.org/10.2760/350656
Marcus JS (2024) Digital aspects of the EU single market: still an incomplete work in progress?* CEPS In-Depth Analysis 2024/06. Centre for European Policy Studies. Published April 2024. Available at: https://cdn.ceps.eu/wp-content/uploads/2024/04/2FAajR4z-CEPS-InDepthAnalysis-2024-06_EU-Single-Mkt-digital.pdf
Mihu C, Pitic A, Bayraktar D (2023) Drivers of digital transformation and their impact on organisational management. Studies in Business and Economics 18(1):149–170. https://doi.org/10.2478/sbe-2023-0009
Ministerul Cercetării, Inovării şi Digitalizării (2024) Planul Naţional de Acţiune privind Deceniul Digital pentru România. https://www.mcid.gov.ro/wp-content/uploads/2024/04/Plan-national-de-actiune-roadmap-pentru-publicare.pdf
Păceşilă M (2007) E-government services at European level—features and trends [Serviciile de guvernare electronică la nivel European—caracteristici şi tendinţe]. Theoretical and Empirical Researches in Urban Management (Cercetări practice şi teoretice în Managementul Urban) 2(5):1–11. https://um.ase.ro/v02i4/1.pdf
Pradhan RP, Arvin MB, Nair MS, Hall JH, Bennett SE (2021) Sustainable economic development in India: The dynamics between financial inclusion, ICT development, and economic growth. Technol Forecast Soc Change 169:120758. https://www.sciencedirect.com/science/article/abs/pii/S0040162521001906
PwC Hungary (2019) How will AI impact the Hungarian labour market? https://www.pwc.com/hu/en/publications/assets/How-will-AI-impact-the-Hungarian-labour-market.pdf
Sturgeon TJ (2021) Upgrading strategies for the digital economy. Glob Strateg J 11(1). https://doi.org/10.1002/gsj.1364, https://sms.onlinelibrary.wiley.com/doi/abs/10.1002/gsj.1364
Twizeyimana JD, Andersson A (2019) The public value of e-government: A literature review. Gov Inf Q 36(3):167–178. https://doi.org/10.1016/j.giq.2019.01.001
Vărzaru A, Bocean C (2024) Digital transformation and innovation: the influence of digital technologies on turnover from innovation activities and types of innovation. Systems 12(395):1–25. https://doi.org/10.3390/systems12090359
Zdražil P, Kraftová I (2022) The determinants of competitive advantage for Europe's Regions: digital economy at the start of the fourth industrial revolution. J Econ [Ekonomicky casopis], Institute of Economic Research, Slovak Academy of Sciences 70(5):450–471. https://doi.org/10.31577/ekoncas.2022.05.04

Governmental Initiatives and EU-Funded Projects

Anca Otilia Dodescu and Laurențiu Droj

Abstract Anchored in the EU's vision for digital transformation and ethical AI governance, this chapter examines how Romania's AI path is shaped by European strategies, policy frameworks, and funding opportunities. Government policies, national programmes, and EU-funded projects support AI and digital economy growth within a multi-level governance structure linking EU directives with national strategies and local initiatives. European frameworks set direction, national policies translate priorities into action and regional and local actors- innovation hubs, universities, public institutions, and public–private partnerships-play a key role. Ultimately, progress toward an AI-driven economy depends not only on technological advancement but also on skills, cooperation and institutional capacity as well as on the ability to align infrastructure, talent and policy into a sustainable vision for digital transformation.

1 European-Level Initiatives and Funding for Artificial Intelligence and Digital Economy

The growing use of AI across the economy has become one of the EU's most significant priorities for the coming years. In April 2018, all EU Member States and Norway signed the *Declaration of Cooperation on Artificial Intelligence*, marking a shared political commitment to develop AI together while managing its opportunities and challenges (European Commission 2018). Building on this commitment, the European Commission proposed a *European strategy on Artificial Intelligence*, which was endorsed by the European Council in June 2018. To strengthen coordination between national and EU actions, the Commission adopted a *Coordinated Plan on Artificial Intelligence* in December 2018 with the goals such as aligning investments in AI research and innovation, fostering cooperation across Member States, promoting trustworthy and ethical use of AI and facilitating the exchange of knowledge and

A. O. Dodescu (✉) · L. Droj
Faculty of Economic Sciences, University of Oradea, Oradea, Romania
e-mail: adodescu@uoradea.ro

C. Sabău-Popa (ed.), *Artificial Intelligence in Finance, Accounting and Business Administration*, Contributions to Finance and Accounting,
https://doi.org/10.1007/978-3-032-22737-9_3

best practices across the EU. The plan was updated in 2021 (European Commission 2021a).

The *2021 Coordinated Plan on Artificial Intelligence* (European Commission 2021a) was developed in close cooperation with the Member States (and inclusive of Norway and Switzerland) and sets out an agenda for joint actions aimed at strengthening and streamlining cooperation between Member States and the European Commission. It focuses on key areas such as increasing investment, improving data availability, fostering talent and ensuring trust in AI. Among its central objectives is the encouragement of all Member States to design and implement their own national AI strategies, thereby aligning national efforts with the broader European framework.

Moreover, in the updated version of the plan (European Commission 2021a), the Commission, together with the Member States reaffirmed their commitment "accelerate private and public investments leveraging EU funding available, for example, through Digital Europe Program (DEP) and Horizon Europe Program (HE) and the Recovery and Resilience Facility (RRF)" (European Commission 2021a). The plan further specifies that the European Commission should allocate "at least EUR 1 billion per year from Horizon Europe and the Digital Europe programs under the programming period 2021–2027" (European Commission 2021a). The objective of this strategy is to "gradually increase public and private investment in AI to a total of EUR 20 billion per year over the course of this decade" (European Commission 2021a).

The *Coordinated Plan on Artificial Intelligence* is complemented by the *White Paper on Artificial Intelligence—A European Approach to Excellence and Trust*, published in February 2020 (European Commission 2020), which elaborated the Union's vision for a trustworthy AI ecosystem. The core elements of the *Coordinated Plan on Artificial Intelligence* include the main policy priorities and strategic actions designed to foster AI development and adoption across the European Union. Figure 1 illustrates the key policy objectives of the Coordinated Plan, emphasising investment coordination, the creation of enabling conditions for AI uptake, and ensuring that AI technologies are developed and used in ways that are trustworthy, human-centric, and aligned with European values.

As the use of AI expanded rapidly across the EU, the European Commission reinforced its strategic approach to ensure that innovation in AI contributes to economic growth, societal well-being, and sustainable development across all Member States. A key step in implementing the plan was the proposal of the first comprehensive EU regulations on AI in April 2021 (European Commission 2021b).

The Artificial Intelligence Act (AI Act) introduces a risk-based classification system for AI applications, establishing obligations proportionate to their potential impact (European Union 2024). Moreover, the AI Act builds on existing EU legislation, frameworks, and regulatory practices, reflecting the EU's commitment to ensuring that AI technologies are safe, trustworthy, and aligned with fundamental rights (European Union 2024; Future of Life Institute 2025).

Building upon this regulatory foundation, the institutional landscape that supports the implementation and governance of the AI Act is outlined in Fig. 2. It illustrates

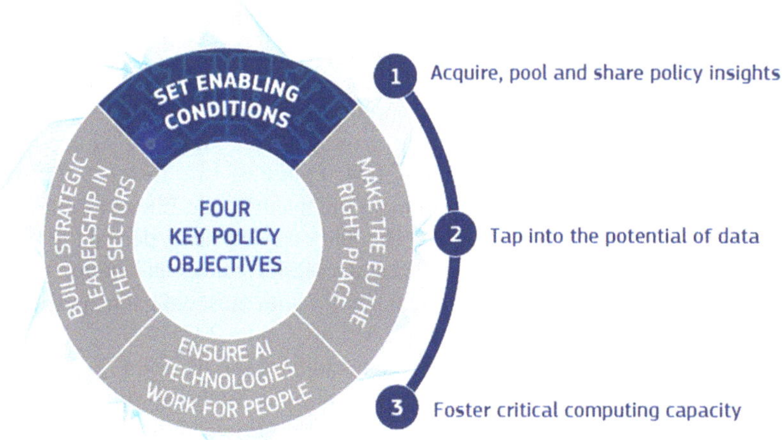

Fig. 1 AI key policy objectives. *Source* European Commission (2021a)

the interconnections among the European institutions, agencies, and advisory bodies involved in overseeing compliance, ethical standards, and the coordinated application of AI-related policies across Member States.

The AI risk-based classification categorises AI applications according to the level of risk they pose to users. Applications identified as posing higher risks are subject to stricter regulatory requirements. Building on the regulatory framework established by the AI Act, the risk-based classification categorises AI applications according to the potential impact they may have on users and society (European Union 2024).

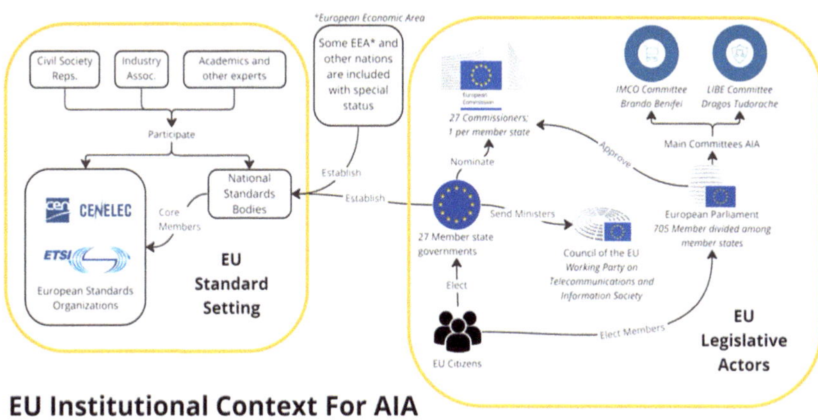

Fig. 2 EU institutional context for the Artificial Intelligence Act (AIA). *Source* Future of Life Institute, EU Artificial Intelligence Act, https://artificialintelligenceact.eu/about/ (accessed 03.09.2025)

Table 1 illustrates the four main risk categories defined in the Act—unacceptable risk, high risk, limited risk, and minimal risk—along with the corresponding obligations for providers and users.

As highlighted above, this risk-based approach is central to the AI Act, as it ensures that regulatory attention is proportionate to the potential impact of AI applications on users and society (European Union 2024; Future of Life Institute 2025). The EU Artificial Intelligence Act was formally adopted by the European Parliament in June 2024 (European Union 2024). The ban on AI systems deemed to pose an unacceptable risk came into effect on 2 February 2025 (European Union 2024). The implementation of the Act is currently underway, with most obligations expected to take full effect from August 2026 (Orrick AI Law Centre 2025).

To better understand the phased implementation of the AI Act, Fig. 3 presents a timeline of key obligations, from the formal adoption by the European Parliament in June 2024 to the full enforcement of regulatory requirements expected in August 2026 (Orrick AI Law Centre 2025). This timeline highlights the progressive rollout of compliance measures, including the immediate ban on AI systems deemed to pose an unacceptable risk, as well as the staggered application of obligations for high-risk and other AI systems (European Union 2024).

The development of advanced AI techniques remains extremely limited in the project area at present. According to the report *AI Watch—National Strategies on Artificial Intelligence: A European Perspective* (European Commission 2021c), both Romania and Hungary exhibit low adoption of AI tools in key areas, including business growth, research and development, innovation, education and training, lifelong learning, future market needs, and networking (European Commission 2021). The report recommends that, in order to ensure high-quality education in AI, countries should implement policies to strengthen teachers' competencies in digital and AI technologies and introduce AI-related subjects at universities, facilitating the transfer of expertise to broader society (European Commission 2021c; Galindo et al. 2021).

2 European Financing Mechanisms for AI and Digital Transformation

The European Union supports the development, adoption, and large-scale deployment of AI and digital technologies through a variety of funding instruments aimed at strengthening research, innovation, and deployment capacities across Member States. These programmes foster collaboration between universities, research centres, industry, and governments, contributing to Europe's competitiveness, innovation, and technological sovereignty (European Commission 2021d–h; European Commission and JRC 2025).

Several key European funding programmes play a central role in achieving these objectives:

Table 1 Risk-based classification of AI applications

Risk category	Description	Applications/examples	Regulatory obligations/exceptions
Unacceptable risk	AI systems considered a clear threat to safety, fundamental rights, or democratic values; prohibited in the EU	• Cognitive or behavioural manipulation of individuals or vulnerable groups (e.g., voice-activated toys encouraging dangerous behaviour in children) • Social scoring AI evaluating people based on behaviour, socio-economic status, or personal characteristics • Biometric identification and categorisation of individuals • Real-time and remote biometric identification in public spaces, including facial recognition • Compilation of facial recognition databases to infer emotions in workplaces or educational institutions (except for medical or safety purposes)	Exceptions may be granted only for law enforcement purposes, and under strict limitations

(continued)

Table 1 (continued)

Risk category	Description	Applications/examples	Regulatory obligations/exceptions
High-risk AI systems	AI systems that may negatively affect safety or fundamental rights; subject to stringent regulatory oversight	1. Integrated into products covered by EU product safety legislation 2. Operating in high-risk sectors (must be registered in an EU database), including: • Management and operation of critical infrastructure • Education and vocational training • Employment, worker management, and access to self-employment • Access to and enjoyment of essential private and public services • Law enforcement • Migration, asylum, and border control • Assistance in legal interpretation and application of the law	• Conformity assessment required • Approval required prior to market placement
Limited and Minimal Risk AI Systems	Applications generally safe but requiring ongoing oversight for transparency and compliance	• Disclosing AI-generated content • Informing users when interacting with AI systems (e.g., chatbots) • Implementing spam filters • Designing models to prevent illegal content generation	• Ensure transparency • Monitor and maintain compliance with AI Act requirements

Source Created by authors based on the European Union 2024

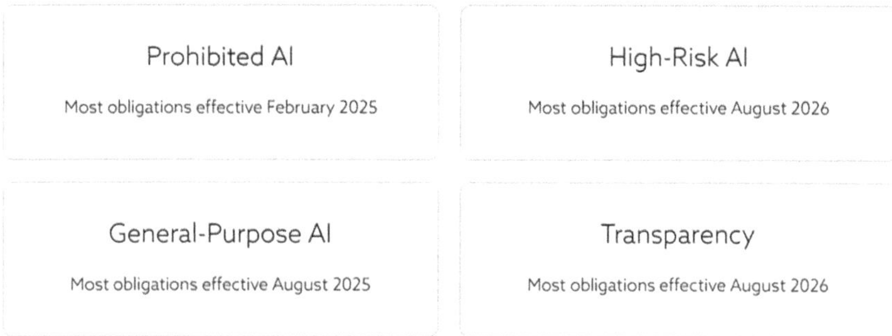

Fig. 3 Timeline of obligations for implementing EU AI Act. *Source* Orrick AI Law Centre, https://ai-law-center.orrick.com/ (accessed 04.09.2025)

1. *Horizon Europe (HE)—Framework Programme for Research and Innovation (2021–2027)*
   HE is the EU's primary funding programme for AI-related research and innovation projects. It supports the development of trustworthy, human-centric AI and facilitates integration across sectors such as industry, healthcare, transport, and public administration. Under Cluster 4: Digital, Industry, and Space, multiple calls target next-generation AI technologies (European Commission 2021d). A notable initiative under HE is **GenAI4EU** (2025), which promotes the adoption of generative AI solutions across manufacturing, healthcare, public services, creative industries, and education. The first call for proposals was opened in June 2025, with a submission deadline of 16 September 2025 (European Commission and JRC 2025).
2. *Digital Europe Programme (DEP)—Building Strategic Digital Capacities*
   DEP complements HE by financing the large-scale deployment of digital technologies, bridging the gap between research and market implementation. With a budget of €7.5 billion for 2021–2027, DEP supports AI testing and experimentation facilities, cybersecurity, digital skills development, deployment of digital infrastructure, and assistance for SMEs in adopting AI solutions (European Commission 2021e).
3. *Recovery and Resilience Facility (RRF)*
   RRF provides financial support for digital and green transformation projects, including AI-driven modernisation of public services and strategic investments in digital infrastructure across Member States (European Commission 2021f).
4. *European Territorial Cooperation (INTERREG)*
   Interreg supports the twin green and digital transition in health, environment, transport, sustainable energy, research, and education, promoting regional collaboration to find shared solutions and facilitating the implementation of joint actions and policy exchanges. They foster cooperation between local authorities, research centres, and businesses to strengthen regional competitiveness and digital capacity (European Commission 2021g).
5. *Made in Europe Partnership—Driving European Industrial Leadership*

Under Horizon Europe's industrial policy, this programme advances digital transformation in the manufacturing sector. It supports the integration of AI, robotics, and data-driven technologies and the development of "Factories of the Future," where human–machine collaboration and smart automation are central enablers (European Commission 2021h).

To provide a clear overview, Table 2 summarises these programmes, highlighting their objectives, key areas of activity, funding periods, and further resources.

3 Governmental Initiatives and National-Level Support Programs for Artificial Intelligence and Digital Economy in Romania

The adoption of Artificial Intelligence (AI) and the digital economy in Romania is driven by a combination of *national strategies, governmental policies,* and *EU-funded programmes.* Together, these initiatives aim to foster research and innovation, increase investment in AI, develop digital skills, and strengthen collaboration between public and private stakeholders. The success of AI integration depends not only on technological innovation but also on the creation of a supportive ecosystem that connects research institutions, industry, public administration, and civil society.

3.1 National Strategies

Romania's national approach to artificial intelligence is firmly aligned with the European Union's strategic framework, particularly the EU Artificial Intelligence Act (European Union 2024), the Coordinated Plan on Artificial Intelligence (European Commission 2021a). Building on the insights from the European-level AI initiatives and European funding programmes supporting AI and digital transformation (European Commission 2021d–h; European Commission and JRC 2025), Romania has developed its own comprehensive framework to foster the adoption and implementation of AI across public and private sectors (European Commission 2021c; Galindo et al. 2021).

This alignment ensures that European guidelines, funding mechanisms, and ethical standards complement national priorities, promoting a coherent, responsible, and human-centric AI ecosystem. By integrating EU objectives into domestic policy, Romania contributes to a unified European AI landscape grounded in transparency, accountability, and innovation that serves society.

The cornerstone of Romania's framework is the *National Strategy for Artificial Intelligence 2024–2027*, approved in July 2024 (Government of Romania 2024). The strategy sets a framework for AI implementation in sectors such as taxation, public administration, risk analysis, public tenders, and optimisation of public spending. It

Table 2 European funding programmes supporting AI and digital transformation

Programme/initiative	Objective/focus	Key areas/activities	Period	Further information
Horizon Europe (HE)	Research and innovation in AI, trustworthy and human-centric AI	Cluster 4: Digital, Industry, and Space; next-gen AI technologies	2021–2027	Horizon Europe
GenAI4EU	Integrate Generative AI across key sectors	Manufacturing, healthcare, public services, creative industries, education	2025	GenAI4EU Programme
Digital Europe Programme (DEP)	Large-scale deployment of digital technologies	AI testing and experimentation facilities, cybersecurity, digital skills, digital infrastructure, support for SMEs	2021–2027	Digital Europe Programme
Recovery and Resilience Facility (RRF)	Digital and green transformation support	AI-driven modernisation of public services, strategic investments in digital infrastructure	2021–2027	Recovery and Resilience Facility
INTERREG	Regional collaboration and innovation	AI adoption in SMEs, cooperation between authorities, research, and business	2021–2027	Interreg
Made in Europe Partnership	Industrial digital transformation	AI, robotics, data-driven technologies, Factories of the Future	Horizon Europe period	Made in Europe Initiative

Source Created by authors based on European Commission (2021d–h) and European Commission and JRC (2025)

anticipates that around 70% of private companies and government institutions will adopt AI technologies in the near future. The *National Strategy for Artificial Intelligence 2024–2027* defines the following general objectives, aligned with the priority action axes included in EU strategic documents and with national development needs and opportunities:

1. Supporting R&D education and the development of AI-specific skills;
2. Developing and efficiently using infrastructure and datasets;

3. Developing the national Research–Development–Innovation system in the field of AI;
4. Ensuring technology transfer through partnerships;
5. Facilitating the adoption of AI across society;
6. Developing a governance and regulatory system for AI.

The strategy underscores Romania's commitment to integrating AI in both public services and the private sector, emphasising ethical AI, data protection, innovation, and competitiveness.

Several other national policies and strategic documents complement Romania's AI strategic framework, shaping the broader environment for AI adoption and deployment across public and private sectors:

- *Recovery and Resilience Plan (PNRR)*—supports digitalisation and adoption of AI-driven solutions in public administration and industry (Government of Romania 2021a).
- *National Strategy for Research, Innovation, and Smart Specialisation 2022–2027*—promotes AI in research, innovation, and economic development, supporting knowledge transfer and smart specialisation (Government of Romania 2022a).
- *Romania's Cybersecurity Strategy 2022–2027*—addresses AI-driven cybersecurity challenges, data protection, and secure deployment of AI applications (Government of Romania 2022b).
- *Employment Strategy 2021–2027*—integrates AI in workforce planning, skill development, and labour market adaptation (Government of Romania 2021b).
- *Strategy for the Digitalisation of Education in Romania 2021–2027* (SMART.Edu), addresses the need for digital transformation in education, focusing on two main pillars: developing competencies relevant to digital transformation, and creating a high-performing digital education ecosystem. AI plays a central role in the second pillar, optimising resource allocation, monitoring student progress, personalising learning, and providing predictive and vocational guidance (Romanian Ministry of Education 2020).
- *National Defence Strategy 2020–2024* recognises AI as both a development driver and a source of potential hybrid and informational risks to national security. The *White Paper on Defence* (2021) calls for the creation of an AI utilisation strategy within the Ministry of National Defence, aiming to enhance Romania's participation in NATO and EU research and innovation initiatives focused on emerging and disruptive technologies (Romanian Ministry of National Defence 2021).

These strategies collectively provide a comprehensive overview of Romania's AI priorities, emphasising human resource development, education enhancement, entrepreneurship, and investment in cybersecurity mechanisms to manage the growing volumes of data processed by AI applications.

3.2 Governmental Policies and National Programmes

At the national level, Romania's governmental policies translate strategic objectives into concrete measures designed to stimulate innovation, investment, and digital transformation. These programmes, often co-funded by the European Union, ensure coherence between national and European priorities. Complementing the strategic framework, Romania has introduced a series of *governmental policies, programmes* and *initiatives* that support the development and application of AI across various sectors. They focus on funding, incentives, and capacity-building to accelerate AI integration within the economy and public administration.

National Research, Development and Innovation Plan (PNCDI IV) 2022–2027, Romania's central framework for RDI funding, plays a key role in supporting AI research, innovation, and collaboration. According to the Executive Unit for Financing Higher Education, Research, Development and Innovation (UEFISCDI 2023), PNCDI IV provides targeted support for AI research, startup creation, and collaborative initiatives, promoting AI activities across universities, research centres, and industry, while fostering technological excellence and applied AI solutions. Several subprograms and instruments are particularly relevant for AI, notably 5.9.8 Artificial Intelligence and 5.9.9 Autonomous Systems (UEFISCDI 2023). Table 3 summarises the main PNCDI IV programs, subprograms, and funding instruments with direct relevance to AI.

Other key national programmes and initiatives include:

- *Skills Development Programs*—National-scale initiatives focusing on digital and emerging technology competences (including AI), targeting university students, professionals and educators, with emphasis on lifelong learning, teacher training and high-quality digital education such us *National Digital Skills Programme for employees in small and medium-sized enterprises*—a government program for SME employees aimed at developing digital skills (Romanian Ministry of Education and Research 2020), and *SMART-Edu Strategic Initiative for Digitization of Education 2021–2027*—an initiative coordinated by the Ministry of Education that includes digital training for teachers and the development of digital competences at all levels of education (Eurofound 2020).
- *Tax Incentives and Digitalisation Support*—Encourage the adoption of AI and Industry 4.0 technologies by offering fiscal benefits to companies investing in digital transformation. The report *Investing in Romania 2024* highlights that the additional 50% deduction for R&D expenditures and accelerated depreciation for technological equipment are among the main fiscal incentives (KPMG 2024). Thus, a company investing in AI algorithms, computing infrastructure, or Industry 4.0 systems can benefit from these incentives, lowering net investment costs and making AI projects more attractive.
- *Public–Private Partnerships (PPPs)*—Facilitate joint projects among universities, research institutions, startups, and corporations to develop and implement AI-driven solutions (Law 178/2010). The Romanian government recently launched an initiative via the Ministry of Finance to identify a national portfolio of projects

Table 3 PNCDI IV programs and funding instruments relevant to AI

Program/subprogram	Scope/objective	Key instruments	Relevance to AI
5.1 Ideas	Support high-performing research teams to generate new theories, methods, or directions	Exploratory Research Projects, Frontier Research Projects, ERC-like projects, Workshops	Frontier AI research, interdisciplinary studies, algorithm development, foundational AI research
5.2 Human Resources	Develop researchers, early-career scientists, and research capacity	5.2.1 Start in Research (PhD/postdoc grants), 5.2.2 Mobilities (researcher exchanges, diaspora), 5.2.3 Support (publication/patent rewards, IP protection)	Building AI teams, training PhD/postdocs in AI, international collaboration
5.3 High-Performing Research Organisations (partial)	Strengthen institutional research excellence	Institutional performance grants, capacity building	Establish AI research centres, improve institutional excellence
5.5 Research Infrastructures (partial)	Develop and efficiently use research infrastructures	Infrastructure grants, access to computing/data platforms, EOSC participation	AI computing clusters, cloud services, data platforms, lab infrastructure
5.6 Challenges (partial)	Address societal/economic challenges through RDI	5.6.1 Strategic Agenda Partnerships, 5.6.2 National Missions, 5.6.3 Solutions	AI applied to societal challenges (e.g., Smart Villages, rural digitalisation, health, sustainability)
5.7 Innovation Partnership	Support public–private partnerships and innovation ecosystems	5.7.1 Competitiveness (demonstrators, vouchers), 5.7.2 Innovative Entrepreneurship (seed/accelerator grants), 5.7.3 Innovative Companies (spin-offs, market support), 5.7.4 Technology Transfer (Twinning, tech transfer fund)	Translating AI research into products/services, AI startups, spin-offs, industry collaboration

(continued)

Table 3 (continued)

Program/subprogram	Scope/objective	Key instruments	Relevance to AI
5.8 European and International Cooperation	Integrate Romanian RDI into European/ international networks	5.8.1 Horizon Europe, 5.8.2 European and International Initiatives, 5.8.3 Bilateral/Multilateral, 5.8.4 Cooperation Support	International AI projects, EU consortia, networking, co-financing, joint research
5.9 Research in Strategic Fields (partial)	Enhance national technological potential and competitiveness	5.9.8 Artificial Intelligence, 5.9.9 Autonomous Systems	Core AI funding: research, applications, algorithms, autonomous systems
5.10 Science and Society	Promote responsible research, dissemination, societal engagement	Outreach programs, ethical research initiatives	AI ethics, community engagement, societal impact projects (e.g., AI in Smart Villages)

Source Created by authors based on UEFISCDI (2023)

suitable for PPP development, involving private capital and industrial expertise (Romania Insider 2025). Therefore, a university, research centre, and technology company collaborating to develop an AI solution for a community can access PPP mechanisms that facilitate funding, risk-sharing, infrastructure, and market deployment.

3.3 EU-Funded Programmes Supporting AI and Digital Transformation

To ensure the successful adoption of AI in Romania, European funding programmes play a crucial role. Romania benefits from several *EU-funded programmes* that directly support its national strategy for digital transformation. These programmes are implemented at the national and regional levels and are designed to strengthen digital infrastructure, enhance skills, and accelerate innovation through co-financing mechanisms that reinforce national efforts.

Key Romanian EU-Funded Programmes supporting AI are:

- *PNRR—Component 7 "Digital Transformation"*—Financed through the Recovery and Resilience Facility (RRF), this component supports AI integration in public administration and SMEs, aiming to modernise services, improve efficiency, and promote data-driven governance (Ministry of Investments and European Projects 2025a).
- *Operational Programme for Smart Growth, Digitisation, and Financial Instruments (POCIDIF 2021–2027)*—Focuses on creating digital innovation hubs, AI

testing and experimentation platforms, and technology transfer networks that bridge academia and industry (Ministry of Investments and European Projects 2025b).
- *Regional Operational Programmes (ROPs)*—Promote regional smart specialisation strategies, innovation-driven SMEs, and digital public services, reinforcing cohesion and balanced territorial development (Ministry of Investments and European Projects 2025c).

In addition to national operational programmes, *EU-level funding frameworks* are essential for advancing AI and digital innovation. The *EU Framework Programme for Research and Innovation (2021–2027), Digital Europe Programme, GenAI4EU Programme, European Territorial Cooperation* complement national initiatives by promoting research excellence, developing strategic digital capacities, and facilitating cross-border collaboration, thereby accelerating AI adoption and strengthening innovation ecosystems (European Commission 2021d, e, g; European Commission and JRC 2025). By combining national operational programmes, EU-level funding frameworks, and cross-border initiatives, Romania is positioned to accelerate AI deployment and foster sustainable innovation ecosystems across the country and the wider CEE region.

4 Conclusions

Romania's AI and digital transformation ecosystem benefits from coordinated support at the EU and national levels, which provides strategic investments, capacity-building, and a framework for innovation. EU-level funding frameworks, including Horizon Europe, the Digital Europe Programme, and European Territorial Cooperation initiatives, complement national operational programmes such as PNRR, POCIDIF, and Regional Operational Programmes, fostering research excellence, technological adoption, and collaboration between academia, industry, and public institutions.

Key factors contributing to effective AI adoption include:

- Strategic alignment between national policies and EU priorities, ensuring that national AI initiatives complement European objectives in digital transformation, research, and innovation.
- Targeted funding programmes that support AI research, startup development, infrastructure, and collaborative projects between universities, research centres, and industry.
- Skills development initiatives, which enhance AI literacy and workforce readiness, ensuring that both public and private sectors can effectively deploy AI technologies.
- Public–private collaboration, facilitating knowledge transfer, innovation, and commercialisation of AI solutions.

Despite these strengths, challenges persist:

- Limited absorption capacity may constrain full utilisation of available EU and national funding.
- Alignment between national priorities and EU strategic goals must be maintained to ensure efficient implementation.
- Monitoring and evaluation mechanisms need to be strengthened to measure the impact of AI programmes and ensure accountability.

To further enhance Romania's AI ecosystem, several recommendations emerge:

Strengthen coordination across EU and national frameworks to ensure effective design, funding, and implementation of AI projects.
Encourage multi-stakeholder initiatives integrating universities, public authorities, and private sector actors to foster comprehensive innovation ecosystems.
Implement robust monitoring and evaluation frameworks to track outcomes, enhance accountability, and support evidence-based decision-making.
Promote workforce development and AI literacy to secure long-term innovation capacity and competitiveness.
Leverage EU co-financing strategically to maximise the adoption of AI technologies across public administration, industry, and research sectors.

Overall, Romania's experience demonstrates that strategic coordination, EU-national synergy, and capacity-building are essential to accelerate AI adoption, strengthen innovation ecosystems, and support a human-centric and responsible digital transformation.

References

Ernst I (2025, July 22) Romanian government launches initiative to identify viable public-private partnership projects. Romania Insider. Retrieved from https://www.romania-insider.com/romania-viable-public-private-partnerships-program-2025

Eurofound (2020) EU PolicyWatch, Digital training of SMEs employees—Romania: National Program "Competențe digitale pentru angajații din sectorul întreprinderilor mici și mijlocii" (Government Decision no. 599/July 2020). https://static.eurofound.europa.eu/covid19db/cases/RO-2020-32_1405.html

European Commission (2018) Coordinated Plan on Artificial Intelligence (COM(2018) 795 final). Brussels. Retrieved August 16, 2025, from https://digital-strategy.ec.europa.eu/en/news/eu-member-states-sign-cooperate-artificial-intelligence

European Commission (2020) White Paper on Artificial Intelligence: A European approach to excellence and trust (COM(2020) 65 final). Brussels, 19 February 2020. Retrieved from https://eur-lex.europa.eu/legal-content/EN/TXT/PDF/?uri=CELEX%3A52020DC0065

European Commission (2021a) Coordinated Plan on Artificial Intelligence 2021 Review (COM(2021) 205 final). Brussels. Retrieved August 16, 2025, from https://digital-strategy.ec.europa.eu/en/library/coordinated-plan-artificial-intelligence-2021-review

European Commission (2021b) Proposal for a Regulation of the European Parliament and of the Council laying down harmonised rules on artificial intelligence (Artificial Intelligence Act) and amending certain Union legislative acts (COM(2021) 206 final). Brussels, 21 April

2021. Retrieved from https://eur-lex.europa.eu/legal-content/EN/TXT/?uri=CELEX%3A52021PC0206
European Commission (2021c) AI watch—National Strategies on Artificial Intelligence: A European Perspective. Retrieved from https://ai-watch.ec.europa.eu/publications/ai-watch-national-strategies-artificial-intelligence-european-perspective-2021-edition_en#files
European Commission (2021d) Horizon Europe: The Framework Programme for Research and Innovation 2021–2027. Brussels: European Commission. Retrieved from https://commission.europa.eu/funding-tenders/find-funding/eu-funding-programmes/horizon-europe_en?prefLang=ro
European Commission (2021e) Digital Europe Programme. Brussels: European Commission. Retrieved from https://digital-strategy.ec.europa.eu/en/activities/digital-programme
European Commission (2021f) Recovery and Resilience Facility. Brussels: European Commission. Retrieved from https://commission.europa.eu/business-economy-euro/economic-recovery/recovery-and-resilience-facility_en
European Commission (2021g) Interreg—European Territorial Cooperation: Programme 2021–2027. Brussels: European Commission. Retrieved from https://social-economy-gateway.ec.europa.eu/eu-funding-programmes/european-territorial-cooperation-interreg_en
European Commission (2021h) Made in Europe Initiative. Brussels: European Commission. Retrieved from https://research-and-innovation.ec.europa.eu/knowledge-publications-tools-and-data/publications/all-publications/made-europe_en
European Commission & Joint Research Centre (JRC) (2025) GenAI4EU Programme. Brussels: European Commission. Retrieved from https://digital-strategy.ec.europa.eu/en/policies/genai4eu
European Union (2024) Regulation (EU) 2024/1689 of the European Parliament and of the Council of 13 June 2024 laying down harmonised rules on artificial intelligence (Artificial Intelligence Act) and amending certain Union legislative acts. Official Journal of the European Union, L 168:1–137. Retrieved from https://eur-lex.europa.eu/eli/reg/2024/1689/oj
Executive Unit for Financing Higher Education, Research, Development and Innovation (UEFISCDI) (2023) National Research, Development and Innovation Plan (PNCDI IV) 2022–2027 (updated 14 December 2023). https://uefiscdi.gov.ro/pncdi-iv
Future of Life Institute (2025) EU Artificial Intelligence Act—overview and resources. Retrieved September 3, 2025, from https://artificialintelligenceact.eu/
Galindo L, Perset K, Sheeka F (2021). An overview of national AI strategies and policies (OECD Going Digital Toolkit Note No. 14). OECD Publishing. https://doi.org/10.1787/c05140d9-en
Government of Romania (2021a) Planul Național de Redresare și Reziliență (PNRR). Bucharest: Government of Romania. Retrieved from https://www.mfe.gov.ro/pnrr/
Government of Romania (2021b) Employment Strategy 2021–2027. Bucharest: Government of Romania.
Government of Romania (2022a) National Strategy for Research, Innovation, and Smart Specialization 2022–2027. Bucharest: Government of Romania. Retrieved from https://www.mcid.gov.ro/programe-nationale/strategia-nationala-de-cercetare-inovare-si-specializare-inteligenta-2022-2027/mcid.gov.ro+1
Government of Romania (2022b) Cybersecurity Strategy of Romania 2022–2027. Bucharest: Government of Romania.
Government of Romania (2024) National Strategy for Artificial Intelligence 2024–2027. Bucharest: Government of Romania. Retrieved from Strategia Națională în Domeniul Inteligenței Artificiale 2024–2027—Autoritatea Națională pentru Cercetare: www.research.gov.ro
KPMG in Romania (2024, June) Investment in Romania 2024. https://kpmg.com/ro/en/home/insights/2024/06/investment-in-romania.htm
Law 178/2010—Public-Private Partnership in Romania (2010) Retrieved from https://www.ppp-romania.eu/law-178-2010/
Ministry of Education (2020) SMART.Edu – Strategy for the digitalisation of Education in Romania 2021–2027. Bucharest: Ministry of Education. Retrieved from https://www.edu.ro

Ministry of Education and Research (Romania) (2020, October 26) SMART.Edu—Strategia privind digitalizarea educației din România 2021–2027. https://www.edu.ro/smartedu-strategia-privind-digitalizarea-educației-din-România-2021-2027edu.ro+2Digital%20Skills%20and%20Jobs%20Platform+2

Ministry of Investments and European Projects (2025a) National Recovery and Resilience Plan (PNRR)—"Funds for a modern and reformed Romania!". Retrieved from https://mfe.gov.ro/pnrr/

Ministry of Investments and European Projects (2025b) Operational Programme for Smart Growth, Digitization and Financial Instruments (POCIDIF) 2021–2027. Retrieved from https://mfe.gov.ro/pocidif/despre-programul-pocidif/

Ministry of Investments and European Projects (2025c) Regional Programmes 2021–2027. Retrieved from https://mfe.gov.ro/programe-regionale-21-27/

Ministry of National Defence (2021) White Paper on Defence. Bucharest: Ministry of National Defence

Orrick AI Law Center (2025) Timeline of obligations for implementing EU AI Act. Retrieved September 4, 2025, from https://ai-law-center.orrick.com/

AI-Enabled Efficiency in Public Sector Processes: Pilot Projects in Local Government

Olimpia Iuliana Ban and Diana Claudia Perţicaş

Abstract This chapter examines how artificial intelligence (AI) and RFID technologies enhance efficiency, transparency, and sustainability in public sector processes, focusing on municipal waste management. Using the city of Oradea, Romania, as a case study, the chapter analyses the design, implementation, and outcomes of a Pay-As-You-Throw pilot project based on RFID-enabled identification and AI-supported monitoring. The analysis shows that integrating AI and RFID improves waste traceability, enables fair and data-driven billing, optimizes collection routes, and supports environmentally responsible behaviour. AI-based object recognition and predictive analytics further automate operational processes and reduce costs. Despite technical, organisational, and investment-related challenges, the Oradea pilot demonstrates the scalability of AI-enabled solutions and provides practical insights for municipalities seeking to modernize public services through digital transformation.

1 Introduction

This chapter aims to examine how Artificial Intelligence (AI) can enhance operational efficiency in public sector processes by analysing pilot projects implemented at the local government level. The case study of Oradea illustrates how AI-based solutions, combined with RFID technologies, have been tested in waste management to improve traceability, optimise routes, increase billing transparency, and support environmental sustainability. By focusing on a concrete local initiative, the chapter not only assesses the operational benefits and limitations of AI adoption in municipal services but also provides insights into how such pilot projects can serve as scalable models for other cities seeking to digitalise and modernise public sector processes.

Its primary objectives are to:

O. I. Ban (✉) · D. C. Perţicaş
Faculty of Economic Sciences, University of Oradea, Oradea, Romania
e-mail: oban@uoradea.ro

D. C. Perţicaş
e-mail: dperticas@uoradea.ro

C. Sabău-Popa (ed.), *Artificial Intelligence in Finance, Accounting and Business Administration*, Contributions to Finance and Accounting,
https://doi.org/10.1007/978-3-032-22737-9_4

- Review the theoretical background of AI in waste management.
- Explore the theoretical rationale for using AI technologies to improve municipal services, particularly waste management.
- Present and analyse an example of Oradea's AI-enabled waste-management pilot, highlighting the technology deployed, implementation steps and measurable outcomes.
- Identify the benefits, challenges and critical success factors encountered during the pilot.
- Derive practical insights and policy recommendations for other municipalities considering similar initiatives.

The scope of the chapter is deliberately focused on local government applications, and it does not attempt to cover national-level AI strategies or private-sector implementations. While the discussion draws on broader literature to contextualise AI adoption in public administration, the empirical analysis centres on the Oradea case, with attention to technical, organisational and socio-political dimensions. As such, the chapter provides both a conceptual framework and an evidence-based assessment of AI's potential to improve public-service delivery at the municipal level.

The public sector, both municipal and national, differs from the private sector in that it is funded by taxpayer contributions; therefore, the equitable and efficient use of resources is crucial. AI offers opportunities for optimal resource allocation, process simplification, and increased efficiency in the management of public funds, which can strengthen public trust.

Implementing artificial intelligence (AI) in the public sector can generate substantial benefits, but also complex challenges. At a conceptual level, AI contributes to the creation of public value when integrated into service design, generating innovation and improving its quality and efficiency. Studies such as Wang et al. (2021) and Fatima et al. (2021) show that tools such as knowledge management, process automation, virtual agents, predictive analytics or robots can increase public value. In terms of efficiency, Ågerfalk et al. (2022) and Schaefer et al. (2021) emphasise that AI allows the automation of repetitive tasks and generates cost savings; thus, the saved resources can be reallocated to value-added services. Vassilakopoulou et al. (2023) show that the adoption of internal AI-based tools reduces the workload for service customers and stimulates digital transformation. In addition, AI can function as a decision support tool. Gualdi and Cordella (2021), Asatiani et al. (2021) and Dwivedi et al. (2021) highlight that AI models can collect information and provide relevant arguments for civil servants, providing support in decision-making, but insist on the need to maintain human control to prevent bias and ensure accountability. Henk and Nilssen (2021) show that using AI as an internal tool, such as chatbots, stimulates employee creativity and autonomy, and Schmager et al. (2023) demonstrate that human involvement in automated processes increases public trust. In terms of economic benefits, Alsheiabni et al. (2019), Lyu et al. (2023), and Schaefer et al. (2021) argue that AI can improve organisational performance, reduce costs and increase revenues, including through the use of service robots for repetitive tasks.

However, the adoption of AI in the public sector is also accompanied by significant challenges. A major barrier is the lack of internal expertise and managerial support. Alsheiabni et al. (2019) emphasise that skills shortages and integration with legacy systems make implementation difficult. Ethical issues are another obstacle, along with issues related to data security and privacy (de Cerqueira et al. 2021). Trust and accountability are crucial, as is the importance of transparency in automated decision-making (Asatiani et al. 2021). Dwivedi et al. (2021) emphasise that employee resistance to change and shared values in the organisation can hinder AI adoption because the success of AI depends on the availability of qualified human resources and continuous training.

One of the applications of AI in public services concerns waste management. AI in waste management takes many forms, and the results show a considerable improvement in the entire process.

2 Theoretical Background of AI in Waste Management

According to the European Commission (2020), effective waste management is crucial today as global waste generation is expected to increase by 70% by 2050, making it essential to transition toward a more circular economy to reduce environmental and health risks. Although Artificial Intelligence (AI) is not explicitly highlighted as a central component in the *"New Circular Economy Action Plan"* of the European Commission, it plays a crucial role in supporting and accelerating many of the proposed measures. AI is an important tool in the digitalisation process, contributing to the development of digital product passports that include information about product composition, recyclability, reparability, and life cycle. These data can be automatically processed using AI algorithms, facilitating material traceability and transparency along the value chain.

Another key area where AI is relevant is waste management. The Commission promotes the modernisation of waste collection and sorting infrastructure, and AI-based technologies are already being used for automatic waste type recognition, route optimisation for collection vehicles, and increased efficiency in recycling facilities. In this way, AI directly contributes to higher recycling rates and the reduction of valuable material loss.

Furthermore, AI can support public authorities and companies in decision-making by providing predictive models, data analysis, and simulations of the impact of various environmental policies. In industry, AI is integrated into solutions that enable the transition to circular business models, such as product-as-a-service systems, predictive maintenance, and resource optimisation. Therefore, AI is not merely a technological tool, but a catalyst for the European circular economy.

Abdallah et al. (2020) conducted a systematic literature review to map how artificial-intelligence techniques have been used to tackle problems in solid-waste management (SWM). Recognising that waste management processes are influenced by many technical, environmental, demographic and regulatory factors and are hard to model with conventional methods, the authors argued that AI can handle such complex, noisy data. The review surveyed 85 research articles published between 2004 and 2019, offering a comprehensive analysis of the AI models employed, the SWM domains addressed, and the performance metrics reported. Four research questions guided the review: identifying the application areas of AI in waste management; cataloguing the AI models and algorithms used; comparing their performance with non-AI techniques; and assessing the strengths and limitations of AI approaches. Six principal application areas emerged: forecasting waste characteristics (generation rates, composition, heating value and co-melting temperature), bin-level detection, process-parameter prediction, process-output prediction (e.g., biogas or leachate), vehicle-routing optimisation and SWM planning. The most common AI techniques were artificial neural networks (ANNs), support-vector machines (SVMs), linear regression (LR), decision trees (DTs) and genetic algorithms (GAs). ANNs were the predominant model across almost all application areas because of their ability to capture nonlinear relationships; GAs were widely used for optimisation tasks such as route planning; LR and DTs were favoured for their simplicity and interpretability despite limitations with non-linear data; and SVMs offered robust classification and regression performance with low risk of over-fitting, though they were sensitive to kernel selection. Numerous hybrid models combined AI techniques to overcome the limitations of single models, and most reported improved accuracy.

Artificial Intelligence technologies play a crucial role in optimising waste management systems through various innovative applications. These include (Andeobu et al. 2022): bin-level monitoring to detect when containers are full, efficient waste collection, route planning for waste collection vehicles (vehicle routing), automated waste sorting, appropriate waste treatment based on type and hazard level, and strategic waste management planning. By integrating AI into these processes, operational efficiency is enhanced, costs are reduced, and environmental sustainability is promoted.

In Elia et al. (2015) it presents an integrated framework for designing and managing Pay-As-You-Throw (PAYT) systems in municipal solid waste management (MSWM). PAYT schemes, which charge users based on the amount of waste they generate, aim to promote more sustainable waste practices by encouraging reduction, reuse, and recycling. However, their implementation introduces significant complexity, particularly regarding user identification, accurate waste measurement, and fee calculation. The authors propose a holistic model that incorporates economic pricing structures (fixed and variable fees), technologies for identifying users (e.g., RFID, QR codes, mobile devices), and systems for measuring waste volume or weight. They emphasise the growing role of Internet of Things (IoT) technologies—such as sensors, cameras, and smart bins—in enhancing service efficiency and transparency. The study also outlines a multi-criteria evaluation of technology solutions based on user convenience, service reliability, and cost-effectiveness. To ensure long-term success, the authors recommend applying the Deming Cycle (Plan–Do–Check–Act) for continuous improvement and adaptation. Overall, the paper highlights that the effectiveness of PAYT schemes depends heavily on local service conditions and the thoughtful integration of technological, organisational, and economic elements.

There are not many studies on waste management in Romania. However, there is a very useful study, even on the city of Oradea in its efforts to become a smart city (Popescu et al. 2016). The article analyses the waste management strategy at the University of Oradea in the broader context of the city's transformation into a "smart city". The study evaluates the existing waste collection, storage and recycling system in the period 2010–2015 and proposes modern solutions to improve efficiency, environmental protection and the involvement of the university community. The authors propose an innovative approach based on Internet of Things (IoT) technologies, by equipping the collection points with smart sensors (for volume, weight, temperature) and video cameras, connected to a central computer that monitors in real time the degree of filling of the containers and streamlines the collection routes. The SIGUREC system in Oradea is mentioned as an example of smart collection with reward, and its replication on campus is suggested.

3 An Example of AI and RFID Application in Oradea

Oradea, a rapidly developing city in north-western Romania near the Hungarian border, has over 180,000 inhabitants and serves as the administrative and economic centre of Bihor County, being recognised for its cultural heritage, tourism potential, and innovative urban development projects.

At the level of the municipality of Oradea, waste collection is carried out by specialised companies under the coordination and supervision of the local authorities on the basis of contracts with private individuals, homeowners' associations or economic operators.

From an economic point of view, waste collection operators endeavour to reduce the amount of waste deposited in landfills, as this generates additional costs. The separation of recyclable waste and residual waste directly at source (households, homeowners' associations, businesses) is therefore encouraged. The collection of recyclable fractions is associated with lower costs compared to residual waste; however, non-compliance with sorting regulations can lead to penalties. Overall, both the waste management companies' customers and the operators themselves are pursuing a common goal: minimising the amount of residual waste generated and reducing the quantities destined for landfill.

In order to ensure fair and efficient billing for the services provided, the "pay-as-you-throw" principle is applied, whereby the tariff is set in relation to the quantity actually generated by each user. In this respect, some operators determine the amount of waste based on the weight collected by the vehicle, while others use the volume collected. It is in this context that the topic of the present chapter falls, namely the analysis and development of methods to automate the process of recording collections and their correct allocation to the corresponding customers.

3.1 Description of RFID Technology

A technological solution widely used in waste management to ensure traceability and accountability of waste producers is the use of RFID (Radio Frequency Identification) tags (Islam et al. 2012) on containers distributed to customers. The main purpose of this approach is to uniquely and automatically identify each container at the time of collection. When the waste is collected, the RFID sensors attached to the vehicle read the tag attached to the container (Kumar et al. 2023). Once read, a digital record is created containing information such as: the unique bin code, the time of collection and the association with the customer to whom the bin was allocated (Mudra et al. 2023). This method enables the creation of a real-time database of the quantity and frequency of collections.

The advantages of this solution are manifold:

- Traceability (Tichoniuk and Wiszumirska 2024), each container is assigned to a user, which enables unique identification of the waste producer;
- Operational efficiency (Khan et al. 2022; Assis et al. 2022; Chai et al. 2023; Sarg 2025), manual checks are no longer required and processing time is reduced;
- Billing transparency (Luo and Yang 2019; Czekała et al. 2023; Ghule et al. 2024; Bolke 2024), facilitates the application of the "pay-as-you-throw" principle by correlating the collected volume or weight with each customer;
- Support environmental policy (Kang et al. 2023; Ahmed and Cheelu 2024), provides useful data to analyse and optimise collection processes and promote proper waste segregation.

The digitisation system as a whole consists of hardware and software. The hardware part includes a video camera running an artificial intelligence algorithm (Figs. 1 and 2). The task of this algorithm is to address a desired use case, in this case the identification of collected containers and bins, and to report any incidents detected during the collection process.

However, this technology is not without its limitations (Gendy et al. 2023; Habib et al. 2023; Abugabah et al. 2022). The functionality of RFID tags can be impaired by technical or external factors: malfunction of vehicle sensors, wear and tear of the tags or even intentional damage or removal by users who want to avoid being charged for the waste they create. These risks require the introduction of additional verification mechanisms, such as the integration of video systems and artificial intelligence algorithms, to increase the reliability of the process.

3.2 Application of AI Based on RFID Technology in Waste Management in Oradea

The application of RFID technology in the field of waste management in Oradea (The City of Hall 2021, 2022a, b, 2025) was implemented for the first time through a

Fig. 1 Screenshot of the Trackosoft Solutions. *Source* The image was provided by the company responsible for managing the hardware and software infrastructure of the sanitation services in Oradea (RER Vest)

Fig. 2 Screenshot of the onboard camera mounted on a garbage truck. *Source* The image was provided by the company responsible for managing the hardware and software infrastructure of the sanitation services in Oradea (RER Vest)

pilot project launched in December 2021, called "Pay As You Throw". This initiative was carried out in the Prima neighbourhood and aimed to introduce a modern waste collection system based on radio frequency identification, enabling residents to pay according to the amount of waste they generated. Within the project, access to metal waste collection enclosures was conditioned by scanning the RFID code printed on the collection bags, and only waste collected in authorised bags could be picked up by the sanitation operator. The distribution of RFID-tagged bags began in February 2022, and the pilot program ran for 90 days, from January 25 to April 25, 2022. During this period, the system was tested to evaluate its efficiency in selective collection and to encourage citizens' responsibility regarding the amount of waste they produced. Additionally, starting in March 2022, the metal collection enclosures in the pilot area were equipped with surveillance cameras and RFID scanning systems.

In the following years, the municipality continued the process of expanding the use of RFID technology in sanitation services. According to the updated Regulation of the

Waste Management Service of Oradea Municipality (2024–2025), the use of RFID tags for identifying collection containers and personalised bags became mandatory, and the operator now collects only the containers registered in the system database. For households that do not have standard containers (120 l or 240 l), the regulation allows the use of smaller containers equipped with RFID tags or prepaid personalised bags, aligned with the "Pay As You Throw" principle. These provisions confirm the local authorities' intention to extend the RFID system beyond the pilot phase toward large-scale implementation, in order to optimise waste management and ensure fair billing based on the actual amount of waste generated by each user.

The need to increase the accuracy of the identification of bins and containers has led to the development of an additional recognition mechanism based on an artificial intelligence algorithm. Its task is to analyse the video streams generated by the cameras mounted on the collection vehicles and correlate the identified objects with the RFID tags detected by the other sensors installed on the vehicle (Kasteren et al. 2010; Aguileta et al. 2019).

Compared to classic algorithms, artificial intelligence offers considerable advantages in situations where no clear heuristics can be formulated and implemented in code, provided that sufficient data is available to extract relevant features. For example, an AI model has the ability to generalise and extrapolate from one situation to another, which makes it scalable (Schuett 2023; Hampiholi 2023; Baqal et al. 2024). It can detect not only bins and containers, but also other types of objects, such as rubbish bags, mis-sorted waste, atypical objects or even irregular actions of operators. However, these advantages come with a number of disadvantages, such as higher complexity, higher error rates and higher development and implementation costs compared to the original RFID solution.

In order to determine the optimal operating parameters, a pilot programme was carried out in collaboration with a local sanitation company. This involved monitoring and analysing the operation of a collection vehicle and installing special equipment to test the detection algorithms.

From a technical perspective, the project raised the following issues:

– The waste collection sector is not treated as a general interest by the organisations developing AI-based models for object recognition, so it was necessary to train their own models adapted to the specificities of this sector. The process required the creation of a comprehensive and diverse dataset that could capture the characteristics of the bins and containers collected by vehicles.

In waste collection, objects must be recognised not only in static images, but also in continuous video sequences (Fig. 3), which requires an analysis of the behaviour of the object (bin or container). With regard to the main objective - to accurately count the number of collections- it was therefore necessary to correlate the behaviour of the object with its identity.

The main goal of the project was to accurately recognise objects of the bin and container type. In this respect, the process went through several successive iterations of annotation—training—validation—testing. During these cycles, both new test

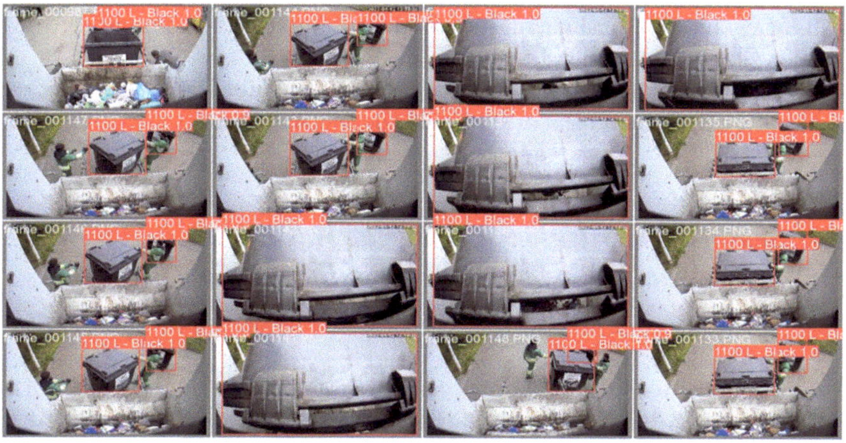

Fig. 3 Results from the automated testing of the annotation model. *Source* The image was provided by the company responsible for managing the hardware and software infrastructure of the sanitation services in Oradea (RER Vest)

cases and procedural deviations were identified by the collection vehicle operators, which provided the opportunity to refine the algorithm and adapt the workflows.

Another objective of the project was to develop the ability to identify and track a recognised object in order to ensure traceability and provide evidence of the collection of the contents of a specific bin or container. To this end, common features associated with the collection process were extracted and analysed to differentiate between the containers detected in the background and those actually collected.

Once the collection of a bin was confirmed, an automatic workflow was triggered that generated a collection notification with the corresponding street address and the video recording of the collected bin.

3.3 How Artificial Intelligence Can Further Improve Waste Management Practices

The use of artificial intelligence (AI) technologies to optimise waste management, reduce environmental impact and increase overall efficiency is essential to achieving sustainable development goals in the waste transport sector. Here are some ways in which AI can support environmentally friendly waste transport: *route optimisation* (Guo et al. 2024; Zhou et al. 2014; Liu 2024; Cornea and Obretin 2023); *predictive maintenance* (Landaluce et al. 2020; Coito et al. 2021); *dynamic scheduling* (Fu et al. 2011; Chen et al. 2012; Ntakolia and Iakovidis 2021); *intelligent container monitoring* (Nursuwars et al. 2023; Calo et al. 2021; Ran et al. 2024); *data analysis* (Zhao 2024; Patel et al. 2023); *vehicle automation* (Samuel and Sebastian 2019; Asfoura et al. 2021); *emissions reduction* (Yusoff et al. (2021) and *public engagement.*

By integrating artificial intelligence technologies into waste transport networks, stakeholders can realise significant improvements in terms of environmental sustainability, efficiency and costs. AI has the potential to revolutionise waste management and facilitate the achievement of sustainable development goals.

3.4 Seasonal Distribution of Collected Waste in the Municipality of Oradea and Related Consumption Trends

Analysing the seasonal distribution of collected waste volumes is an essential tool for understanding the dynamics of consumption processes and supporting planning decisions in the field of waste management (Yılmaz et al. 2023). At the level of Oradea municipality (Fig. 4), the available data show the presence of recurring monthly fluctuations that reflect both the specific characteristics of the population's consumption behaviour and the influence of contextual factors such as the seasonality of economic activities and the growing attractiveness of the city as a tourist destination.

The identification of these patterns allows not only the correlation of waste generation with consumption trends, but also the development of strategies to optimise collection processes, resource allocation and the dimensioning of logistical capacities. In addition, a comparative multi-year analysis shows the stability of these trends,

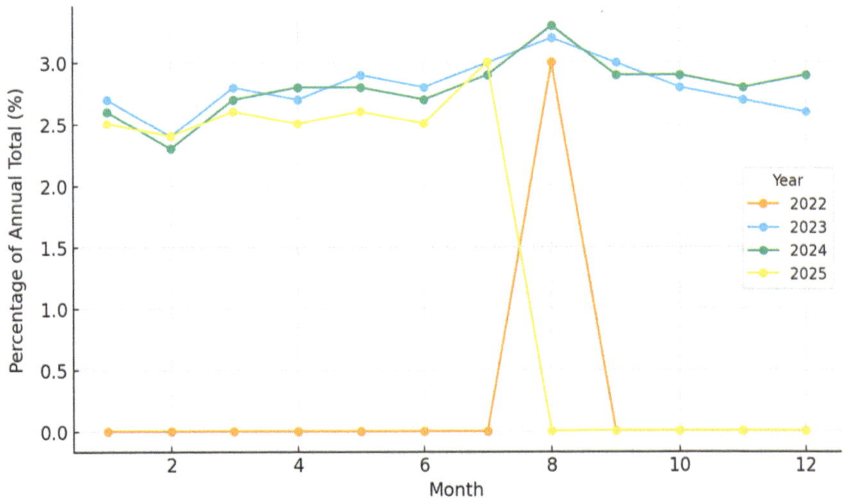

Fig. 4 Monthly percentage distribution of collected quantities (%).*The figure contains only information from the period of implementation of the 'Pay-as-You-Throw' project. *Source* Prepared by the authors on the basis of data provided by the company responsible for waste management in Oradea (RER Vest)

which facilitates the development of forecasting models for medium and long-term planning.

The analysis of the collected data (Fig. 4) shows a pronounced seasonality of waste generation in the municipality of Oradea. The summer months, especially July and August, represent a peak season and account for between 9 and 9.5% of the total annual volume. This increase can be attributed both to the intensification of economic and consumer activities during the holiday season and to the growing attractiveness of the city as a tourist destination. In contrast, the winter months (January-March) are characterised by lower figures, below 8% of the total, with a minimum in February (6.93%).

A comparison of the data series for 2023 and 2024 shows that the proportions are stable, confirming the persistent nature of this seasonality. In addition, the available data for 2025 show a similar trend in the first months, which underlines the consistency of the observed pattern.

Overall, the results show a clear seasonal model characterised by increases in summer and decreases in winter. The relatively even distribution of annual percentages suggests that the total volume of waste collected is not subject to significant year fluctuations; however, the monthly fluctuations are both recurring and predictable (Fig. 5). These results are of practical importance to the waste management industry as they provide a basis for planning measures such as the allocation of additional resources during the peak season and the optimisation of operational processes throughout the year.

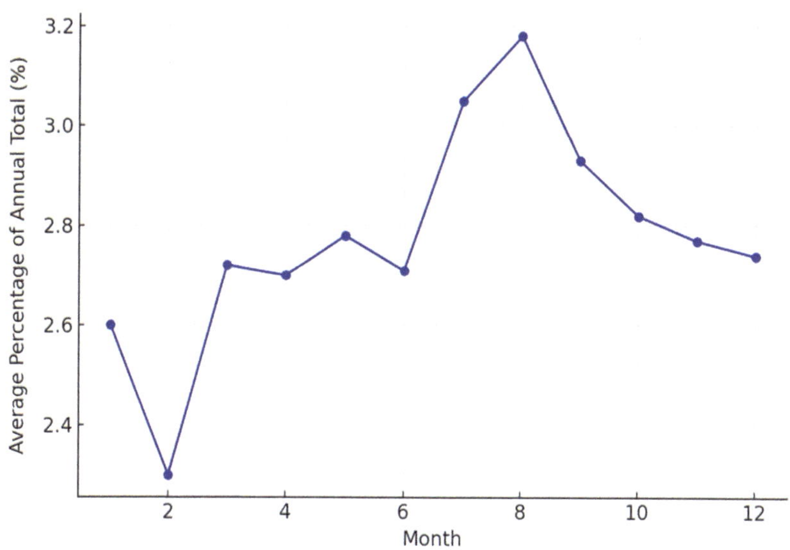

Fig. 5 Multi-annual monthly average distribution of collected quantities (%).*The figure contains only information from the period of implementation of the 'Pay-as-You-Throw' project. *Source* Prepared by the authors on the basis of data provided by the company responsible for waste management in Oradea (RER Vest)

The graph illustrates a clear seasonality in the development of the indicator, which indicates a strong correlation between the annual dynamics and the economic factors specific to each period.

The lower values in the first quarter (January-March), which are below 3%, could be related to the adjustment phase after the public holidays, when consumption and economic activity traditionally decline. In addition, the beginning of the year coincides with a phase of budget and investment planning, which explains the lower values of the indicator.

Between May and July, a gradual increase can then be observed, linked to the intensification of domestic and foreign demand and the activation of sectors dependent on the warm season, such as agriculture, tourism and related services. This upward trend culminates in the annual peak recorded in July–August, when values exceed the 3% threshold.

The growth in summer can be explained, among other things, by the increase in tourist flows. The municipality of Oradea has increasingly become an interesting tourist destination thanks to extensive investment in the restoration of historic buildings and the redevelopment of the city centre, which has helped to strengthen its cultural and architectural image. At the same time, the development of new attractions- such as water parks- and the proximity of the spa town of Băile Felix, known nationally and internationally for its thermal waters and located around 10 kms from the city, have increased the attractiveness of the region, especially during the summer season. These factors largely explain the high figures recorded in the summer months.

A moderate adjustment can be observed between September and December, with values remaining stable (around 2.6–2.9%). This trend reflects the return to more moderate values after the peak tourist season, together with the consolidation of economic activity at the end of the year, without major fluctuations.

Overall, the pattern identified confirms the existence of a clearly defined seasonal economic cycle, in which fluctuations in consumption, tourism and investment lead to periods of pronounced growth (especially in summer) and periods of stabilisation. Oradea is a convincing example of how urban development strategies and investments in tourism infrastructure can positively influence regional dynamics and reinforce the effects of economic seasonality.

4 Conclusions

The integration of artificial intelligence (AI) and RFID technologies into public sector processes, particularly in waste management, has demonstrated significant potential to transform the efficiency, transparency, and sustainability of municipal services. The Oradea case study illustrates how innovative solutions such as RFID-enabled tracking and AI-based object recognition can improve traceability, automate data collection, and support the implementation of the "Pay-As-You-Throw" principle. These technologies not only facilitate more accurate billing based on actual waste generation but also foster greater accountability among citizens and service providers, contributing to improved environmental outcomes and better resource utilisation.

The deployment of AI in waste management brings several key advantages, including route optimisation, predictive maintenance, dynamic scheduling, and intelligent monitoring of containers. Together, these applications enable municipalities to reduce operational costs, minimise environmental impact, and improve service quality. Additionally, the ability of AI systems to process large volumes of data and generate predictive insights supports more informed decision-making, enhances strategic planning, and strengthens the capacity of local governments to address complex urban challenges.

However, the adoption of AI and RFID technologies also presents challenges that must be addressed to fully realise their benefits. Technical issues, such as sensor failures and intentional tampering, require robust verification systems, while the complexity and high cost of AI implementation demand continuous investment and specialised expertise. Furthermore, ethical considerations, data privacy, and the need for transparency in automated decision-making processes remain critical factors for public acceptance and trust.

Despite these obstacles, the experience of Oradea demonstrates that AI-enabled solutions are scalable and replicable, offering a model for other municipalities aiming to modernise their waste management systems and broader public services. By embracing these technologies, local governments can advance toward more sustainable urban management, improve the quality and efficiency of public services, and strengthen citizen engagement and trust in municipal institutions. Ultimately, the combination of AI and IoT-based tools has the potential to redefine public sector service delivery, turning cities into more adaptive, data-driven, and environmentally responsible communities.

References

Abdallah M, Talib MA, Feroz S, Nasir Q, Abdalla H, Mahfood B (2020) Artificial intelligence applications in solid waste management: a systematic research review. Waste Manage 109:231–246

Abugabah A, Sanzogni L, Houghton L, AlZubi A, Abuqabbeh A (2022) RFID adaption in healthcare organizations: an integrative framework. Comput Mater Contin 70(1):1335–1348. https://doi.org/10.32604/cmc.2022.019097

Ågerfalk PJ, Conboy K, Crowston K, Eriksson Lundström J, Jarvenpaa SL, Ram S, Mikalef P (2022) Artificial intelligence in information systems: state of the art and research roadmap. Commun Assoc Inf Syst 50(1):420–438. https://doi.org/10.17705/1CAIS.05017

Aguileta A, Brena R, Mayora O, Minero E, Trejo L (2019) Virtual sensors for optimal integration of human activity data. Sensors 19(9):2017. https://doi.org/10.3390/s19092017

Ahmed H, Cheelu D (2024) A reliable message broadcast protocol using active RFID mechanism in vehicular ad hoc networks. J Adv Inf Technol 15(5):580–590. https://doi.org/10.12720/jait.15.5.580-590

Alsheiabni S, Cheung Y, Messom C (2019) Factors inhibiting the adoption of artificial intelligence at organisational-level: a preliminary investigation. În: Proceedings of the 25th Americas Conference on Information Systems (AMCIS).

Andeobu L, Wibowo S, Grandhi S (2022) Artificial intelligence applications for sustainable solid waste management practices in Australia: a systematic review. Sci Total Environ 834:155389

Asatiani A, Malo P, Nagbøl PR, Penttinen E, Rinta-Kahila T, Salovaara A (2021) Sociotechnical envelopment of artificial intelligence: an approach to organisational deployment of inscrutable artificial intelligence systems. J Assoc Inf Syst 22(2):325–352. https://doi.org/10.17705/1jais.00664

Asfoura E, Abdel-Haq M, Kassem G (2021) Conceptualization of smart system based on RFID technologies for controlling vehicle speed. Tem J 192–196. https://doi.org/10.18421/tem101-24

Assis T, Abreu V, Costa M, D'Agosto M (2022) Methodology for prioritizing best practices applied to the sustainable last mile—the case of a brazilian parcel delivery service company. Sustainability 14(7):3812. https://doi.org/10.3390/su14073812

Baqal O, Habib E, Hasabo E, Galasso F, Barry T, Arsanjani R, et al (2024) Artificial intelligence-enabled electrocardiogram (AI-ECG) does not predict atrial fibrillation following patent foramen ovale closure. IJC Hear Vasc 51:101361. https://doi.org/10.1016/j.ijcha.2024.101361

Bolke O (2024) Smart trolley using RFID & GSM. Interantional J Sci Res Eng Manag 8(4):1–5. https://doi.org/10.55041/ijsrem32226

Calo A, Barbosa J, Llevado J (2021) In-classroom faculty attendance monitoring system based on ultra high frequency (UHF) radio frequency identification (RFID) with captured image cross-verification mechanism. Indian J Sci Technol 14(45):3335–3343. https://doi.org/10.17485/ijst/v14i45.1782

Chai T, Haw S, Jahangir M, Hoe K, Heng L, Vellaisamy M (2023). Advancing retail operations: a customizable IoT-based smart inventory system. Int J Membr Sci Technol 10(3):1885–1897. https://doi.org/10.15379/ijmst.v10i3.1848

Chen K, Chen J, Cox R (2012) Real time facility performance monitoring system using RFID technology. Assem Autom 32(2):185–196. https://doi.org/10.1108/01445151211212334

City Hall of Oradea (2021, December) Pilot project "Pay As You Throw" in the Prima neighbourhood: Waste containers can be accessed only by scanning the RFID code on the bags. Oradea.ro. Retrieved September 29, 2025, from https://oradea.ro/stiri/proiectul-pilot-platesti-pentru-cat-arunci-in-cartierul-prima-incintele-pentru-deseuri-menajere-pot-fi-accesate-doar-scanand-codul-rfid-de-pe-saci

City Hall of Oradea (2022a, February) Distribution of RFID-coded bags begins within the pilot project implemented in the Prima neighborhood. Oradea.ro. Retrieved September 29, 2025, from https://oradea.ro/stiri/incepe-distribuirea-sacilor-cu-coduri-rfid-in-cadrul-proiectului-pilot-desfasurat-la-asociatia-cartier-prima

City Hall of Oradea (2022b, January) Pilot project on selective waste collection at a homeowners' association in Oradea. Oradea.ro. Retrieved September 29, 2025, from https://oradea.ro/stiri/proiect-pilot-de-colectare-selectiva-a-deseurilor-la-o-asociatie-de-proprietari-din-oradea

City Hall of Oradea (2025, August) Updated regulation of the Waste Management Service of Oradea Municipality (version 01.08.2025). Oradea.ro. Retrieved September 29, 2025, from https://oradea.ro/wp-content/uploads/2025/08/REGULAMENT-ACTUALIZAT-FINAL-_01.08.2025.pdf

Coito T, Firme B, Martins M, Vieira S, Figueiredo J, Sousa J (2021) Intelligent sensors for real-time decision-making. Automation 2(2):62–82. https://doi.org/10.3390/automation2020004

Cornea A, Obretin A (2023) Technical review of radio frequency identification and internet of things technologies in business operations and automated indoor location. Tem J 1233–1241. https://doi.org/10.18421/tem123-01

Czekała W, Drozdowski J, Łabiak P (2023) Modern technologies for waste management: a review. Appl Sci 13(15):8847. https://doi.org/10.3390/app13158847

de Cerqueira JAS, dos Althoff LS, de Almeida PS, Canedo ED (2021) Ethical perspectives in AI: a two-folded exploratory study from literature and active development projects. În: Proceedings of the 54th Annual Hawaii International Conference on System Sciences, pp 5240–5249

Dwivedi YK, Hughes L, Wade MR et al (2021) Artificial intelligence (AI): multidisciplinary perspectives on emerging challenges, opportunities, and agenda for research, practice and policy. Int J Inf Manage 57:101994. https://doi.org/10.1016/j.ijinfomgt.2019.08.002

Elia V, Gnoni MG, Tornese F (2015) Designing Pay-As-You-Throw schemes in municipal waste management services: a holistic approach. Waste Manage 44:188–195

European Commission (2020) Communication from the commission to the European parliament, the council, the European economic and social committee and the committee of the regions a new circular economy action plan for a cleaner and more competitive Europe

Fatima S, Desouza KC, Buck C, Fielt E (2021) Business model canvas to create and capture AI-enabled public value. În: Proceedings of the 54th Annual Hawaii International Conference on System Sciences, pp 2317–2326

Fu Y, Jiang P, Li Y (2011) The study on RFID middleware for real-time monitoring in manufacturing. Adv Mater Res 314–316:2491–2494. https://doi.org/10.4028/www.scientific.net/amr.314-316.2491

Gendy M, Tham P, Harrison F, Yuce M (2023) Comparing efficiency and performance of IoT BLE and RFID-based systems for achieving contact tracing to monitor infection spread among hospital and office staff. Sensors 23(3):1397. https://doi.org/10.3390/s23031397

Ghule P, Mane V, Revankar V, Pusegaonkar A (2024) Versatile smart carts: redefining the retail experience. Int J Res Appl Sci Eng Technol 12(5):1348–1351. https://doi.org/10.22214/ijraset.2024.61814

Gualdi F, Cordella A (2021) Artificial intelligence and decision-making: The question of accountability. În: Proceedings of the 54th Annual Hawaii International Conference on System Sciences, pp 2297–2306

Guo J, Wang Y, Guo Y, Dai S, Yan R, Shi Z (2024) Exploring logistics transport route optimization: an algorithmic study based on RFID technology. Int J RF Technol 14(2):107–124. https://doi.org/10.3233/rft-230059

Habib A, Akram S, Ali M, Muhammad T, Zainab S, Jehangir S (2023) Radio frequency identification temperature/CO_2 sensor using carbon nanotubes. Nanomaterials 13(2):273. https://doi.org/10.3390/nano13020273

Hampiholi N (2023) Medical imaging enhancement with AI models for automatic disease detection and classification based on medical images. IJEAST 8(5):31–37. https://doi.org/10.33564/ijeast.2023.v08i05.005

Henk A, Nilssen F (2021) Can AI become a state servant? A case study of an intelligent chatbot implementation in a Scandinavian public service. În: Proceedings of the 54th Annual Hawaii International Conference on System Sciences, pp 5515–5524. https://eur-lex.europa.eu/legal-content/EN/TXT/HTML/?uri=CELEX%3A52020DC0098&utm_source=chatgpt.com, Accessed on 31 July 2025

Islam MS, Arebey M, Hannan MA, Basri H (2012) Overview for solid waste bin monitoring and collection system. Int Conf Innov Manag Technol Res 2012:258–262. https://doi.org/10.1109/icimtr.2012.6236399

Kang Y, Shi X, Liu S (2023) Sales channel competition for supply chain with the blockchain technology. Int Trans Oper Res 31(6):4068–4104. https://doi.org/10.1111/itor.13370

Kasteren T, Englebienne G, Kröse B (2010) An activity monitoring system for elderly care using generative and discriminative models. Pers Ubiquit Comput 14(6):489–498. https://doi.org/10.1007/s00779-009-0277-9

Khan M, Huda N, Zaman U (2022) Smart warehouse management system: architecture, real-time implementation and prototype design. Machines 10(2):150. https://doi.org/10.3390/machines10020150

Kumar K, Singh V, Raja L, Bhagirath S (2023) A review of parking slot types and their detection techniques for smart cities. Smart Cities 6(5):2639–2660. https://doi.org/10.3390/smartcities6050119

Landaluce H, Arjona L, Perallos A, Falcone F, Angulo I, Muralter F (2020) A review of IoT sensing applications and challenges using RFID and wireless sensor networks. Sensors 20(9):2495. https://doi.org/10.3390/s20092495

Liu Q (2024) Logistics distribution route optimization in artificial intelligence and internet of things environment. Decis Mak Appl Manag Eng 7(2):221–239. https://doi.org/10.31181/dmame7220241072

Luo J, Yang M (2019) A secure partial RFID ownership transfer protocol with multi-owners. Sensors 20(1):22. https://doi.org/10.3390/s20010022

Lyu F, Wang M, Choi J (2023) Detection of interaction-based knowledge for reclassification of service robots: Big data analytics perspective. În: Proceedings of the 56th Annual Hawaii International Conference on System Sciences, pp 1591–1600

Mudra G, Cui H, Johnstone M (2023) Survey: an overview of lightweight RFID authentication protocols suitable for the maritime internet of things. Electronics 12(13):2990. https://doi.org/10.3390/electronics12132990

Ntakolia C, Iakovidis D (2021) A route planning framework for smart wearable assistive navigation systems. SN Appl Sci 3(1). https://doi.org/10.1007/s42452-020-04038-6

Nursuwars F, Audika R, Sutisna S, Taufiqurrahman I (2023) Smart labouratory using radio frequency identification (RFID) based on the internet of things. COELITE 1(2):75–90. https://doi.org/10.17509/coelite.v1i2.51618

Patel B, Katariya L, Upadhyay C (2023) RFID sensing & its data analysis using micro-controller for vehicle security & its tracking. JRTDD. https://doi.org/10.53555/jrtdd.v6i1.2703

Popescu DE, Bungau C, Prada M, Domuta C, Bungau S, Tit DM (2016) Waste management strategy at a public university in smart city context. J Environ Prot Ecol 17(3):1011–1020

Ran S, Wang Q, Wang J, Ni Y, Guo Z, Luo Y (2024) A concise state-of-the-art review of crack monitoring enabled by RFID technology. Appl Sci 14(8):3213. https://doi.org/10.3390/app14083213

Samuel A, Sebastian S (2019) An algorithm for IoT based vehicle verification system using RFID. Int J Electr Comput Eng (IJECE) 9(5):3751. https://doi.org/10.11591/ijece.v9i5.pp3751-3758

Sarg M (2025) Emergency drug box accuracy: analysis of manual replenishment errors and the use of RFID as a preventative strategy. J Pharm Technol 41(5):212–216. https://doi.org/10.1177/87551225251344143

Schaefer C, Lemmer K, Kret KS, Ylinen M, Mikalef P, Niehaves B (2021) Truth or dare? How can we influence the adoption of artificial intelligence in municipalities? În: Proceedings of the 54th Annual Hawaii International Conference on System Sciences, pp 2347–2356

Schmager S, Grøder CH, Parmiggiani E, Pappas I, Vassilakopoulou P (2023) What do citizens think of AI adoption in public services? Exploratory research on citizen attitudes through a social contract lens. În: Proceedings of the 56th Annual Hawaii International Conference on System Sciences, pp. 4472–4481

Schuett J (2023) Three lines of defense against risks from AI. AI & Soc 40(2):493–507. https://doi.org/10.1007/s00146-023-01811-0

Tichoniuk M, Wiszumirska K (2024) Packaging supporting food sustainability, pp 54–70. https://doi.org/10.18559/978-83-8211-209-2/4

Vassilakopoulou P, Haug A, Salvesen LM, Pappas IO (2023) Developing human/AI interactions for chat-based customer services: lessons learned from the Norwegian government. Eur J Inf Syst 32(1):10–22

Wang C, Teo TSH, Janssen M (2021) Public and private value creation using artificial intelligence: an empirical study of AI voice robot users in Chinese public sector. Int J Inf Manage 61:102401. https://doi.org/10.1016/j.ijinfomgt.2021.102401

Yılmaz R, Tamer Ö, Kut A, Fidan N (2023) Body temperature related risk factor assessment using RFID sensor tags. Çukurova Üniversitesi Mühendislik Fakültesi Dergisi 38(2):585–592. https://doi.org/10.21605/cukurovaumfd.1334191

Yusoff Z, Ishak M, Alezabi K (2021) The role of RFID in green IoT: a survey on technologies, challenges and a way forward. Adv Sci Technol Eng Syst J 6(1):17–35. https://doi.org/10.25046/aj060103

Zhao M (2024) Positioning sensor data mining and correlation analysis based on multi-mode radio frequency identification. Int J RF Technol 15(2):86–106. https://doi.org/10.1177/17545730241297787

Zhou Y, Dong Y, Xia H, Gu J (2014) Routing optimisation of intelligent vehicle in automated warehouse. Discret Dyn Nat Soc 2014:1–14. https://doi.org/10.1155/2014/789754

The Entrepreneurial Tech Ecosystems and AI Potential

Elena Aurelia Botezat and Anca Otilia Dodescu

Abstract This chapter outlines the transition toward AI driven entrepreneurial ecosystems, highlighting both the opportunities for innovation and competitiveness and the challenges created by uneven technological adoption. It shows how AI can strengthen startups and SMEs, while emphasizing the need for coordinated strategies to prevent widening digital disparities. The Romanian case demonstrates how national and local initiatives mirror global trends yet also expose gaps in coherence and strategic alignment. The integration of infrastructure, talent, and governance emerges as a decisive factor for sustainable, AI driven growth. Innovation hubs and digitalization programs serve as living laboratories where the relationships among talent, infrastructure, and policy frameworks unfold and can be assessed, offering practical insights for policies aligned with international best practices and tailored to Romania's socio-economic conditions.

1 Introduction

Technology, including artificial intelligence (AI) and global connectivity, has transformed entrepreneurial ecosystems from localised, static models into dynamic, fluid, and borderless global networks, thereby necessitating more holistic frameworks to grasp their increasing complexity (Etemad 2025). The entrepreneurial tech ecosystem refers to the interconnected network of people, organisations, resources, and processes in which digital technologies are prioritised as the primary means of interaction, communication, and operation, making entrepreneurship happen within a community or region (Muldoon et al. 2022; Etemad 2025). In the entrepreneurship context, artificial intelligence (AI) is related to the use of machine learning and natural language processing tools to optimise operations, boost productivity, and

E. A. Botezat (✉) · A. O. Dodescu
Faculty of Economic Sciences, University of Oradea, Oradea, Romania
e-mail: elenabotezat1@gmail.com; ebotezat@uoradea.ro

A. O. Dodescu
e-mail: adodescu@uoradea.ro

C. Sabău-Popa (ed.), *Artificial Intelligence in Finance, Accounting and Business Administration*, Contributions to Finance and Accounting,
https://doi.org/10.1007/978-3-032-22737-9_5

drive strategic value (IBM, n.d.). Artificial intelligence has rapidly evolved from a functional tool into a catalyst for systemic transformation, redefining entrepreneurial ecosystems through real-time, data-driven decision-making, seamless digital engagement, and the reconfiguration of business operations around cloud technologies and personalised marketing strategies. However, this shift also presents significant vulnerabilities ranging from data-driven prejudice, algorithmic bias and ethical concerns to unequal digital access among individuals and organisations—highlighting the critical need for an adaptable and holistic framework. Given entrepreneurial ecosystems stem from natural phenomena, scholars have researched entrepreneurial ecosystems as geographic regions, highlighted that they are shaped by region-specific material, social, and cultural attributes—such as talent, universities, role models, and access to resources—which collectively influence human capital, policy, and market dynamics (Liguori et al. 2019; Kang et al. 2021).

2 The Concept of Entrepreneurial Tech Ecosystems and Platform-Based Collaboration

Traditional entrepreneurial ecosystems have been conceptualised as interdependent networks of actors, organisations, institutions, and entrepreneurial processes that interact within a regional framework characterised by geographic proximity, physical infrastructure, and face-to-face interactions (Kansheba and Wald 2020). Entrepreneurial tech ecosystems, supported by digital technologies and characterised by global access, digital scalability, data, algorithms, and virtual networks, represent emergent entrepreneurial systems in which interactions and entrepreneurial processes increasingly take place via digital platforms and online environments (Bejjani et al. 2023). More importantly, it should be noted that the effective functioning of a tech entrepreneurial ecosystem depends not only on the presence of the key antecedents proposed by Isenberg (2010)—namely, policy, finance, culture, support, human capital, and markets—but also on how these elements interact dynamically to create new structures for interaction and innovation (Bejjani et al. 2023). Consequently, we are witnessing a growing interest from communities and regions in leveraging technology to build and sustain entrepreneurial activity, considering the positive effects of digital entrepreneurship—from sustainable job creation to large-scale socioeconomic improvement (Muldoon et al. 2022; Etemad 2025).

In technology-based entrepreneurship, part or all of what would be physical in a traditional organisation is digitised—starting with the pursuit of opportunities, which becomes closely linked to the use of digital media, and extending to products, marketing, and workspaces (Kraus et al. 2019). Existing or newly created digital enterprises create the jobs and growth opportunities of the future using novel digital technologies to improve business operations and propose new business models to engage with customers and stakeholders (European Commission 2015). Thus, it is easy to observe that in this type of entrepreneurship, the emphasis is placed on interactions and relationship networks within the digital context, noting that environmental resources play a role equivalent to entrepreneurial abilities. Emerging domain literature (e.g., Spigel 2017; Du et al. 2018) emphasises the importance of online communities and resources derived from professional and social networks as key elements for the success of tech-based entrepreneurship. Specifically, Elia et al. (2020) examined how digital technologies and collective platform intelligence are transforming the entrepreneurial process. They view the tech entrepreneurship ecosystem as the result of interactions between humans and machines that drive startup creation and genuine business innovation. According to the above-mentioned authors, digital actors—such as entrepreneurs, platforms, and communities—engage in activities like product development and resource coordination, motivated by value creation. These processes are structured through organisational forms such as platforms, networks, and meta-organisations, which aim to create new ways of satisfying consumer needs and ultimately generating profit.

The changes brought by tech entrepreneurial ecosystems target some of the foundational business aspects (Sahut et al. 2021). For example, one key aspect involves a shift in the way value is created, specifically moving from a business model orientation based on a traditional value chain to one rooted in networks. Moreover, the innovative tools offered by digital technologies, by enabling the revelation of consumers' intrinsic motivations in a world increasingly driven by self-expression, lead to the emergence of new products designed to meet the most diverse and nuanced needs—thereby generating new market demand. Another important aspect concerns the fact that the digitalisation of entrepreneurial processes has made these processes less confined than in the traditional economy, in the sense that everything unfolds much faster, often perceived as instantaneous. Thus, the path from idea to business is significantly shorter (Huang et al. 2017), and the entrepreneurial success is determined both by the ability to maintain a constant presence on digital platforms and by the capacity to adapt one's actions in response to those of others, entrepreneurs, and consumers (Srinivasan and Venkatraman 2018). Collaboration and knowledge sharing with and among users of digital platforms—whether they are suppliers or demand carriers—raises the issue of risk. This aspect is organically tied to entrepreneurship as we traditionally know it. Within entrepreneurial tech ecosystems, digital entrepreneurs can craft strategies through their online presence to mitigate risks both upstream and downstream of the offering. Upstream, the use of digital technologies enables entrepreneurs to respond in real time to specific problems, to create, customise, and promote their offerings. Downstream, digital entrepreneurs can leverage these technologies to co-produce services with consumers, to understand the value attributed by them to the offering and digital presence, and to extract meaningful insights aimed at improving the quality of their products delivered to the market (Abbes and Troudy 2017). Another sensitive aspect of entrepreneurship, namely funding, also seems to benefit from the use of platforms associated with Entrepreneurial Tech Ecosystems. Through crowdfunding platforms and social networks, digital entrepreneurs can more easily find investors. Of course, this also comes with certain risks, such as the possibility of having their business idea copied (Jaouat 2021).

3 Challenges of the Platform-Based Economy for Romania's Entrepreneurial Tech Ecosystems

One significant challenge Romania faces is building and demonstrating its capacity to participate in the emerging platform-based economy, directly linked with entrepreneurial tech ecosystems. This challenge is heightened by Romania's low level of digital integration and its limited ability to support such ecosystems, as measured by the Digital Economy and Society Index (DESI). Romania's estimated total score stands at just 0.47 out of a maximum of 1.00—significantly below the EU average of 0.65 and lower than most Central and Eastern European countries, except for Bulgaria, as illustrated in Table 1.

As shown in Table 1, Romania's Tech Entrepreneurship sub-index is estimated at 0.48, which is over 27% below the EU average. Except for Bulgaria—lagging just three percentage points behind—all other Central and Eastern European countries outperform Romania in the following order: Slovakia, Hungary, Poland, and the Czech Republic. Looking at the DESI'sub-indices, the most pressing issue appears to be the human factor and the slow adoption of the platform economy, both of which require targeted policies and smart investments. Only through addressing these challenges can Romania realistically reach a score of 0.52–0.53 by 2026, catching up with Slovakia and Hungary.

The enabling factors of a business strategy focused on maintaining harmony between established and emerging economic actors are strongly tied to the cultivation of a healthy entrepreneurial ecosystem, with emphasis on the role of place and contextual factors in entrepreneurial dynamics, as well as on national economic productivity (Maul et al. 2024). In this sense, the focus may fall on both the living elements of the entrepreneurial ecosystem, such as entrepreneurs, social networks, mentors, and innovation communities, as well as on the non-living elements, including digital

Table 1 Estimated total score and sub-indices of the digital platform economy (DPE)

Country	Estimated Total Score (*)	Digital Tech Infrastructure	Digital User Citizenship	Multi-sided Platforms (*)	Tech Entrepreneurship (*)
Romania	**0.47**	**0.52**	**0.45**	**0.42**	**0.48**
Poland	**0.58**	0.62	0.58	0.54	0.56
Hungary	**0.53**	0.57	0.52	0.50	0.53
Bulgaria	**0.43**	0.48	0.42	0.38	0.45
Czechia	**0.60**	0.65	0.60	0.56	0.61
Slovakia	**0.52**	0.60	0.50	0.46	0.52
EU Average	**0.65**	0.68	0.64	0.61	0.66

Note Values marked with (*) are estimates based on trend analysis and secondary sources
Source Own elaboration, based on Digital Economy and Society Index (DESI) 2024, DataReportal, and Digital Decade Reports data and trend analysis

infrastructure, legislative frameworks, economic policies, and access to funding (Ali and Jabeen 2024).

Although entrepreneurial tech ecosystems evolve around the non-living element of platforms—due to their capacity to enable collaborative innovation, product and service sharing, and knowledge transfer—the leading role among the living elements is taken by the ecosystem leader. Specialised literature (e.g., Schäfer and Kuebart 2024) highlights that the ecosystem leader is the primary socio-economic actor who facilitates efficient flows of information and knowledge among participants, thereby enabling the development of shared learning opportunities, innovation, and the beneficial reconfiguration of value propositions. Furthermore, the leader plays a vital role in cultivating trust between parties—specifically among collaborators and users.

Unfortunately, authentic leadership is rare in Romania, with the lack of leaders being more a matter of psychocultural context than of actual capability (David et al. 2015). Moreover, according to David, the absence of trust and cooperation blocks much of the high intellectual and creative potential of Romanians, distorted by the projection of an idealised leadership model that is difficult, if not impossible, to find in reality, thus generating disappointment and passivity. Therefore, only through smart and targeted psychocultural interventions could Romania cultivate authentic leaders capable of effectively mobilising the collective resources of tech-driven entrepreneurial ecosystems.

4 The Transformative Impact of Artificial Intelligence on Entrepreneurial Tech Ecosystems

Artificial intelligence (AI) is a technology based on the ability of computational systems to imitate intelligent human behaviour to create new forms of value in the economy (Etemad 2025). Through various innovations such as machine learning or natural language processing, artificial intelligence processes vast amounts of data in record time, interacts with customers, detects patterns in consumer and employee behaviour, selects and trains new employees, and automates routine tasks in any organisation (Muldoon 2022; Bejjani et al. 2023). However, like anything else, artificial intelligence also has its downsides, closely tied to algorithmic opacity, which can lead to prediction errors with harmful consequences for human subjects, such as the reduction of individual autonomy and human choice. The benefits of artificial intelligence for the internal functioning of organisations and their increased ability to create a competitive advantage lead actors within entrepreneurial ecosystems to place disadvantages related to costs, adaptability, or ethics in the background, focusing increasingly on the opportunities for innovation, efficiency, and scalability that this general-purpose technology offers (Uriarte et al. 2025). A summary of AI in Entrepreneurial Ecosystems is presented in Table 2.

In conclusion, artificial intelligence, with its huge impact, enhances decision-making, streamlines business operations, and enables predictive data analytics,

Table 2 Artificial intelligence (AI) in entrepreneurial ecosystems: summary table

Aspect	Advantages	Disadvantages
Productivity and Efficiency	Automates repetitive tasks, enhances operational speed, accelerates decision-making	Over-automation can diminish human creativity and reduce human oversight in decision-making
Business innovation	Enables the development of new business models and innovative products	Innovations can disrupt traditional industries and contribute to increased market volatility
Data Analysis	Enhance data utilisation by enabling real-time analysis, uncovering patterns, and predicting outcomes	AI-powered data analysis may raise significant concerns regarding data privacy and cybersecurity vulnerabilities
Cost Reduction	Lowers operational costs through automation and efficiency	High initial investment, ongoing maintenance costs to ensure system performance, updates, and security
Customer Experience	Improves customer personalisation and responsiveness, enabling businesses to deliver tailored experiences that boost satisfaction and engagement	Risk of depersonalization, lack of human empathy in interactions between organisations and customers
Scalability	Facilitates rapid data-driven platforms and rapidly responds to market changes without needing extensive human resources	Contributes to a growing divide between AI-fluent and conventional entrepreneurs
Decision Support	Provides a strategic advantage by delivering data-driven insights and accurate forecasting to support informed decision-making	Introduces challenges such as algorithmic bias and lack of transparency in decision-making
Accessibility	Democratizes access to advanced tools such as predictive analytics, automation, and customer intelligence for small businesses	Implies the risk of widening gaps between businesses, excessive reliance on unclear AI systems, and the replacement of human workers without proper support or training

(continued)

Table 2 (continued)

Aspect	Advantages	Disadvantages
Knowledge Creation	AI supports learning and adaptive systems by continuously processing data, identifying patterns, and refining algorithms	It contributes, to some extent, to the fragmentation of expertise in entrepreneurial ecosystems and a growing dependence on external AI providers
Ethical and Social Impact	Promotes responsible innovation when guided by ethical frameworks, fostering positive societal outcomes and inclusive technological progress	Raises ethical dilemmas and concerns over potential job displacement, with significant social consequences

Source Created by authors after Uriarte S, Baier-Fuentes H, Espinoza-Benavides J, Inzunza-Mendoza W (2025) Artificial intelligence technologies and entrepreneurship: a hybrid literature review. Rev Manag Sci. https://doi.org/https://doi.org/10.1007/s11846-025-00839-4

empowering entrepreneurs as core actors of entrepreneurial tech ecosystems to scale rapidly and adapt more efficiently to market changes. However, its integration into entrepreneurial tech ecosystems also introduces challenges such as algorithmic bias and unequal access to AI tools (Uriarte et al. 2025). To fully benefit from AI's transformative potential in business, it is essential to develop holistic frameworks that account for both physical and digital entrepreneurial ecosystems dimensions, and to better understand their hybrid nature, consisting of spaces where digital and physical interactions converge (Muldoon et al. 2022; Etemad 2025). This aspect also calls for inclusive policies that address the growing digital divide and ensure equitable access to technological resources for entrepreneurs. Governments and institutions must rethink support mechanisms by integrating digital literacy initiatives, remote incubation models, and virtual funding platforms, so that entrepreneurial ecosystems remain resilient, innovative, and equitable in a digitally-driven world.

5 Tech-Enabled Regions in the Age of AI: Toward Inclusive and Adaptive Policy Recommendations

The rapid rise of artificial intelligence (AI) is profoundly reshaping the landscape of regional development, opening new avenues for economic growth, social inclusion, and adaptive governance. In this context, tech-enabled regions emerge as living laboratories where digital transformation intersects with policy innovation, demonstrating how AI can be harnessed to build more inclusive, resilient, and adaptive ecosystems.

As a general-purpose technology with disruptive implications for markets, institutions, and business models, AI is increasingly viewed as one of the most transformative forces of our time, reshaping the competitive landscape for entrepreneurial ecosystems and challenging traditional governance (McAfee and Brynjolfsson 2017; Agrawal et al. 2019). At the same time, the innovation systems literature underlines the critical interplay between infrastructure, human capital, and governance, which together sustain entrepreneurial ecosystems and foster long-term development (Lundvall 1992, 2016; Carayannis and Campbell 2009).

The concept of innovation ecosystems emphasises interdependencies among actors, resources, and institutions that foster innovation.

The *Triple Helix model* (Etzkowitz and Leydesdorff 2000) and its extensions, the *Quadruple Helix model* and *Quintuple Helix innovation model* (Carayannis and Campbell 2009, Carayannis et al. 2012), highlight the importance of collaboration among universities, industry, government, and civil society. In the digital age, regional competitiveness increasingly depends on the capacity to create tech-enabled entrepreneurial ecosystems and to integrate AI across economic, educational, and institutional domains.

Within the European Union, strategic frameworks such as the *Oslo Manual* (OECD/Eurostat 2018) and the proposed *Artificial Intelligence Act* (European Commission 2021) highlight the need for anticipatory and adaptive policies—ones that not only promote innovation but also ensure inclusiveness and fairness in the transformation process.

AI policy frameworks increasingly adopt this ecosystem perspective. The OECD (2019) underscores the need for *AI policy frameworks* that balance technological experimentation with ethical and inclusive standards. The *Digital Government Policy Framework* proposed by OECD (2020) includes six dimensions of a fully digital government: digital by design, data-driven public sector, government as a platform, open by default, user-driven, proactiveness. The Digital Government Index (DGI) score of a country is the average score of all six dimensions. Similarly, the European Union's *AI Act* proposal advocates for harmonised regulation that simultaneously encourages innovation and protects citizens' rights (European Commission 2021).

The emergence of AI-driven entrepreneurial tech ecosystems calls for policies that are not only forward-looking but also adaptive to continuous technological disruption (Nambisan et al. 2019; OECD 2020, 2021). In tech-enabled regions, competitiveness increasingly depends on the ability of public and private stakeholders to co-create an environment that supports innovation, ensures equitable access to resources, and builds resilience against socio-economic shocks (Carayannis et al. 2012; European Commission 2020).

An effective policy mix for assessing AI ecosystems should integrate three core pillars: *infrastructure, human capital,* and *governance*—dimensions consistently identified in both the innovation systems literature (Lundvall 2016; Edquist 2005) and European policy frameworks (OECD/Eurostat 2018; OECD 2019, 2020; European Commission 2020, 2021).

First, *infrastructure* must evolve beyond physical connectivity to encompass high-speed broadband, cloud computing capacity, and secure data-sharing frameworks. This is particularly critical for rural and peripheral regions, where connectivity gaps risk excluding communities from AI-enabled growth opportunities.

Second, investment in *human capital* should prioritise AI literacy and digital entrepreneurship skills across all education levels, complemented by lifelong learning programs for the workforce. Public–private partnerships can foster AI training labs, accelerators, and online learning platforms that democratize access to cutting-edge tools.

Third, *governance* frameworks must encourage collaborative experimentation while safeguarding ethical standards. Regulatory sandboxes, for example, can enable startups to test AI solutions under controlled conditions, accelerating innovation without compromising consumer rights or data protection. Additionally, regional innovation councils—composed of entrepreneurs, researchers, policymakers, and citizen representatives—can help align AI strategies with local socio-economic priorities.

5.1 Global Cases

Several global experiences underscore that the success of AI-driven ecosystems relies on the simultaneous consolidation of infrastructure, human capital, and governance frameworks (Carayannis et al. 2012; OECD 2021). The following cases present policy-oriented lessons that demonstrate how these pillars can be effectively operationalised across different national contexts.

Estonia has consistently outperformed the OECD average in the Digital Government Index. According to the OECD (2023) assessment, Estonia ranked 6th out of 33 countries, achieving a score of 74.2% versus the OECD average of 60.5%, with its strongest performance in the "Data-Driven Public Sector" dimension (OECD 2023). These results highlight the country's advanced data interoperability, high level of transparency, and citizen-centric public services (OECD 2023; e-Estonia 2023). In Estonia, the integration of AI across public services, fintech, and startups illustrates how a digitally mature ecosystem—supported by robust infrastructure, AI training programs, and strong public–private collaboration—can accelerate national digital transformation (European Commission 2023; E-Governance Academy 2021; OECD 2015). The key lessons include the importance of integrating AI into public administration to improve efficiency, fostering digital literacy programs for SMEs, and creating governance structures that facilitate cross-sector experimentation.

Ranking among the top OECD countries in venture capital activity (OECD 2025a, b). Israel offers another compelling example, where dense innovation networks, strong university–industry partnerships, venture capital availability, and mentorship programs accelerate technology commercialisation and have created one of the most dynamic AI hubs globally (OECD 2025a, b; Israel Innovation Authority 2024). Government Approves Transformative Stimulus Package to Boost Israeli High-Tech Industry (OECD 2016). Israel's approach demonstrates the power of AI-driven innovation hubs, early-stage funding availability, and collaborative research environments that promote rapid AI adoption.

These global examples serve as reference points for Romanian regions, highlighting strategies that can be adapted to local socio-economic contexts to accelerate AI-driven innovation and inclusive growth.

5.2 The Case of Romania

In this context, Romania finds itself in an early but dynamic stage of developing AI ecosystems (OECD 2025a, b; World Bank 2023). Regional hubs such as Cluj-Napoca, Bucharest, Timişoara, and Oradea illustrate that emergent ecosystems can function as drivers of economic and social transformation (European Digital Innovation Hubs Network 2025). Yet, persistent regional disparities, digital infrastructure gaps, and the absence of a coherent national AI strategy risk producing fragmented and uneven development (OECD 2025a, b).

The examples below demonstrate that tech-enabled regional hubs in Romania are already experimenting with adaptive AI ecosystems. By combining robust digital infrastructure, investments in human capital, and flexible governance mechanisms, these tech-enabled regions are creating environments where AI-driven innovation can flourish while remaining inclusive and socially responsible (Table 3).

These Romanian examples demonstrate that adaptive AI ecosystems are already emerging, showing the benefits of combining robust infrastructure, human capital development, and flexible governance mechanisms.

5.3 Toward an Inclusive and Adaptive AI Policy Framework

Inclusive and adaptive policy recommendations must recognise the heterogeneity of tech-enabled regions: what works in a metropolitan hub may not be suitable for a mid-sized industrial city or a rural innovation cluster. Tailored policy roadmaps, informed by continuous monitoring of ecosystem performance, can ensure that the benefits of AI are equitably distributed and contribute to sustainable regional development.

Building on this perspective, a coherent framework for inclusive policy design must translate general recommendations into context-sensitive actions. This requires a systematic approach that prioritises bridging digital divides, expanding AI and entrepreneurship education across diverse demographic groups, institutionalising participatory governance through regional innovation councils, and establishing adaptive monitoring mechanisms that align strategies with local socio-economic realities. In this way, regions can evolve into resilient AI-enabled ecosystems capable of sustaining long-term economic growth, social inclusion, and regional competitiveness.

To conceptually capture these dynamics, the following infographic illustrates the interconnections between Romania's regional hubs and the four core pillars of inclusive and adaptive policy:

Table 3 Romanian tech-enabled regional hubs: good practices

Region/hub	Key focus areas	Infrastructure/tools	Human capital initiatives	Governance and innovation support	Notable achievements/ impact
Cluj-Napoca/Digital Innovation Hub for Society, Transilvania Digital Innovation Hub	Digital Health, Industry 4.0	IT clusters, universities, research institutes, pre-investment testing	AI and entrepreneurship labs, accelerators, online learning	EU networking, collaboration with local government	Strengthened AI ecosystem; multi-sector partnerships
Bucharest-Ilfov / Wallachia eHub	Eco-digital transformation, sustainability	Co-working spaces, tech infrastructure	Training programs for digital skills	Public–private collaboration	Addresses economic and sustainability challenges in the metropolitan area
Oradea Tech Hub	Local startups, community capacity-building	Online learning platforms, incubators	"Online Teacher" initiative (25,000+ educators trained)	Local engagement, global outreach	Engaged 336 tech professionals; global impact
Timişoara / Vox Technology Park and Incuboxx	IT&C innovation	BREEAM-certified infrastructure, incubators	Startup mentorship and training	Collaboration with universities and corporates	Supports new ventures in AI, digital innovation
Nationwide (Emerging Hubs: Iaşi, Braşov, Sibiu, Craiova, Constanţa)	Multi-sector AI adoption	IT&C infrastructure	Workforce development programs	Regional innovation councils	Growing startup ecosystems, AI adoption across sectors

(continued)

Table 3 (continued)

Region/hub	Key focus areas	Infrastructure/tools	Human capital initiatives	Governance and innovation support	Notable achievements/ impact
National Public Administration (AFIR)	EU fund automation for farmers	UiPath robots, automated workflows	Training for staff in AI tools	Process automation governance	Saved 784 workdays; improved service delivery for 50,000+ applications (€5.32B)
Leading Startups	AI across fintech, HR, edtech	Cloud-based AI platforms, proprietary software	Company-led training and internships	Startups' governance, accelerators	Sectoral innovation, scaling of AI solutions nationally

Source Created by authors based on Agency for Rural Investments Financing (AFIR) (2025), Digital Innovation Hub for Society (2025), European Digital Innovation Hubs Network—Romania (2025), Incuboxx (2025), Oradea Tech Hub (2025), Romania Insider (2025), Romania Journal (2025), StartupBlink. (2025), Tech Talent (2025), The Recursive (2022), Transilvania Digital Innovation Hub (2025), Vox Technology Park (2025), Wallachia eHub (2025),World Bank (2023)

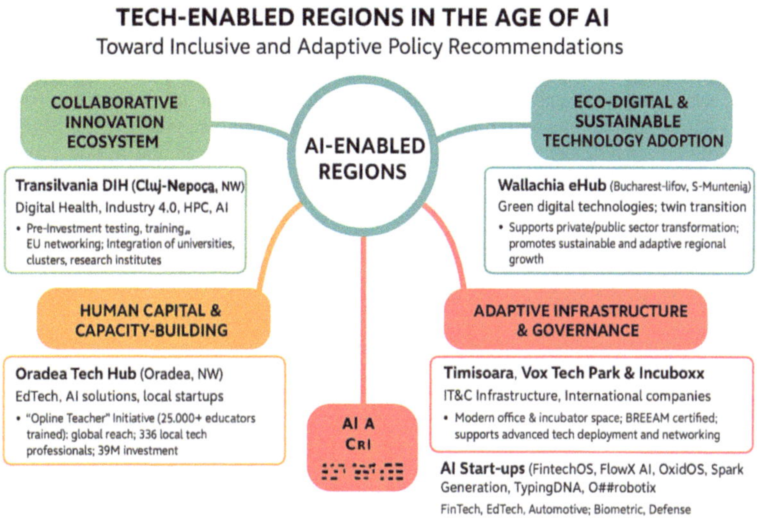

Fig. 1 Romanian Regional Hubs Good Practices: Interconnections with the four main pillars of inclusive and adaptive policies. *Source* Created by authors

(1) Collaborative Innovation Ecosystem,
(2) Eco-Digital and Sustainable Technology Adoption,
(3) Adaptive Infrastructure and Governance,
(4) Human Capital and Capacity-Building (Fig. 1).

6 Conclusions

The transformation of entrepreneurial ecosystems into integrated, AI-driven networks represents both a historic opportunity and a multidimensional challenge. AI provides unprecedented potential for innovation, operational efficiency, and scalable growth. Start-ups and SMEs that adopt AI can optimise supply chains, personalise customer experiences, and access international markets more effectively. However, uneven technology adoption risks widening disparities in access to digital resources, talent distribution, and investment flows. Therefore, coordinated strategic action is essential to ensure inclusive and sustainable AI integration.

International experiences show that AI success emerges from the interplay of infrastructure, human capital, and governance. Estonia and Israel exemplify how nations can leverage these pillars to accelerate innovation. Table 4 illustrates key strategies and outcomes in these countries:

As we observe these international benchmarks, a pattern emerges: AI ecosystems thrive where digital infrastructure, human capital, and governance reinforce each

Table 4 Global cases: lessons for policy design

Country	Key AI strategies	Outcomes/benefits	Implications for Romania
Estonia	AI integration in public services, fintech, and startups through mature digital ecosystems, robust infrastructure, AI training programs, and public–private collaboration	Increased efficiency in public services, higher SME competitiveness, widespread AI literacy	Develop national and regional digital infrastructure; expand AI training programs for SMEs and public administration; promote cross-sector data sharing
Israel	AI innovation hubs, strong university-industry collaboration, venture capital networks, and mentorship programs	Rapid commercialisation of technologies, vibrant startup ecosystem, accelerated innovation	Foster university-industry-government partnerships; create mentorship and regional investment networks; support incubation and acceleration programs

Source Created by authors

other. These lessons offer a valuable compass for Romania, guiding the design of regional and national strategies.

Romania has begun translating these global insights into tangible regional initiatives. Each hub demonstrates unique strengths, while collectively highlighting a growing national AI ecosystem. Table 5 summarises these initiatives and their impacts:

The Romanian examples reveal how local initiatives can echo international strategies, yet they also highlight the need for coherence and coordination. The Romanian examples reveal how local initiatives can echo international strategies, yet they also highlight the need for coherence and coordination. These hubs function as living laboratories, where the interplay between human capital, infrastructure, and governance can be tested and scaled. In this sense, they provide both evidence and experimentation grounds for designing policies that are not only aligned with global best practices but also responsive to Romania's specific socio-economic context.

To gain deeper insight, it is useful to juxtapose Romania's emerging AI hubs with the established ecosystems of Estonia and Israel. The comparison underscores both progress and gaps (Table 6).

This comparative lens clarifies that Romania's regional hubs have achieved notable success, yet a national strategic framework is essential to amplify their impact. The integration of infrastructure, talent, and governance emerges as a decisive factor for sustainable AI-driven growth.

Table 5 The case of Romania: lessons for policy design

Region	Key AI initiatives	Observed impact	Lessons learned
Cluj-Napoca / Transilvania Digital Innovation Hub	AI in healthcare data analysis, Industry 4.0; AI and entrepreneurship labs, accelerators	Strengthened cross-sector partnerships, increased startup activity	Cross-sector collaboration and dedicated AI labs accelerate knowledge transfer and innovation adoption
Bucharest-Ilfov / Wallachia eHub	Eco-digital transformation, digital training programs	Addressed urban economic and sustainability challenges	Public–private collaboration and inclusive training programs are critical for metropolitan regions
Timişoara / Vox Technology Park and Incuboxx	University-SME collaboration for AI-driven logistics and manufacturing	Improved operational efficiency, human-centred AI solutions tested	Human-centred AI design combined with academic collaboration increases SME adaptability
Oradea Tech Hub	Local startup support, online learning platforms	336 tech professionals engaged, increased global visibility	Inclusive AI education programs enhance regional capacity and community engagement
Emerging National Hubs (Iaşi, Braşov, Sibiu, Craiova, Constanţa)	Multisector AI adoption, workforce development	Growing startup ecosystems, sectoral AI adoption	Workforce training and participatory governance foster inclusive regional innovation

Source Created by authors

6.1 *Strategic Roadmap for Romania*

Drawing upon lessons from both international benchmarks and domestic initiatives, Romania can chart a roadmap for inclusive AI ecosystems:

(1) **Infrastructure Development:** Expand broadband, cloud services, and secure data-sharing platforms, particularly in rural and peripheral regions.
(2) **Investing in Human Capital:** Scale AI literacy programs, entrepreneurial training, and lifelong learning initiatives; foster mentorship networks inspired by Israeli hubs.
(3) **Governance and Collaboration:** Establish regional innovation councils, regulatory sandboxes, and adaptive policies to allow experimentation while maintaining ethical standards.
(4) **Cross-Sector Integration:** Promote collaboration among SMEs, startups, universities, and public institutions to facilitate knowledge transfer and innovation adoption.

Table 6 Comparative analysis: Global vs. Romanian ecosystems

Dimension	Estonia	Israel	Romanian hubs	Conclusions
Infrastructure	Mature digital ecosystems, strong public–private connectivity	Innovation hubs, robust VC and research networks	Regional IT clusters, co-working spaces, incubators	Investment in broadband, cloud, and collaborative regional platforms is fundamental
Human Capital	AI training programs in the public sector	Mentorship, university-industry pipelines	AI and entrepreneurship labs, online platforms, accelerators	Continuous AI education for students, SMEs, and public officials ensures sustainable adoption
Governance and Policy	Cross-sector collaboration, regulatory frameworks	Flexible experimentation, venture support	Regional innovation councils, partnerships with local authorities	Adaptive governance encourages experimentation while respecting ethical and social inclusion standards
Innovation Outcomes	Increased efficiency, SME competitiveness	Rapid technology commercialisation, vibrant ecosystem	Multisector partnerships, AI pilot projects	Technology adoption must align with local socio-economic priorities

Source Created by authors

(5) **Monitoring and Adaptation:** Implement performance metrics to track AI adoption, cross-sector collaboration, and social inclusion, adjusting strategies based on regional realities.

By blending international best practices with domestic ingenuity, Romania has the potential to construct AI ecosystems that are not only globally competitive but also socially inclusive. In this endeavour, the triad of infrastructure, human capital, and governance is not merely a framework—it is the connective tissue that binds vision to action, enabling a sustainable and prosperous AI-driven entrepreneurial landscape.

References

Abbes I, Troudy Y (2017) Co-création de valeur et technologie digitale: Quel design pour ces plateformes d'engagement? Le cas du Photomaton 2.0. Manag Avenir 94:153–175. https://doi.org/10.3917/mav.094.0153
Acs ZJ, Autio E, Szerb L (2014) National systems of entrepreneurship: measurement issues and policy implications. Res Policy 43(3):476–494. https://doi.org/10.1016/j.respol.2013.08.016
Agency for Rural Investments Financing (AFIR) (2025) https://www.afir.info/
Agrawal A, Gans J, Goldfarb A (2019) Prediction machines: the simple economics of artificial intelligence. Harvard Business Review Press, Boston
Ali J, Jabeen Z (2024) Digital ecosystem, entrepreneurial ecosystem and economic development as enablers of digital technology entrepreneurship. Manag Decis Econ 45(6):3929–3941. https://doi.org/10.1002/mde.4233
Bejjani M, Göcke L, Menter M (2023) Digital entrepreneurial ecosystems: a systematic literature review. Technol Forecast Soc Chang 189:122372. https://doi.org/10.1016/j.techfore.2023.122372
Carayannis EG, Campbell DFJ (2009) "Mode 3" and "Quadruple Helix": toward a 21st Century Fractal Innovation Ecosystem. Int J Technol Manage 46(3–4):201–234. https://doi.org/10.1504/IJTM.2009.023374
Carayannis EG, Barth TD, Campbell DF (2012) The Quintuple Helix innovation model: global warming as a challenge and driver for innovation. J Innov Entrep 1(2). https://doi.org/10.1186/2192-5372-1-2
David D, Iliescu D, Matu S, Balaszi R (2015) The national psychological/personality profile of Romanians: an in-depth analysis of the regional national psychological/personality profile of Romanians. RomIan J Psychol 17(2). https://doi.org/10.24193/rjp.2015.2.01
Digital Innovation Hub for Society (2025) https://dih4society.ro/
Du W, Pan SL, Zhou N, Ouyang T (2018) From a marketplace of electronics to a digital entrepreneurial ecosystem (DEE): the emergence of a meta-organization in Zhongguancun, China. Inf Syst J 28(6):1158–1175
Edquist C (2005) Systems of innovation: perspectives and challenges. In: Fagerberg J, Mowery D, Nelson R (eds) The Oxford handbook of innovation. Oxford University Press, Oxford
e-Estonia (2023) Estonia among the best countries to provide digital public services according to the OECD. https://e-estonia.com/
E-Governance Academy (2021) Artificial intelligence strategy in Estonia. EGA Publications. Retrieved from https://ega.ee/publications/
Elia G, Margherita A, Passiante G (2020) Digital entrepreneurship ecosystem: How digital technologies and collective intelligence are reshaping the entrepreneurial process. Technol Forecast Soc Chang 150:119791. https://doi.org/10.1016/j.techfore.2019.11979
Etemad H (2025) The artificial intelligence, digital economy, and global connectivity: implications and lessons for international entrepreneurship. J Int Entrep 22:409–432. https://doi.org/10.1007/s10843-025-00388-7
Etzkowitz H, Leydesdorff L (2000) The dynamics of innovation: from National Systems and "Mode 2" to a Triple Helix of university–industry–government relations. Res Policy 29(2):109–123. https://doi.org/10.1016/S0048-7333(99)00055-4
European Commission (2020) A European strategy for data. European Commission, Brussels
European Commission (2021) Proposal for a regulation laying down harmonised rules on artificial intelligence (Artificial Intelligence Act). European Commission, Brussels
European Commission (2015) Digital transformation of European industry and enterprises: a report of the strategic policy forum on digital entrepreneurship. https://ec.europa.eu/DocsRoom/documents/9462/attachments/1/translations/en/renditions/native
European Commission (2023) Digital Government Index 2023: Estonia Country Report. European Commission, Brussels

European Digital Innovation Hubs Network—Romania (2025) https://european-digital-innovation-hubs.ec.europa.eu/edih-catalogue/countries/romania
Huang JC, Henfridsson O, Liu M, Newell S (2017) Growing on steroids: rapidly scaling the user base of digital ventures through digital innovation. MIS Quarterly 41(1):301–314. https://doi.org/10.25300/MISQ/2017/41.1.15
IBM (n.d.) Artificial intelligence in business. IBM Think. https://www.ibm.com/think/topics/artificial-intelligence-business. Accessed July 28, 2025
Incuboxx (2025) https://timisoara2023.eu/ro/loca%C8%9Bii/incuboxx/
Isenberg DJ (2010) The big idea: how to start an entrepreneurial revolution. Harv Bus Rev 88(6):40–50. https://hbr.org/2010/06/the-big-idea-how-to-start-an-entrepreneurial-revolution
Israel Innovation Authority (2024) Government approves transformative stimulus package to boost Israeli high tech industry
Jaouat F (2021) One (provider) to rule them all: white-label platforms in crowdfunding—an exploratory case study. ECIS 2021 Research-in-Progress Papers, 4. https://doi.org/10.51399/ECIS2021.1083
Kang Q, Li H, Cheng Y, Kraus S (2021) Entrepreneurial ecosystems: analysing the status quo. Knowl Manag Res Pract 19(1):8–20. https://doi.org/10.1080/14778238.2019.1701964
Kansheba JMP, Wald AE (2020) Entrepreneurial ecosystems: a systematic literature review and research agenda. J Small Bus Enterp Dev 27(6):943–964. https://doi.org/10.1108/JSBED-11-2019-0364
Kraus S, Palmer C, Kailer N, Kallinger FL, Spitzer J (2019) Digital entrepreneurship: a research agenda on new business models for the twenty-first century. Int J Entrep Behav Res 25(2):353–375. https://doi.org/10.1108/IJEBR-06-2018-0425
Liguori E, Bendickson J, Solomon S, McDowell WC (2019) Development of a multi-dimensional measure for assessing entrepreneurial ecosystems. Entrep Reg Dev 31(1–2):7–21. https://doi.org/10.1080/08985626.2018.1537144
Lundvall BÅ (1992) National systems of innovation: towards a theory of innovation and interactive learning. Pinter Publishers, London
Lundvall BÅ (2016) The learning economy and the economics of hope. Anthem Press, London
Mason C, Brown R (2014) Entrepreneurial ecosystems and growth-oriented entrepreneurship. OECD LEED Programme. https://doi.org/10.13140/RG.2.1.1849.1607
Maul V, Rose R, Hölzle K (2024) Revising digital entrepreneurial ecosystems: an integrative framework and future research agenda. In: Research handbook on entrepreneurial ecosystems. Edward Elgar Publishing, pp 371–393. https://doi.org/10.4337/9781802208949.00032
McAfee A, Brynjolfsson E (2017) Machine, platform, crowd: harnessing our digital future. W. W. Norton
Muldoon J, Liguori EW, Solomon S, Bendickson J (2022) Technological innovation and the expansion of entrepreneurship ecosystems. RMS 17(6):1789–1808. https://doi.org/10.1007/s11846-022-00573-1
Nambisan S, Wright M, Feldman M (2019) The digital transformation of innovation and entrepreneurship: progress, challenges and key themes. Res Policy 48(8):103773. https://doi.org/10.1016/j.respol.2019.03.018
OECD (2015) OECD public governance reviews: Estonia and Finland: fostering strategic capacity across governments and digital services across borders, OECD public governance reviews. OECD Publishing, Paris. https://doi.org/10.1787/9789264229334-en
OECD (2016) SME and entrepreneurship policy in Israel 2016. In: OECD studies on SMEs and entrepreneurship. OECD Publishing, Paris. https://doi.org/10.1787/9789264262324-en
OECD (2019) OECD principles on artificial intelligence. OECD Publishing, Paris
OECD (2020) The OECD digital government policy framework: six dimensions of a digital government. OECD Public Governance Policy Papers, No. 02, OECD Publishing. https://doi.org/10.1787/f64fed2a-en
OECD (2021) OECD science, technology and innovation outlook 2021: times of crisis and opportunity. OECD Publishing, Paris

OECD (2023) Digital Government Index 2023: country results. https://www.oecd.org/gov/digital-government/
OECD (2025) Benchmarking government support for Venture Capital: a comparative analysis. OECD SME and Entrepreneurship Papers. OECD Publishing, Paris. https://doi.org/10.1787/81e53985-en
OECD (2025) Romania's National Artificial Intelligence Strategy. Organisation for Economic Co-operation and Development. https://oecd.ai/en/dashboards/policy-initiatives/romanias-national-ai-strategy-3795
OECD/Eurostat (2018) Oslo Manual 2018: guidelines for collecting, reporting and using data on innovation. In: The measurement of scientific, technological and innovation activities, 4th edn. OECD Publishing, Paris. https://doi.org/10.1787/9789264304604-en.
Oradea Tech Hub (2025) https://oth.shopia.ro/despre-noi
Romania Insider (2025) Romania's green startup ecosystem gaining momentum, report shows. https://www.romania-insider.com/romania-green-startup-ecosystem-report-2025
Romania Journal (2025) Romania drops 4 spots in global startup rank, Leads in AI. https://www.romaniajournal.ro/business/romania-drops-4-spots-in-global-startup-rank-leads-in-ai/
Sahut JM, Iandoli L, Teulon F (2021) The age of digital entrepreneurship. Small Bus Econ 56(3):1159–1169. https://doi.org/10.1007/s11187-019-00294-3
Schäfer S, Kuebart A (2024) A typology of trans-local knowledge circulation between entrepreneurial ecosystems. In: Research handbook on entrepreneurial ecosystems. Edward Elgar Publishing, pp 279–293. https://doi.org/10.4337/9781800378988.00021
Spigel B (2017) The relational organization of entrepreneurial ecosystems. Entrep Theory Pract 41(1):49–72. https://doi.org/10.1111/etap.12167
Srinivasan A, Venkatraman N (2018) Entrepreneurship in digital platforms: a network-centric view. Strateg Entrep J 12(1):54–71. https://doi.org/10.1002/sej.1272
Stam E (2015) Entrepreneurial ecosystems and regional policy: a sympathetic critique. Eur Plan Stud 23(9):1759–1769. https://doi.org/10.1080/09654313.2015.1061484
StartupBlink (2025) 31 Top Startups in Timişoara for August 2025. https://www.startupblink.com/top-startups/timisoara-ro
Tech Talent (2025) Why Romania is emerging as Europe's AI-ready R&D powerhouse. https://www.techtalent.ro/why-romania-is-emerging-as-europes-ai-ready-rd-powerhouse/
The Recursive (2022) Mapping of Romanian cities: who is shaping tech and innovation? https://therecursive.com/mapping-romanian-cities-that-are-shapping-tech-innovation/
Transilvania Digital Innovation Hub (2025) https://transilvaniadih.ro/en/homepage-en/
Uriarte S, Baier-Fuentes H, Espinoza-Benavides J, Inzunza-Mendoza W (2025) Artificial intelligence technologies and entrepreneurship: a hybrid literature review. RMS. https://doi.org/10.1007/s11846-025-00839-4
Vox Technology Park (2025) https://voxtechnologypark.ro/
Wallachia eHub (2025) https://wallachiaehub.ro/
World Bank (2023) Starting up Romania: entrepreneurship ecosystem diagnostic. https://openknowledge.worldbank.org/entities/publication/ce6b5004-d2de-5b9c-997e-5858e2ccd935

The Romanian Labour Market and Its Response to Digital Transformation

Elena Aurelia Botezat and Olimpia Iuliana Ban

Abstract This chapter examines the Romanian labor market and the ways in which it seeks to address the challenges generated by the rapid integration of digital technologies and artificial intelligence, while simultaneously confronting significant demographic and structural constraints. These include substantial emigration of skilled workers, an aging population, persistently high rates of NEET youth (not in education, employment, or training), widespread informal employment, and limited access to the formal labor market for several vulnerable groups. The analysis concludes that Romanian authorities and employers must invest in programs that develop employees' digital competencies. Such programs should focus on integrating digital technologies into everyday work processes and on cultivating the advanced skills needed to support organizational innovation, productivity growth, and long-term economic resilience.

1 Introduction

The labour market in Romania, as the intersection between labour demand and supply, presents a multifaceted and evolving reality—one increasingly shaped by both a shortage of workforce and a deficit in critical skills (Vasile et al. 2021). Despite that Romania's labour market may seem acceptable at first glance—thanks to an employment rate of over 63% and an unemployment rate below 4%—a closer look reveals deep structural issues, such as high youth unemployment, demographic aging, the lack of effective educational reforms, all accompanied by persistent regional disparities (European Labour Authority 2024; Dumitrescu 2024). Additionally, the continuous emigration of the skilled labour force puts pressure on Romania's socio-economic adaptability, which is further intensified by global competition, economic

E. A. Botezat (✉) · O. I. Ban
Faculty of Economic Sciences, University of Oradea, Oradea, Romania
e-mail: elenabotezat1@gmail.com; ebotezat@uoradea.ro

O. I. Ban
e-mail: oban@uoradea.ro

C. Sabău-Popa (ed.), *Artificial Intelligence in Finance, Accounting and Business Administration*, Contributions to Finance and Accounting,
https://doi.org/10.1007/978-3-032-22737-9_6

challenges, shifting employee expectations, and rapid technological advancements (Benta et al. 2024).

The digital transformation wave is generating disruptions across the labour market. These changes manifest through the disappearance of many traditional roles, the emergence of new job categories, the urgent need to restructure existing skill sets, and the acquisition of new competencies that are generated and oriented toward technology.

To remain competitive on today's global market, Romanian employers have begun investing in employee development programs, with the integration of digital technology in daily work processes emerging as a cornerstone of business transformation, as emphasised in *the World Economic Forum's 2025* Future of Jobs Report. According to data released by the European Labour Authority in 2025, 94% of Romanian companies plan to invest in employee training, an aspect which reflects a commitment to upskilling and a proactive approach to digital economy transformation.

2 Overview of the Present Labour Market

At the end of 2024, Romania's active population was estimated by the Romanian National Institute of Statistics to be 8.3 million people, representing 43.56% of the total population recorded in the 2021 national census. The number of employed people was 7.85 million, while the number of unemployed reached 451.000. By age group, the employment rate among people aged 20–64 was 69% (approximately 73% for men and 55% for women), which is 6.3% higher than the rate for those aged 15–64. The employment rate in 2023 for Romania's working-age population (15–64 years) was 63% overall, with rates of 71.7% for men and 54.3% for women. According to data provided by the Romanian National Institute of Statistics (2025), based on educational level, university graduates registered an employment rate of 90%, individuals with a medium level of education reached 66.5%, while those with a low level of education had only 36.9%. The employment rate in urban areas was 69.8%, compared to 57.0% in rural areas.

The latest data for 2025, provided by Eurostat and the European Labour Authority, reveal a 0.4% decrease in the employment rate compared to 2024. Romania has the lowest job vacancy rate in the EU27, at 0.6%. At the same time, Romania recorded the highest increase in hourly labour costs in the European Union, namely 16.1%. The unemployment rate fluctuates slightly around 4.3%, which is below the EU average. However, youth unemployment reached 14.1% in 2024, an increase of 1 percentage point compared to 2023. Moreover, Romania had the highest rate in the EU of young people who are neither working, studying, nor participating in training: 19.4% in 2024. In addition to the youth unemployment issue, Romania also faces challenges related to migration—especially among qualified workers—and demographic ageing. In figures, this means that one in four mobile workers in the EU is Romanian, and Romania could potentially triple the number of active people over the age of 65 in the next decade (Eurostat 2025; European Labour Authority 2024). To address labour force shortages, Romania issued over 77,000 work permits in the previous year and is projected to need between 200,000 and 300,000 foreign workers in 2025 to maintain economic activity (Shabani 2024). A summary of the main labour market indicators for Romania compared to the EU27 is presented in Table 1.

Romanian literature (e.g., Benta et al. 2024; Dumitrescu 2024) shows that although Romania's GDP has doubled since joining the EU, labour productivity remains among the lowest in the Union. The active population is expected to continue declining, with an estimated drop of one million more people by 2030. The labour shortages that hinder economic efficiency are currently most acute in Bucharest, Cluj, Timiş, and Braşov. According to Benta et al. (2024), the sectors with the highest job vacancy rates are manufacturing, IT, and public administration. Similarly, the study conducted by Dumitrescu (2024) highlights several Romanian labour market strengths, including the low unemployment rate, increased investments in the green economy and digitalisation, government measures aimed at raising the employment rate to 75% for the 20–64 age group, and efforts to upgrade the education system. The same study also highlighted weaknesses in the labour market, including labour shortages and the mismatch between skills supply and demand, as well as persistent regional disparities, limited inclusion of vulnerable groups, and the social costs associated with digital transition.

Table 1 Comparative labour market data: EU27 vs. Romania

Indicator	EU27 value	Romania value	Difference
Employment rate (20–64 age group)	76.1%	62.7%	−13.7%
Overall unemployment rate (March 2025)	5.8%	5.8%	0
Youth unemployment rate (under 25)	14.5%	26.3%	+11.8%
Nominal productivity per employee	100%	80% of the EU27 average	−20%
Wages	100%	35% of the EU27 average	−65%
Hourly labour costs Growth rate (2025 vs 2024)	+4.1%	+16.1%	An increase in RO nearly four times higher than EU27

Source Created by the authors based on data from Eurostat 2024, 2025

3 The Impact of Digital Transformation

The shift toward a technology-driven economy is redefining existing industries and giving rise to new ones. As a result, traditional retail (brick-and-mortar stores), conventional banking services, non-automated industrial production, digitally unadapted transport and logistics, and traditional education are at risk of disappearing, as can be seen in Table 2, along with thousands of jobs. This transformation affects cashiers, travel agents, bank consultants and tellers, factory workers, postal service employees, traditional librarians, data operators in educational institutions, administrative secretaries, archivists, and others in similar roles. On the other hand, new industries are flourishing, including the tech and digital sectors, such as software development, fintech, and AI engineering; the green transition sectors of renewable energy, environmental engineering, and sustainability consulting; as well as the care economy and e-education (see Table 2). Consequently, professionals who work with AI, augmented reality, and interactive platforms are increasingly in demand. These include AI and machine learning engineers, designers of intuitive and engaging interfaces, virtual and augmented reality specialists, renewable energy engineers, green project managers, teachers who embrace technology, digital content developers, wellness and healthcare specialists, e-commerce professionals, and experts in smart logistics (World Economic Forum 2025; European Labour Authority 2025).

A study conducted in Romania between February and March 2024, based on an online questionnaire applied to a sample of 512 respondents aged between 19 and 65, mainly from economic and technical areas, investigated the perception of Artificial Intelligence as a possible threat or support for human skills in the workplace, depending on the field of activity and professional experience of the participants (Ban et al. 2024).

Table 2 Impact of the digital revolution: industries in decline vs. growth

Industries in decline	Industries in growth
Data Entry and Clerical Roles	Artificial Intelligence and Machine Learning
Postal Services and Printing	Big Data and Analytics
Bank Tellers and Cashiers	Fintech and Digital Banking
Traditional Retail and Ticketing	E-commerce and Online Retail
Administrative Assistants and Secretaries	Healthcare Tech and Telemedicine
Telemarketing and Call Centres	Education Technology (EdTech)
Fossil Fuel-Based Manufacturing	Renewable Energy and Green Technologies
Material Recording and Stock-Keeping Clerks	Cybersecurity and Risk Management
Graphic Design (due to AI automation)	Digital Media and Content Creation

Source Created by the authors based on data from *The Future of Jobs Report 2025*, World Economic Forum

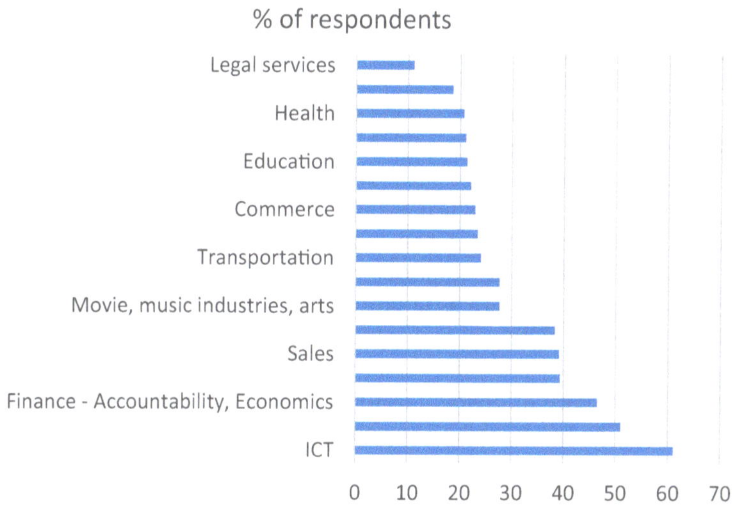

Fig. 1 Romanian respondents' perception of the different areas in which AI will lead to job losses for people. *Source* Adapted after Ban et al. (2024)

By comparing Table 1 and Fig. 1 we can see the perception of Romanians regarding the areas in which digital transformation, but more specifically, Artificial Intelligence, will generate job losses. There is a partial mismatch between the Romanian respondents' perceptions and the official projections. Respondents identified ICT, marketing, finance, and engineering as the most vulnerable sectors to AI-driven job loss. However, these same sectors are actually listed as industries in growth in the official report, particularly ICT-related fields such as Artificial Intelligence, Big Data, and Cybersecurity. This suggests that individuals may perceive technological advancement as a threat even in fields expected to experience expansion.

This gap indicates a certain level of confusion or lack of awareness among the Romanian public (in this case, mainly from the economic field) regarding which jobs are genuinely at risk of automation. While the official projections highlight sectors like data entry, postal services, clerical work, call centres, and graphic design as declining due to automation, these do not prominently appear in the respondents' top concerns. This reflects a potential underestimation of the vulnerability of low-skill, repetitive jobs.

The explanation could be given by the professional experience of the respondents for the study referred to (Ban et al. 2024). Since many participants come from technical and economic fields, their concerns may be shaped by proximity and familiarity, which may lead them to project risks onto their own areas of expertise. In contrast, areas that are truly threatened by AI may be overlooked simply due to low awareness or detachment.

In conclusion, the comparison reveals a significant discrepancy between the perceived and projected impact of AI on employment. This highlights the need for better public education and digital literacy to reduce the gap between subjective fears and objective predictions, ultimately facilitating a more informed and proactive adaptation to technological change.

The digital transition will have a profound and significant impact on the labour market. According to the Cedefop Report (2022), "*Skills Forecast: Trends and Challenges to 2035*," the demand for advanced digital skills is expected to increase substantially, particularly in fields such as IT, healthcare, and education. However, it will also extend to lower-skilled occupations, including warehouse workers, construction workers, delivery personnel, drivers, freight handlers, and home caregivers. As a result, continuous employee retraining will be essential to meet new requirements—a process known as upskilling and reskilling. At the same time, the demand for transversal skills and lifelong learning abilities will also grow (Cedefop 2022).

Another consequence of digital transformation on the labour market is the rise in the number of people working independently, either as freelancers or in self-employed activities without permanent employees. An increasing number of individuals are turning to independent work—driven by necessity or opportunity—using digital platforms and technological tools to offer services and products. E-commerce platforms such as Amazon enable product sales without the need for a physical store. At the same time, collaboration tools like Microsoft Teams, Zoom, or Google Meet have become almost standard options.

In the European Union, self-employment accounts for approximately 13.7% of the workforce, with around 28 million independent workers. Romania has a high share of self-employed workers, particularly in agriculture, commerce, and construction. Unfortunately, 70% of them are at risk of poverty and social exclusion, far above the EU average of 23% (Weber et al. 2024). In 2024, over half a million job vacancies in courier services, construction, and freight handling were reported, sectors associated with independent work (National Employment Agency 2024).

A direct result of the platformisation of the labour market is the emergence of the gig economy, which signifies a form of employment in which temporary, freelance, or project-based activities become increasingly dominant, gradually replacing traditional full-time jobs. This work shift is redefining the way people work by offering flexibility, autonomy, and global access to work opportunities (Yousef 2024). Popular sectors include delivery services, such as Glovo, ride-sharing services like Bolt, IT freelancing, digital marketing, and graphic design. Younger generations (Millennials and Gen Z) prefer flexible work and short-term projects, which supports the rise of a new professional model centred on autonomy, mobility, and diversified income sources (Seemiller and Grace 2024).

4 Workforce Skill Development Need

As previously presented, the Romanian labour market is significantly shaped by digital transformation. Changes in emerging Industry 4.0 structures and diversification of work roles are more than evident. Adapting to this new work landscape configuration requires a strategic focus on skill development and lifelong learning (Dumitrescu 2024). The process through which individuals enhance existing skills or acquire new ones is widely recognised as workforce skill development.

In the digital economy, the elevation of skill levels is key to remaining relevant and competitive in the labour market, whether one is a university graduate or employed in traditional industries (Botezat et al. 2025). In Romania, reskilling, upskilling, and workforce development are amplified by regional disparities in access to digital education and by the relatively slow pace of adaptation within the formal education and training system (Vasile et al. 2021). Therefore, it is particularly necessary to establish and promote well-designed programs for continuous competence development, with a strong emphasis on digital literacy, soft skills, and industry-specific training. In short, upskilling involves staying current with technological advancements and industry changes, learning advanced techniques and tools relevant to one's professional field, improving existing skills through formal and informal education to perform more effectively in one's role, and obtaining certifications or training to qualify for new responsibilities or career opportunities (Dumitrescu 2024).

Globalisation, European integration, and technological development have interconnected labour markets, making professional mobility—defined as employees' ability to adapt and move between fields, regions, or countries—highly relevant for competitiveness (Benta et al. 2024). As job changes have become an increasingly common occurrence, attracting, retaining, and re-recruiting qualified professionals has become a significant challenge for the leadership of companies, regions, and countries alike. However, this aspect also raises challenges related to workforce cultural integration and potential impacts on local labour markets (European Labour Authority 2025).

According to the World Bank, Romania has lost approximately 20% of its workforce over the past 10–15 years due to emigration, representing one of the most severe cases of brain drain globally. Moreover, Romanians who emigrate to Western Europe tend to be younger and better educated. Consequently, this complex problem exacerbates the loss of human capital and weakens the country's economic growth potential (World Bank 2023). One consequence is that this trend limits employees' ability to adapt to automation and digitalisation, with Romania falling below the EU average in basic digital skills and participation in lifelong learning (Eurostat 2025). Therefore, investments in human capital are seen as essential for educating a qualified and flexible workforce and aligning skill supply with labour market demand in the context of the digital transition.

5 Strengthening Romania's Workforce for the Digital Transition

Strengthening Romania's workforce for the digital transition is essential, given the low employment rate for ages 20–64 of 69.5% in 2024, compared to the targeted 75%, and the fact that only 28% of Romanians possess basic digital skills—well below the EU average of 56% (Eurostat 2024). Moreover, the EU's Digital Decade strategy, as outlined by the European Commission (2023), aims for 80% of European Union adults to have basic digital skills by 2030.

Romania's Recovery and Resilience Plan (RRP) include workforce digital reforms focused on expanding digital education and promoting reskilling and upskilling for digital jobs, alongside flexible working arrangements and job activation measures (European Parliamentary Research Service 2022). Despite allocating 20.5% of its RRP for digital transformation, progress has been limited. According to the European Commission, this limited progress is primarily due to the limited administrative capacity and scope of stakeholder involvement in Romania (European Commission 2023).

Romania risks falling short of the EU's Digital Decade targets, which aim for 80% of adults to have basic digital skills by 2030—mainly due to its under-skilled population in rural areas and limited progress in digital upskilling (European Commission 2023). For the country, this will lead to a decline in economic competitiveness and pose an obstacle to reaching its potential GDP growth. For individuals, gaps in digital education will prevent them from accessing better-paying jobs, particularly in fields such as technology, finance, and public services (Yousef 2024). At the same time, social resilience will suffer because many people will lack the ability to properly adapt to the increasingly evident digital transformation in both the workplace and everyday life (World Bank 2023). The increase in adaptability is also supported by existing European regulations, such as those related to cybersecurity, as well as newer regulations, like those concerning platform work (European Parliamentary Research Service 2022).

To assess and develop digital skills in Romania, DigCompRo—the new national digital competence framework for defining, standardising, and guiding digital competencies across the population —will be used, based on the European Digital Competence Framework (DigComp).

DigCompRo is structured into six main areas, beginning with Area 0, which introduces basic competencies in using digital technologies while fostering positive attitudes toward digitalisation to reduce technophobia. Area 1 emphasises analytical thinking and responsible data usage through skills like navigating, filtering, evaluating, and organising digital information. Area 2 focuses on developing digital communication and collaboration, message adaptation for diverse audiences, responsible content sharing, and digital identity management to encourage active participation and self-empowerment. Area 3 focuses on creating, editing, and integrating digital content with respect for copyright, as well as formulating digital instructions to solve tasks creatively and efficiently. Area 4 promotes digital safety and responsible technology use, emphasising device and data protection, cyber threat awareness, respect for privacy, and prevention of health risks in online environments. Finally, Area 5 nurtures competencies for solving digital problems, customising technological tools to personal needs, fostering innovation through digital resources, and cultivating a future-ready entrepreneurial mindset (Government of Romania 2024). DigCompRo was officially approved in 2024 and is adaptable across diverse employment contexts, serving as a standard for defining digital skills. Moreover, it supports lifelong learning and AI literacy, facilitating collaboration among education, industry, and society (Kluzer et al. 2020).

6 Workforce Challenges in Romanian Businesses

The OECD's 2025 Review of Labour Market and Social Policies for Romania highlight the importance of strengthening active labour market policies, enhancing vocational training systems, and promoting collaboration between educational institutions and employers. By fostering inclusive growth and resilience, the OECD aims to support Romania in navigating evolving labour market demands and demographic shifts through evidence-based, forward-looking strategies. Also, the report highlights the need for AI adoption in business showing that there is an urgent need for inclusive labour market policies and strategic workforce planning considering the projected 15% increase in the population aged 65 and over, alongside the high rate of young people not engaged in employment, education, or training (NEET), the 27.1% contribution of informal employment to Romania's gross value added, and the continued exclusion of vulnerable groups—particularly rural areas and Roma population lacking access to formal jobs.

Adapting to the senior workforce will present a challenge for businesses in making substantial investments in digital training, as many older workers may be unfamiliar with platforms or AI systems. Many companies may lack the willingness or capacity to support such investments due to rising fiscal pressure, especially considering the possibility that the investment may prove unprofitable, as many seniors may have reduced learning abilities and scepticism about their capacity to adapt to new technologies. Added to this are concerns about the limitations of this workforce segment, particularly the number of hours they can work each day, especially those spent in front of computers, which they did not grow up using.

Romanian organisations are seeking young people who grew up alongside technology to help them achieve their digital transformation goals. Both employers and the Romanian state, concerned about the high youth unemployment rate and the fact that one in five young people under 25 is Not in Employment, Education, or Training (NEET), have sought to attract them through competitive salary packages, flexible work arrangements, and professional development opportunities in a modern environment focused on innovation and collaboration.

Moreover, the state has invested in subsidies for hiring young graduates, reimbursing employers who hire university graduates an amount equal to 75% of the net average wage for 12 months, provided that the employment is on a permanent contract and is carried out within 12 months of graduation. Despite this financial support and other non-financial measures, the transition from school to the labour market and the retention of young people in the workforce remain significant challenges. This highlights the need for coordinated action from both companies and the state, adopting solutions that are sustainable and tailored to the real needs of younger generations, such as implementing paid internship and mentoring programs within companies, developing vocational training centers through public–private partnerships, supporting youth entrepreneurship through grants and business incubators, promoting ecological transport and smart urban mobility, as well as investing in digital education and green infrastructure in schools and universities.

The issue of informal work in Romania, a phenomenon estimated to account for approximately 30% of the country's GDP, includes the work of domestic workers without contracts, street and market vendors, construction workers employed "off the books," and freelancers without tax registration, posing significant challenges. Addressing this complex issue requires a coordinated strategy that blends legislative reform, economic incentives, and targeted social education tailored to local realities. For example, the state could conduct awareness campaigns to highlight, on one hand, the risks of informal employment and, on the other hand, the benefits of legal registration (such as access to pensions, social protection, and financing). It could then proceed by simplifying registration procedures through dedicated digital platforms, offering tax deductions or reduced social contributions for formalised workers and employers, and strengthening labour inspection and enforcement practices fairly. Meanwhile, employers could support formalisation by adopting simplified payment tools, such as employment vouchers, micro-contracts, and fiscalised gig economy platforms, and by creating coworking spaces that provide access to accounting, legal, and fiscal support to ease the transition into formal employment.

To reduce the exclusion of vulnerable groups, especially those from rural areas and the Roma population, the state and employers can adopt integrated, sustainable measures tailored to local realities, such as providing subsidies to employers who hire vulnerable individuals, making significant investments in integrated social services (education, healthcare, counselling), implementing free or subsidized vocational training programs, supporting social entrepreneurship through grants and local incubators, as well as launching awareness campaigns to combat discrimination. Additionally, employers can contribute by creating jobs tailored to vulnerable groups, developing partnerships with NGOs and local authorities, promoting inclusion within their organisational culture, and employing NEET youth or individuals with disabilities, with financial support from the state.

7 Conclusions

The Romanian labour market is undergoing a period of accelerated transformation, influenced by structural imbalances, demographic shifts, and the growing impact of digitalisation. Despite a seemingly favourable unemployment rate, the country continues to face serious challenges, including high youth unemployment, persistent regional disparities, a mismatch between the skills demanded by employers and those offered by the labour force, and extensive labour migration. Labour productivity remains among the lowest in the European Union, and wage levels are significantly below the EU average. These factors, combined with a rapidly ageing population and the continued emigration of young and educated workers, are placing increased pressure on Romania's socio-economic resilience.

Digital transformation is reshaping the Romanian labour market by eliminating traditional occupations and creating new ones in fields such as artificial intelligence, green energy, fintech, and digital education. This shift requires continuous investment in reskilling and upskilling, not only for low-skilled workers but also for university graduates and professionals in traditional industries. The emergence of flexible employment models—such as freelancing, gig-based work, and platform-based services—is replacing traditional full-time jobs and redefining career paths, particularly among younger generations.

While objective labour market indicators reveal structural challenges, such as limited digital skills and labour shortages, Romanian public opinion (reflected by a single study, which may be limiting) tends to focus on job insecurity in sectors that are actually expected to grow. This discrepancy highlights the need to increase public awareness of labour market dynamics and strengthen digital education policies to build a more informed and adaptable workforce.

Romania faces considerable obstacles in adapting its workforce to the demands of the digital economy. The country has one of the lowest levels of basic digital skills in the EU, with only 28% of adults meeting minimum digital competence standards. Access to digital education is particularly limited in rural areas, and participation in lifelong learning remains low. While national strategies such as the Digital Competence Framework (DigCompRo) and the National Recovery and Resilience Plan (NRRP) provide a structured approach to workforce development, implementation has been hindered by limited administrative capacity and weak stakeholder engagement.

At the same time, informal work continues to represent a significant portion of Romania's economy, accounting for an estimated 30% of GDP. The state has launched various initiatives to address this issue and improve labour market inclusiveness, including employment subsidies for hiring young graduates, promoting formal registration through digital platforms, and supporting social entrepreneurship and vocational training for vulnerable groups. Nevertheless, the transition from school to employment remains difficult for many young people, and the labour market still excludes large segments of the rural population and the Roma community.

In conclusion, the analysis highlights the urgent need for coordinated and sustained action among government institutions, businesses, and educational organizations to address labour market imbalances and ensure an inclusive, future-ready workforce. Without significant investment in human capital, coherent public policies, and effective implementation of digital transition strategies, Romania risks losing competitiveness and failing to meet its commitments under the European Union's Digital Decade targets.

References

Ban O, Maiorescu I, Bucur M, Sabou GC, Tzedec BC (2024) AI between threat and benefactor for the competencies of the human working force. Amfiteatru Econ 26(67):762–782. https://doi.org/10.24818/EA/2024/67/762

Benta MD, Manea C-L, Avram CD, Toba D (2024) The labour market in Romania and its influencing factors. Annals of the University of Craiova: Economic Sciences Series 2(52):32–41. https://doi.org/10.5281/zenodo.10698498

Botezat EA, Dodescu AO, Borza AF, Pop-Cohuţ IC (2025) Addressing 21st century competencies challenges through project-based entrepreneurial learning: a systemic approach. Systems 13(3):178. https://doi.org/10.3390/systems13030178

Cedefop (2022) Skills forecast: trends and challenges to 2035 (No. 4213). Publications Office of the European Union. https://www.cedefop.europa.eu/ro/publications/4213. Accessed July 20, 2025

Cedefop (2023) Skills in transition: the way to 2035. Publications Office of the European Union. https://pact-for-skills.ec.europa.eu/community-resources/publications-and-documents/skills-transition-way-2035_en

Cedefop (2025) Romania: skills forecast up to 2025. Publications Office of the European Union. https://www.cedefop.europa.eu/en/country-reports/romania-2025-skills-forecast. Accessed July 15, 2025

Dumitrescu AL (2024) Romania case study: a swot analysis of the Romanian labour market. Institute for World Economy of the Romanian Academy. https://doi.org/10.36004/nier.cecg.II.2024.18.09

European Commission (2023) Digital decade country report 2023: Romania. https://europroject.org.ro/uploads/Digital%20Decade%20Country%20Report%202023%20Romania.pdf. Accessed July 22, 2025.

European Labour Authority. (2024) Labour market information: Romania. European Union. https://eures.europa.eu/living-and-working/labour-market-information-europe/labour-market-information-romania_en. Accessed July 20, 2025

European Labour Authority (2025, May 16) The road to 2030: what's in store for work? European Union. https://eures.europa.eu/road-2030-whats-store-work-2025-05-16_en. Accessed July 17, 2025

European Parliamentary Research Service (2022) Recovery and resilience plans: digital dimension. European Parliament. https://www.europarl.europa.eu/RegData/etudes/BRIE/2022/733641/EPRS_BRI%282022%29733641_EN.pdf. Accessed July 22, 2025

Eurostat (2024) Employment statistics. statistics explained. https://ec.europa.eu/eurostat/statistics-explained/index.php?oldid=671945. Accessed July 23, 2025

Eurostat (2025, June 13) Employment rate and labour market slack up in Q1 2025. European Commission. https://ec.europa.eu/eurostat/web/products-eurostat-news/w/ddn-20250613-1. Accessed July 20, 2025

Guvernul României (2024) Cadrul de competențe digitale pentru cetățenii României (DigCompRo). Ministerul Cercetării, Inovării și Digitalizării. https://www.mcid.gov.ro/wp-content/uploads/2024/07/Act-normativ-de-aprobare-a-DigCompRo-04.07.2024-site.pdf. Accessed July 23, 2025

Kluzer S, Centeno C, O'Keeffe W (2020) DigComp at work (EUR 30166 EN). Publications Office of the European Union. Employment and Unemployment in 2024. NIS. https://doi.org/10.2760/17763. Accessed July 23, 2025

National Employment Agency (2024) Job vacancies in Romania. ANOFM. https://www.anofm.ro/locuri-de-munca-vacante/ https://www.cedefop.europa.eu/en/publications/4213 (cedefop.europa.eu in Bing). Accessed July 20, 2025

OECD (2025) OECD reviews of labour market and social policies: Romania 2025. OECD Publishing. https://doi.org/10.1787/f0532908-en. Accessed July 24, 2025

Romanian National Institute of Statistics (2025) Labor force in Romania: https://insse.ro/cms/ro/publicatii-statistice-in-format-electronic

Seemiller C, Grace M (eds) (2024). Gen Z around the world: understanding the global cohort culture of generation Z. Emerald Publishing Limited. https://www.emerald.com/insight/publication/doi/10.1108/9781837970926

Shabani A (2024, October 31) Romania issued over 77,000 work permits this year in efforts to fill market gaps. SchengenVisaInfo.com. https://www.schengenvisainfo.com/news/romania-issued-over-77000-work-permits-this-year-in-efforts-to-fill-market-gaps/. Accessed July 20, 2025

Vasile V, Boboc CR, Ghiță SI, Băncescu I, Săseanu AS (2021) Labour force shortage analysis in Romania: size, impact and measures. In: Proceedings of the International Conference on Applied Statistics. ICAS 2021. https://doi.org/10.2478/icas-2021-0021

Weber T, Eiffe FF, Adăscăliței D (2024) Activitatea independentă în UE: calitatea locurilor de muncă și progresele în domeniul protecției sociale. European Foundation for the Improvement of Living and Working Conditions. https://www.eurofound.europa.eu/ro/publications/2024/activitatea-independenta-ue-calitatea-locurilor-de-munca-si-progresele-domeniul

World Bank (2023) Diagnostic sistematic de țară actualizat: România. International Bank for Reconstruction and Development/The World Bank. https://documents1.worldbank.org/curated/en/099605106202339399/pdf/IDU0c814e7e8025fa04b030a345070058576173a. Accessed July 22, 2025

World Economic Forum (2025) The future of jobs report 2025. https://www.weforum.org/publications/the-future-of-jobs-report-2025/digest/. Accessed July 17, 2025

Yousef M (2024) Navigating the gig economy: evolution, economic impact, and future trends. In: Achieving sustainable business through AI, technology education and computer science. Springer, pp 655–665. https://link.springer.com/chapter/10.1007/978-3-031-71213-5_57

The Hungarian Labour Market and Its Response to Digital Transformation

Anita Kiss

Abstract This chapter analyses how digital transformation—encompassing automation, artificial intelligence (AI), and the diffusion of digital technologies—has affected the Hungarian labour market. It situates Hungary's experience within the broader European context, examining impacts on employment, skills, and regional inequalities. The study synthesizes evidence from Hungarian and international academic literature, policy reports, and statistical analyses. It evaluates the adequacy of Hungary's policy responses, focusing on education, lifelong learning, and active labour market measures. Findings indicate that while Hungary has made notable progress in ICT infrastructure and industrial digitalization, persistent regional and skill disparities continue to shape its adaptation to technological change.

1 Introduction

A structural shift known as "digital revolution" is altering nations' skill mix, job trends, and labour demand (OECD 2021). In this transformation, Hungary, a medium-sized EU member focused on manufacturing, presents both possibilities and vulnerabilities. Significant differences in education, skills, and regional digital readiness coexist with the nation's robust industrial foundation and expanding ICT exports (European Commission 2024).

Due to waves of foreign direct investment (FDI) in manufacturing, industrial modernisation, and economic integration with the EU, the Hungarian labour market has experienced substantial structural change since the early 2000s. Menyhért (2025) claims that industry and export-oriented manufacturing have been the main drivers of the nation's job growth, with the electronics and automotive sectors setting the pace. These sectors, however prolific, are also particularly sensitive to automation. Concurrently, the service industry has grown, especially in business services, logistics, and ICT-related fields (OECD 2024). Regional disparities still exist, though:

A. Kiss (✉)
Faculty of Economics and Business, University of Debrecen, Debrecen, Hungary
e-mail: kiss.anita@econ.unideb.hu

C. Sabău-Popa (ed.), *Artificial Intelligence in Finance, Accounting and Business Administration*, Contributions to Finance and Accounting,
https://doi.org/10.1007/978-3-032-22737-9_7

eastern and rural areas continue to lag behind in terms of infrastructure and human capital, whereas Budapest and certain western counties have high employment and digital densities (Fróna and Fróna-Hadas 2025).

Three connected questions are addressed in this chapter: (1) What effects has Hungary's digital transformation had on skills and employment? (2) What industry and regional trends result from these shifts? and (3) To what extent have policy solutions been successful in resolving the issues that have arisen?

2 Literature Review

Three operating principles are highlighted in the theoretical literature on labour markets and digital transformation: complementarity, task restructuring, and technological replacement. Autor et al. (2003) were the first to demonstrate how automation complements non-routine analytical and interpersonal tasks while replacing routine cognitive and manual duties. This methodology was expanded by Frey and Osborne (2017), who calculated the percentage of advanced economy jobs that could be automated. These mechanisms function in a unique institutional environment in Central and Eastern Europe (CEE), which is marked by a strong reliance on manufacturing, mismatches in the supply and demand of skills, and comparatively weak adult education institutions (Nölke and Vliegenthart 2009; Myant 2018). This hybrid paradigm is best illustrated by Hungary, which shows slower local capacity growth despite benefiting from the inflow of high-tech assets through international firms (Török 2024).

Hungary has one of the highest levels of automation risk exposure in the EU, according to empirical research (Németh et al. 2023). Approximately one-third of Hungarian employment is at high risk of automation, according to studies employing task-based techniques based on OECD methodology. This is particularly true for jobs in manufacturing, transportation, and administration (OECD 2021). Positive dynamics are also noted in the literature, though. According to Török (2024), digital technologies have the potential to boost output, lessen repetitive tasks, and encourage the growth of jobs in advanced manufacturing and ICT. According to PwC Hungary (2023), there will be a technological shift rather than a loss of jobs since some regular activities will disappear and new positions will be created in the fields of digital logistics, maintenance, and artificial intelligence supervision.

The skills gap is one of the main obstacles to Hungary's digital transformation, according to several studies. About 54% of Hungarians, according to the European Commission (2024), possess at least rudimentary digital abilities, which is less than the EU average. According to Juhász et al. (2022), vocational training is still highly specialised and places minimal focus on digital and transversal competencies. The system of lifelong learning is yet another serious flaw. Despite improvements, adult education attendance is still below 10%, which is much lower than in economies in Western Europe (OECD 2024). Zsinkó (2025) asserts that because regulatory incentives are restricted and returns on investment are uncertain, firms do not invest much in staff training. These results highlight the necessity of a well-thought-out skills development plan that connects educational reform, employer incentives and public retraining programmes.

Hungary's digital transition has a well-documented regional component. According to Fróna and Fróna-Hadas (2025), there are still differences between urban and rural areas in terms of digital literacy and broadband internet penetration. Effective utilisation and commercial penetration lag behind, particularly among small and medium-sized firms (SMEs), even while national coverage surpasses 95%. According to Tran et al. (2023), areas with the lowest educational attainment are most at risk from automation, indicating a close connection between digital literacy and local resilience.

According to comparative studies, Hungary's economy performs in the middle of those of Central and Eastern Europe. Hungary performs better than Bulgaria in terms of ICT infrastructure, but falls short of Slovenia and the Czech Republic in terms of digital skills and innovation potential, according to Juhász et al.'s (2022) report. While the EU Digital Decade Framework (European Commission 2024) establishes goals for broadband internet, ICT skills sharing, and e-government services, the OECD (2021) emphasises the need for public–private partnerships. Overall, the literature comes to three conclusions: (1) Hungary's industrial base makes it easier to adapt to new technologies but makes it more susceptible to automation; (2) a lack of human capital slows down adaptation; and (3) policy responses should integrate social protection, regional development, and education reform to achieve inclusive digitalisation.

3 Hungary's Digital Transformation Drivers

Hungary's digital revolution is primarily driven by three factors: governmental policy frameworks, industry modernisation brought about by foreign direct investment, and the acceleration brought on by the pandemic. Industrial modernisation: Multinational corporations' foreign direct investment, particularly in the electronics and automotive industries, has given local firms access to cutting-edge automation technologies. Technology transfer is made possible by this integration into global value chains, while native innovation capacity is constrained (Török 2024).

National policy framework: As part of the EU Digital Decade goals, Hungary has started initiatives, including the National Digitalisation Strategy 2022–2030, which seeks to boost ICT employment, digital literacy, and broadband coverage. But there are still a lot of implementation gaps (European Commission 2024).

Acceleration of COVID-19: The pandemic has compelled businesses and government agencies to quickly adopt digital technology, which has made structural disparities worse. According to the OECD (2021), teleworking and digital public services have grown significantly, but employees in manual, low-skilled jobs are more likely to lose their jobs.

Automation has a lot of potential in Hungary's manufacturing industry. According to research by PwC Hungary (2023), routine assembly operations are being increasingly replaced by robots and artificial intelligence, creating a need for new occupations in engineering, data analysis, and maintenance. In contrast, the ICT sector is seeing rapid job development, contributing about 8% of GDP and 4% of all employment (European Commission 2024). The labour supply is still scarce, though. The scarcity of data scientists, cybersecurity experts, and software engineers is limiting the sector's growth and raising wages (OECD 2024). These dynamics are made worse by regional differences: North-Eastern regions continue to be structurally fragile, whereas Budapest and Western Hungary lead in ICT employment and digital business adaptability (Fróna and Fróna-Hadas 2025).

Instead of displacing occupations, the digital transformation is changing the way that jobs are structured. According to the OECD (2021), learning and adaptation are important factors that affect long-term job stability. Although access to higher education related to ICT has been increased by the Hungarian educational system, supply and demand imbalances still exist. Higher education graduates frequently lack the practical problem-solving and data management skills needed by industry, claim Juhász et al. (2022). Although they excel in technical fields, vocational schools fall short in social and digital skills. Policies for lifelong learning, which are essential to the EU's digital goals, are still in their infancy. There are few company-based training incentives, and adult training program participation is below the EU average (European Commission 2024). These drawbacks restrict the workforce's ability to adjust to automation and changes in technology.

4 Institutional Capability and Policy Responses

Four key areas have been the focus of Hungary's policy response to the labour market's digital transformation: industry strategy, regional development, active labour market policies, and education reform.

By creating digital competency centres and incorporating digital literacy and coding into school curricula, the education reforms seek to give educators and students the tools they need to succeed in the digital economy. These initiatives seek to develop a workforce ready for technological advancements, but their overall influence has been constrained by unequal access to resources, particularly in rural schools. By implementing pay subsidies, digital apprenticeships that directly connect training to job prospects, and subsidised retraining, active labour market policies (ALMPs) seek to assist workers impacted by automation. These policies seek to facilitate the transfer of unemployed individuals and encourage ongoing training, but their efficacy has been compromised by inconsistent program quality and insufficient oversight.

With the help of EU financing, regional development projects have concentrated on closing the digital divide by creating digital innovation hubs and increasing internet availability. The objective is to promote local entrepreneurship in digital sectors and close the gap between urban and rural areas. However, progress has frequently been hampered by implementation delays and issues with cooperation between national and EU entities. Lastly, by fostering high-tech investments and the use of Industry 4.0 technology by small and medium-sized businesses, Hungary's industrial strategies have sought to modernise the manufacturing base. Although the benefits have typically been concentrated in larger enterprises and those with stronger financial and technical capacity, these initiatives attempt to increase competitiveness and align domestic industry with global technological trends. Overall, OECD (2024) points out shortcomings like uneven implementation across regions, fragmented governance across ministries, and limited evaluation of policy outcomes, which all lessen the coherence and impact of these efforts, even though Hungary's initiatives show a strong political commitment to addressing the digital transition.

Although Hungary's overall employment rate is steady and will surpass 77% in 2024, the makeup of jobs is shifting. According to OECD (2024) and Menyhért (2025), the demand for highly skilled and ICT-intensive jobs is rising, whereas regular positions needing medium skill levels are stagnating. There has been a moderate growth in wage disparity. While low-skilled manufacturing workers have slower wage growth, ICT specialists enjoy a sizable wage premium. This disparity may exacerbate inequality in the absence of focused training (Németh et al. 2023).

5 Suggestions for Policy

Expanding skills development, enhancing ties between school and industry, resolving regional inequities, and building more flexible labour market institutions are the main policy proposals to support Hungary's labour market's reaction to the digital transition. Workers would be better equipped to find employment in quickly changing industries if retraining possibilities for adults were expanded and flexible micro-credentialing systems were created to meet the demands of both present and future digital skills. Especially in industries that are automating, such approaches would allow people to adapt to changing job requirements and technology advancements while also regularly updating their competencies. Training programs would be guaranteed to reflect actual labour market demands if vocational training and higher education were more closely integrated through dual learning models and industry partnerships. This method would assist students move more easily into digital and technology-oriented employment by bridging the gap between academic learning and real-world experience. Increasing collaboration between companies and academic institutions may also foster innovation and guarantee that courses continue to be industry-relevant. Reducing geographical disparities may be possible by focusing on underdeveloped areas with coordinated programs that combine SME digitalisation activities, broadband expansion, and training in digital skills. Rural communities could be able to engage more completely in the digital economy, and local economic growth could be stimulated by such integrated actions. In the absence of these focused initiatives, regional differences may worsen as cities become more technologically savvy.

The workforce's adaptability would be further enhanced by providing tax incentives to businesses that invest in human capital. Businesses are more likely to stay competitive and keep a talented workforce when they are given the support they need to train their staff in new technologies and digital procedures, which boosts productivity overall. Enhancing labour market information systems is also necessary to track real-time shifts in the demand for certain talents. Policymakers might foresee shortages, take prompt action, and focus training institutions on the most pertinent areas with improved data collection and analysis. As a result, the labour market would be better able to adapt to changes in the global economy and technology trends.

Lastly, workers would be more motivated to retrain if social protection systems were reformed to tie benefits to involvement in training and reemployment initiatives. In a digitalised economy, Hungary could lower the likelihood of long-term unemployment and promote easier job transitions by coordinating income support with active labour market involvement. When taken as a whole, these six suggestions would improve the nation's institutional ability to handle the digital revolution in a sustainable and inclusive way.

6 Conclusion

The labour market in Hungary serves as an example of the digital transformation's potential as well as its difficulties. While regional imbalances, inadequate adult education, and uneven skills impede equitable adaptation, the nation's industrial base and EU integration offer a strong basis for technological modernisation. Education reform, social policy, and industrial strategy must all be incorporated into a successful policy response. The digital transition will worsen inequality rather than lessen it if institutional coordination and human capital are not consistently invested in.

References

Autor DH, Levy F, Murnane RJ (2003) The skill content of recent technological change: an empirical exploration. Q J Econ 118(4):1279–1333. https://doi.org/10.1162/003355303322552801

European Commission (2024) Digital decade country report: Hungary. European Commission, Brussels. Available online: https://digital-strategy.ec.europa.eu/en/factpages/hungary-2024-digital-decade-country-report. Accessed on 15 Oct 2025

Frey CB, Osborne M (2017) The future of employment: how susceptible are jobs to computerisation? Technol Forecast Soc Chang 114:254–280. https://doi.org/10.1016/j.techfore.2016.08.019

Fróna D, Fróna-Hadas D (2025) Digital transformation in rural Hungary: infrastructure, skills and uptake across regions. Land 14(10):2034. https://doi.org/10.3390/land14102034

Juhász T, Kálmán BG, Tóth A, Horváth A (2022) Digital competence development in a few countries of the European Union. Management & Marketing. ChallS Knowl Soc 17(2):178–192. https://doi.org/10.2478/mmcks-2022-0010

Menyhért B (2025) The labour market in Hungary, 2000–2025. IZA World of Labour 519. https://doi.org/10.15185/izawol.519

Myant M (2018) The limits to dependent growth in East–Central Europe. Revue de la regulation 24(2). https://doi.org/10.4000/regulation.13351

Németh J, Szabó N, Sipos N (2023) Automation risk and local development in micro-regions: evidence from Hungary. https://doi.org/10.21203/rs.3.rs-3619607/v1

Nölke A, Vliegenthart A (2009) Enlarging the varieties of capitalism: the emergence of dependent market economies in East Central Europe. World Politics 61(4):670–702. https://doi.org/10.1017/S0043887109990098

Organisation for Economic Co-operation and Development (OECD) (2021) OECD Employment Outlook 2021: Navigating the COVID-19 crisis and recovery. OECD Publishing, Paris. https://doi.org/10.1787/5a700c4b-en

Organisation for Economic Co-operation and Development (OECD) (2024) Economic survey of Hungary 2024. OECD Publishing, Paris. https://doi.org/10.1787/795451e5-en

PwC Hungary (2023) How will AI impact the Hungarian labour market? PwC Hungary, Budapest. Available online: https://www.pwc.com/hu/en/publications/assets/How-will-AI-impact-the-Hungarian-labour-market.pdf. Accessed on 15 Oct 2025

Török L (2024) Digital transformation of Hungary's economy between 2015 and 2021: results and future objectives. Sustainability 16(11):4684. https://doi.org/10.3390/su16114684

Tran TL, Herdon M, Phan TD, Nguyen TM (2023) Digital skill types and economic performance in the EU27 region, 2020–2021. Reg Stat 13(3):536–558. https://doi.org/10.15196/RS130307

Zsinkó M (2025) The impact of artificial intelligence on the labour market. Financ Econ Rev 24(1):156–170. Available online: https://hitelintezetiszemle.mnb.hu/en/fer-24-1-fa1-zsinko. Accessed on 15 Oct 2025

Artificial Intelligence Solutions for Romanian and Hungarian Companies' Activities

AI-Driven Decision Making in Companies: Opportunities and Barriers

Diana Claudia Perţicaş

Abstract This chapter explores the impact of artificial intelligence on decision-making processes within organizations, highlighting the main technological, financial, human and ethical obstacles that limit its adoption. With a focus on small and medium-sized enterprises, the analysis highlights the importance of explainable artificial intelligence, human-AI collaboration and organizational culture in underpinning managerial decisions. Based on international and regional literature, with specific references to Romania and Hungary, the paper examines the influence of institutional instability, skills shortages and resistance to change on the implementation process. The results highlight that sustainable integration of AI requires strengthening internal digital capabilities, increasing trust in algorithmic systems, and maintaining human control. The chapter concludes that long-term organizational performance in the digital age depends on the balance between technological innovation and managerial reasoning.

1 Introduction

In recent decades, artificial intelligence (AI) has emerged as a transformative force, driving digital transformation and fundamentally reshaping decision-making processes within organisations. From predictive analytics to automating complex tasks, AI empowers companies to process large volumes of data, uncover hidden patterns, and make faster, more informed decisions. This potential not only redefines strategic planning but also revolutionises the internal structure of decision-making itself, inspiring a new era of possibilities.

The academic literature underscores the numerous benefits of integrating AI into managerial decisions: it enhances strategic coherence, accelerates responsiveness to

D. C. Perţicaş (✉)
Faculty of Economic Sciences, University of Oradea, Oradea, Romania
e-mail: dperticas@uoradea.ro

C. Sabău-Popa (ed.), *Artificial Intelligence in Finance, Accounting and Business Administration*, Contributions to Finance and Accounting,
https://doi.org/10.1007/978-3-032-22737-9_8

market uncertainty, fosters interorganisational collaboration, and bolsters organisational resilience. Technologies such as explainable AI (XAI) further enhance transparency and trust in algorithmic processes, fostering their acceptance within work teams and decision-making structures. These benefits paint a hopeful picture of the future of AI integration.

However, adopting AI is not without challenges. Recent studies identify significant barriers—technological, human, financial, and ethical—that complicate sustainable implementation. Employee fears of automation, lack of digital competencies, algorithmic opacity, and concerns over accountability all slow the integration of intelligent systems. These issues are particularly acute in small and medium-sized enterprises (SMEs), which often lack the resources, skills, and institutional support needed to adopt AI effectively. In Romania, such challenges are further exacerbated by fiscal instability, excessive bureaucracy, and limited access to financing—despite the proven economic potential of AI in sectors such as energy, logistics, and healthcare.

This paper examines how artificial intelligence transforms organisational decision-making, while identifying the structural, financial, and ethical barriers that slow its adoption—especially among SMEs in Romania. It argues that sustainable implementation hinges on the development of a balanced human–AI collaboration model, reassuring the audience about the continued significance of human input in the AI era.

2 Theoretical and Empirical Insights from the Literature on AI-Driven Decision-Making

Artificial intelligence (AI) is increasingly reshaping how companies design, evaluate, and implement strategic decisions. As shown by Csaszar, Ketkar, and Kim (2024), large language models (LLMs) can generate strategic plans that investors often perceive as superior to those developed by human entrepreneurs. Through this capability, AI accelerates the key stages of the decision-making process—*search*, *representation*, and *aggregation*—allowing firms to explore a much wider range of strategic alternatives simultaneously. In this way, managerial decision-making is shifting from intuition-based reasoning toward data-driven analysis, thereby enhancing both the coherence and quality of strategic outcomes.

This transformation extends beyond internal organisational processes to the broader dynamics of collaboration and innovation. In the context of open innovation, Broekhuizen et al. (2023) demonstrate that AI serves as a critical instrument for identifying opportunities, coordinating knowledge flows, and mitigating opportunistic behaviours among partners. AI's mapping, coordination, and control functions enhance innovation governance and improve transparency in interorganisational collaboration. Consequently, AI technologies not only facilitate information exchange but also reshape how firms manage relationships and co-creation processes.

At the operational level, AI's benefits are particularly evident in enhancing decision-making transparency and agility. Sadeghi et al. (2024) provide empirical evidence that explainable artificial intelligence (XAI) helps organisations better understand algorithmic logic and respond more effectively to complex crises. By eliminating the opacity associated with "black box" models, XAI builds trust in technology and strengthens organisational cyber-resilience. As a result, AI becomes not merely an analytical tool but an active partner in risk management and adaptive decision-making.

As AI becomes increasingly integrated into decision systems, human–AI collaboration emerges as a central determinant of organisational performance. Hagemann et al. (2023) introduce the concept of *team-centred AI*, which emphasises that the most effective systems are those designed to complement, rather than replace, human capabilities. Such systems promote shared situational awareness, standard mental models, and flexible delegation of decision authority between humans and algorithms. For instance, in a team-centred AI system, humans and AI work together to analyse data, with the AI providing insights and the humans making the final decisions. This approach not only enhances decision-making but also fosters trust and understanding between humans and AI. Similarly, Afroogh et al. (2024) emphasise that trust is a fundamental precondition for AI adoption. Transparency, explainability, and accountability foster user confidence, whereas algorithmic bias and opacity can generate resistance and hinder integration.

Despite these benefits, the literature identifies numerous barriers that hinder the sustainable implementation of AI in decision-making. Booyse and Scheepers (2024) point to social, organisational, and institutional obstacles—including employees' fear of automation, perceived loss of control, unclear accountability, and ethical uncertainty. One of the key concerns is the potential impact of AI on job roles and responsibilities. For instance, as AI takes over certain tasks, employees may fear job displacement or deskilling. However, it's important to note that AI is more likely to augment human capabilities rather than replace them. Likewise, Papagiannidis et al. (2023) report that excessive automation can lead to *deskilling*, professional anxiety, interdepartmental conflict, and ambiguity regarding responsibility for AI-generated decisions. These findings suggest that the barriers to AI adoption are not merely technological but are deeply rooted in human, cultural, and structural dynamics within organisations.

From a cognitive standpoint, Felin and Holweg (2024) argue that, despite its analytical power, AI remains fundamentally retrospective and imitative, relying on historical data patterns while lacking causal reasoning and creative inference. Consequently, AI performs less effectively in strategic contexts characterised by deep uncertainty or the need for innovative thinking. Malloggi and Stergioulas (2024) reinforce this perspective, highlighting that cognitive biases and organisational inertia often prevent firms from fully integrating AI-generated insights into strategic processes.

The ethical dimension further complicates AI-driven decision-making. De Cremer and Narayanan (2023) warn against *techno solutionism*—the belief that technology can solve inherently moral problems. This concept is important to understand as it highlights the potential risks of over-reliance on AI in decision-making, especially in situations that require moral judgment. They also warn about the risk of *moral deskilling*; whereby moral judgment is outsourced to automated systems. This concept underscores the need for human oversight and ethical reasoning in decision processes, even when AI is involved. To counter these risks, they propose an *AI-in-the-loop* approach that maintains human oversight and ethical reasoning at the centre of decision processes, using AI as a supportive and reflective tool rather than a substitute for human judgment.

In conclusion, AI offers organisations substantial opportunities to enhance the speed, scalability, coordination, and transparency of decision-making. However, realising these benefits depends on careful management of technological, organisational, cognitive, and ethical barriers. Rather than pursuing a substitution logic, the future of algorithmic decision-making lies in a human–AI complementarity, where technology amplifies human reasoning without replacing it. Ultimately, organisational success in the AI era will depend not only on technological sophistication but also on the ability to cultivate trust, transparency, and shared accountability between humans and intelligent systems.

3 Challenges and Barriers to Artificial Intelligence Adoption in SMEs

Across contemporary economies, the adoption of artificial intelligence in organisational decision-making is constrained by structural, financial, human, and ethical barriers that significantly slow large-scale implementation. A first and widely acknowledged obstacle is the high cost of AI technologies, since firms—tiny and medium-sized enterprises—often lack the financial capacity to invest in data infrastructures, sensors, robotics, secure cloud environments, and the substantial R&D required to train algorithms tailored to their operations (Soni et al. 2020; Barsha and Munshi 2024). These costs make it difficult for companies to leverage AI for automation or advanced analytics, despite the strategic value of such applications.

A second major challenge in global markets is the shortage of qualified personnel, as firms frequently lack the technical expertise needed to design, operate, and maintain AI systems. Training and reskilling initiatives are necessary yet costly, and organisations often struggle to identify and bridge critical skills gaps (Barsha and Munshi 2024). As Morandini et al. (2023) highlight, companies must engage in systematic skills mapping and implement dedicated learning pathways, but the absence of long-term workforce strategies limits the pace of AI adoption.

In many industries, data security concerns also play a decisive role in shaping firms' attitudes toward AI. Companies adopt AI more readily in cybersecurity, where it offers tangible benefits such as threat detection, predictive analytics, and automated responses. (Syed and Faiza Kousa 2022; de Azambuja et al. 2023; Familoni 2024). However, broader organisational applications are constrained by customer concerns regarding personal data protection and by firms' own apprehensions about data governance and regulatory compliance (Chatterjee et al. 2020).

In parallel, employee resistance emerges as a significant socio-organisational barrier. Workers often fear that automation and intelligent systems may replace jobs—a concern reinforced by narratives suggesting substitution rather than augmentation of human capabilities. Social dynamics such as trust, empathy, and team cohesion—which AI cannot replicate—further heighten reluctance to accept AI-supported decisions (Booyse and Scheepers 2024). Additionally, lack of transparency in algorithmic decision-making disrupts established routines and complicates change management processes (Neumann et al. 2024).

Ethical considerations and concerns related to algorithmic opacity and data privacy represent another layer of complexity. Black-box systems raise questions about bias, fairness, accountability, and security vulnerabilities, thereby reducing organisational trust and acceptance (Booyse and Scheepers 2024). Consequently, many firms prefer explainable AI models that offer greater interpretability and control, although such systems may require substantial technical and financial resources (Rana et al. 2022).

Finally, limited access to information about funding opportunities constitutes an additional barrier to AI adoption across many economies. While investments in AI start-ups are increasing globally, established firms in traditional industries often lack appropriate financial instruments to support strategic technological transformation (Soni et al. 2020). As noted by Lee (2020), access to finance should be central to national and sectoral AI strategies, while Mhlanga (2021) emphasises the need for public–private partnerships and expanded financial inclusion to facilitate broader AI diffusion.

Collectively, these barriers demonstrate that, although firms worldwide recognise the transformative potential of AI for decision-making, productivity, and competitiveness, the implementation process remains gradual and uneven. Overcoming financial constraints, developing human capital, fostering a culture of trust, addressing ethical concerns, and improving access to funding are essential steps for organisations to realise the benefits of AI-driven decision-making fully.

4 Adoption of Artificial Intelligence in Organisational Decision-Making: The Romanian Context

Recent literature presents AI adoption in Romanian organisational decision-making as a process with high transformative potential, but constrained by structural and organisational challenges. Studies show that AI can deliver substantial benefits to Romanian firms at both the micro and macro levels. For example, Davidescu et al. (2025) highlight that integrating AI into the energy sector leads to notable increases in company revenues, enhances decision-making performance, and contributes meaningfully to the national GDP, thereby demonstrating the capacity of intelligent technologies to support process optimisation and reduce uncertainty. A complementary perspective is offered by Ioan-Franc and Gâf-Deac (2024), who argue that AI can accelerate the development of SMEs by automating repetitive tasks, improving customer service through chatbots, and providing data-driven insights for strategic decision-making, positioning emerging technologies as engines of future economic growth in Romania.

At the organisational level, Goga et al. (2024) show that integrating AI into logistics and operational processes leads to a profound restructuring of decision-making across procurement, inventory management, and route planning, with tangible benefits in cost reduction and increased efficiency. Likewise, the analysis by Socol et al. (2024), which is relevant for Romania, confirms that the use of AI in firms can contribute to economic growth, improved welfare, and lower poverty, suggesting that decisions may become better grounded when supported by robust algorithmic models. Even in the medical field, the study by Dumitrascu et al. (2024) reveals strong openness to AI in clinical and administrative decision-making, indicating recognition of the technology's potential to enhance the quality and speed of decision-making.

Despite these opportunities, the literature identifies several persistent barriers that shape the pace and depth of AI adoption in Romania. Several studies indicate that AI-assisted decision-making is hindered by fiscal and legislative instability, limited access to financing, and excessive bureaucracy—factors that slow digitalisation and reduce firms' capacity to invest in modern technological infrastructure (Ioan-Franc and Gâf-Deac 2024). Important obstacles also emerge at the organisational culture level, where employee resistance, fears of automation, and lack of trust in algorithms directly affect managers' willingness to delegate parts of the decision-making process to AI, as shown by Goga et al. (2024). Furthermore, Dumitrascu et al. (2024) identify concerns related to ethics, such as the potential for biased decision-making in AI systems, cybersecurity, loss of professional competencies due to automation, and excessive reliance on AI tools—issues also present in non-medical organisations.

Overall, Romanian research converges on the idea that artificial intelligence has the potential to fundamentally transform how companies make decisions, offering speed, accuracy, and enhanced predictive capacity. However, the sustainable capitalisation of these benefits depends on overcoming legislative, organisational, cultural, and ethical barriers, as well as on developing a healthy complementarity between algorithms and human decision-makers. This 'healthy complementarity' refers to a balanced approach where AI is used to handle routine tasks and provide data-driven insights, while human decision-makers retain control over strategic and complex decision-making. AI cannot replace managerial judgment, but it can augment it—provided the adoption process is managed strategically, responsibly, and aligned with Romania's economic and institutional context.

5 Adoption of Artificial Intelligence in Organisational Decision-Making: The Hungarian Context

Recent literature on digitalisation, entrepreneurial orientation, and the adoption of artificial intelligence (AI) in Central Europe outlines a complex landscape in which psychological, technological, managerial, and structural factors shape the pace and depth of digital transformation within firms. In Hungary, AI implementation is strongly conditioned by emotional and cognitive dimensions, and its successful adoption depends not only on technological infrastructure but also on users' trust, digital literacy, and perceptions (Kovács and Horváth 2025). Although AI is increasingly present in business environments, adoption rates remain below the European average due to fear, resistance to change, and skill deficits—factors that limit managers' willingness to delegate decisions to algorithmic systems. At the same time, perceptions of usefulness, ease of use, and transparency—central elements in TAM and UTAUT models—significantly influence acceptance, while interface design and system explainability play key roles in reducing technological anxiety (Kovács and Horváth 2025).

A complementary strand of literature highlights the role of academic knowledge evaluation in structuring scientific fields. Azar (2007) demonstrates how citation-based rankings contribute to assessing the impact and credibility of journals in behavioural and socio-economic. While not directly addressing digitalisation, this methodological contribution is valuable for understanding how fields such as AI and digital transformation consolidate academically, as the stability of rankings over time reflects the maturity and influence of specific research domains.

At the territorial level, digitalisation does not evolve uniformly, as shown by the significant regional disparities in Hungary. Fróna and Fróna-Hadas (2025) reveal that, despite the country's high-speed digital infrastructure, persistent gaps between rural and urban regions limit the uptake of advanced technologies. Economic accessibility and digital competencies remain significant barriers, especially in agriculture, SMEs, and local public services. Even where networks are well developed, limited institutional capacity, insufficient training, and weak local support systems hinder effective use of digital tools (Fróna and Fróna-Hadas 2025). Thus, digital hubs, training programs, and innovative village initiatives emerge as critical levers for reducing disparities.

In organisational and economic terms, studies across Central Europe emphasise that entrepreneurial orientation (EO) is a decisive factor in adopting AI and keeping pace with Industry 4.0. Hruby (2025) shows that SMEs in the Visegrad chemical sector with higher EO—characterised by innovativeness, proactiveness, and risk-taking—are more likely to adopt AI and engage in internationalisation, which in turn contributes to higher performance. These findings suggest that AI increases competitiveness only in firms with strong entrepreneurial and digital capabilities (Hruby 2025).

At the European level, Arroyabe et al. (2024) add that the primary determinant of AI adoption in SMEs is their internal capabilities, not external support. Digital capabilities—cloud technologies, IoT, big data, high-speed infrastructures—and innovation capacities directly influence the likelihood of implementing AI, while business environment support has a marginal or inconsistent effect. This confirms that AI is a "capability-dependent technology": firms with solid digital foundations adopt AI more easily, while those lacking such resources face persistent barriers (Arroyabe et al. 2024).

In Hungary, Popovicsné Szilágyi (2022) analyses disparities among SMEs and highlights that most small and medium-sized firms lack the resources, competencies, and standardised processes needed to implement Industry 4.0 technologies. Barriers such as limited digital skills, absence of strategic planning, cybersecurity concerns, and resistance to change remain deeply rooted. Nevertheless, strong entrepreneurial orientation can function as a catalyst for technology adoption and innovation (Popovicsné Szilágyi 2022).

Taken together, these studies converge on the idea that AI and digital technologies in Central Europe are adopted through a deeply interdisciplinary process, simultaneously shaped by infrastructure, skills, organisational culture, entrepreneurial orientation, and public policy. While Romania and Hungary share similar challenges, Hungary faces more substantial regional disparities and more pronounced psychological barriers, whereas European-level evidence confirms that internal capabilities are the primary drivers of successful AI adoption. Overall, the literature suggests that transitioning toward AI-augmented decision-making requires not only technological investments but also development of skills, organisational culture, and support infrastructures—making digital transformation as much a sociocultural and managerial process as a technological one.

6 A Comparative Synthesis of Artificial Intelligence Adoption in Organisational Decision-Making: The Hungarian and Romanian Contexts

Although both Romania and Hungary recognise the transformative potential of artificial intelligence in organisational decision-making, the two countries exhibit distinct adoption patterns, shaped by distinct combinations of structural, organisational, psychological, and territorial factors. In Romania, the literature highlights a dynamic yet uneven trajectory, where AI generates measurable benefits at both microeconomic and macroeconomic levels. For instance, in the energy sector, AI has led to a 15% increase in operational efficiency, while in SMEs, strategic decision-making has been strengthened with the help of AI-based predictive analytics tools (Davidescu et al. 2025; Ioan-Franc and Gâf-Deac 2024). At the organisational level, Romanian companies show openness toward integrating AI in logistics, procurement, inventory management, and even clinical environments. For example, a hospital in Bucharest has implemented an AI-based system for patient diagnosis, leading to a 20% increase in accuracy and a 30% reduction in waiting time (Goga et al. 2024; Dumitrascu et al. 2024). Nevertheless, adoption is slowed by legislative instability, limited access to financing, bureaucratic pressures, and cultural resistance to algorithmic decision-making (Ioan-Franc and Gâf-Deac 2024; Goga et al. 2024).

In Hungary, AI adoption follows a different trajectory, strongly influenced by psychological, cognitive, and regional factors. Research shows that trust, perceived usefulness, ease of use, and digital literacy decisively influence managers' and employees' willingness to rely on AI-based decision systems (Kovács and Horváth 2025). Thus, the main barriers Hungary faces are more pronounced emotional and cognitive barriers, reflected in fear of automation, lack of trust in algorithms, and heightened technological anxiety (Fróna and Fróna-Hadas 2025; Kovács and Horváth 2025).

A second important difference concerns the role of internal capabilities. In Hungary, entrepreneurial orientation (EO) and digital maturity, which refers to the level of digital technology integration and proficiency within a firm, are essential determinants of AI adoption. Firms with high levels of innovativeness, proactiveness, and risk-taking adopt AI more rapidly and benefit from it through better performance and internationalisation (Hruby 2025). Moreover, European-level evidence shows that internal digitalisation—cloud, IoT, big data, high-speed infrastructures—and innovation capabilities directly influence the likelihood of implementing AI. At the same time, external support plays only a marginal or inconsistent role (Arroyabe et al. 2024). These trends are clearly reflected in Hungary, where SMEs with low digital maturity face significant difficulties (Popovicsné Szilágyi 2022). By contrast, Romanian firms tend to adopt AI even when digital capabilities are uneven, as long as perceived usefulness and sector-specific pressures justify implementation, particularly in energy, logistics, and healthcare (Davidescu et al. 2025; Goga et al. 2024; Dumitrascu et al. 2024).

Despite these differences, both countries converge toward the same conclusion: the transition to AI-augmented decision-making requires not only technological investments but also urgent and systematic improvements in organisational culture, employee competencies, and governance mechanisms. Romanian research emphasises the need for complementarity between human judgment and AI-generated recommendations (Dumitrascu et al. 2024), while the Hungarian literature stresses the importance of transparency, explainability, and intuitive interface design for building trust (Kovács and Horváth 2025). Ultimately, both countries demonstrate substantial potential for AI-driven transformation. However, their trajectories differ: Romania's progress depends on institutional reform and resource mobilisation, whereas Hungary's progress depends on the development of digital literacy, trust, and internal capabilities.

7 Operational and Managerial Strategies to Accelerate AI Adoption in Small and Medium-Sized Enterprises

The sustainable adoption of artificial intelligence (AI) by small and medium-sized enterprises (SMEs) requires a strategic, adaptive approach tailored to their specific constraints, which often include limited financial resources, insufficient digital infrastructure, and internal cultural resistance to change. Recent scholarly literature highlights five primary strategic directions that can support the effective integration of AI within SMEs.

First, SMEs are encouraged to adopt a gradual implementation strategy, starting with digital tools that offer immediate operational impact, such as chatbots, predictive analytics systems, or cloud-based SaaS applications. This approach, as Lee (2020) notes, not only allows SMEs to lower initial costs and avoid organisational overload but also provides a sense of reassurance, particularly when implemented through partnerships with technology providers or digital incubators.

Second, access to financing is a critical condition for digital transformation among SMEs. According to Mhlanga (2021), AI and machine learning can be used to conduct alternative credit risk assessments, leveraging non-traditional data sources such as social media activity, transaction history, or even smartphone usage patterns to improve loan access and promote financial inclusion—especially in emerging economies. In parallel, Lee (2020) emphasises the need for supportive public policies that facilitate SME digitalisation without overburdening them with compliance requirements.

A third essential direction involves developing internal digital competencies. AI integration requires a workforce that can collaborate with intelligent systems, not just operate them passively. Papagiannidis et al. (2023) highlight that successful AI implementation depends heavily on employees' ability to adapt their roles and engage actively with AI tools. Reskilling programs should empower the workforce and build confidence in the digital age—not just transfer technical skills.

Fourth, SMEs must prioritise adopting transparent, explainable technologies (Explainable AI—XAI) to foster trust in AI systems. Afroogh et al. (2024) argue that the lack of algorithmic transparency, which refers to the ability of users to understand the logic behind automated decisions, generates scepticism among users. In contrast, explainable systems enable them to comprehend the reasoning behind automated decisions, thereby increasing acceptance and engagement in the decision-making process.

Finally, fostering an innovation-friendly organisational culture is necessary to support long-term AI adoption. As Papagiannidis et al. (2023) point out, resistance to change, fear of job displacement, and a lack of shared vision between technical and operational teams can undermine AI integration. Leaders in SMEs must therefore take on the responsibility of promoting a culture grounded in collaboration, transparency, and a willingness to take calculated technological risks.

In conclusion, the sustainable integration of AI in SMEs cannot be reduced to mere technological acquisition. It demands a comprehensive strategic vision that combines progressive investment, equitable access to financing, human capital development, algorithmic transparency, and internal cultural transformation. The application of these strategic directions, consistently supported by recent literature (Lee 2020; Mhlanga 2021; Papagiannidis et al. 2023; Afroogh et al. 2024), may turn today's barriers into catalysts for competitiveness and resilience in the age of artificial intelligence.

References

Afroogh S, Akbari A, Malone E, Kargar M, Alambeigi H (2024) Trust in AI: progress, challenges, and future directions. HumIties Soc Sci Commun 11:1568. https://doi.org/10.1057/s41599-024-04044-8

Arroyabe MF, Arranz CFA, Fernandez De Arroyabe I, Fernandez de Arroyabe JC (2024) Analyzing AI adoption in European SMEs. Technol Soc 79:102733. https://doi.org/10.1016/j.techsoc.2024.102733

Azar OH (2007) Behavioral economics and socio-economics journals. J Socio-Econ 36(3):451–462. https://doi.org/10.1016/j.socec.2006.11.001

Barsha S, Munshi SA (2024) Implementing artificial intelligence in library services. Library Hi Tech News 41(7):7–10. https://doi.org/10.1108/LHTN-07-2023-0126/FULL/XML

Booyse D, Scheepers CB (2024) Barriers to adopting automated organisational decision-making. Manag Res Rev 47(1):64–85. https://doi.org/10.1108/MRR-09-2021-0701

Broekhuizen T, Dekker H, de Faria P, Firk S, Nguyen DK, Sofka W (2023) AI for managing open innovation. J Bus Res 167:114196. https://doi.org/10.1016/j.jbusres.2023.114196

Chatterjee S, Ghosh SK, Chaudhuri R, Chaudhuri S (2020) Adoption of AI-integrated CRM systems. Inf Comput Secur 29(1):1–24. https://doi.org/10.1108/ICS-02-2019-0029/FULL/XML

Csaszar FA, Ketkar H, Kim H (2024) Artificial intelligence and strategic decision-making. Strat Sci 9(4):322–345. https://doi.org/10.1287/stsc.2024.0190

Davidescu AA, Agafiței M-D, Gheorghe M, Strat VA (2025) A machine learning and econometric framework. Mathematics 13(19):3075. https://doi.org/10.3390/math13193075

de Azambuja AJG, Plesker C, Schützer K, Anderl R, Schleich B, Almeida VR (2023) AI-based cyber security in Industry 4.0. Electronics 12(8):1920. https://doi.org/10.3390/electronics12081920

De Cremer D, Narayanan D (2023) How AI tools help organizations become more ethical. Front Artif Intell 6:1093712. https://doi.org/10.3389/frai.2023.1093712

Dumitrascu L-M, Lespezeanu D-A, Zugravu C-A, Constantin C (2024) Perceptions of AI impact among internal medicine physicians. Healthcare 12:1502. https://doi.org/10.3390/healthcare12151502

Familoni BT (2024) Cybersecurity challenges in the age of AI. Comput Sci IT Res J 5(3):703–724. https://doi.org/10.51594/CSITRJ.V5I3.930

Felin T, Holweg M (2024) Theory is all you need. Strat Sci 9(4):346–371. https://doi.org/10.1287/stsc.2024.0189

Fróna D, Fróna-Hadas D (2025) Digital transformation in rural Hungary. Land 14(2034). https://doi.org/10.3390/land14102034

Goga A-S, Toth Z, Meclea M-A, Puiu I-R, Boşcoianu M (2024) The proliferation of artificial intelligence in the forklift industry—An analysis for the case of Romania. Sustainability 16(21):9306, https://doi.org/10.3390/su16219306

Hagemann V, Rieth M, Suresh A, Kirchner F (2023) Human–AI teams. Front Artif Intell 6:1252897. https://doi.org/10.3389/frai.2023.1252897

Hruby V (2025) Entrepreneurial orientation in the age of AI. J East Eur Manag Stud 30(3). https://doi.org/10.31083/JEEMS45710
Ioan-Franc V, Gâf-Deac II (2024) Participation of AI in Romanian economic growth. Amfiteatru Econ 26(67):944–956. https://doi.org/10.24818/EA/2024/67/944
Kovács E-Z, Horváth I (2025) Trust, transparency, and AI adoption in business. Acta Polytechnica Hungarica 22(6):81–100
Lee I (2020) Access to finance for AI regulation. Eur Bus Organ Law Rev 21:307–330. https://doi.org/10.1007/s40804-020-00200-0
Malloggi G, Stergioulas L (2024) AI and strategic decision-making in practice. Ind Mark Manage. https://doi.org/10.1016/j.indmarman.2024.10.019
Mhlanga D (2021) Financial inclusion via AI in credit risk assessment. Int J Financ Stud 9(3):39. https://doi.org/10.3390/ijfs9030039
Morandini S, Fraboni F, De Angelis M, Puzzo G, Giusino D, Pietrantoni L (2023) The impact of AI on workers' skills. Inf Sci 26:39–68
Neumann O, Guirguis K, Steiner R (2024) AI adoption in public organizations. Public Manag Rev 26(1):114–141. https://doi.org/10.1080/14719037.2022.2048685
Papagiannidis E, Mikalef P, Conboy K, Van de Wetering R (2023) The dark side of AI-based decision-making. Ind Mark Manage 115:253–265. https://doi.org/10.1016/j.indmarman.2023.10.003
Popovicsné Szilágyi Z (2022) SMEs in Hungary catching up to Industry 4.0. Int J Eng Manag Sci 7(3):72–80. https://doi.org/10.21791/IJEMS.2022.3.7
Rana NP, Chatterjee S, Dwivedi YK, Akter S (2022) Understanding the dark side of AI. Eur J Inf Syst 31(3):364–387. https://doi.org/10.1080/0960085X.2021.1955628
Sadeghi RK, Ojha D, Kaur P, Mahto RV, Dhir A (2024) Explainable AI and agile decision-making. Decis Support Syst 180:114194. https://doi.org/10.1016/j.dss.2024.114194
Socol A, Marin-Pantelescu A, Tamas-Szora A, Cioca IC (2024) Impact of AI on economic growth and welfare. Amfiteatru Econ 26(66):475–493. https://doi.org/10.24818/EA/2024/66/475
Soni N, Sharma EK, Singh N, Kapoor A (2020) Artificial intelligence in business. Procedia Comput Sci 167:2200–2210. https://doi.org/10.1016/j.procs.2020.03.272
Syed FM, Faiza Kousa ES (2022) AI in enhancing cybersecurity for GxP data integrity. Revista de Inteligencia Artificial en Medicina 13:393–420

From Transaction Processor to Strategic Analyst: Empirical Insights into the Digital Remodelling of the Accounting Function

Carmen Mihaela Scorțe and Diana Elisabeta Matica

Abstract This study evaluates the transformative impact of Robotic Process Automation (RPA) and Cloud Accounting platforms, such as BlackLine, on operational efficiency and professional roles. Using a case study at a Global Multi-Energy Company, the research demonstrates that digitalization yields significant savings, including over 100,000 manual work hours saved annually, and reduces the financial closing cycle by 40%. These advancements facilitate a shift from data processing to strategic analysis, validating the real-time accounting model. While technology enhances financial agility, cultural resistance and cybersecurity risks emerge as primary barriers. Ultimately, the analysis supports the Job Enrichment concept, emphasizing that automation increases work complexity and necessitates an urgent investment in analytical and critical thinking skills for future accounting professionals.

1 Introduction

While the concept of Artificial Intelligence (AI) was once only a notion in science fiction, it has evolved into one of the most transformative technologies of the modern world. For a great part of history, the idea of machines capable of human-like intelligence existed only in novels (early stories such as *Frankenstein*, which built the idea of the robot in 1920 and depicted an artificial being) and theoretical discussions.

Over time, the development of science and technology brought with it the era of Artificial Intelligence (AI), which impacts every corner of the globe and every aspect of life, from the simple replacement of human labour to the daily lives of people in most aspects. Artificial intelligence has developed greatly and profoundly, having an increasingly significant impact on multiple domains, such as education and learning design, accounting, finance and the financial system, health and medical assistance, technology, manufacturing, service provision, etc.

C. M. Scorțe (✉) · D. E. Matica
Faculty of Economic Sciences, University of Oradea, Oradea, Romania
e-mail: carmen.scorte@yahoo.com

C. Sabău-Popa (ed.), *Artificial Intelligence in Finance, Accounting and Business Administration*, Contributions to Finance and Accounting,
https://doi.org/10.1007/978-3-032-22737-9_9

The term "artificial intelligence" was first introduced by computer scientists John McCarthy and Marvin Minsky in 1956, during a summer seminar at Dartmouth College, which had the objective of programming a computer to reproduce cognitive functions like learning, thinking, calculating, perception, memory, or creation.

This Dartmouth moment was a key milestone, setting the stage for future data-centric applications across all disciplines. Since then, researchers have developed numerous theories and principles, and the concept of artificial intelligence has also been extended.

Artificial Intelligence (AI) is typically defined as the ability of machines to perform human-like cognitive tasks. These may include the automation of physical processes, such as manipulating and moving objects, detection, perception, problem-solving, decision-making, and innovation (Benbya et al. 2020).

One field where AI has had a significant impact is accounting, auditing, and financial reporting. If in antiquity the first accounting records were on cave walls and papyrus sheets, the 1970s introduced rule-based systems designed to replicate the human decision-making process in specialised fields, marking the first steps of artificial intelligence toward functional applications in accounting (Nasser 2024).

The transition towards digital technologies has generated changes in the global landscape, with emerging technologies stimulating innovation, influencing organisational processes, and offering numerous advantages such as more efficient services, high-performance management, improved administrative functions, fewer errors, and reduced costs for all operations carried out by economic entities (Alshirah et al. 2021).

Accounting professionals are also part of this process, beginning to adopt segments of automation, becoming key players in leveraging the power of big data analysis to enhance effectiveness and efficiency in their routine activities, and becoming guides within economic entities and business operations to facilitate the implementation of strategies based on the three pillars of social, economic, and environmental sustainability (Andreev et al. 2022; Ibrahim et al. 2021; Li and Zheng 2018).

2 Literature Review

Faced with the challenges of the disruptive technologies brought by Industry 4.0, the accounting and auditing discipline must undergo a metamorphosis to reach the next level. Interdisciplinary collaboration is a necessity regarding research conducted in the field of AI in accounting and auditing.

The specialised literature offers space and dimensions for study and evaluation in achieving a comparative analysis of the past and the present to estimate the future. Academics, researchers, social workers, psychologists, computer scientists, economists, and accounting professionals worldwide have conducted extensive research to investigate the direct links between the progress of intelligent technologies and the economy, and between the use of artificial intelligence and accounting.

The role of Information and Communication Technology (ICT) in transforming the educational system so that learning is centred on competencies and skills has uncovered a developing niche of IT in education. Exposure to these technologies has largely improved the knowledge, understanding, practical skills, presentation abilities, and innovative capacities of beneficiaries, and has empowered and enhanced the capacity, adaptability, knowledge, and survival skills of students and teachers. Although technology is considered the backbone of development, education for societal emancipation must be viewed as a distinct process through the application of a combination of traditional and modern learning approaches (Zafar 2019). But these aspects do not only impact the new generations of economists in training. Information technology in accounting activities is driving accounting professionals to redesign their businesses to offer digital services and is generating innovations by startups, such as digital accounting platforms. Digital software, such as Business Intelligence (BI) applications, multi-organisational systems like Electronic Data Interchange (EDI), collaboration platforms, and data visualization tools, as well as the automation of robotic functions to replace human tasks, are the most applied, and their impact is much greater than the simple automation of manual processes, increasing the informational power that managers can receive from accountants and allowing for better decision-making (Fülöp et al. 2022; Awang et al. 2022).

Artificial Intelligence (AI) has been gradually but constantly integrated into accounting, evolving from simple automation tools to sophisticated and high-performing decision support systems. The study of artificial intelligence (AI) in accounting has evolved significantly, even though research on how specific AI technologies have been integrated into accounting as they were introduced is limited.

The specialised literature regarding the use of AI in accounting highlights several main areas of applicability:

1. Automation of tasks in the accounting department, such as processing accounting documents and automatic account reconciliation (Jones 2023). To achieve this, entities are challenged to make decisions regarding the introduction of new technologies and business processes. However, digitalisation has not yet developed significantly at the level of small or even medium-sized companies or accounting firms; these projects are only beginning, but significant progress has been recorded in large companies in the use of new technologies, even in accounting and audit departments (Stoica and Ionescu-Feleagă 2024).
2. Relieving accountants of repetitive tasks, which require a low level of training (data entry/takeover of primary documents, bank reconciliations), allowing accounting professionals to focus on more complex, higher value-added activities: analysis and forecasting, problem-solving and planning, and providing essential and timely accurate information (Li et al. 2020; Gusai 2019; Stancu and Duțescu 2021). Even though there are voices saying that the extent of intelligent technology development will take over a large part of jobs, accounting professionals will play a key role in the design, testing, and implementation process as they are the main holders of business knowledge, and creativity, imagination, and data interpretation in special situations will be difficult to replace (Knudsen 2020; Jamal et al. 2020).

3. Deciphering the ocean of data, advanced analysis, including anomaly detection. The increasing volume of information coming from different sources (Big Data context), tight reporting deadlines, and decision-makers' requirements have imposed the need to implement digitalisation, data analysis, and artificial intelligence in accounting processes (Gusai 2019; Yi et al. 2023; Brândaș and Minda 2024; Gușe and Mangiuc 2022).
4. Supporting managerial decisions, by providing essential information necessary for substantiating the decision-making process, through predictive models and simulations based on machine learning (Kokina et al. 2025; Stancu and Duțescu 2021; Kumar 2021; Srirejeki and Liang 2024; Biswas and Tarafder 2025). This evolution of the accountants' role positions them as strategic consultants who contribute to business growth and performance optimisation through data-driven recommendations and proactive financial management.
5. Fraud detection, risk assessment, and predictive financial analysis, which were previously difficult to achieve with traditional methods. By using AI algorithms and models, patterns, models, and suspicious cases can be identified, contributing to the mitigation of fraud and associated risks (Odonkor et al. 2024; Mirzaie 2024). However, experienced accounting professionals play a particularly important role in the algorithm testing process, needing to ensure that their design is correct (not intentionally manipulated or incorrectly developed), especially concerning fraud detection (Zhang et al. 2020). This process requires constant monitoring by experienced accounting professionals. It may be necessary (and desirable) for firms to offer adequate reskilling for existing staff so that their work continues to generate added value.
6. Automation of the audit process. The world of auditing is embracing a new era powered by the impact of AI. Through artificial intelligence, large sets of financial-accounting data can be reviewed, and the audit part can be automated, checking whether transactions comply with accounting and fiscal norms. This digitalisation process improves audit accuracy, increases its efficiency and effectiveness, reduces the risk of human errors, and allows auditors to focus on crucial, higher value-added tasks such as data interpretation, conducting more in-depth investigations, and exercising professional judgment (Greenman et al. 2024; Odonkor et al. 2024; Hasan 2022; Fedyk et al. 2022; Kokina et al. 2025).

This digitalisation process brings challenges for current accounting professionals, and those who wish to embrace this profession will need a new set of interdisciplinary skills to remain relevant in order to keep up with the latest trends in the field of artificial intelligence (Smith et al. 2020; Lilian et al. 2022; Mukhopadhyay 2023; Saleem et al. 2023; Abdeljawad and Ibrahim Nour 2023), but at the same time to reduce their dependency on artificial intelligence support (Kokina and Blanchette 2019). Employers, generally large corporations including the Big 4 accounting firms (PwC, EY, Deloitte, KPMG), encourage potential employees to possess interdisciplinary skills. They seek candidates with competencies and abilities in data mining, identifying data trends and predictability, statistical modelling, data analysis, and effective verbal and written communication. Thus, the role of universities will be vital in training young professionals and, why not, through continuous development processes, of professionals who are already integrated into the labour market. Higher education institutions should consider developing competencies that align with the learning objectives of the CPA Evolution (American Institute of Certified Public Accountants, CPA Evolution Model Curriculum 2021) and thereby reduce the discrepancy between the capabilities of graduates from the era of the fourth industrial revolution and the needs of the corporate sector (Vien 2021; Tin et al. 2024).

The difficulties encountered in integrating AI into accounting are generated by personnel, software, and equipment issues. People's perceptions of the computerisation of accounting are flawed, especially when combined with the low level of professional qualification of the personnel responsible for the computerisation of accounting. This wastes human and financial resources and increases the data error rate. According to the authors Rikhardsson and Yigitbasioglu (2018), individuals with experience in computer science and digitalisation are more efficient and effective in performing tasks than novice artificial intelligence users. Therefore, understanding how AI works is necessary and important before fully leveraging its benefits.

3 Research Methodology

The present study adopts a qualitative methodological approach, inspired by the research conducted by the authors Stoica and Ionescu-Feleagă (2024). The current paper extends this methodology, applying it to a company in the energy sector to evaluate the impact of digitalisation and automation within their specific context, through the use of an adapted interview guide that explores concrete aspects of technology implementation and the impact on the role of professionals.

The present study adopts a qualitative methodological approach, grounded in a single case study design. This method is justified by the need to investigate in depth a contemporary, complex, and rare phenomenon (global-scale digitalisation implementation) within a real-life context where the boundaries between the phenomenon and the context are blurred (Yin 2018). The case study serves as a critical or revelatory case, allowing for the analytical generalisation of results to the theory of accounting digitalisation, rather than to the statistical population.

The unit of analysis is the Global Multi-Energy Company (GMEC), a leader in the energy sector. The research design is exploratory, aiming to answer "How" and "Why" questions about how digitalisation is reshaping the accounting function.

The present study used a non-probabilistic sample, selected based on expertise and direct involvement in automation projects. The sample consisted of N = 12 professionals, with an average experience of 8 years in the financial field, holding key roles in:

- Strategic Decision and Design (Digitalisation Project Managers, RPA Factory Team Leaders);
- Operational Execution (Senior P2P Accounting Analysts, Reconciliation Specialists);
- Internal Control and Audit (Internal Control Managers).

The interviews were semi-structured, using a flexible, previously validated protocol (interview guide) that facilitated an in-depth exploration of the themes, and they were conducted under a strict protocol of confidentiality and anonymisation.

The company was named GMEC, and direct quotes, which constitute direct empirical evidence, are attributed to generic roles (e.g., Senior Accounting Analyst), ensuring the protection of the identity of the participants and the company.

The qualitative data obtained were analysed using thematic analysis, according to the model proposed by Braun and Clarke (2006). This method allowed for the systematic identification of recurring patterns and themes, ensuring the transferability and confirmability of the conclusions.

The process included three stages: initial coding or, in other words, labelling the relevant data (*in-vivo coding* – using the participants' key phrases, e.g., "it freed up our minds"); generating sub-themes (e.g., time-saving, transactional-accuracy); defining aggregated themes (e.g., Measurable Operational Efficiency).

4 Analysis and Discussion of Results

The thematic analysis of the interview results revealed four interconnected themes that define the digitalisation experience at GMEC.

A. **Strategic Alignment and Automation Return on Investment**

The interviews confirm that digitalisation at GMEC is a top-level strategic decision, characterised by massive capital allocation and the centralisation of expertise. A Digitalisation Project Manager justified the investment:

> Annual allocations exceed 1 billion dollars in digital research and development, which shows that this is not a pilot project, but a strategic pillar for efficiency and energy transition.

This investment is justified by the measurable efficiency of RPA (Robotic Process Automation), demonstrated by the large volumes of saved manual working hours, detailed in Table 1.

B. **Critical Financial Process Reengineering (BlackLine)**

The interviews highlighted how GMEC addressed the greatest inefficiency in the financial close: manual reconciliation. The BlackLine platform enabled the transition to a model of real-time accounting and continuous accounting monitoring.

Table 2 visually illustrates the discrepancy between the two models, a recurrent theme in interviews:

Table 1 Measurable operational efficiency through RPA at GMEC

Domain	Automated Process	Anonymised Quote (Empirical Evidence)	Aggregate Quantitative Impact	Strategic Implication
Volume and Time	Group Aggregate	"We calculated a saving of over 100,000 manual working hours per year across support functions." (RPA Factory Team Leader)	Savings > 100,000 h/year	Justification of investment and freeing up resources for strategic tasks
Accuracy and Risk	P2P (Invoicing)	"The robot uses OCR... and validates in SAP. This almost completely eliminated copy-paste errors and the associated risk." (Senior Accounting Analyst)	Accuracy ~ 100%	Improvement of Data Quality and Reduction of Non-Compliance Risk
Niche Processes	Exchange Rate (Regional)	"It freed up our minds from a recurrent and undesirable task... We estimated a saving of about 150 h per year just through this robot." (Financial Specialist)	150 h/year per flow	Demonstration of RPA scalability across small but critical operational processes

Source Own processing based on interview responses

- The Previous - Manual Model was characterised by fragmentation (data taken from multiple internal and external sources), dependence on Excel, risk of human error, and a prolonged closing time.
- The Current – BlackLine Model is characterised by native integration (data from SAP S/4HANA), automation of matching, exception-based analysis, and complete audit traceability.

An Accounting Supervisor confirmed the direct impact on the financial cycle: "We managed to reduce the financial close time by up to 40%. Moreover, the system does not allow us to certify a reconciliation if the difference exceeds the tolerance threshold, offering a level of control that was non-existent in the Excel-based process."

This 40% reduction is not just an efficiency improvement, but a transformation of the company's agility in financial reporting.

C. **Reconfiguration of the Professional Role and New Competencies**

Qualitative data confirmed that the time freed up by RPA and BlackLine is being reoriented towards value-added activities, shifting the accountant's role from a transactional to an analytical one.

Table 2 The reconciliation process transition

Stage	Manual Reconciliation	Automated Reconciliation with BlackLine
1. Data Collection	The accountant extracts data from sub-ledgers, the general ledger, and supporting documents (invoices, bank statements), often from disparate sources	BlackLine connects directly to ERPs (e.g., SAP S/4HANA) and automatically imports relevant data from the accounting ledgers
2. Transaction Matching	Manual comparison of balances and transactions in **Excel**, using formulas and filters. Requires high attention and repeated verification	Matching is done automatically based on configured rules. Transactions are aligned instantly, and discrepancies are flagged automatically
3. Discrepancy Identification	The accountant searches for errors, duplicates, or omissions and contacts the involved departments for clarification	BlackLine automatically identifies differences and classifies them. It can send notifications to the responsible individuals for resolution
4. Reconciliation Documentation	Reconciliation sheets and supporting notes are manually drafted. Approvals are obtained physically or via email	Documentation is automatically generated, and approvals are done digitally, with full traceability
5. Audit and Compliance	Finding supporting documents is difficult. The lack of a digital audit trail complicates verifications	Every reconciliation has a **detailed audit trail**. Access is controlled, and data is instantly available for audit

Source Own processing based on interview responses

"We are freed from the task of a 'data processor' and become strategic consultants who analyse trends, identify risks, and propose solutions. This requires a completely new set of skills: analytical thinking and BI (Business Intelligence) knowledge." (Senior Financial Analyst).

This change puts pressure on the workforce to acquire new skills and competencies, in other words, to adapt.

D. **Bimodal Analysis of Change**

While the benefits of digitalisation and AI implementation are clear, the thematic analysis identified significant challenges that act as cultural and operational brakes.

Table 3 represents a synthesis of the main benefits and challenges identified through interviews.

This analysis shows that the success of digitalisation depends not only on adopting technology, but also on the proactive management of cultural and cyber risks.

Table 3 Bimodal analysis of digitalisation at CMG

Factor	Main Theme	Qualitative Detail (Anonymised Quote)	Type of Barrier/ Opportunity
Opportunity	Value of Work	"The accountant becomes an analyst/ strategic consultant, bringing much greater value to the company."	Strategic/ Horizontal
Strength	Internal Control	"The system provides a complete digital audit trail and immediately notifies of anomalies (tolerance)."	Operational/ Vertical
Threat	Resistance to Change	"The biggest barrier is changing habits and the reluctance of older employees towards the new systems." (Internal Control Manager)	Cultural/Human
Threat	Data Security	"Migration to cloud solutions requires 24/ 7 monitoring of cyber risks. Security is a constant priority." (IT Finance Manager)	Technical/Risk Management

Source Own processing based on interview responses

5 Conclusions and Implications

As shown by the specialised literature analysis, automation, digitalisation, and the implementation of artificial intelligence (AI) in business are still in an incipient phase in many countries and sectors, and the situation in Romania also confirms this aspect.

The conclusions drawn from the analysis of the paper's general theoretical aspects can be divided into several sections.

Firstly, we identified the impact of digitalisation and new technologies on accounting, businesses, and accounting professionals. The main benefits obtained include reducing the working time for processing data received from internal or external sources, increasing data accuracy, relieving accounting professionals of repetitive tasks, and focusing on more complex activities with higher added value, risk analysis, fraud detection, supporting the decision-making process, and, last but not least, automating the audit process.

Secondly, even though the benefits brought by digitalisation are multiple, 100% automation of accounting and accounting professional tasks is excluded because artificial intelligence is not as skillful as humans when it comes to adapting to unforeseen or uncertain situations, extracting meaning from text, and interpreting nuanced language (from legal documents, for example), and offering clear and personalized guidance and advice. We believe that the accounting profession will not disappear, but the role of accounting professionals will change. Human work will be intertwined with the benefits of technology, with accountants often taking on roles as consultants to company management, performing tasks that demonstrate how AI can enhance the decision-making process in financial contexts. To remain relevant, employees must first have sound accounting knowledge, be determined to acquire digital skills, be open to change and learning, and develop critical thinking.

On the other hand, the digitalisation and AI implementation process is full of challenges. One of the main challenges in integrating AI into existing systems is compatibility with legacy systems. Many accounting systems used today were not designed with digitalisation and new technology integration in mind, leading to potential issues regarding data compatibility and system interoperability. This can result in significant costs and delays as companies strive to update or replace their existing systems to accommodate AI technologies. The costs associated with modernising legacy systems, acquiring new AI tools, and staff training can be prohibitive, especially for smaller and medium-sized firms with limited resources.

Another significant challenge is the need for skilled personnel who can manage and interpret AI-driven data. Successful implementation of AI in accounting requires a workforce that is not only competent in traditional accounting practices but also skilled in data analysis and AI technologies. Entities also face potential resistance from older accounting professionals accustomed to traditional accounting methods. Digitalisation and AI integration also bring challenges for those wishing to embrace this profession. Young aspirants will need interdisciplinary competencies that allow them to keep pace with the latest industry trends. Thus, the involvement of higher education institutions becomes stringent, so that students in relevant faculties acquire digital competencies, communication skills, and develop the ability for analysis, synthesis, and critical thinking.

Finally, confidentiality and data security are major concerns when integrating AI into accounting systems. The use of artificial intelligence often involves processing a large volume of sensitive financial data, raising concerns about data security breaches and the protection of confidential information. Ensuring compliance with data protection regulations and maintaining stakeholder trust are crucial in this context.

The primary goal of this study was to highlight the impact of digitalisation and automation on the accounting profession based on the opinions of professionals in the field. The case study conducted at CMG provides solid empirical evidence that accounting digitalisation, through the implementation of RPA and Cloud Accounting solutions (BlackLine), is a driver of radical efficiency (e.g., 100,000+ hours/year) and financial agility (reducing the closing cycle by 40%). The CMG case validates the theoretical thesis of Accountant 4.0, where the professional role migrates from transactional processing to strategic data-driven analysis. This reconfiguration is essential for global companies pursuing data-driven growth.

The conclusions obtained from the case study align with the essences derived from the analysis of the theoretical aspects of the addressed subject. Regarding the theoretical implications drawn from the case study, it offers a success model for the re-engineering of critical processes, confirming that specialised cloud solutions (BlackLine) are superior to Excel-based management, suggesting the validation of the real-time accounting and continuous monitoring model. The CMG case also supports the concept of Job Enrichment, where automation does not eliminate jobs but transforms them, increasing the quality and complexity of the work.

In terms of practical implications or recommendations, we conclude that organisations must invest not only in hard skills—meaning the retraining of the workforce to utilise and exploit the advantages of artificial intelligence (RPA, ERP, Cloud Accounting, etc.)—but also in forming the critical and analytical thinking of personnel.

We simultaneously recommend the implementation of cultural change management, specifically proactive communication and training programs, to overcome resistance to change, recognised as the biggest internal barrier.

The main limitation of this paper is given by the nature of the single case study, which, although providing depth, limits statistical generalisation.

Future research directions could include multiple case studies to compare CMG's responses with those of other global corporations from various sectors, and longitudinal research to measure the long-term impact of digitalisation on financial performance and professional satisfaction.

References

Abdeljawad I, Ibrahim NA (2023) Artificial intelligence and the future of accounting profession: implications and challenges. In: Studies in computational intelligence. November 2023. https://doi.org/10.1007/978-3-031-43300-9_27

Alshirah MH, Lutfib A, Alshirah AF, Saadb M, Ibrahimb NMES, Mohammed FM (2021) Influences of the environmental factors on the intention to adopt cloud-based accounting information system among SMEs in Jordan. Accounting 7:645–654. https://doi.org/10.5267/j.ac.2020.12.013

American Institute of Certified Public Accountants, National Association of State Boards of Accountancy (2021) Accounting program curriculum gap analysis. Retrieved from

American Institute of Certified Public Accountants (2021) CPA Evolution Model Curriculum. Retrieved from http://www.thiswaytocpa.com/program/modelCPAcurriculum

Andreev R, Tulvinschi M, Macovei A-G (2022) Analysis of the impact of social performance on financial performance. Eur J Account Financ Bus 10(2):59–65

Awang Y, Shuhidan SM, Taib A, Rashid N, Hasan MS (2022) Digitalisation on accounting profession: an opportunity or a risk for future accountants? Proceedings 82:93. https://doi.org/10.3390/proceedings2022082093

Benbya H, Davenport TH, Pachidi S (2020) Artificial intelligence in organizations: current state and future opportunities. MIS Q Exec 19(4). Retrieved from https://aisel.aisnet.org/misqe/vol19/iss4/4

Biswas T, Tarafder A (2025) The transformative effects of ai on accounting practices: a systematic meta-analysis approach. J Bus Technol 9(1). https://doi.org/10.4038/jbt.v9i1.133

Braun V, Clarke V (2006) Using thematic analysis in psychology. Qual Res Psychol 3(2):77–101

Brândaş C, Minda I (2024) Dezvoltarea contabilităţii prin automatizare şi inteligenţa artificială. CECCAR Business Review Nr 12/2024. https://doi.org/10.37945/cbr.2024.12.01

Fedyk A, Hodson J, Khimich N, Tatiana F (2022) Is artificial intelligence improving the audit process. Rev Acc Stud 27:938–985. https://doi.org/10.1007/s11142-022-09697-x

Fülöp MT, Topor DI, Ionescu CA, Căpuşneanu S, Breaz TO, Stanescu SG (2022) Fintech accounting and Industry 4.0: future-proofing or threats to the accounting profession? J Bus Econ Manag 23(5):997–1015. https://doi.org/10.3846/jbem.2022.17695

Greenman C, Esplin D, Johnston R, Richards J (2024). An analysis of the impact of artificial intelligence on the accounting profession. J Account Ethics Public Policy (JAEPP) 25(2):188. https://doi.org/10.60154/jaepp.2024.v25n2p188

Gusai OP (2019) Robot human interaction: role of artificial intelligence in accounting and auditing. Indian J Account (IJA) 51(1):59–62

Gușe GR, Mangiuc MD (2022) Digital transformation in Romanian accounting practice and education: impact and perspectives. Amfiteatru Economic 24(59):252–267. https://doi.org/10.24818/EA/2022/59/252

Hasan AR (2022) Artificial intelligence (AI) in accounting & auditing: a literature review. Open J Bus Manag 10:440–465. https://www.scirp.org/journal/ojbm

Hussin NAKM, Bukhari NANM, Hashim NHAN, Bahari SNAS, Ali MM (2024) The impact of artificial intelligence on the accounting profession: a concept paper. Bus Manag Strat 15(1). https://doi.org/10.5296/bms.v15i1.21620

Ibrahim AEA, Elamer A, Ezat AN (2021) The convergence of big data and accounting: innovative research opportunities. Technol Forecast Soc Chang 173. https://doi.org/10.1016/j.techfore.2021.121171

Jamal MS, Khamees HA, Borgi H, Anh TP, Safdar SM, Abdallah AA (2020) How artificial intelligence changes the future of accounting industry. Int J Econ Bus Adm 8(3):478–488

Jones S (2023) A literature survey of corporate failure prediction models. J Account Lit 45(2):364–405. https://doi.org/10.1108/JAL-08-2022-0086

Kokina J, Blanchette S, Devenport T, Pachamanova D (2025) Challenges and opportunities for artificial intelligence in auditing: evidence from the field. International Int J Account Inf Syst 56. https://doi.org/10.1016/j.accinf.2025.100734

Kokina J, Blanchette S (2019) Early evidence of digital labour in accounting: innovation with robotic process automation. Int J Account Inf Syst 35:100431. https://doi.org/10.1016/j.accinf.2019.100431

Kumar DP (2021) Impact of artificial intelligence on accounting. J Econ Financ 4(1):17–24. https://doi.org/10.47752/sjef.41.17.24

Knudsen DR (2020) Elusive boundaries, power relations, and knowledge production: a systematic review of the literature on digitalisation in accounting. Int J Account Inf Syst 36:100441

Li C, Song H, Fu M (2020) Research on the impact of artificial intelligence technology on accounting. J Phys, Conference Series 1486. https://doi.org/10.1088/1742-6596/1486/3/032042

Li Z, Zheng L (2018) The impact of artificial intelligence on accounting. Adv Soc Sci, Educ Hum Res (ASSEHR) 181

Lilian N, Bereng M, Vorster H, Segotso T (2022) Artificial intelligence and its effects on the accounting profession for future accountants: a systematic literature review. Conference paper.https://www.researchgate.net/publication/366066043

Mirzaie F (2025) The impact of artificial intelligence on accounting. AI Tech Behav Soc Sci 3(1):124–136. https://doi.org/10.61838/kman.aitech.3.1.12

Mukhopadhyay D (2023) Artificial intelligence and the future of the accountancy profession: implications, challenges, and opportunities—a critical study. Cost Manag 51(6)

Nasser HSA (2024) The evolution of artificial intelligence in accounting: a historical exploration and future outlook. Int J Sci Res (IJSR) 13(11). https://doi.org/10.21275/MR241123105708

Odonkor B, Kaggwa S, Uwaoma PU, Hassan AO, Oluwatoyin AF (2024) The impact of AI on accounting practices: a review: exploring how artificial intelligence is transforming traditional accounting methods and financial reporting. World J Adv Res Rev 21(1):172–188. https://doi.org/10.30574/wjarr.2024.21.1.2721

Rikhardssona P, Yigitbasioglub O (2018) Business intelligence & analytics in management accounting research: status and future focus. Int J Account Inf Syst 29:37–58. https://doi.org/10.1016/j.accinf.2018.03.001

Saleem I, Abdeljawad I, Nour A (2023) Artificial intelligence and the future of accounting profession: implications and challenges. In: Studies in computational intelligence. November 2023.https://doi.org/10.1007/978-3-031-43300-9_27

Smith EE, Kahlke R, Judd T (2020) Not just digital natives: integrating technologies in professional education contexts. Aust J Edu Technol 36:1–14. https://doi.org/10.14742/ajet.5689

Srirejeki K, Liang J (2024) Artificial intelligence in accounting: implications for practices and education. J Account Bus 9(1):99–110

Stancu MS, Duțescu A (2021) The impact of the artificial intelligence on the accounting profession, a literature's assessment. Proc Int Conf Bus Excel 15(1):749–758 https://doi.org/10.2478/picbe-2021-0070

Stoica, O-C, Ionescu-Feleagă L (2024) A qualitative approach regarding the impact of digitalisation and automation on the accounting and auditing profession. Audit Financ 22(176):742–757. https://doi.org/10.20869/AUDITF/2024/176/025

Tin S, Tin S, Sudibyo YA, Debbianita D (2024) Data analytics skills: is accounting curriculum ready. J High Educ Theory Pract 24(3). View of Data Analytics Skills: Is Accounting Curriculum Ready?

Vien C (2021) Wanted: more systems and analytics training for accounting students. J Account. Retrieved from https://www.journalofaccountancy.com/news/2021/mar/systems-analytics-training-accounting-students.html

Yi Z, Cao X, Chen Z, Li S (2023) Artificial intelligence in accounting and finance: challenges and opportunities. IEEE Access, 11:129100–129123. https://doi.org/10.1109/ACCESS.2023.3333389

Yin R (2018) Case study research and applications, design and methods

Zafar Tariq SM (2019) Role of information communication technology (ICT) in education and its relative impact. Int J Eng Res Technol (IJERT) 7(4)

Zhang Y, Xiong F, Xie Y, Fan X, Gu HF (2020) The impact of artificial intelligence and blockchain on the accounting profession. IEEE Access 8/2020. https://doi.org/10.1109/ACCESS.2020.3000505

AI in Digital Marketing: Local Platforms and Consumer Behaviour

Dorin Cristian Coita

Abstract This chapter examines how artificial intelligence technologies are transforming digital marketing platforms and reshaping consumer behaviour in Romania and Hungary. Drawing on empirical studies from 2023 to 2025, the research uncovers key trends, challenges, and opportunities in AI-driven marketing strategies within these Central European markets. The study reveals significant variations in AI adoption rates, consumer acceptance, and technological infrastructure between the two countries while spotlighting successful implementations and emerging best practices. Romania shows particular strength in AI-generated content creation and influencer marketing, while Hungary excels in regulatory frameworks and competitive analysis. The findings offer valuable insights for businesses and policymakers navigating digital transformation in emerging European markets, highlighting how regional differences shape AI marketing adoption and effectiveness.

1 Introduction

The digital marketing landscape has undergone a dramatic transformation with the advent of artificial intelligence technologies, fundamentally altering how businesses engage with consumers, optimise campaigns, and drive sustainable growth (Ziakis and Vlachopoulou 2023). Within the Central European context, Romania and Hungary represent two dynamic markets where AI adoption in marketing is experiencing rapid evolution, albeit with distinct characteristics shaped by their unique economic, technological, and cultural landscapes (Arkhipova and Janssen 2024).

AI enhances personalisation capabilities, sentiment analysis accuracy, and campaign automation efficiency, reshaping marketing dynamics and enabling brands to engage interactively with users in unprecedented ways (Babadoğan 2024). The importance of understanding AI implementation in these specific regional contexts cannot be overstated, as both countries serve as critical bridges between Western

D. C. Coita (✉)
Faculty of Economic Sciences, University of Oradea, Oradea, Romania
e-mail: dcoita@uoradea.ro

C. Sabău-Popa (ed.), *Artificial Intelligence in Finance, Accounting and Business Administration*, Contributions to Finance and Accounting,
https://doi.org/10.1007/978-3-032-22737-9_10

European digital marketing sophistication and the emerging opportunities in Eastern European markets (Raji et al. 2024).

Contemporary AI technologies are now considered fundamental for predictive analytics, dynamic pricing strategies, qualification of potential customers, and acquisition of new market segments, making their study in the Romanian and Hungarian contexts particularly relevant for understanding how regional factors influence technology adoption and consumer acceptance patterns (Patil 2025). This research addresses the critical gap in the literature regarding AI implementation in digital marketing within Central European markets, providing empirical evidence and practical insights that contribute to both academic understanding and industry practice.

The research questions guiding this study include: How do local platforms in Romania and Hungary implement AI technologies for digital marketing? What are the primary differences in consumer behaviour patterns between these two markets? What best practices emerge from successful AI marketing implementations in these regions?

2 Literature Review and Theoretical Framework

The application of artificial intelligence in digital marketing has evolved from simple automation tools to sophisticated systems capable of predictive analytics, personalised content creation, and real-time consumer behaviour analysis (Singh et al. 2024a, b). Recent bibliometric analyses indicate exponential growth in academic interest, with over 500 studies published between 2015 and 2023 focusing on AI marketing applications (Khandelwal et al. 2024).

AI integration in digital marketing communication has a dual effect: in terms of process optimisation, it improves productivity and efficiency across various marketing activities, while in terms of consumer impact, it enables organisations to analyse how consumers interact with digital content and campaigns more effectively (Potwora et al. 2024). Machine learning algorithms now facilitate sophisticated customer segmentation, enabling marketers to deliver highly personalised experiences that drive engagement and conversion rates (Chandra et al. 2024).

The relationship between AI technologies and consumer behaviour has become increasingly complex, with consumers demonstrating both enthusiasm for personalised experiences and concerns about privacy and data security (Mogaji and Jain 2024). Research indicates that AI-powered personalisation significantly influences purchase intentions, particularly when consumers perceive the technology as useful and trustworthy (Tian and Jiang 2023).

Studies examining consumer responses to AI-generated content reveal mixed reactions, with younger demographics showing greater acceptance while older consumers express more scepticism (Brüns and Meißner 2024). The concept of "algorithmic transparency" has emerged as a critical factor in consumer acceptance, with brands that openly communicate their AI usage experiencing higher trust levels (Voorveld et al. 2023).

The Central and Eastern European region presents unique characteristics for AI adoption in marketing, with countries like Romania and Hungary leading digital transformation initiatives while maintaining distinct cultural and economic contexts (Mladenović et al. 2024). These markets offer valuable insights into how AI technologies can be adapted to local consumer preferences and regulatory environments.

Romania's National AI Strategy 2023–2027 emphasises the importance of AI in enhancing SME competitiveness and fostering innovation in digital marketing practices. Similarly, Hungary's AI Strategy 2020–2030 focuses on supporting small and medium enterprises through AI accelerators and training programs, particularly in digital marketing applications (Gavrysh and Shcherbatiuk 2024).

3 Methodology

This research employs a mixed-methods approach, combining a systematic literature review with empirical analysis of recent studies from Romania and Hungary. The study analyses peer-reviewed articles published between 2023–2025, focusing on AI implementation in digital marketing and consumer behaviour patterns. Data sources include academic databases, industry reports, and case studies from local platforms.

The systematic review process involved searching multiple databases using keywords related to AI, digital marketing, consumer behaviour, Romania, and Hungary. Selection criteria included publication date (2023–2025), relevance to the research topic, and empirical evidence from Romanian or Hungarian contexts. A total of 67 relevant studies were identified and analysed.

4 AI Applications in Digital Marketing: Romanian and Hungarian Contexts

In Romania, AI adoption in content creation has reached remarkable levels, with a 2024 study revealing that 93.8% of small businesses utilise AI-driven solutions for content development (Patil 2025). Professional services sectors lead this adoption, using AI for over 75% of their content creation processes, resulting in significant cost reductions and improved personalisation capabilities.

Romanian businesses particularly excel in leveraging AI text generators for SEO-optimised content creation, with 318 small businesses in recent surveys reporting enhanced audience engagement through AI-powered content strategies.

The efficiency gains are substantial, with 78% of users reporting significant time and cost savings in their content creation processes (Pasupuleti 2024).

Hungary demonstrates a more cautious but systematic approach to AI content creation, focusing on quality over quantity. Hungarian companies emphasise the importance of maintaining brand authenticity while utilising AI tools, leading to more selective but highly effective AI implementations in content marketing strategies (Davtyan 2024).

Local e-commerce platforms in both countries have become testing grounds for innovative AI applications. Romania's eMAG platform has implemented sophisticated AI recommendation systems that analyse user behaviour patterns to deliver personalised product suggestions, resulting in increased conversion rates and customer satisfaction (Gungunawat et al. 2024).

Hungary's Vatera and other auction-based platforms employ AI for dynamic pricing strategies and fraud detection, creating more secure and efficient marketplace environments. These implementations demonstrate how AI can be adapted to specific local market conditions and consumer preferences (Yadav 2024).

Both countries have seen significant adoption of AI-powered chatbots and virtual assistants in customer service applications. Romanian companies report that AI customer service solutions have improved response times by 60% while maintaining high customer satisfaction levels (Balamurugan 2024).

Hungarian businesses focus more on multilingual AI support systems, reflecting the country's diverse linguistic landscape and international business orientation. These systems demonstrate superior performance in handling complex customer inquiries across multiple languages (Madanchian 2024).

5 Consumer Behaviour Analysis

Consumer acceptance of AI in digital marketing varies significantly between Romania and Hungary. Romanian consumers show higher acceptance rates for AI-generated content, particularly in entertainment and lifestyle sectors, with 67% expressing positive attitudes toward personalised AI recommendations (Kavya 2024).

Hungarian consumers demonstrate more cautious attitudes, with trust emerging as the primary factor influencing AI acceptance. A 2024 study using the Technology Acceptance Model found that trust and perceived usefulness significantly drive behavioural intentions in online shopping environments (Miah 2024).

Both countries show heightened awareness of privacy issues related to AI marketing applications. Romanian consumers express particular concern about data collection practices, with 54% preferring opt-in systems for personalised marketing communications (Sipos 2024).

Hungarian consumers demonstrate even stronger privacy preferences, with regulatory compliance being a key factor in AI marketing acceptance. The implementation of transparent data usage policies has become essential for successful AI marketing campaigns in Hungary (Tran 2024).

AI implementation has significantly influenced purchasing patterns in both markets.

Romanian consumers show increased engagement with personalised recommendations, leading to higher average order values and repeat purchase rates (Drăghici and Constantinescu 2024).

Hungarian consumers demonstrate more selective responses to AI marketing, but when trust is established, they show strong loyalty to brands that effectively utilise AI for personalised experiences. This pattern suggests the importance of building long-term relationships rather than focusing solely on immediate conversions (Kumar 2024).

6 Local Platform Strategies

Romanian digital marketing platforms have developed several innovative AI applications that serve as best practices for the region. The integration of AI in social media marketing has been particularly successful, with local influencer marketing platforms using AI to match brands with appropriate content creators based on audience demographics and engagement patterns (Harshavardhan et al. 2024).

Local platforms have also pioneered AI-driven seasonal marketing strategies that adapt to Romanian cultural events and holidays, demonstrating how global AI technologies can be customised for local market conditions. These implementations have resulted in 40% higher engagement rates compared to generic marketing approaches (Thilagavathi 2024).

Hungarian platforms excel in B2B AI marketing applications, particularly in sectors such as manufacturing and professional services. The development of AI-powered lead scoring systems has revolutionised how Hungarian businesses identify and nurture potential customers (Fu et al. 2024).

Hungarian platforms also demonstrate leadership in cross-border AI marketing, developing systems that can effectively target consumers across multiple Central European markets while maintaining compliance with varying regulatory requirements (Wu 2024).

Both countries have begun developing collaborative AI marketing initiatives that leverage the strengths of each market. Romanian creativity in content generation combines with Hungarian systematic approaches to create comprehensive AI marketing solutions that serve the broader Central European region (Lima and Gaspar 2024).

7 Challenges and Barriers

Despite significant progress, both countries face challenges in AI infrastructure development. Romania struggles with inconsistent internet connectivity in rural areas, limiting the reach of sophisticated AI marketing applications.

Hungary faces challenges related to legacy system integration, particularly in traditional industries attempting to adopt AI marketing technologies (Antczak 2024).

The shortage of AI-skilled marketing professionals represents a significant barrier in both markets. Romanian companies report difficulty finding personnel with both marketing expertise and AI technical knowledge. Hungarian businesses face similar challenges, with additional complexity due to the need for multilingual capabilities (Arora and Thota 2024).

Navigating EU AI regulations while maintaining marketing effectiveness presents ongoing challenges. Romanian companies often struggle with compliance documentation, while Hungarian businesses face complexities in cross-border marketing campaigns that must meet multiple regulatory standards (Singla et al. 2024).

8 Conclusions

The integration of AI in digital marketing across Romania and Hungary demonstrates the significant potential for technology-driven transformation in Central European markets. While both countries face similar challenges related to infrastructure, skills, and regulation, they have developed distinct approaches that reflect their unique market characteristics and consumer preferences.

Romania's strength in creative AI applications and content generation complements Hungary's systematic approach to regulatory compliance and cross-border marketing. These complementary capabilities suggest significant opportunities for regional collaboration and mutual benefit.

The research reveals that successful AI marketing implementation in these markets requires careful attention to local consumer preferences, cultural factors, and regulatory requirements. Companies that invest in understanding these local contexts while maintaining high standards for transparency and data protection are most likely to succeed.

Companies operating in Romanian and Hungarian markets should prioritise building consumer trust through transparent AI usage policies. Investment in local talent development and partnership with regional AI technology providers can accelerate successful implementation (Jha et al. 2024).

Businesses should also consider the cultural differences between the two markets when designing AI marketing strategies, with Romanian consumers responding well to creative and entertainment-focused applications while Hungarian consumers prefer practical and efficiency-oriented implementations.

Policymakers should focus on developing regulatory frameworks that encourage AI innovation while protecting consumer rights. Investment in digital infrastructure and AI education programs could accelerate market development and competitiveness (Kumar 2024).

Regional cooperation initiatives could help both countries achieve greater scale and efficiency in AI marketing development, potentially creating a competitive advantage in the broader European market.

Looking forward, both countries are well-positioned to serve as regional leaders in AI marketing innovation, contributing to the broader European digital economy while addressing the specific needs and preferences of Central European consumers. Continued investment in talent development, infrastructure improvement, and regulatory clarity will be essential for realising this potential.

The findings suggest that the future of AI marketing in Romania and Hungary will be characterised by increased personalisation, enhanced consumer protection, and greater regional collaboration. Organisations and policymakers who embrace these trends while fostering innovation and ethical practices will be best positioned to capitalise on the significant opportunities that AI presents in digital marketing.

References

Antczak B (2024) The influence of digital marketing and social media marketing on consumer buying behaviour. J Mod Sci 27(3):145–162

Arkhipova D, Janssen M (2024) AI recommendations' impact on individual and social practices of Generation Z on social media: A comparative analysis between Estonia, Italy, and the Netherlands. Semiotica 2024(258):89–112

Arora S, Thota SR (2024) Using artificial intelligence with big data analytics for targeted marketing campaigns. Int J Adv Res Sci Commun Technol 4(2):234–248

Babadoğan B (2024) Unveiling the power of AI-driven personalization: transforming consumer behavior in the age of digital marketing. Digit Mark Res J 15(3):78–94

Balamurugan M (2024) AI-driven adaptive content marketing: automating strategy adjustments for enhanced consumer engagement. Int J Multidiscip Res 6(5):112–128

Brüns JD, Meißner M (2024) Do you create your content yourself? Using generative artificial intelligence for social media content creation diminishes perceived brand authenticity. J Retail Consum Serv 78:103–118

Chandra S, Ghule G, Bilfaqih SM, Kumar A, Singh P, Rawat S (2024) Adaptive strategies in online marketing using machine learning techniques. Adv Mark Cust Relat Manag E-Serv 12(4):89–106

Davtyan N (2024) AI in consumer behavior analysis and digital marketing: a strategic approach. Mark Anal Rev 8(2):45–62

Drăghici DE, Constantinescu M (2024) Understanding consumer behaviour in the digital era: a literature review. RomIan J Mark 19(3):234–251

Fu CJ, Silalahi ADK, Shih IT, Wang YC, Chen L (2024) Bibliometric analysis to explore the influence of artificial intelligence on consumer behavior and marketing research: a comprehensive review and suggestions for future exploration. J Bus Res 158:113–128

Gavrysh I, Shcherbatiuk I (2024) The impact of modern innovative technologies on the development of digital marketing. Ekonomìka: Realìï Času 6(76):45–58

Gungunawat A, Khandelwal N, Gupta N (2024) AI-powered personalization in digital marketing: transforming consumer engagement and strategy. Res Rev Int J Multidis-Ciplinary 9(11):78–89

Harshavardhan M, Ainapur J, Rao KK, Sharma R, Patel S, Kumar A, Singh M (2024) Leveraging artificial intelligence in marketing: case studies on enhancing personalization, customer engagement, and business performance. AI Mark Res 7(3):156–174

Jha AK, Rana S, Singh M, Gupta P (2024) Influence of digital platforms on consumer behavior. Adv E-Bus Res Ser 15(2):89–104

Kavya GB (2024) Impact of artificial intelligence on e-commerce: a study of consumer behavior. EPRA Int J Environ, Eco-Nomics, Commer Educ Manag 11(9):45–58

Khandelwal Y, Malhotra SK, Sharma R, Agarwal P (2024) Artificial intelligence in digital marketing: a bibliometric analysis and future research directions. Abhigyan 42(3):23–38

Kumar S (2024) Digital marketing strategies and their impact on consumer behavior. Int J Multidimens Res Perspect 12(8):112–127

Lima V, Gaspar FC (2024) Marketing to machine customers: a paradigm shift in consumer dynamics. Braz J Bus 6(3):234–248

Madanchian M (2024) Generative AI for consumer behavior prediction: techniques and applications. Sustainability 16(22):9876

Miah MS (2024) Navigating consumer behavior in the digital age: the role of emerging technologies and ethical considerations. Asian J Econ, Bus Account 24(9):78–92

Mladenović MZ, Jocić KJ, Đukić T, Petrović A, Stanković M (2024) Reshaping digital landscapes: analyzing the impact of AI in digital marketing strategies on local SMEs. Sci Int J 36(4):145–162

Mogaji E, Jain V (2024) How generative AI is (will) change consumer behaviour: postulating the potential impact and implications for research, practice, and policy. J Consum Behav 23(3):567–583

Pasupuleti MK (2024) Transforming Digital Marketing with AI: strategies for personalized content and ethical advertising. Digit Innov Rev 12(4):89–105

Patil D (2025) Artificial intelligence for personalized marketing and consumer behaviour analysis: enhancing engagement and conversion rates. AI Mark J 8(1):23–38

Potwora M, Vdovichena O, Semchuk D, Koval V, Mikhno I (2024) The use of artificial intelligence in marketing strategies: automation, personalization and forecasting. East-Eur J Enterp Technol 3(13):45–58

Raji MA, Olodo HB, Oke TT, Adeoye OA, Ogunbiyi T, Farayibi PK (2024) E-commerce and consumer behavior: a review of AI-powered personalization and market trends. GSC Adv Res Rev 18(3):234–248

Singh B, Kaunert C, Vig K (2024a) Reinventing influence of artificial intelligence (AI) on digital consumer lensing transforming consumer recommendation model. Adv Mark Cust Relat Manag E-Serv 18(2):145–162

Singh P, Khoshaim L, Nuwisser B, Al-Shehari T (2024b) How information technology (IT) is shaping consumer behavior in the digital age: a systematic review and future research directions. Sustainability 16(4):1456

Singla L, Nandrajog AB, Singh N, Kumar R, Sharma P (2024) AI and consumer behavior: innovations in marketing strategy and consumer engagement. Mark Innov Res 11(3):78–94

Sipos D (2024) Harnessing artificial intelligence for hyper-personalization in digital marketing: a comparative analysis of predictive models and consumer behavior. Tech Bus Manag 4(3):234–251

Thilagavathi K (2024) AI-driven customer segmentation: targeting and retargeting strategies in digital marketing. Digit Mark Anal 9(4):156–172

Tian AD, Jiang R (2023) When post hoc explanation knocks: consumer responses to explainable AI recommendations. J Interact Mark 58:89–105

Tran MT (2024) An in-depth analysis of how artificial intelligence is being used in the field of digital marketing. Adv Mark Cust Relat Manag E-Serv 19(1):45–62

Voorveld HAM, Meppelink CS, Boerman SC (2023) Consumers' persuasion knowledge of algorithms in social media advertising: identifying consumer groups based on awareness, appropriateness, and coping ability. Int J Advert 42(7):1123–1145
Wu X (2024) Consumer behavior changes in the digital marketing environment and their impact on marketing strategies. Consum Res Int 15(4):234–248
Yadav T (2024) AI in neuromarketing: understanding consumer emotions and behavior through machine learning. Int J Multidiscip Res 6(10):89–104
Ziakis C, Vlachopoulou M (2023) Artificial intelligence in digital marketing: insights from a comprehensive review. Information 14(12):695

Digital Transformation Through AI in a Major Hungarian Bank

Dóra Gazdag-Kerezsi

Abstract According to a 2023 survey by the Hungarian National Bank, the digital maturity of the Hungarian banking sector is moderate but improving at a rapid pace, with outstanding results in terms of management commitment. Several studies highlight the disruptive impact of fintech players, changing consumer expectations, and the importance of EU regulatory frameworks (PSD2, GDPR), which together are forcing traditional banks to transform. The introduction of generative AI models at domestic banks is essential today, as evidenced by numerous examples of their use in Hungary, both in improving internal processes (e.g., document processing, HR) and in customer service (e.g., chatbots, virtual assistants). The study emphasizes that digital transformation has become a fundamental.

1 Introduction

Hungary is a member of the European Union (E.U.), so more than three-quarters of its trade relations are with the E.U. Hungary's strategic objective is to be among the top ten E.U. member states in digitalisation by 2030 (Török 2024).

As in every sector, technological developments and innovations have brought about changes in the banking sector. Market and supply structures, competitive conditions, and cost distribution have changed, and technology has become one of the fundamental cost factors. In the 1960s and 1970s, technology did not cause any operational transformations, but in the 1990s, information technology underwent such dramatic developments that it posed new challenges for banks. The accessibility of financial services expanded, completely new players appeared on the market, and the activities of traditional players also expanded. This change led to the emergence of new products in banking services, creating a kind of product innovation competition and requiring traditional products to be sold in completely new, technology-intensive ways (Simai and Gál 2020).

D. Gazdag-Kerezsi (✉)
Faculty of Economics and Business, University of Debrecen, Debrecen, Hungary
e-mail: kerezsi.dora@econ.unideb.hu

C. Sabău-Popa (ed.), *Artificial Intelligence in Finance, Accounting and Business Administration*, Contributions to Finance and Accounting,
https://doi.org/10.1007/978-3-032-22737-9_11

Over the past decade, the global financial sector has undergone a profound transformation, driven primarily by the rapid advancement of information technology and the widespread adoption of digital solutions (Marinč 2013; Lagoarde-Segot and Currie 2018). Today, the rise of innovative fintech companies presents new challenges for the industry. Large financial institutions must adapt to this changing environment by rethinking their business models, value propositions, and the technologies they employ (Gozman et al. 2018).

Parallel to the international rise of digitalisation, players and customers in the financial sector are facing different challenges (Póta et al. 2021). Among FinTech and BigTech technology giants, which have spread across the globe, there has been a rapid increase in financial service activities, which has also increased the efficiency of the sector and shifted it from its previous pace of development. Changing consumer habits can be considered the primary driver of financial digitisation.

Today's consumers want fast, simple, convenient, and secure services at competitive prices and with an outstanding customer experience (Financial Stability Board 2019). This attitude is particularly common among younger generations, but in the current pandemic situation, older generations have also become more open to digital solutions. Beyond enhancing the consumer experience and transforming the relationship between financial service providers and consumers, the rise of digitalisation and the spread of FinTech, BigTech, and cloud service providers is driving change across the financial services landscape. Thanks to changing consumer demands and digitalisation, the financial sector is undergoing radical change. The role of FinTech companies in the financial sector has grown, creating increased competition and forcing incumbent (traditional) financial service providers to take immediate action, as it has threatened the dominance of banks in the financial market (Droppa and Becsky-Nagy 2019).

2 Current State of Digitalisation in the Hungarian Banking Sector

Digitisation has significantly transformed transaction costs in the sector. Outsourcing certain banking activities results in lower costs than if they were carried out internally by the incumbent institution. According to Coase's (1937) theory of transaction costs, there are costs associated with using the market price mechanism, and transaction costs influence the formation and boundaries of businesses. In transaction cost-based corporate theories, the corporate institution appears as a coordination mechanism that can carry out certain transactions at a lower cost than the market price mechanism directly. The fact that digitalisation reduces interorganisational transaction costs can lead to the outsourcing of banking processes, the lengthening of value chains, and increased interdependence between institutions. In addition, the opening up of regulation to new market players also creates the legal possibility for similar integrations (Navaretti et al. 2017).

From its inception, the financial sector—particularly the banking industry—has operated on a foundation of trust. Consequently, it possesses extensive experience in acting ethically and in building and maintaining the confidence of customers and markets, fully aware of how quickly that trust can be lost. Rebuilding credibility and reliability is a slow and difficult process, as has been repeatedly demonstrated in the aftermath of economic crises. Trust, reliability, ethics, and business reputation are invaluable assets and, at the same time, essential tools for sustainable success and profitability (Müller and Kerényi 2019). However, the question arises as to how ethical expectations, professional standards, and relevant regulations evolve when financial innovation brings new solutions into the sector. Such developments compel traditional credit institutions, banks, insurance companies, and other financial organisations to transform their business models—particularly in light of challenges such as the impact of the COVID-19 pandemic on digitalisation. Digital technologies are reshaping our lives: artificial intelligence, big data analytics, blockchain, and cloud-based solutions are enhancing our world in countless ways. Yet, alongside new opportunities, they also introduce fresh vulnerabilities, possibilities for error, and previously unknown risks. In the financial sector, the rise of digital technologies has brought significant benefits worldwide, such as improved customer experience, rapid customer acquisition, reduced operating costs, increased efficiency, and the elimination of financial exclusion. At the same time, however, the sector is facing new competition and unprecedented risks due to the disruptive entry of FinTech companies into the market, which has accelerated in recent years, particularly because of the COVID-19 pandemic. The emergence of FinTech players is breaking the monopoly of traditional banking services. Digital solutions, especially open banking and close integration with financial institutions, have opened a new dimension in operational risks. Access to customer data (sensitive payment data and information classified as financial secrets) typically takes place via the internet and interfaces (APIs), while data storage and processing is increasingly carried out using cloud services. This complex infrastructure, involving multiple subcontractors, presents new points of attack and security risks. The introduction of AI-based solutions (e.g., customer risk analysis, robot advisory services) increases efficiency but also raises the issue of unclear legal liability. The functioning of AI is complex and not always transparent, so in the event of a possible error or distortion, it is not clear who bears legal responsibility (Harkácsi and Szegfű 2021).

The European Union responded to risk management and the regulation of innovation with uniform tightening. The second Payment Services Directive (PSD2), which came into force in 2018, created a regulated environment for digital services. It enabled Third Party Providers (TPPs) to securely access customer payment accounts (strictly with the customer's consent), which fundamentally changed the dynamics of competition. PSD2 also requires the use of strong customer authentication (SCA). The General Data Protection Regulation (GDPR) has tightened the protection of personal data. Banks are responsible for ensuring that data is adequately protected: they must assess their entire data assets (personal data, banking secrets, trade secrets) and classify them into appropriate security categories. The transposition of stricter EU directives on anti-money laundering and counter-terrorist financing (AML) has enabled remote, electronic customer due diligence (KYC). Legal simplifications (video chat, selfie solutions, e-ID cards) have made it possible to carry out the entire customer acquisition process online and without interruption, which has significantly supported FinTech players in acquiring customers (PSD2 2015; GDPR 2016; MNB rendelet 2020).

The complex interaction between technology and regulation gives rise to several challenges that hinder the digitisation of banking operations. One such challenge is the uneven playing field. PSD2 requires banks to make significant investments in developing interfaces, which is costly. In addition, the diversity of banking interfaces (lack of standardisation) represents a high barrier to entry for TPPs. Some credit institutions have used unethical means to try to prevent TPPs from joining (the EBA and the MNB have issued guidelines to clarify what constitutes "obstruction"). Furthermore, fraud prevention and instant payments. With the spread of digital technologies and instant payment systems, new types of instant fraud risks are emerging. The system's vulnerability increases due to the large number of participants involved in the payment transaction. Although PSD2 requires fraud monitoring, the operation of a real-time supervisory system covering all digital channels and TPPs is not currently a general legal requirement, which represents a shortcoming (Harkácsi and Szegfű 2021).

According to the 2023 digital development survey conducted by the Magyar Nemzeti Bank (MNB), the digital maturity of the domestic banking sector has continued to improve at an accelerated pace compared to the previous year. The survey covered more than 90% of the banking system's total assets and examined digital development along seven main pillars. This complex examination showed significant progress on average in all areas, but the sector remains at a moderate level of digital development. The management pillar achieved outstanding results, reflecting management commitment to digital transformation, and reached a high level in 2023. The goal of banks' digital developments is to improve customer experience and expand their product portfolio. There are significant differences between the retail and corporate segments in this area. The complete digitisation of retail customer service has been achieved in several basic services. At all banks surveyed, opening a current account and applying for a personal loan can be done entirely digitally, in many cases via a mobile app, with selfie identification. This trend is consistent with the fact that, in line with international trends, domestic banks are primarily focusing on mobile banking platforms, with continuous functional expansion and customer experience enhancement. The use of mobile banking channels has increased among the population. Digital payment solutions are also becoming more widespread, with mobile payments (such as Apple Pay and Google Pay) widely available and several banks developing unique mobile payment solutions.

Banks are also strengthening digital information and incentives for customers, including digital educational materials, frequently asked questions, and incentive systems for using digital products, which contribute to the growth of digital product sales revenues. Developing financial awareness among younger generations is particularly important, which is why many banks support the dissemination of financial knowledge through educational programs and gamification platforms. The median value of service outages is steadily declining, reflecting banks' more effective defence and recovery capabilities amid growing cybersecurity challenges.

At the same time, cooperation agreements related to open banking are becoming increasingly common among banks, which points to a future of innovation and personalised services. The development of employees' digital skills has also become a focus, as updating knowledge that supports digitalisation is essential for maintaining the competitiveness of organisations. In addition, more banks are adopting artificial intelligence-based solutions and creating separate teams for AI research and development, while digitalisation-related tasks are also included in employee performance evaluations. However, the technological infrastructure still needs improvement. At the same time, the number of service outages has decreased in recent years, indicating better system management and operational efficiency.

3 Adoption of Generative AI in Leading Hungarian Banks: Case Studies

The latest technological focus is on exploring artificial intelligence (AI)-based solutions. The domestic banking sector has also responded to the emergence of Generative AI, although the depth of the response varies from institution to institution. Two-thirds of banks are considering the application of AI at both the strategic and operational levels, and the most active players have set up dedicated teams for research and development (MNB 2023).

Generative artificial intelligence (genAI) models have emerged in everyday life less than three years ago, yet they have rapidly gained strategic importance within corporate environments. The banking sector has been among the earliest adopters, initially testing and subsequently deploying genAI-based solutions. At present, most Hungarian banks actively utilise these technologies to enhance internal operations and customer engagement. The Portfolio (2025) survey provides a comprehensive overview of the AI-based systems employed by the largest financial institutions in Hungary.

According to the study, Hungarian banks predominantly employ generative AI to improve efficiency across internal processes (Portfolio 2025). At CIB Bank, genAI is currently applied to translation and translation verification tasks, where human employees oversee quality assurance. The institution is also assessing AI-driven automation in broader document-processing activities, including virtual assistance, communication, and creative content generation. Erste Bank began its organisational preparation for AI integration three years ago. In 2024, the bank equipped all its more than 3000 employees with personal AI "assistants." These systems collect and structure publicly available data, generate written content, analyse information, prepare meeting summaries, and synthesise discussion points. The in-house developed application—built on OpenAI's language model—integrates the bank's regulatory documents, product guidelines, and contractual terms, allowing for instantaneous responses to staff queries.

GRÁNIT Bank leverages generative AI agents to improve operational efficiency, particularly in the verification and processing of loan-related documentation.

At K&H Bank, the originally customer-facing chatbot *Kate* has been extended for internal use. It now manages hundreds of HR-related queries daily and supports internal human resource procedures. The bank intends to expand this functionality further, thereby providing all 3800 employees with a comprehensive digital workplace assistant.

MBH Bank has established a dedicated AI division responsible for strategy development, the creation of methodological and testing frameworks, and employee training. More than 2000 employees have already completed AI-focused education programs. Recently, a pilot AI-based digital tool was introduced to assist staff in daily tasks and decision-making.

OTP Bank has implemented, or is in the advanced stages of developing, several genAI-based applications, including a *Retrieval-Augmented Generation (RAG)*-powered unified knowledge base that supports branch operations, contact centres, and back-office functions, as well as self-service customer platforms. AI technologies are also employed in credit line applications, risk analytics, document processing, and standardised report generation.

Raiffeisen Bank utilises generative AI to enhance both branch-level operations and HR processes. Within the IT domain, AI is applied throughout the development lifecycle—from business requirement analysis and testing to code generation and documentation. Optical Character Recognition (OCR) technologies play a pivotal role in document management, yielding significant improvements in text-processing efficiency.

Regarding customer service, Erste Bank envisions expanding its digital platform *George* with AI-driven capabilities that will enable clients to access personalised financial advice and execute certain banking operations autonomously.

GRÁNIT Bank launched its generative AI-powered virtual assistant, *Gránit Guru*, on its website in late 2024. By August 2025, the system had already handled over 25,000 customer inquiries concerning the bank's products and services. K&H Bank's voice- and chat-based digital financial assistant, *Kate*, currently supports both retail and SME clients across 362 distinct functions, covering banking and insurance operations, and has facilitated over two million interactions. At MBH Bank, an AI assistant provides information to clients interested in Worker's loans. Additionally, in May 2025, the bank launched an AI-based service within its *BUPA* digital platform to assist micro, small, and medium-sized enterprises in navigating state funding opportunities. OTP Bank employs AI technologies for voice-based customer service, automated inquiry classification, and response generation. The bank is also developing a generative AI assistant capable of managing complex customer needs across both text- and voice-based communication channels. Raiffeisen Bank's customer service currently integrates a generative AI-powered chatbot with limited functionality on its website; however, the institution is actively expanding its use to encompass broader service domains (Portfolio 2025).

Overall, the digital transformation of the domestic banking sector is underway, with the average digital composite index of banks rising significantly from 62 to over 66. This development clearly reflects the fact that digital transformation is no longer just a competitive advantage but a fundamental element of operations. Further expansion of management commitment, technological developments, and customer-centric digital services is expected, which will lay the foundation for the sector's long-term competitiveness and innovation.

References

Coase RH (1937) The nature of the firm. Economica 4(16):386–405. https://doi.org/10.1111/j.1468-0335.1937.tb00002.x

Droppa D, Becsky-Nagy P (2019) A pénzvilág üdvöskéi: a FinTech-megoldások. Pécsi Tudományegyetem Közgazdaságtudományi Kar. ISBN: 978-963-429-456-6

Financial Stability Board (2019) FinTech and market structure in financial services: Market developments and potential financial stability implications. https://www.fsb.org/wp-content/uploads/P140219.pdf

GDPR (2016) Az (EU) 2016/679 rendelet (GDPR)—a természetes személyek adatainak védelméről és az ilyen adatok szabad áramlásáról

Gozman D, Liebenau J, Mangan J (2018) The innovation mechanisms of fintech start-ups: insights from SWIFT's Innotribe competition. J Manag Inf Syst 35(1):145–179. https://doi.org/10.1080/07421222.2018.1440768

Harkácsi GJ, Szegfű LP (2021) A megfelelőségbiztosítási funkció szerepe a digitalizáció, mesterséges intelligencia és robotizáció idején a pénzügyi szektorban. Hitelintézeti Szemle 20(1):152–170

Lagoarde-Segot T, Currie WL (2018) Financialization and information technology: a multi-paradigmatic view of IT and finance: Part II. J Inf Technol 33:1–8. https://doi.org/10.1057/s41265-017-0045-7

Magyar Nemzeti Bank (2023) Jelentés. MNB. https://www.mnb.hu/kiadvanyok/jelentesek/fintech-es-digitalizacios-jelentes

Marinč M (2013) Banks and information technology: marketability vs. relationships. Electron Commer Res 13(1):71–101. https://doi.org/10.1007/s10660-013-9107-2

MNB rendelet (2020) 26/2020. (VIII.25.) MNB rendelet a pénzmosás és a terrorizmus finanszírozása megelőzéséről és megakadályozásáról szóló törvény végrehajtásáról. https://njt.hu/jogszabaly/2020-26-20-2C

Müller J, Kerényi Á (2019) A bizalom és etika igénye a digitális korszakban—Napfény és árnyék a FinTech világában. Hitelintézeti Szemle 18(4):5–34. https://doi.org/10.25201/HSZ.18.4.534

Navaretti GB, Calzolari G, Mansilla-Fernandez JM, Pozzolo AF (2017) FinTech and banking: friends or foes? Eur Economy—Banks Regul Real Sect 2017(2):9–39. https://doi.org/10.2139/ssrn.3099337

Portfolio (2025) Nagyot szól az AI-boom a magyar bankokban—Így használják most a genAI technológiát. Portfolio.hu. https://www.portfolio.hu/bank/20250929/nagyot-szol-az-ai-boom-a-magyar-bankokban-igy-hasznaljak-most-a-genai-technologiat-789034

Póta C, Veres M, Dávidházy G, Becsky-Nagy P (2021) Kényszeradta lehetőség a pénzügyi digitalizációban. Controller Info 9(1–2):2–7

PSD2 (2015) Az (EU) 2015/2366 irányelv (PSD2)—A belső piaci pénzforgalmi szolgáltatásokról

Simai M, Gál P (2020) Új trendek és stratégiák a világgazdaságban. Akadémiai Kiadó

Török L (2024) Digital transformation of Hungary's economy between 2015 and 2021: results and future objectives. Sustainability 16(4684). https://doi.org/10.3390/su16114684

AI-Supported HR Management: Insights from Romania and Hungary

Gergő Tömöri and Elena Aurelia Botezat

Abstract The introduction of AI in Hungarian and Romanian HR practice opens up new opportunities and debates. Automation, machine learning, and predictive analytics are transforming recruitment, with a demonstrable increase in efficiency as a result, while raising questions about ethical governance, data protection, and employee autonomy. Despite the supportive attitude of domestic experts, professional retraining, the development of ethical standards, and the preservation of the human factor remain challenges. As numerous studies have highlighted, the transformation of the Hungarian labour market is reflected in the structure of employment and skill requirements, and the key to sustainable implementation is retaining the human factor, developing ethical frameworks, and applying AI in an employee-centred manner.

1 Introduction to AI in HR Management

Artificial Intelligence (AI) has emerged as a transformative force in human resource management (HRM), reshaping how companies and other organisations recruit, manage, and develop their workforce. AI technologies, such as machine learning, natural language processing (NLP), and predictive analytics, are increasingly integrated into HR processes to enhance efficiency, reduce biases, and improve decision-making (Bencsik 2021). These tools enable HR professionals to automate repetitive tasks, analyse vast datasets, and provide personalised employee experiences, thereby revolutionising traditional HRM practices.

According to Aon (2024), predictive AI, which uses machine learning to identify future patterns, has long supported talent management, compensation, health insurance, and retirement, while generative AI accelerates recruitment (automatic job

G. Tömöri (✉)
Faculty of Economics and Business, University of Debrecen, Debrecen, Hungary
e-mail: tomori.gergo@econ.unideb.hu

E. A. Botezat
Faculty of Economic Sciences, University of Oradea, Oradea, Romania

C. Sabău-Popa (ed.), *Artificial Intelligence in Finance, Accounting and Business Administration*, Contributions to Finance and Accounting,
https://doi.org/10.1007/978-3-032-22737-9_12

posting) and performance management (predicting employee attrition risk) through content creation. Chatbots improve the employee experience in retirement processes and reduce costs by identifying high-cost healthcare needs (in a case study, involving a 20% risk group resulted in savings of $2,000 per person). The benefits of AI include increased productivity (shortening drug development from 12–15 years to 8 years), better decision-making, and engagement, but it also presents challenges: minimising ethical biases, data security, cyberattacks, data privacy, and generative AI "hallucinations" (misinformation). In the future, HR leaders will need to ensure responsible implementation, provide technology training (91% on demand), and build governance, while 51% of professionals are not prepared, offering an opportunity to transform the workforce through reskilling.

2 AI in Employee Performance Management and Development

AI is revolutionising employee performance management and development by enabling data-driven insights, real-time feedback, and personalised learning experiences. In Hungarian organisations, where digital transformation is gaining momentum, AI applications in performance management are emerging as critical tools to address workforce challenges like skill gaps and retention (Dajnoki and Boros 2024).

Selejó et al. (2024) provide a comprehensive analysis of the application of artificial intelligence (AI) in human resource management (HRM), emphasising its revolutionary role in data-driven decision-making and the optimisation of employee processes in the context of the Fourth Industrial Revolution. According to their findings, AI supports resume screening (ATS systems, e.g., Breezy HR), video interviews, and predictive aptitude forecasts in recruitment and selection, while performing turnover prediction and 360-degree evaluations in performance assessment. In training, it offers personalised modules (e.g., competency development, attitude reinforcement), and in onboarding, it reduces anxiety as a mentor with emotionally intelligence-based content. Practical examples enrich the analysis: SAP SuccessFactors talent management (Vodafone, Nestlé), Textkernel CV evaluation (Randstad), Jobvite job ad optimisation (LinkedIn), and IBM Watson, which saved 12,000 working hours through automation. Among the challenges, ethical dilemmas (data protection, transparency) and the impossibility of AI replacing the human factor are mentioned, emphasising that AI is a tool to assist, not a substitute. Overall, according to their findings, "artificial intelligence is already having a big impact on many of our lives, but in the future, it can be said that artificial intelligence will greatly influence the work environment, but it cannot completely replace the human factor. In fact, processes using artificial intelligence may create new job opportunities" (Selejó et al. 2024).

Munnisunker (2023) highlights the transparency of ethical AI as an advantage, which provides a competitive edge in forecasting market trends and gaining consumer insights, as well as cost efficiency, but identifies errors resulting from a lack of data and feedback as a challenge that can damage reputation. In conclusion, Munnisunker (2023) emphasises the need for continuous learning and monitoring to overcome biases and unexpected circumstances, warning that without a strategy, the use of AI will lose employee and customer trust. As Munnisunker (2023) highlights that „evidence had been provided by various examples such as data leaks, supply decisions and through the case study. The case showed that more knowledge is required about AI to support the decision to implement an AI system, along with the possible pros and cons of using such a system. The potential threats and opportunities must be well thought through before implementing a system. A clear strategy that is drawn from the company's vision is needed before the use of AI should be considered. Constant learning and monitoring of AI are required to overcome the effects of biases and unforeseen circumstances" (Munnisunker 2023).

In Hungary, where reskilling is a pressing need due to technological advancements, AI-driven training tools are being explored to address skill shortages in industries like IT and manufacturing (Marciniak 2020). Studies highlight that Hungarian organisations are beginning to adopt these tools to foster employee growth, though implementation remains limited compared to global leaders (Ferenczy 2025).

3 Current Developments in AI Adoption Within Romanian HR

At present, AI-supported HR management, including that of Romania, is positioned at the intersection of technology, economy, and society, transforming the way companies organize their people and processes (Rădulescu et al. 2025). This naturally follows from the main objective of adopting AI in organizations, consisting in reaching the level of 'AI systems with human-competitive intelligence,' an aspect that blurs the boundaries between artificiality and human intelligence.

At the current stage of AI adoption within Romanian HR, specialized literature highlights that recruiters and HR managers primarily perceive efficiency gains from the integration of AI, whereas employees remain cautious regarding fairness and potential job displacement (e.g., Năstase et al. 2024; Briciu et al. 2025). This dual perception is reflected in the *National Strategy on Artificial Intelligence 2024–2027*, developed by the Authority for Romania's Digitalization (2024), which seeks to establish a national framework aimed at reducing the tension between the pressure for economic competitiveness and the imperative to protect human capital (Ciocodeică et al. 2024).

The strategy proposes an integrated framework to support both organizations in adopting AI for increased efficiency and innovation, and employees, through training, reskilling, and upskilling programs designed to reduce the risk of digital exclusion.

In Romanian HR, this framework is essential for the development of digital skills, the responsible integration of AI into recruitment, evaluation, and employee management processes, and alignment with European standards on ethics and transparency (Iuga and Brad 2022).

Recent studies, such as Ciocodeică et al. (2024), reveal a workforce in Romania that is cautious yet optimistic. Respondents recognize both the opportunities, including job creation, efficiency, and digitalization, and the risks, such as job displacement, skill mismatches, and increased pressure to adapt to rapid technological change. Particularly important are:

- Understanding the importance of individual adaptability at work, which competes alongside task performance and contextual performance as a third type of workplace performance shaped by emerging technologies (Botezat et al. 2023).
- Maintaining a balance between the pressures of economic competitiveness and the protection of human capital. This is evidenced by Ciocodeică et al. (2024), who found that 95% of respondents believe government regulations on AI are necessary in the workplace, while 75% think Romanian companies should invest more in employee training in AI.

Human resource management literature discusses prioritization tools that can be highly effective when integrating AI into HR functions (Noe et al. 2017). Accordingly, the Eisenhower Matrix facilitates operational prioritization by distinguishing tasks that AI can automate from those requiring human judgment, while the Covey Matrix ensures strategic alignment by supporting long-term HR objectives such as employee engagement, organizational culture, and talent development. Taken together, these frameworks enable HR leaders to balance efficiency with organizational values, positioning AI not merely as a productivity enhancer but as a catalyst for sustainable, human-centered HR practices.

Based on studies related to Romanian organizations (e.g., Mihai and Duţescu 2022; Pop et al. 2023; Goga et al. 2024; Năstase et al. 2024), we applied the principles of the two matrices to provide both an operational and a strategic perspective on how AI supports organizations in addressing these important aspects, as illustrated in Tables 1 and 2.

To provide a strategic perspective, we applied the Covey Matrix to illustrate where AI serves as a strategic partner and where human expertise remains irreplaceable. The matrix also highlights automation opportunities and identifies low-value tasks that HR should minimize.

By combining the Eisenhower Matrix and the Covey Matrix, HR managers can better prioritize tasks, leverage AI where it adds the most value, and ensure that human expertise is focused on areas where it is truly irreplaceable.

Table 1 Applying the Eisenhower Matrix to HR functions with AI to enhance operational prioritization

Quadrant	What it means	HR functions	How AI helps
Urgent and Important (Do Now)	Immediate issues that affect employees or compliance	Handling employee relations crises Correcting payroll errors Monitoring compliance risks	AI chatbots triage urgent employee complaints AI payroll systems flag anomalies instantly AI compliance tools detect policy or legal violations in real time
Not Urgent but Important (Plan)	Strategic, long-term HR priorities	Workforce planning Talent development and succession Diversity and inclusion initiatives	Predictive analytics forecast turnover and skill gaps AI learning platforms personalize training paths AI dashboards track diversity metrics and bias risks
Urgent but Not Important (Delegate)	Time-sensitive but routine tasks	Resume screening Interview scheduling Benefits inquiries	AI recruitment tools rank candidates automatically AI assistants schedule interviews across calendars Chatbots answer benefits and policy questions 24/7
Not Urgent and Not Important (Automate/ Eliminate)	Repetitive admin work with little strategic value	Timesheet approvals Routine FAQs Document filing	AI auto-validates timesheets Knowledge bases answer FAQs instantly Document management systems auto-tag and retrieve files

4 Critical Challenges of AI Integration in Romanian HR Systems

The analysis of specialized literature on the adoption of AI in human resource management within Romanian companies shows that it is applied to the automation of repetitive tasks, including accounting and logistics operations such as forklift management (Mihai and Duţescu 2022; Goga et al. 2024), enhancing productivity in areas like e-commerce (Nistor and Zadobrischi 2024), personalizing employee and customer experiences (Simion and Popescu 2023; Cozmescu et al. 2025), and attracting digital talent (Pop et al. 2023). Across all these domains, AI is regarded

Table 2 Applying the Cover Matrix to HR functions with AI to enhance strategic prioritization

Quadrant	What it means	HR functions	How AI helps
High Strategic Impact/ High AI Enablement (AI as a Strategic Partner)	Critical for long-term HR strategy and strongly supported by AI	Workforce planning, succession planning, talent analytics	Predictive analytics forecast turnover and skill gaps AI dashboards provide real-time workforce insights
High Strategic Impact/ Low AI Enablement (Human Expertise Irreplaceable)	Strategic priorities that still rely heavily on human judgment	Culture building, leadership development, employee engagement	AI offers sentiment analysis and engagement surveys, but HR leaders interpret results and drive action
Low Strategic Impact/ High AI Enablement (Automation Opportunities)	Operational tasks with limited strategic value but easily automated	Recruitment screening, interview scheduling, benefits administration	AI recruitment tools rank candidates Assistants coordinate interviews Chatbots handle benefits queries
Low Strategic Impact/ Low AI Enablement (Low-Value Tasks to Minimize)	Routine tasks with little strategic importance and minimal AI leverage	Policy drafting, complex employee relations cases, sensitive negotiations	AI provides document templates and compliance checks, but nuanced handling remains human-driven

as a driver of efficiency and innovation, though challenges persist both from the perspective of organizations and from that of employees.

A synthesis of these challenges of AI integration in Romanian HR systems, together with recommendations for success, is presented in Table 3.

In conclusion, beyond the allure created by the promise of efficiency, increased productivity, and time savings through the rapid execution of repetitive tasks and the processing of large volumes of data, the responsibility falls to HR to manage the balance between human competencies and those generated by intelligent systems. This highlights the need to reposition employees not as rivals of machines, but as complementary partners, capable of adding value through creativity, empathy, critical thinking, and adaptability.

5 Impact of AI on Hungarian Labour Market Dynamics

The integration of AI into various sectors is profoundly reshaping labour market dynamics worldwide, and Hungary is no exception. AI technologies, such as automation, machine learning, and predictive analytics, are transforming job roles, skill

Table 3 AI integration in Romanian HR systems: organizational and employee challenges with pathways to success

Sector	Challenges from the organization's perspective	Challenges from the employees' perspective	Recommendations for success
Ecommerce	High implementation costs, need for continuous updates to AI systems, risk of over-reliance on automation	Reluctance toward algorithms that decide selection and evaluation	Combine AI with human oversight in recruitment; invest in scalable AI solutions; provide employee training to build trust and reduce fear of automation
Accounting	Integration difficulties with legacy systems, compliance with financial regulations, need for specialized IT staff	Distrust in automated decisions and lack of transparency	Establish clear transparency policies; run workshops showing error reduction benefits; allocate resources for system integration and compliance alignment
Digital Marketing	Difficulty in measuring ROI of AI-driven creativity, risk of homogenized campaigns, need for constant innovation	Perception that AI directly competes with human creativity	Launch pilot projects blending AI with human creativity; set KPIs to measure ROI; reward employee contributions to maintain motivation and originality
Dental Activities	High costs of digital infrastructure, data privacy concerns in medical records, lack of technical expertise	Resistance to change in a traditional field	Implement AI gradually with clear communication of patient benefits; provide staff training; ensure compliance with medical data privacy regulations
Social Enterprises	Limited budgets for AI adoption, lack of technical know-how, risk of alienating volunteers who value human interaction	Difficulties in accepting AI due to limited resources and organizational culture	Use AI only for repetitive tasks; keep final decisions human-led; seek low-cost AI tools; foster a supportive culture through awareness programs

requirements, and employment structures, presenting both opportunities and challenges (Transforming our jobs: Automation in Hungary 2024). In Hungary, where labour market challenges like skill shortages and high turnover rates are prevalent, AI is emerging as a tool to enhance workforce efficiency while necessitating significant reskilling efforts (From AI to Demography 2025). This chapter examines the impact of AI on Hungarian labour market dynamics, focusing on job transformation, skill demands, and the broader socio-economic implications, drawing on local and global insights.

AI's influence on the Hungarian labour market is evident in the automation of routine tasks and the creation of new job roles. Automation technologies, including robotic process automation (RPA) and AI-driven decision-making systems, are replacing repetitive tasks in industries such as manufacturing and business services, leading to job displacement in some sectors (Marciniak 2020). For instance, a

McKinsey report highlights that up to 30% of current jobs in Hungary could be automated by 2030, particularly in sectors like logistics and administration (Transforming our jobs: Automation in Hungary 2024). However, AI also fosters job creation in areas like data science and AI system maintenance, aligning with Hungary's push for digital transformation (Hungary's artificial intelligence strategy 2020). Studies indicate that Hungarian organisations are increasingly adopting AI to address labour shortages, particularly in IT and engineering, where demand for skilled professionals outstrips supply (Szabó-Szentgróti 2023).

Karacsony (2022) analysed the attitudes of Hungarian HR practitioners and trainees towards AI. This analysis was conducted on 191 individuals, all of whom were HR managers. Based on the results of the author's research, „it can be said that the attitude of HR professionals in the survey towards AI is mostly supportive, and its role in HR management is considered positive. Based on the results obtained, there is no evidence of a general fear that AI intelligence would jeopardise jobs in the future" (Karacsony 2022). According to this analysis, „therefore it cannot be clearly stated that the employment situation of the surveyed professionals would be negatively affected by the spread of AI" (Karacsony 2022).

Comparative analyses suggest that Hungary lags behind global leaders like Singapore in AI-driven workforce development, highlighting the urgency of reskilling initiatives (Ferenczy 2025). Ferenczy (2025) formulates targeted recommendations for the upcoming Hungarian AI strategy, such as adapting large language models, restructuring the triple helix network of government, industry, and academia for better dialogue, and positioning Hungary as an East–West bridge in automotive AI experiments, thereby increasing competitiveness and innovation opportunities.

Socio-economic implications of AI adoption in Hungary include changes in employment structures and wage dynamics. AI's ability to enhance productivity can lead to higher wages for skilled workers, but it risks exacerbating income inequality for those in low-skill roles (Szabó-Szentgróti 2023). Mélypataki (2024) emphasises the need for reskilling employees to acquire AI competencies, while employers must take responsibility for the ethical introduction of technology, thus building a bridge between technological innovation and social justice in the future labour market. Overall, the study outlines not only a diagnostic but also a proactive labour law framework, encouraging legislation to address the challenges of digital transformation so that AI serves the interests of workers rather than undermining their legal security. Additionally, AI's integration into HR practices, such as performance monitoring and recruitment, raises concerns about worker autonomy and job security, particularly in Hungary's non-inclusive industrial relations system (Makó et al. 2025).

In conclusion, AI is reshaping Hungarian labour market dynamics by driving automation, creating new job opportunities, and necessitating reskilling. While Hungary faces challenges like skill shortages and ethical concerns, national strategies and innovative HR practices are fostering AI adoption (Hungary's artificial intelligence strategy 2020; Dajnoki and Boros 2024). Addressing these challenges through targeted education and policy measures will be crucial for Hungary to leverage AI's potential while mitigating its risks.

6 Future Trends and Challenges for AI in HR Management

The rapid evolution of AI is poised to transform HRM globally, with significant implications for Hungarian organisations. Emerging trends, such as generative AI, advanced predictive analytics, and AI-driven employee engagement tools, promise to enhance HR efficiency and strategic decision-making (Poór et al. 2025). In Hungary, where digital transformation is a national priority, AI adoption in HRM is expected to accelerate, driven by initiatives like Hungary's Artificial Intelligence Strategy (Hungary's Artificial Intelligence Strategy 2020). However, challenges such as ethical concerns, workforce reskilling, and regulatory compliance must be addressed to ensure sustainable integration. This chapter explores future trends and challenges for AI in Hungarian HR management, emphasising local contexts and drawing on global insights.

Izsó (2023) discusses the application of artificial intelligence (AI)-based expert systems in predicting employee success, with a particular emphasis on the concept of the ATOM (Artificial Intelligence for Testing Occupational success of Manpower) system developed by him. The author points out that in the field of human resource management (HRM), especially in recruitment and selection, the use of AI tools is still limited, while traditional methods often underperform, for example, personnel decision-makers inaccurately assess the future performance of candidates. The ATOM system was designed to address these issues: it is an expert system based on machine learning (ML) that learns from empirical data the correlations between candidates' predictor variables (personality traits, abilities) and job-specific success criteria, thereby more accurately predicting employee success. The article highlights the potential expansion of AI in HRM—including employment, training, performance evaluation, wage policy, labour relations, and occupational safety—while also emphasising limitations such as dependence on data quality and ethical issues. ATOM primarily supports not only selection but also recruitment and, to a lesser extent, occupational safety, thus bridging the gap between psychological research and practical HRM tools, helping to increase decision-making efficiency. In the introduction to the article, Izsó describes the operating principles of ATOM in detail, emphasising its innovative multi-machine learning algorithm-based approach, where multiple ML models run in parallel, and the system dynamically selects the best-performing algorithm for predictions, ensuring flexibility and efficiency tailored to different job roles. This method allows ATOM to develop predictive models based on real historical data rather than rigid rules, thus overcoming the limitations of traditional psychological tests or human expert judgments.

Izsó (2023) discusses the results of the ATOM's implementation, although he refers to the other articles in the special issue for empirical data, while highlighting the practical advantages of ATOM: it can reduce selection errors, optimise the recruitment process, and even help predict occupational safety risks by identifying success factors. The discussion critically analyses the barriers to the spread of AI in HRM, such as professional concerns, data protection, and cultural resistance, while also outlining an optimistic outlook that such systems could revolutionise applied psychology, increasing employee fit and organisational performance. In summary, Izsó's work not only presents a technical concept but also offers a comprehensive framework for the psychological application of AI, encouraging further research and implementation in Hungarian HRM practice.

In conclusion, the future of AI in Hungarian HR management holds immense potential, with trends like generative AI and predictive analytics poised to enhance efficiency and employee engagement. However, challenges such as ethical concerns, reskilling needs, and regulatory compliance must be navigated carefully. By leveraging national strategies and innovative tools, Hungarian organisations can position themselves as leaders in AI-driven HRM (Poór et al. 2025; Izsó 2023).

References

Alsulami A, et al (2021) The adoption of artificial intelligence in human resource management: Application of machine learning algorithms to an intelligent recruitment system. Found Manag 13(1):151–166. https://ojs.wsb.edu.pl/index.php/fso/article/download/348/264/596

Aon (2024) How artificial intelligence is transforming human resources and the workforce. Aon Insights. https://www.aon.com/en/insights/articles/how-artificial-intelligence-is-transforming-human-resources-and-the-workforce

Autoritatea pentru Digitalizarea României (2024) Strategia națională în domeniul inteligenței artificiale 2024–2027. ADR. https://www.adr.gov.ro/wp-content/uploads/2024/06/Strategia-Nationala-pentru-Inteligenta-Artificiala.pdf

Bencsik A (2021) The sixth generation of knowledge management: the headway of artificial intelligence. J Int Stud 14(2):6–21. https://www.centreofexcellence.net/index.php/JIS/article/view/jis.2021.14.2.6.1/401

Botezat E, Fotea SL, Crisan D, Fotea IS (2023) Individual adaptability to work: scale validation on the Romanian population. Studia Universitatis Vasile Goldiş Arad, Seria Ştiinţe Economice 33(3):37–60. https://doi.org/10.2478/sues-2023-0013

Briciu VA, Catargiu AC, Briciu A (2025) Artificial intelligence adoption in corporate recruitment and selection processes: a qualitative investigation of Romanian recruiters. In: Ara A (ed), Human resource management in the age of generative AI. IGI Global, pp 133–156. https://doi.org/10.4018/979-8-3693-7693-5

Ciocodeică DF, Berbece ŞA, Pestrea CD (2024) The impact of artificial intelligence on the labor market in Romania. Proc Int Conf Bus Excel 18(1):198–208. https://doi.org/10.2478/picbe-2024-0017

Cozmescu AF, Cernega A, Mincă DG, Didilescu AC, Imre MM, Totan AR, Piţuru SM (2025) Embracing artificial intelligence in dental practice: an exploratory study of Romanian clinicians' perspectives and experiences. Dentistry J 13(9):390. https://doi.org/10.3390/dj13090390

Dajnoki K, Boros J (2024) 'Innovative HR challenges in the 21st century': conference and professional forum—conference report. University of Debrecen Repository. https://dea.lib.unideb.hu/bitstreams/704897c5-5cf6-4dd2-963a-6997506af4e5/download

Ferenczy A (2025) Hungary and AI: efforts and opportunities in comparison with Singapore. arXiv. https://arxiv.org/abs/2507.05280

From AI to demography—what's reshaping Hungary's labour market? (2025) Hungarian Conservative. https://www.hungarianconservative.com/articles/culture_society/labour-market-hungary-trends-challenges-oeconomus-whc/

Goga AS, Toth Z, Meclea MA, Puiu IR, Boşcoianu M (2024) The proliferation of artificial intelligence in the forklift industry—an analysis for the case of Romania. Sustainability 16(21):9306. https://doi.org/10.3390/su16219306

How will AI impact the Hungarian labour market? (n.d.) PwC Hungary Publications. https://www.pwc.com/hu/en/publications/assets/How-will-AI-impact-the-Hungarian-labour-market.pdf
Hungary's artificial intelligence strategy (2020) AI-Hungary.com. https://ai-hungary.com/files/api/v1/companies/15/files/146074/view.pdf
Iuga M, Brad S (2022, September) Adoption of artificial intelligence in Romania: innovative policies to overpass vulnerabilities with TRIZ and deep-thinking tools. In: International TRIZ future conference. Springer International Publishing, Cham, pp 296–311
Izsó L (2023) The concept of an AI-based expert system (ATOM) for predicting job success. Appl Psychol Hung. https://real.mtak.hu/181328/
Karacsony P (2022) Analysis of the attitude of Hungarian HR professionals to artificial intelligence. Naše gospodarstvo/Our Economy 68(2):43–52. https://sciendo.com/2/v2/download/article/10.2478/ngoe-2022-0011.pdf
Koteczki R, Csikor D, Balassa BE (2024) The role of generative AI in improving the sustainability and efficiency of HR recruitment process. Discov Sustain 5(1):Article 204. https://link.springer.com/article/10.1007/s43621-024-00204-0
Legnerová K (2024) The impact of AI implementation on job transformation and competency requirements: Prioritising reskilling and soft skills development. ResearchGate. https://www.researchgate.net/publication/381429589_The_Impact_of_AI_Implementation_on_Job_Transformation_and_Competency_Requirements_Prioritising_Reskilling_and_Soft_Skills_Development
Makó C, Illéssy M, Pap J, Farkas É, et al (2025) Algorithmic management in traditional workplaces: the case of high vs. low involvement working practices—the context of the non-inclusive industrial relations. J Labour Soc. Advance online publication. https://brill.com/view/journals/jlso/aop/article-10.1163-24714607-bja10182/article-10.1163-24714607-bja10182.xml
Marciniak R (2020) Promotion of an industry—trends and expectations of digital transformation in the Hungarian business services sector. In: Proceedings of the 4th Central European PhD Workshop on Technological Change and Development. https://www.academia.edu/82808834/Analysing_Digital_Transformation_among_Hungarian_Organizations
Mélypataki G (2024) The future of artificial intelligence (AI) in the workplace: the perspective of labour law. Revista Curentul Juridic 24(3):68–80. https://revcurentjur.ro/old/pms/uploads/recjurid243_3.pdf
Mihai MS, Duţescu A (2022) Artificial intelligence solutions for Romanian accounting companies. In: Proceedings of the International Conference on Business Excellence, vol 16, no 1. Sciendo, pp 859–869. https://doi.org/10.2478/picbe-2022-0081
Munnisunker S (2023) GiLE journal of skills development: AI in HR training. MTA Repository. https://real.mtak.hu/152369/1/document-5_Munnisunker.pdf
Năstase M, Croitoru G, Florea NV, Cristache N, Lile R (2024) The perceptions of employees from Romanian companies on adoption of artificial intelligence in recruitment and selection processes. Amfiteatru Economic 26(66):421–439. https://doi.org/10.24818/EA/2024/66/421
Nistor A, Zadobrischi E (2024, July) The scale-up of e-commerce in Romania generated by the pandemic, automation, and artificial intelligence. Telecom 5(3):680–705. https://doi.org/10.3390/telecom5030039
Noe RA, Hollenbeck JR, Gerhart B, Wright PM (2017) Fundamentals of human resource management, 7th ed. McGraw-Hill Education
Poór J, et al (2025) The role of human resource consultants in digital transformation. Óbuda University e-Bulletin. https://journals.bme.hu/oee/article/download/40448/23862/223424
Pop MV, Tont G, Şandor A (2023, June) Innovation management opportunities of artificial intelligence social enterprises in Romania. In: 2023 17th International Conference on Engineering of Modern Electric Systems (EMES). IEEE, pp 1–4. https://doi.org/10.1109/EMES57872.2023.10194765
Rădulescu CV, Gâf-Deac II, Bran F, Burlacu S, Bodislav DA, Buzoianu OCA (2025) Cybernetic contributions of artificial intelligence to economic development in Romania. Econ Comput Econ Cybern Stud Res 59(1):139–155. https://doi.org/10.24818/18423264/59.1.25.09

Săniuță A, Filip SO (2021) Artificial intelligence: an overview of European and Romanian startups landscape and the factors that determine their success. In: Strategica. Shaping the future of business and economy, pp 872–884

Selejó J, Bence T, Komóczi M, Csukonyi C (2024) The use of artificial intelligence in human resource management. University of Debrecen Repository. https://dea.lib.unideb.hu/bitstreams/10ed24f9-d6e8-46ba-b649-e05c81538f87/download

Simion PC, Popescu MAM (2023) Assessing the use of artificial intelligence in digital marketing: evidence from Romanian companies. In: Proceedings of the International Conference on Business Excellence, vol 17, no 1. Sciendo, pp 1128–1138

Szabó-Szentgróti G (2023) Artificial intelligence in a transforming labour market. Index Copernicus Journals. https://journals.indexcopernicus.com/api/file/viewByFileId/1809416

Szappanyos M (2023) Artificial intelligence and human rights. Acta Humana 1.93–110. https://real.mtak.hu/164151/1/06_szappanyos_93-110_ActaHumana2023_1.pdf

Transforming our jobs: automation in Hungary (2024) McKinsey & Company. https://www.mckinsey.com/~/media/McKinsey/Locations/Europe%2520and%2520Middle%2520East/Hungary/Our%2520Insights/Transforming%2520our%2520jobs%2520automation%2520in%2520Hungary/Automation-report-on-Hungary-EN-May24.pdf

Data Analysis and Visualisation in the AI Era

AI in Data Visualisation

Codruța Mare

Abstract This chapter focuses on one of the most important and used Data Visualization software—Tableau. The goal is to show how AI tools in general, and Generative AI ones in particular, may be used in creating data visuals in an efficient manner. After a quick introduction into importing data in Tableau and preparing the data visualization process, the discussion moves to using AI with Tableau. There are two major options presented: (1) using GenAI tools like Google AI (Gemini), Microsoft Copilot or ChatGPT (just to name a few), and (2) using the Tableau built in AI tools like Tableau Agent (Einstein Copilot) and Tableau Pulse to create built in dashboards through Tableau Cloud.

1 Introduction

Data visualisation has become of most importance in the late twentieth century. This is due to several reasons, like:

The human brain processes visual information approximately 60,000 times faster than text;
Approximately 90% of the information the human brain processes is visual;
Approximately 80% of the information people remember is visual;
If you add visuals in a presentation, the retention of information is 6 times higher;
Data visualisation is the first step in data exploration, having an important role in data preparation.

The most famous data visualisation software applications are Tableau and Power BI (according to Forbes Advisors: https://www.forbes.com/advisor/business/software/best-data-visualization-tools/), each having advantages and disadvantages.

C. Mare (✉)
Faculty of Economics and Business Administration, Babeş-Bolyai University, Cluj Napoca, Romania
e-mail: codruta.mare@econ.ubbcluj.ro

C. Sabău-Popa (ed.), *Artificial Intelligence in Finance, Accounting and Business Administration*, Contributions to Finance and Accounting,
https://doi.org/10.1007/978-3-032-22737-9_13

The most important disadvantage for Tableau is higher prices in comparison to competitors, while for Power BI that it does not have a Mac desktop version.

In respect to AI usage in data visualisation, Tableau has it implemented in Tableau Cloud as Tableau Agent or Tableau Pulse. But it can also be used with any GenAI tool now existing on the market, like Google AI (Gemini), Copilot (Microsoft) or ChatGPT (OpenAI). Power BI has it directly implemented in the desktop version. The focus of this part will be Tableau.

2 Getting Stated with Tableau

Tableau can connect to a wide range of data sources. A synthesis is presented in Fig. 1. After selecting the data sources, they are uploaded into the software, and you can start creating the relationships by drag and drop (Fig. 2). In order to be able to create the relationships, you need to have merging keys in the data sources.

There are several types of merging possibilities in Tableau:

1. Many to many (full join)
2. One-to-one (inner join)
3. Many to one (left join)
4. One to many (right join).

Tableau has 4 types of worksheets that you can find in the lower left corner of the working page (Fig. 3):

1. Data Source sheet—is the one in which the data sources are imported and relationships created.

Fig. 1 Data sources in Tableau

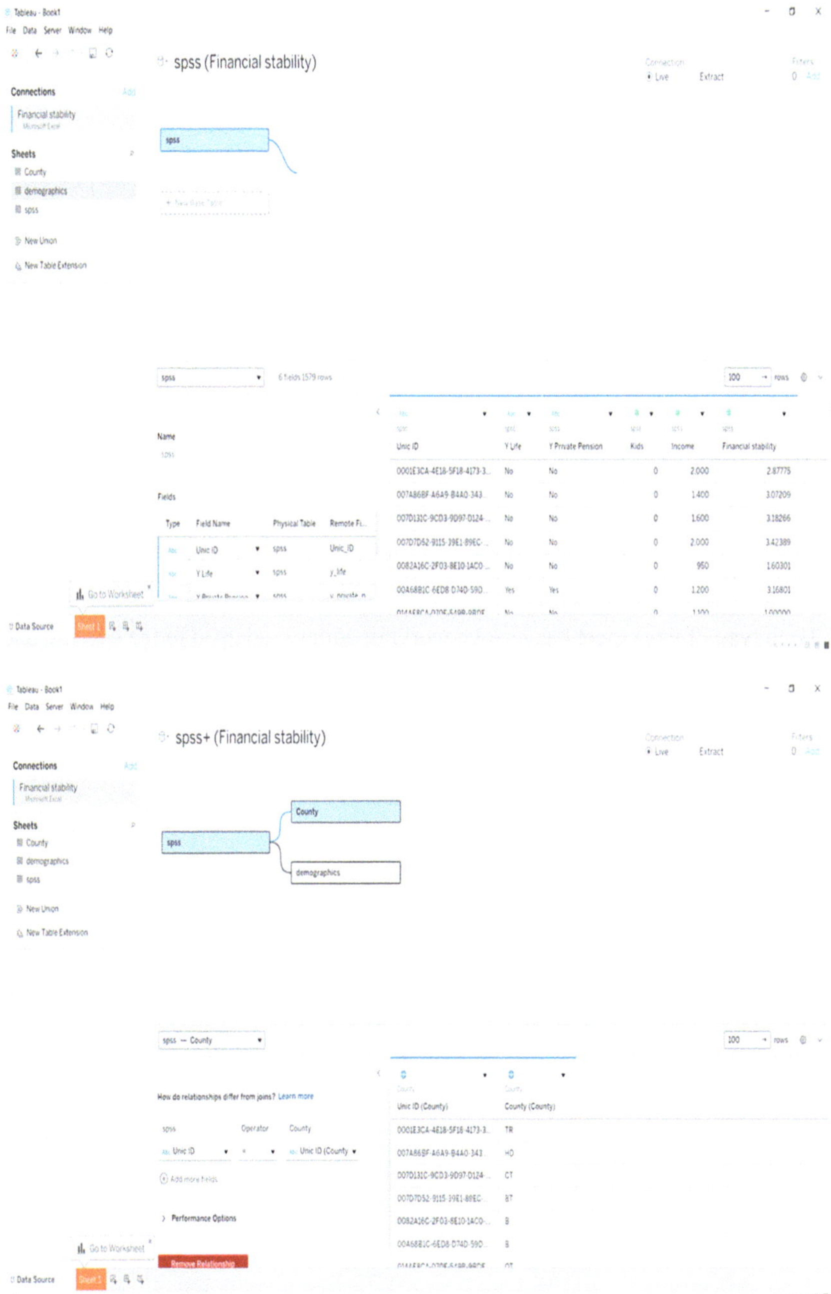

Fig. 2 Creating relationships in Tableau

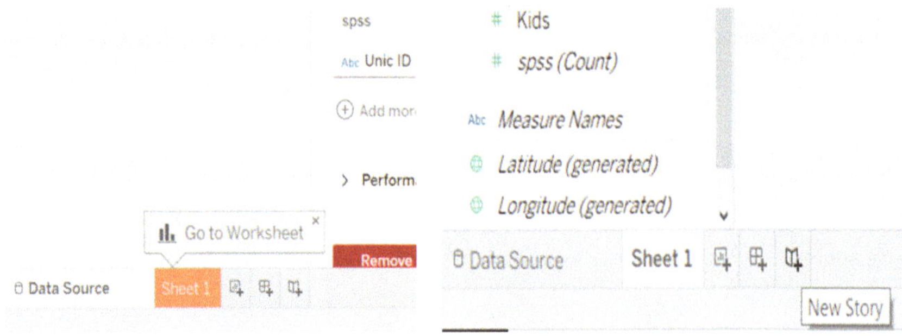

Fig. 3 Types of worksheets in Tableau

2. Worksheet—is the actual worksheet for each data visualisation object that you create.
3. Dashboard—is the worksheet in which dashboards are created from the visual objects in the worksheets.
4. Story—is the storyboard worksheet that allows the user to create data story (data storytelling) from visual objects and dashboards.

Each type of worksheet has its own working options, adapted to the specific data visualisation output that may be created in it.

In the Data Source worksheet, the user may work with variable options. The same may be done from the actual Worksheet, in the variable list in the left-most part of the sheet (Fig. 4). Before starting the data visualisation process, the user has to control that all variables have been correctly identified as a type.

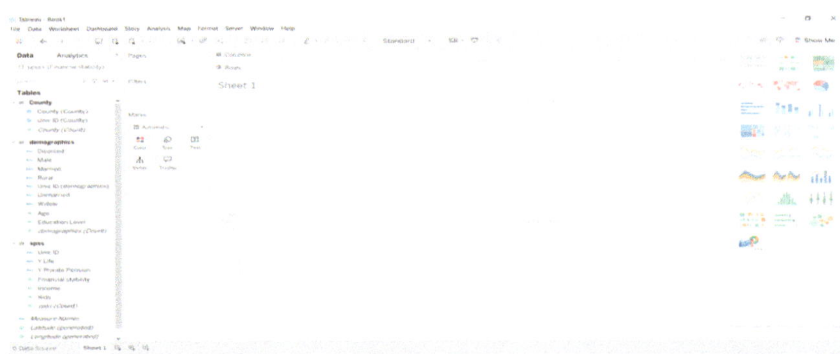

Fig. 4 Worksheet in Tableau

3 Data Visualisation in Tableau

There is a series of data visualisation options in Tableau, from very simple outputs like bar chart or pie chart (available under the Show Me button in the right upper corner of the worksheet). Tableau is known for being quite easy to use, as it works on the "drag and drop" principle, but very limited in terms of default data visualisation options, as you can see in Fig. 4. However, you can import/ add new data visualisation possibilities through the last available button under Show Me, which is launching the Viz Extension (namely, it connects you to Tableau Exchange—see Fig. 5). For example, the doughnut is not by default implemented in Tableau, and to build it, you need to construct 2 pie charts and format them in a specific manner. With the Viz Extension, you can import an already created doughnut, like in Fig. 6, by opening it.

Each such imported data visual comes with instructions on how to use it (Fig. 7).

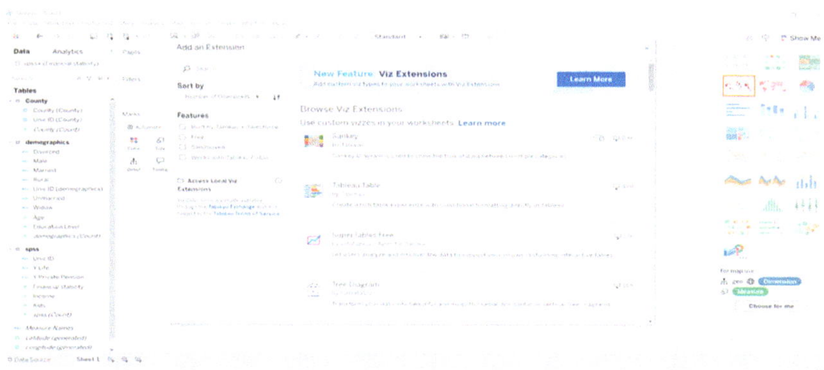

Fig. 5 Tableau Exchange—Viz Extension for visual objects import

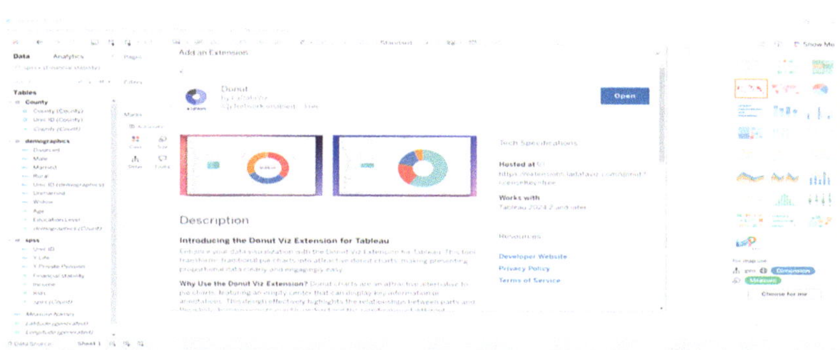

Fig. 6 Importing a doughnut chart from Viz Extension

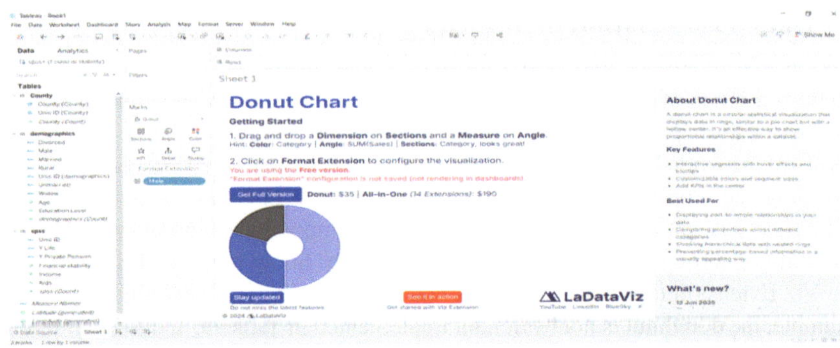

Fig. 7 Example of an imported doughnut

4 AI in Tableau

There are two ways in which Artificial Intelligence may be used in data visualisation with Tableau:

1. Using GenAI tools (Google AI, Copilot, ChatGPT, etc.)
2. Using the Tableau built-in AI tools like Tableau Agent and Tableau Pulse.

4.1 Using GenAI

Google AI, or AI Studio (Gemini), is one of the simplest AI tools that one can use for data visualisation. But the same happens with the other two very famous GenAI tools—Copilot and ChatGPT. All of them already have a series of data visualisation information implemented and, as known, they continuously learn. Additionally, the precision and complexity of the tasks they can suggest depend on the version to be used. Payable versions of GenAI tools are much more complex and may help in different ways, even in code writing for complex data analysis procedures. All these applications work on the chat approach (Fig. 8), but Google AI has the advantage of also working with streaming, even for the most public version.

In the Chat, you can input any question related to data visualisation in Tableau and GenAI software will try to answer. See, for example, Fig. 8 (with an example of all three GenAI tools) and the related reply in Box 1 or the second example in Box 2 (generated by Google AI). However, using the chat is rudimentary, as the user has to read the instructions given and apply them independently.

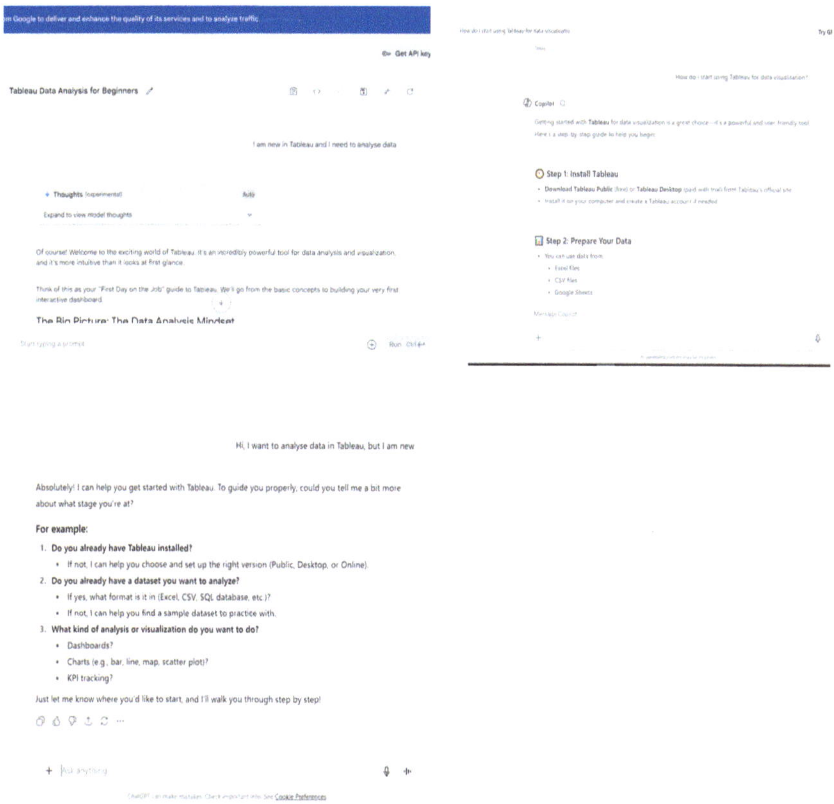

Fig. 8 Chat examples for Google AI (left), Copilot (middle), ChatGPT (right)

Box 1 Google AI studio response to the question "Hi, I am new to Tableau, can you help me?"

Of course! Welcome to the exciting world of Tableau. It's an incredibly powerful tool for data analysis and visualisation, and it's more intuitive than it looks at first glance.

Think of this as your "First Day on the Job" guide to Tableau. We'll go from the basic concepts to building your very first interactive dashboard.

The Big Picture: The Data Analysis Mindset

Before you even open Tableau, remember what you're trying to do. Data analysis is about asking questions and finding answers in your data. A typical workflow looks like this:

1. Ask a Question: What do you want to know? (e.g., "Which of our products are the most profitable?")
2. Gather & Prepare Data: Get the data you need to answer the question.
3. Explore & Visualise: This is where Tableau shines. You'll create charts and graphs to see patterns.

4. Find Insights: What does the visualisation tell you? (e.g., "Wow, Tables are actually losing us money!")
5. Communicate Findings: Share your insights with others, usually in a dashboard.

Step-by-Step Guide to Your First Tableau Analysis

For this guide, we'll use the Sample—Superstore dataset that comes built-in with every copy of Tableau. It's perfect for learning.

Step 1: Connect to Your Data

When you first open Tableau, you'll see a "Connect" pane on the left. This is where you tell Tableau where your data lives.

1. Under "To a File", click on "Microsoft Excel". A window will pop up. Navigate to your My Tableau Repository/Datasources folder. You will find the Sample—Superstore.xls file there. Select it and click Open.
2. Tableau will now show you the Data Source page. You'll see the sheets from the Excel file (Orders, People, Returns). Drag the Orders sheet onto the canvas area that says "Drag tables here".
3. You can now see a preview of your data. This is a good time to check if your columns have the right data types (e.g., numbers are numbers, dates are dates). Tableau is usually very good at guessing correctly.
4. Click on "Sheet 1" at the bottom of the window to go to the main workspace.

Step 2: Understand the Workspace (This is the most important part!)

The Tableau workspace can look intimidating, but it's simple once you understand its parts.

- Left Side (Data Pane): This is your list of available data fields, separated into two crucial categories:
  - Dimensions (Blue): These are qualitative, categorical data. Think of them as the "who, what, when, where." They are the things you slice your data by.

    Examples: Category, Region, Customer Name, Order Date.
  - Measures (Green): These are quantitative, numerical data. They are the things you can do math on (sum, average, etc.).

    Examples: Sales, Profit, Quantity.
- Top (Columns and Rows Shelves): This is where you build your chart.
  - Fields you drag to Columns will create columns in your table or the X-axis of your chart.
  - Fields you drag to Rows will create rows in your table or the Y-axis of your chart.
- Middle (The Canvas): This is where your visualisation appears.
- Marks Card: This is where you control the visual details of your chart—like colour, size, text labels, and chart type (bar, line, etc.).
- Filters Shelf: Drag fields here to filter the data shown in your view.

Step 3: Let's Start Answering Questions!

This is the fun part. We will ask a question and answer it by dragging and dropping.

Question 1: "What are our sales by product category?"

1. From the Data pane (left side), find the Category dimension. Drag it and drop it onto the Columns shelf.
2. Find the Sales measure. Drag it and drop it onto the Rows shelf.

Boom! Tableau automatically creates a bar chart showing the total sales for each product category. It automatically summed up the sales for you (notice it says SUM(Sales)).

- Let's enhance it: How profitable is each category? Drag the Profit measure onto the Colour button on the Marks card. Now your bars are colored based on profitability. You can instantly see that while Technology has high sales, Office Supplies are very profitable for their sales volume.

Step 4: Create a Second Visualisation (A Map!)

Let's create a new sheet. Click the "New Worksheet" icon at the bottom (it looks like a bar chart with a plus sign).

Question 2: "Which states are our most profitable?"

1. In the Data pane, find the State dimension. Notice the little globe icon next to it? Tableau knows this is geographic data.
2. Double-click State. Tableau will automatically create a map and place a dot on each state in your data.
3. Drag the Profit measure onto the Colour button on the Marks card.
4. Drag the Sales measure onto the Size button on the Marks card.

Instantly, you have a map! The colour shows you which states are profitable (blue/green) or unprofitable (orange/red), and the size of the circle shows the total sales volume. You can immediately see that Texas, despite having large sales, is a major problem area for profitability.

Step 5: Build an Interactive Dashboard

A dashboard is a collection of several visualisations on a single screen that allows a user to interact with the data.

1. Click the "New Dashboard" icon at the bottom (it looks like a grid).
2. On the left, you'll see the two sheets you just created (Sheet 1 and Sheet 2).
3. Drag Sheet 2 (your map) onto the dashboard canvas.
4. Drag Sheet 1 (your bar chart) onto the canvas, placing it below the map.
5. Now for the magic. Select the map view on your dashboard. In the top-right corner of that view, a few small icons will appear. Click the "Use as Filter" icon (it looks like a funnel).

Try it out! Click on a state on your map, like "California". Watch how the bar chart below automatically filters to show you the sales and profit for only California. Click on Texas. The bar chart updates again.

Congratulations! You have just built your first interactive dashboard.

Next Steps and Best Practices

1. Practice, Practice, Practice: The best way to learn is by doing. Try to answer other questions with the Superstore data.

- "Who are my top 10 customers by sales?" (Hint: Use a filter)
- "How have sales grown over the months?" (Hint: Drag Order Date to Columns)

2. Learn Calculated Fields: You can create your own measures and dimensions. For example, you could create a Profit Ratio field by creating a calculated field with the formula SUM([Profit]) / SUM([Sales]).
3. Explore "Show Me": In the top-right of the worksheet view, there's a "Show Me" panel. It shows you recommended chart types based on the fields you've selected. It's a great way to learn.
4. Use Online Resources:

- Tableau Public: A free version of Tableau and a gallery of amazing visualisations. It's the best place for inspiration.
- Tableau's Free Training Videos: Tableau provides excellent, short videos on every aspect of the tool.
- Community Forums & Blogs: If you have a question, someone has already asked it. The Tableau community is massive and very helpful.

You've taken the first step. Don't be afraid to experiment. Drag fields everywhere and see what happens. That's the best way to discover the power of Tableau. Good luck!!

Box 2 Response for "How can I build a scatter plot in Tableau Desktop?"
Excellent question! Building a scatter plot is a fundamental skill in Tableau and is perfect for understanding the relationship between two numerical variables.

Let's walk through it step-by-step, using the Sample—Superstore dataset again.

What is a Scatter Plot and Why Use It?

A scatter plot places dots on a graph based on two different numerical values (measures). Its primary purpose is to show you the relationship or correlation between them. For example:

- Does more spending on advertising lead to more sales? (Positive correlation)
- Do higher product discounts lead to lower profits? (Negative correlation)
- Is there any relationship between a customer's age and the quantity of items they buy? (No correlation)

Method 1: The Step-by-Step Build (The Best Way to Learn).

We'll answer the business question: "What is the relationship between the Sales and Profit for our products?"

Step 1: Place Your Measures

1. Open a new worksheet in your Sample—Superstore workbook.
2. Drag the Sales measure to the Columns shelf. (This will become our X-axis).
3. Drag the Profit measure to the Rows shelf. (This will become our Y-axis).

What you see now is the #1 point of confusion for new users: You'll only see one single dot on your chart.

Why? Because Tableau, by default, aggregates your measures. That single dot represents the SUM of ALL sales and the SUM of ALL profit across your entire dataset.

It's accurate, but not what we want. We need to tell Tableau what each individual dot should represent.

Step 2: Disaggregate the Data (The "Magic" Step)

We need to break that single point down into many points. Each point could be a customer, an order, or a product. Let's make each point represent a Product.

1. From the Data Pane on the left, find the Product Name dimension.
2. Drag Product Name and drop it directly onto the Detail button on the Marks Card.

Instantly, your single dot explodes into hundreds of dots! Each dot now represents an individual product, plotted according to its total Sales (on the x-axis) and total Profit (on the y-axis).

You have successfully created a scatter plot!

Method 2: The "Show Me" Shortcut

Tableau's "Show Me" panel is great for quickly creating standard charts.

1. Open a new worksheet.
2. In the Data Pane, select the two measures you want to compare. Hold down the Ctrl key (or Cmd on a Mac) and click on Sales and then on Profit.
3. In the top-right corner of the window, click on the "Show Me" panel.
4. Tableau will highlight the recommended chart types. Click on the scatter plot icon (the one with the dots).

You will get the exact same result as Step 1 above: a single dot. You still need to perform Step 2 (Disaggregate the Data) by dragging a dimension like Product Name or Order ID to the Detail mark to see all the individual points.

Enhancing Your Scatter Plot (Making it more insightful)

A basic scatter plot is good, but a great one tells a richer story. Let's add more layers of information.

Add Colour to Represent a Category

How can we see which product categories are profitable or not?

- Drag the Category dimension to the Colour button on the Marks Card.
  - Insight: Now you can clearly see clusters of products. For example, you might see that many "Technology" products (blue dots) are in the high-sales, high-profit quadrant, while many "Furniture" products (orange dots) have high sales but very low or even negative profit.

Add Size to Represent a Quantity

Which of these transactions had the highest discount?

- Drag the Discount measure to the Size button on the Marks Card.
  - Insight: Now the dots will have different sizes. The larger the dot, the higher the discount applied. You might immediately spot a pattern where the largest dots (highest discounts) are clustered in the negative profit area.

Add Trend Lines for Statistical Analysis

Tableau can automatically calculate a trend line to show the general correlation in your data.

1. Right-click anywhere in the empty space of your chart.
2. Go to Trend Lines > Show Trend Lines.
3. Tableau will draw a line through your data points. If you hover over the line, it will even give you the R-Squared and P-value, which are statistical measures of how strong the relationship is.

Your final, enhanced scatter plot now shows the Sales vs. Profit for every product, colored by its category, with the size of the dot representing the discount applied. This is a very data-rich and insightful visualisation.

A better and more efficient solution is the use of the Stream option in Google AI. This is a very nice option of Google AI and an important advantage with respect to the other options. ChatGPT also has a streaming option, but its usage is not as straightforward as in Google AI. This option allows the user to share the screen with Google AI (Gemini) and ask questions both orally and in writing (Fig. 9). By sharing the screen, the AI response is directly connected to the working session of the user.

Steps in using the Stream interface of Gemini:

1. Log into the Google AI Studio with your Gmail account
2. Select the Stream option in the left part of the screen
3. Open a blank Tableau file
4. Share the screen with the Tableau file through the AI Studio interface
5. Start asking questions—orally or in writing. Gemini will reply orally, coordinating you through the data visualisation process (Fig. 10).

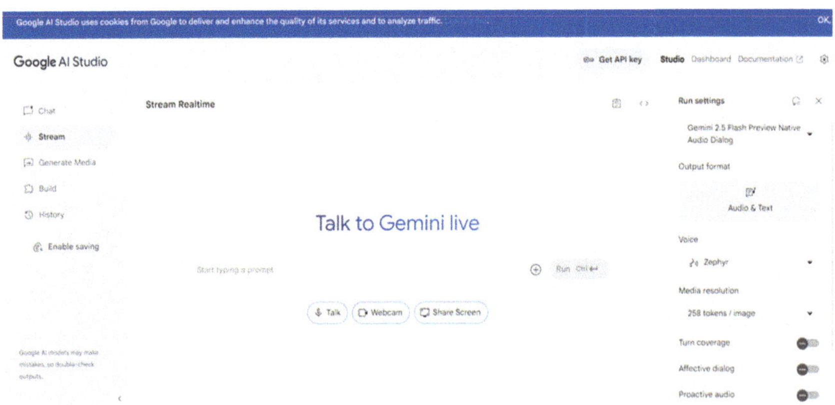

Fig. 9 The Stream interface in Google AI

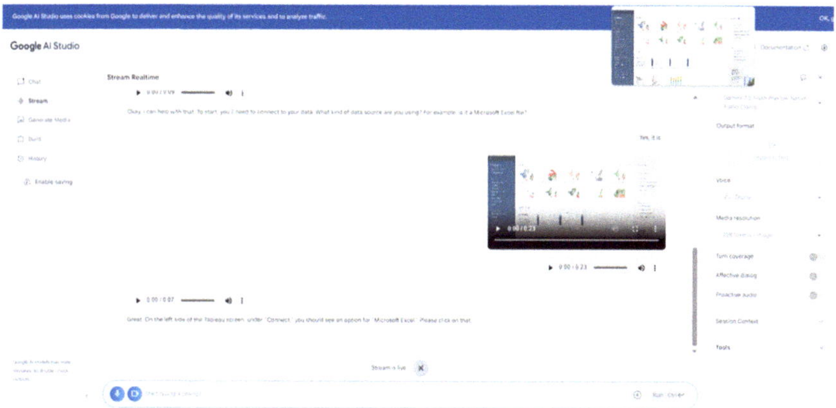

Fig. 10 Output example from Gemini

4.2 Using the Tableau Built-In AI Tools like Tableau Agent and Tableau Pulse

Tableau Agent and Tableau Pulse are two very nice AI features of Tableau. However, they have the disadvantage of not yet being implemented in the Desktop or Prep software, but only in Tableau Cloud, although you have the symbol in Tableau Desktop (Fig. 11). In order to run them under Tableau Desktop, you need to connect to your Tableau Cloud and turn it on from there, in the Settings menu, AI in Tableau section. **Tableau Agent** is the new name of Einstein Copilot, and it is specific to each sheet you have in Tableau. You can ask questions, or you can use the suggestions it gives you. For now, it only works in the written style, with no vocal options.

Tableau Agent may be used in the workbooks in Tableau Cloud. Once you have the data published on the cloud, you can create a new workbook on that set of data, and there you will have Tableau Agent active, like in Fig. 12. From this point on, you can start chatting with the Tableau Agent to run data visualisation and create new measures. However, an important drawback of Tableau Agent is that it does not run in Tableau Desktop with a regular Tableau Cloud license, but you need a Tableau +

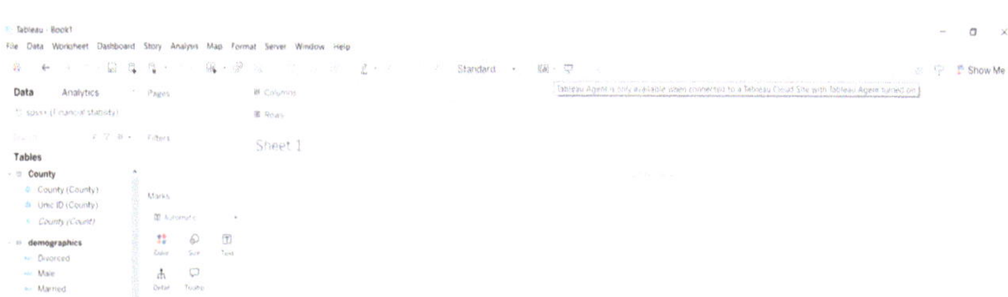

Fig. 11 Tableau Agent in Tableau Desktop

one, which, for the moment, is not available for the Tableau Academic part, as can also be seen in Fig. 12.

Tableau Pulse may be used in any version of the Tableau Cloud license, but it has to be first enabled, just as already stated. To do this, you go on the Settings of your Tableau Cloud account and scroll to the Tableau Pulse and AI in Tableau (Fig. 13). In the left part of the Tableau Cloud interface, you will find the Tableau Pulse option. When selecting it, you will be directed to the Tableau Pulse window to create a new metric or browse through the existing ones (Fig. 14). In order to do that, you need first to connect to a data source. After that, you can start constructing the measure, introducing the information that you see in Fig. 15. Once you start inputting the details in the new metrics, the output appears on the right part of the Tableau Pulse window. An output example is to be found in Fig. 16.

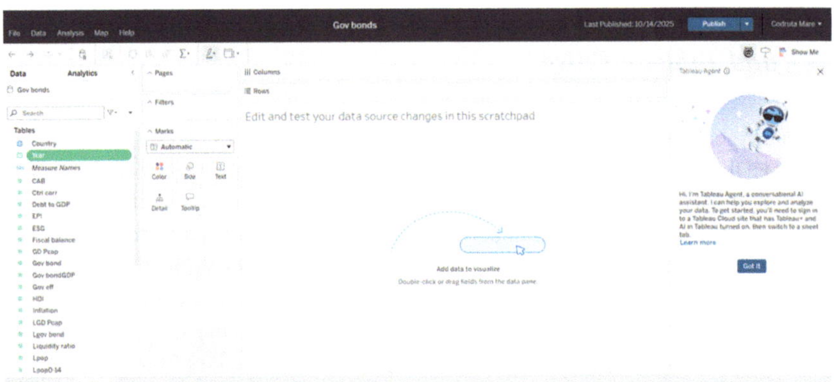

Fig. 12 Tableau Agent in Tableau Cloud

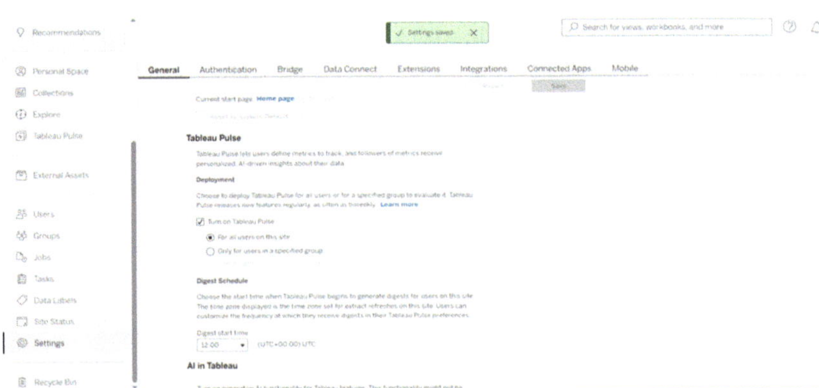

Fig. 13 Activating AI in Tableau in Tableau Cloud

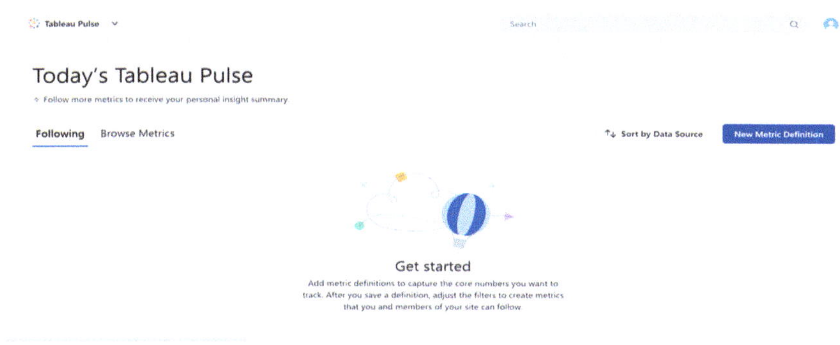

Fig. 14 Tableau Pulse interface

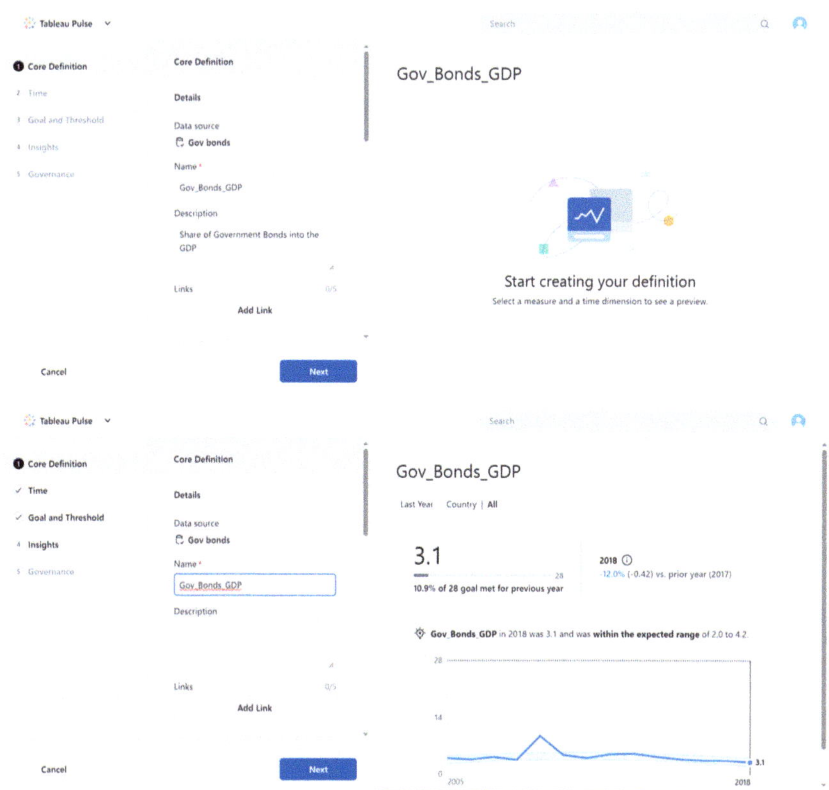

Fig. 15 Defining a new metrics in Tableau Pulse

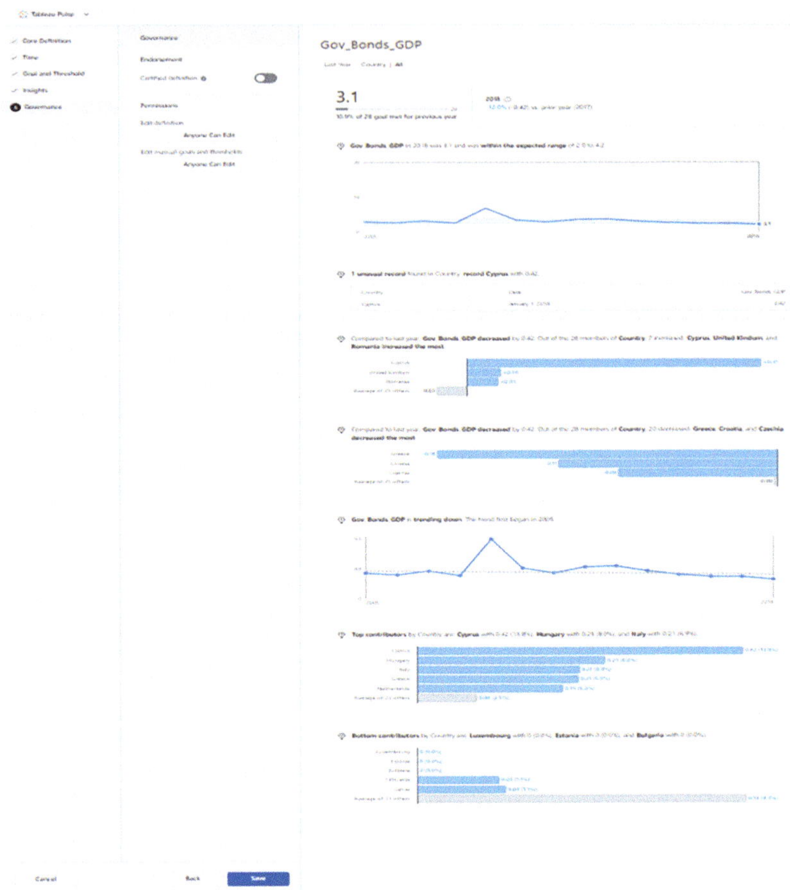

Fig. 16 Final output example in Tableau Pulse

AI in Data Analysis: A STATA Guide

Codruța Mare

Abstract STATA is one of the most famous data analysis software internationally. Its advantage is that it allows for both the menu and programming modes to be used. This chapter opens with a short introduction in STATA—importing the data, data management and transformations, descriptive data analysis. The simplest way to use AI with STATA is by using the Generative AI tools, following the same principles described in Chapter 13 for Data Visualization. Another possibility is to use R or Python related packages adapted for STATA. One option presented is the" chatgpt" command that runs ChatGPT under STATA interface. One important conclusion is that AI tools are quite rudimentary in STATA, but they may be compensated by the existing Generative AI ones.

1 Getting Stated with STATA

Unlike data visualisation applications, data analysis ones have far fewer importing options in terms of data sources (STATA included) (see Fig. 1).

STATA is working on Windows. The main window is the Results one, in which all the output is placed. Additionally, there are the Variables window, Command window, Review window, etc. Working with different windows is user-dependent, each window being dealt with from the Window menu.

STATA is working on a temporary approach—results are not saved for good, but only during the working session. At the end of the working session, the output is lost, unless independently saved using the Log → Begin options in the File menu. A.smcl file is created where all the output is saved during the working session. When a new session is started, the user can just Append the new results to the previous ones.

Importing Excel files is the first data source option. The importing process is given in Fig. 2. Once the dataset is imported, the Variables window is populated, along with

C. Mare (✉)
Faculty of Economics and Business Administration, Babeş-Bolyai University, Cluj Napoca, Romania
e-mail: codruta.mare@econ.ubbcluj.ro

C. Sabău-Popa (ed.), *Artificial Intelligence in Finance, Accounting and Business Administration*, Contributions to Finance and Accounting,
https://doi.org/10.1007/978-3-032-22737-9_14

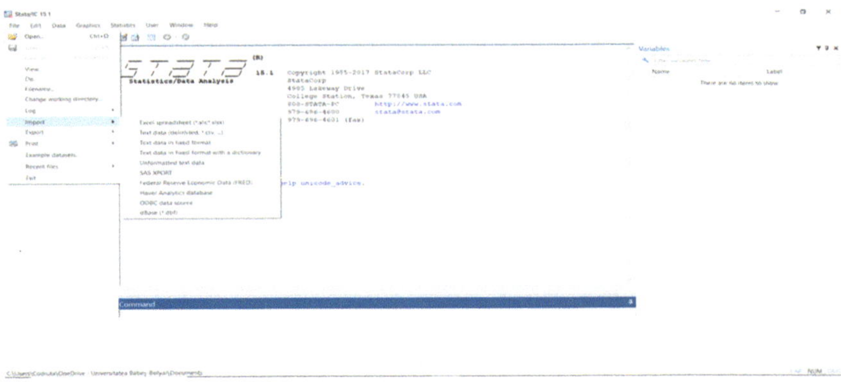

Fig. 1 STATA interface and importing options

the Properties one. From the latter, the user may change the name of the variable, the type, etc., but STATA is usually working in a safe mode, so the user has to Unlock the Properties in order to be able to alter them.

The Review window acts like a content list of all operations that were conducted in STATA. Regardless of whether they are applied from the menu or using the syntax part, the corresponding syntax is saved in the Review window. This enables the user to be able to re-apply the same operation by simply selecting it from there. When this is done, the syntax is automatically shown in the Command window and from there it can be rapidly applied.

The dataset may be viewed in the Data Editor window. This can be activated from the Window menu or from the Data menu → Data Editor option (Fig. 3).

Variables in STATA are presented in black if they are quantitative and in red if they are qualitative. In the importing process, STATA may wrongly categorise the

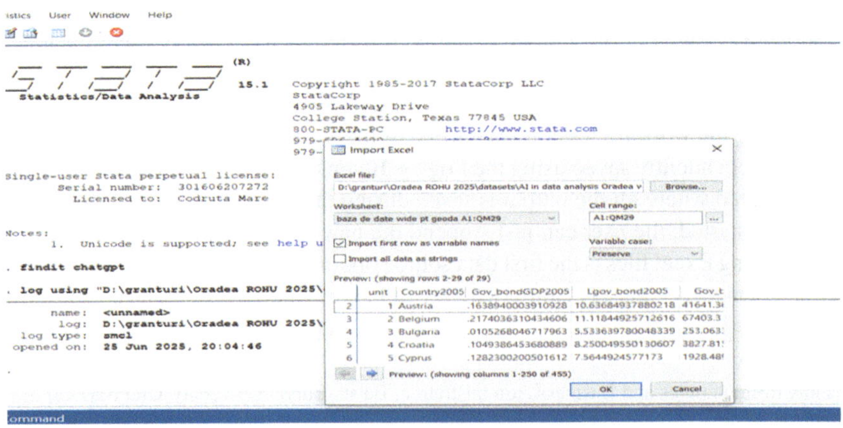

Fig. 2 Importing Excel files in STATA

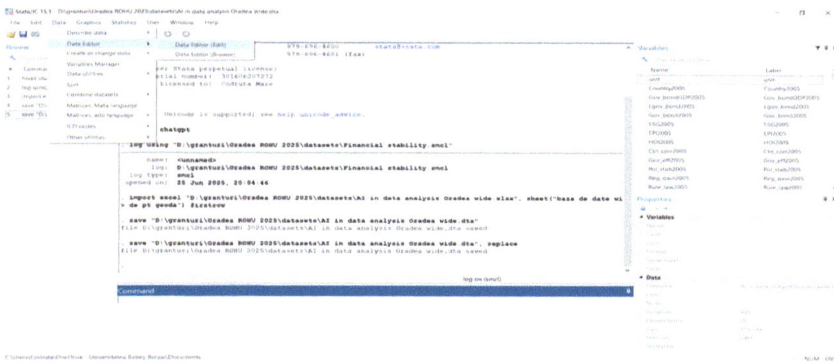

Fig. 3 Activating the Data Editor window

type of variable, such as in Fig. 4. To treat this, in the options related to each variable, the user may find the possibility to convert strings into numeric.

There are several possibilities related to variable properties that you can explore in STATA, including labelling or generating new variable. For example, if the user wants to transform a numerical variable using the natural logarithm, it can be done from the menu or by using the generate command: generate lGDP = ln (GDP).

A very important aspect related to getting data into STATA is the format of the dataset, when time is also involved. For example, panel data is longitudinal, both as an approach and as a way of arranging it. But many secondary data sources export the variables into the wide format (see Fig. 5). STATA offer the possibility to transform the data from wide to long and vice-versa (Fig. 6).

The STATA user may also create the own data visualisation and data analysis sequences using the Do-file options that create and manage the Do-file Editor. All commands that are put in the Do-file may be automatically run as a whole, or only parts of it. Additionally, using a "*" at the beginning of the line allows the user to

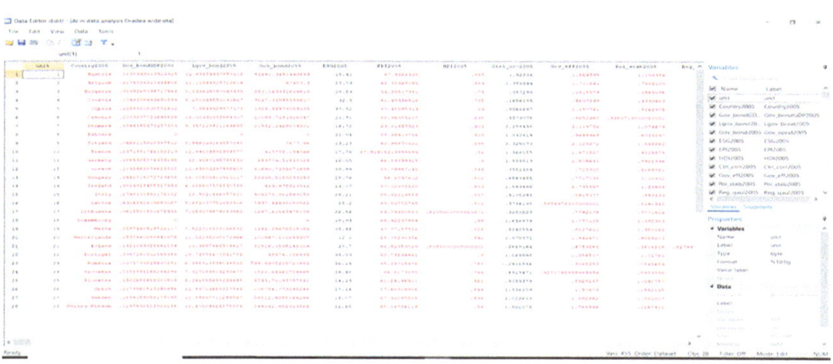

Fig. 4 Dataset in Data Editor window

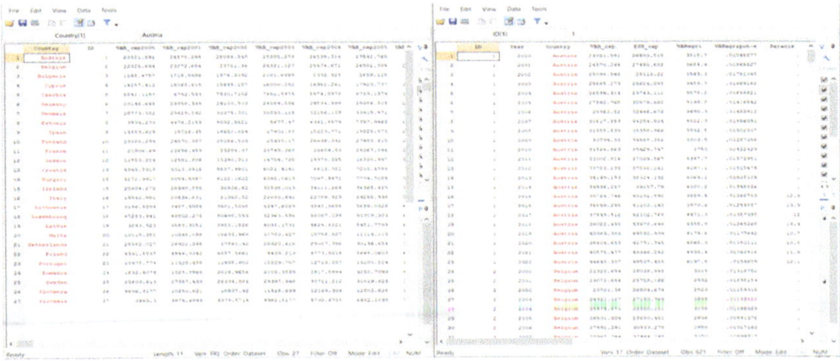

Fig. 5 Wide (left) vs. long (right) format

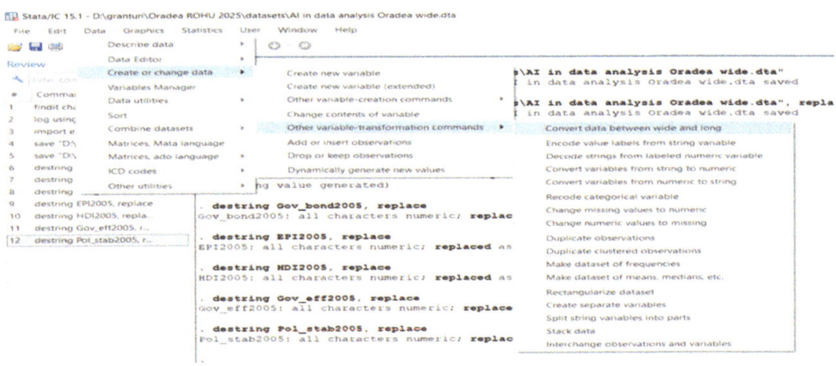

Fig. 6 Data transformation options from wide to long and vice-versa

introduce comments in the Do-file. The Do-file is also permanently saved, like the output one.

2 Data Analysis in STATA

STATA offers a wide range of data visualisation and data analysis methods. There is a dedicated Graphics menu. However, data visualisation is not as straightforward and of good quality as in dedicated data visualisation software like Tableau or Power BI. Additionally, the charts formatting options are also quite user-unfriendly.

In contrast to that, the Statistics menu is very complex, and STATA is one of the licensed data analysis software that updates very quickly in terms of newly developed methodologies. STATA provides users a wide range of methods and methodologies, from descriptive statistics to Machine Learning ones (Fig. 7).

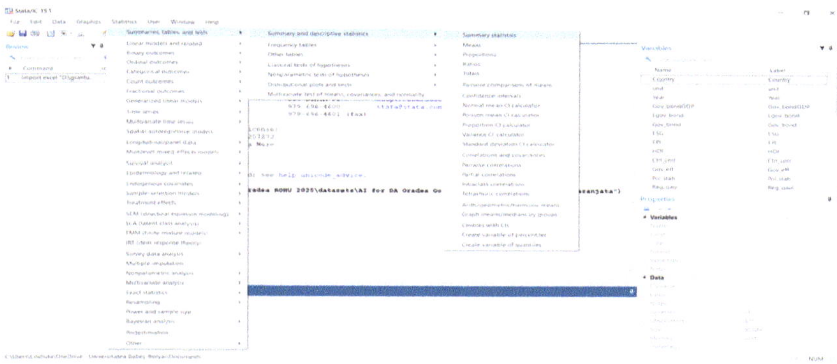

Fig. 7 Summary statistics in STATA

Besides the menu options, there are a series of newly developed and implemented data analysis methods that are available as add-ins and can be installed in different STATA versions. Such examples include the xtabond2 command for dynamic panel data or the ChatGPT one for the use of AI in STATA.

3 AI in STATA

STATA does not have yet standard AI built-in tools. However, there is a series of ML techniques implemented in STATA.

There are two ways in which AI tools, especially Generative AI (GenAI), can be used in STATA:

1. Using GenAI tools with STATA just as described for Tableau in section I.3.1. This means that Gemini or ChatGPT are able to coordinate the user into dealing with STATA tasks, both in the menu and the syntax form.
2. Using Python or R related packages adapted for STATA that ask for GenAI tools like ChatGPT to be used directly in STATA command mode.

For the first situation, all the procedures are similar to those described in the first part of this chapter, related to the data visualisation procedures. Just as an example, Fig. 8 and Box 1 present a more complex situation asked in Copilot (Microsoft) for a spatial panel of the EU countries.

Box 1 Reply of Copilot for the situation *"I am new with STATA and I want to regress Government Bonds on GDP, Economic Freedom and Regulatory Quality on a spatial panel of the EU countries for the 2010–2025 period. How can I do that?"*

Welcome to STATA, Codruta! You're working on a very interesting and advanced

Fig. 8 Reply of Copilot for the situation "*I am new with STATA and I want to regress Government Bonds on GDP, Economic Freedom and Regulatory Quality on a spatial panel of the EU countries for the 2010–2025 period. How can I do that?*"

topic—a **spatial panel regression** involving EU countries over time. Here's a step-by-step guide to help you get started:

1. **Prepare Your Data**

   You'll need a panel dataset with the following structure:

- **Time period**: 2010–2025
- **Units**: EU countries
- **Variables**:
  - Dependent: Government Bonds (e.g., yields or spreads)
  - Independent: GDP, Economic Freedom, Regulatory Quality
  - Spatial information: country adjacency or distance matrix

Make sure your dataset is **balanced** (each country has data for each year) and includes a **country identifier** and **year**.

2. **Set Up Panel Data in STATA**

   xtset country year
   This tells STATA you're working with panel data.

3. **Create a Spatial Weight Matrix**

You need a spatial weights matrix to capture the spatial relationships between countries. You can use:

- **Contiguity matrix** (countries sharing borders)
- **Distance matrix** (based on geographic centroids)

You can create this using the spmat command:
spmat create contiguity W using "eu_shapefile.dta", id(country)
Or if you have a distance matrix:
spmat import text W using "distance_matrix.txt", id(country)

4. **Declare Spatial Panel Settings**

   spxtset country year

5. **Run the Spatial Panel Regression**

   STATA supports spatial autoregressive models via spxtregress. For example:
   spxtregress bonds gdp econ*freedom reg*quality, dvarlag(W) errorlag(W) fe

- dvarlag(W) adds a spatial lag of the dependent variable.
- errorlag(W) adds spatial autocorrelation in the error term.
- fe specifies fixed effects (you can also use re for random effects).

6. **Interpret Results**

STATA will output coefficients, spatial parameters (like rho and lambda), and diagnostics. Pay attention to:

- Significance of spatial lags
- Fixed effects vs. random effects (use Hausman test if unsure)
- Model fit statistics

Optional: Diagnostics and Visualisation

You can run tests for spatial dependence and visualise residuals or fitted values using STATA's graphing tools.

Would you like help with:

- Finding or building the spatial weights matrix for EU countries?
- Getting sample STATA code tailored to your dataset?
- Understanding which spatial model (SAR, SEM, SDM) fits your research best?

Let me know how you'd like to proceed!

In respect to the second possibility, there is the work of Chuck Huber (https://blog.stata.com/2023/07/25/a-stata-command-to-run-chatgpt/) who created the command chatgpt that runs ChatGPT in STATA or the package under the same name created by Chuntao Li and Xueren Zhang (China Stata Club). When typing "findit chatgpt" into the Command window, the latter is to be found for installation in STATA (Fig. 9). You can install it if you have at least STATA 16.

Unfortunately, AI tools are still very rudimentary in STATA and, as the creators of the ChatGPT command state, this is still under construction, so in many cases it may lead to errors like "file c:/ado/plus/c/payload-gpt-4.txt not found". Due to the errors that appear in the running process, it is easier to use GenAI tools outside STATA.

Fig. 9 ChatGPT ado file in STATA

References

Kim NW, Ko HK, Myers G, Bach B (2024, September) Chatgpt in data visualization education: a student perspective. In: 2024 IEEE Symposium on visual languages and human-centric computing (VL/HCC). IEEE, pp 109–120

Koskula J (2024) Generative artificial intelligence in support of analytics: Copilot 365.

Lear BJ (2024) Using ChatGPT-4 to teach the design of data visualizations. J Chem Educ 101(7):2749–2756

Litmanen A (2025) Large language models in graphical data analytics: a comparative study of three popular chatbots

Mora R. (2023) AI in Stata programming: a study on productivity and limitations. In: Spanish Stata Conference 2023 (No. 08). Stata Users Group

Rovetta A, Mansournia MA (2024) Are ChatGPT and copilot reliable for health education on statistical testing? medRxiv, 2024-03

Supriyadi E, Pahmi S (2024) Exploring the potential of AI tools in education: a thematic analysis of Gemini. AI. Gema Wiralodra 15(3):915–923

Wang X, Wu Z, Huang W, Wei Y, Huang Z, Xu M, Chen W (2023) VIS+ AI: integrating visualization with artificial intelligence for efficient data analysis. Front Comp Sci 17(6):176709

Wienholt N (2025) Copilot and data science. In: GitHub copilot and AI coding tools in practice. Apress, Berkeley, CA. https://doi.org/10.1007/979-8-8688-1784-7_10. https://link.springer.com/chapter/10.1007/979-8-8688-1784-7_10

https://www.stata.com/meeting/spain23/slides/Spain23_Mora_AI.html

https://www.tableau.com/products/artificial-intelligence

https://cloud.google.com/use-cases/ai-data-analytics

https://learn.microsoft.com/en-us/fabric/data-engineering/copilot-notebooks-overview

Artificial Intelligence for Enhanced Integrated Reporting in Romania

Victoria Bogdan and Dorina-Nicoleta Popa

Abstract The authors examine the role of Artificial Intelligence (AI) in enhancing integrated reporting quality among Romanian listed companies, employing a hybrid methodology that combines quantitative scoring with qualitative thematic analysis. The research evaluates AI transparency in annual integrated reports and introduces an AI Maturity Index (AMI) to measure advancement across AI integration, transparency, and Fin-ESG data connectivity. Results reveal notable sectoral differences: IT companies stand out in AI strategy and deployment, while energy and healthcare companies lead in assurance and CSRD compliance. Nevertheless, reporting improvements remain constrained when AI initiatives lack KPIs, targets, or controls. The findings underscore the need for robust data governance, transparent reconciliation, and standardized digital alignment, highlighting the importance of comprehensive AI integration for organizational maturity.

1 Introduction

Corporate integrated reporting presents financial and non-financial, or ESG, information in a complex report delivered in a consistent, transparent, and reliable manner. The recent AI-driven technological revolution has demonstrated that Artificial Intelligence (AI) has the potential to enhance the integrated reporting process through automation, anomaly detection, reconciliations, and improved assurance. In other words, AI-based technologies can enhance the quality of reporting, increase transparency of information, and improve the credibility of financial communication with stakeholders. Globally, financial reporting has evolved into the broader concept of integrated reporting. This new reporting model, rather than being an accounting standard, focuses on how a company creates value over time (IIRC 2021). Integrated reporting represents a significant step forward for both financial and non-financial reporting, as it is more than just a simple aggregation of these separate

V. Bogdan (✉) · D.-N. Popa
Faculty of Economic Sciences, University of Oradea, Oradea, Romania
e-mail: vbogdan@uoradea.ro

C. Sabău-Popa (ed.), *Artificial Intelligence in Finance, Accounting and Business Administration*, Contributions to Finance and Accounting,
https://doi.org/10.1007/978-3-032-22737-9_15

reports (Vitolla et al. 2019). The quality of integrated reporting disclosures has a considerable impact on firm valuation, market perception, and investor confidence (Chia et al. 2025). By expanding its vision from a performance indicator to a holistic perspective, integrated reporting has adopted the concept of the "triple outcome," which encompasses economic, social, and environmental performance (Bogdan et al. 2023). This approach emphasises the interdependence between business objectives and their impact on society and the environment in which companies operate (Maama and Mkhize 2020).

Integrated reporting is a forward-looking, multi-stakeholder approach (Farooq et al. 2024) that explains a company's value creation strategy and interconnects financial and non-financial information, including significant past, present, and future data (De Villiers and Dimes 2023; Umair 2023). Integrated reporting enhances transparency, stakeholder engagement, and overall corporate accountability (Nazir 2023). Embedding AI in ESG financial reporting frameworks increases reporting efficiency, improves the reliability of scores, and ensures greater alignment with global standards (Badmus et al. 2025). In their study, the authors propose a multi-layered architecture for integrating artificial intelligence (AI) into ESG financial disclosure processes, which combines several essential components: AI-driven materiality mapping, automated quality assurance mechanisms, and investment-grade analytics. The approach also addresses governance challenges, highlighting the need for algorithmic transparency, auditability, and stakeholder confidence-building. Furthermore, it emphasises that AI integration must be accompanied by ethical safeguards and sector-specific calibration to ensure ESG data accurately reflects sustainable corporate behaviour. As the volume and complexity of data required for reporting continue to grow, and as demands for accuracy and auditability intensify, artificial intelligence (AI) emerges as a key catalyst. Globally, AI is viewed not only as an automation tool but also as a transformative force capable of revolutionising corporate reporting processes. According to the KPMG *AI in Financial Reporting and Audit* report (2023), the global financial reporting landscape is undergoing a profound transformation, transitioning from the digital age to the "AI era." This shift is expected to significantly alter conventional practices. The study shows that approximately 72% of organisations worldwide are either testing or have already integrated AI into their financial reporting processes, with this figure projected to reach 99% in the next three years (KPMG 2023). The use of modern smart technologies enables faster business decisions, leading to increased productivity and profitability (Sarker 2022). Integrating AI models into reporting also helps detect anomalies, anticipate ESG risks, and automate compliance verification (Majekodunmi 2025).

This paper aims to assess the extent to which Romanian companies disclose AI-related practices and how AI transparency contributes to improving financial and ESG data connectivity, as well as the accuracy of the integrated reporting process. A qualitative thematic content analysis was conducted on a small sample of integrated annual reports. For the in-depth qualitative examination of preparedness topics, a grading scale and specific evaluation criteria were used to assess the information identified in the reports. Three main topics were analysed: AI integration in annual reports, AI transparency and data connectivity, and the AI maturity index. The results indicate a very low degree of AI information integration in integrated reports and highlight an early stage of development and maturation regarding AI transparency and accountability in the reporting process for financial and ESG data connectivity. The research aims to find answers to the following questions:

RQ1. To what extent does transparency in AI technologies contribute to improving the connectivity between financial and ESG data in the integrated reporting process?
RQ2. Does assessing and monitoring the evolution of the AI maturity index within the integrated reporting process enhance the quality of annual reporting?

The agenda of this study contains a brief introduction, a literature review on the topic with a focus on the emerging knowledge in the last five years, followed by data collection and research methodology exposure, interpretation of results, discussion on the main findings and concluding remarks, gaps and recommendations, limits and potential further research paths.

2 Retrospective Analysis of the Literature

AI supports integrated reporting by correlating sustainability data with key financial performance indicators, enhancing the coherence of corporate narratives and contributing to long-term value creation and stakeholder impact (Mayegun and Nwanevu 2025). AI models can automate the classification of sustainability indicators, detect anomalies in reporting, and forecast future ESG trends, significantly accelerating the ESG reporting process and improving data accuracy. Several authors (Cojocaru et al. 2024; Aldabbous and Riyath 2024; Alshi 2025; Mustafa et al. 2025) explore the role of digital technologies, outlining both the benefits and challenges of implementing AI in integrated reporting. Advantages include the ability to process and analyse large volumes of data efficiently, facilitate ESG data integration, generate transparent and auditable reports, enhance data accuracy and reliability, provide real-time information for informed decision-making, mitigate risks, and identify emerging trends. Identified disadvantages encompass ethical and data privacy concerns, regulatory uncertainties, complexity and costs of implementation, the need for adequate technological understanding, algorithmic bias, the risk of greenwashing, and shifts in workforce dynamics. Other researchers focus on the adoption of AI technology in integrated reporting audit practices. Majekodunmi (2025) examines the integration of AI into ESG financial reporting systems, highlighting how machine learning, natural language processing, and intelligent automation can be leveraged to enhance the integrity and relevance of non-financial information. The study highlights how greater transparency and contextualization of non-financial indicators can optimise capital allocation and risk management. Critical ethics and governance issues discussed include model explainability, mitigation of algorithmic biases, and system auditability. Alhazmi et al. (2025) propose the use of AI-powered drones by non-Big 4 audit firms to reduce audit fees, enhance the quality of financial reports, and improve audit accuracy. Khan et al. (2024) examine the moderating effect of audit quality on the relationship between AI adoption experience and integrated reporting in firms listed on the Gulf Cooperation Council (GCC) stock exchange, which reflects the characteristics typical of emerging economies.

Deliu and Olariu (2024) emphasise the need for responsible integration of artificial intelligence and big data analytics, particularly in emerging markets. While the adoption of digital technologies prompts a revision of traditional practices and increases efficiency, progress can be hindered by regulatory limitations and gaps in digital literacy. Studies on Chinese companies listed on the stock exchange (Tian et al. 2025; Yu et al. 2025) reveal that the impact of AI on ESG performance is more significant in highly competitive, developed factor markets and asset-based industries, but diminishes under uncertain environmental conditions. Numerous studies (Antwi et al. 2024; Jejeniwa et al. 2024; Cucari et al. 2023; Kumar and Khanna 2023; Gutierrez-Bustamante and Espinosa-Leal 2022) investigate the impact of AI on integrated, financial, or sustainability reporting. These works focus on machine learning (ML), natural language processing (NLP), and robotic process automation (RPA) technologies that, by mimicking human cognitive functions, can solve complex problems and improve decision-making processes. Machine l*earning (ML)* involves training software to identify patterns and make predictions from data. In financial contexts, ML algorithms are highly effective for tasks such as financial forecasting, risk assessment, credit scoring, and fraud detection. They can process high-dimensional data and uncover complex, nonlinear relationships that traditional analytical methods may overlook (Jejeniwa et al. 2024). *Natural language processing (NLP)* enables computers to understand, interpret, and generate human language. This capability is crucial for automating the extraction and classification of key information from extensive textual sources, such as financial reports. NLP also facilitates market sentiment analysis from news articles and social media, and significantly aids in regulatory compliance by efficiently parsing large volumes of legal and policy documents (Gutierrez-Bustamante and Espinosa-Leal 2022). *Robotic process automation (RPA)* automates repetitive, rule-based tasks that have traditionally required human intervention. In financial reporting, RPA systems can efficiently collect and organise financial data, perform calculations, and verify information, thus streamlining many routine operations (Kumar and Khanna 2023). While each of these technologies offers unique benefits, their true potential is realised when they are used in combination (see Fig. 1).

RPA initiates the process by collecting and organising raw financial data from various sources, such as ERP systems, spreadsheets, and databases. Next, NLP analyses unstructured data, including market news and analyst reports, to provide qualitative context and sentiment analysis. ML then combines the structured data from RPA and qualitative insights from NLP to build comprehensive models. These models can predict future performance, identify potential risks, and detect fraudulent activity (Antwi et al. 2024). Predictive analytics leverages statistical modelling, data extraction algorithms, and machine learning to analyse historical data and forecast future trends and outcomes. In financial reporting, predictive analytics is used to forecast key financial indicators, helping organisations optimise resources and

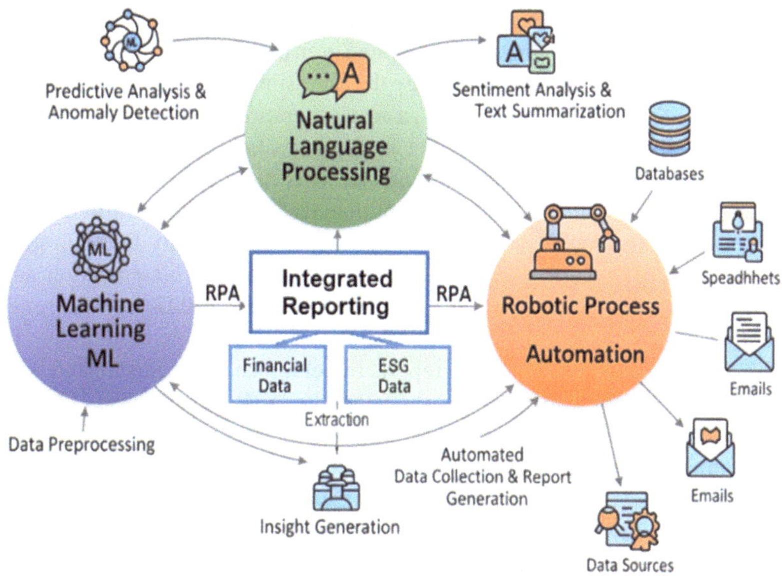

Fig. 1 AI technologies connected to integrated reporting. *Source* Generated by GoogleAI based on authors' requirements (September 15, 2025)

improve performance across various domains (Farayola et al. 2024). This integrated approach creates a robust reporting system that is not only efficient and accurate but also provides deeper insights than traditional manual processes. It automates routine tasks, interprets complex information, and predicts future developments, fundamentally transforming corporate reporting. Cui (2025) argues that integrating artificial intelligence (AI) into financial reporting represents a paradigm shift, optimising the efficiency, accuracy, and value of information for decision-makers. With the ability to process large volumes of data in real time and identify trends and anomalies, AI has the potential to revolutionise the analysis and interaction with financial data. Despite these considerable benefits, implementing AI presents ethical and operational challenges. The success of AI integration depends on inter-institutional collaboration and the development of ethical, effective regulatory frameworks. Striking a balance between innovation and compliance will enable AI to become a foundational tool for a more efficient, transparent, and resilient financial system.

Several recent studies highlight advances in improving integrated reporting through the use of various AI models. Hillebrand et al. (2023) propose *Sustain.AI*, a recommender system based on BERT (Bidirectional Encoder Representations from Transformers), which can associate relevant passages from sustainability reports with GRI standards, thereby facilitating rapid compliance analysis. Sustain.AI is an interactive, AI-based tool designed for the semi-automatic analysis of German sustainability reports. Ni et al. (2023) introduce *ChatReport*, a large language model (LLM) tool that incorporates expert knowledge to automate the assessment of sustainability reports in accordance with TCFD (Task Force for Climate-Related Financial Disclosures) recommendations. *ChatReport* is applied in an initial case to evaluate corporate climate risk disclosures, aiming to increase the accessibility of complex assessments. Huang et al. (2023) developed *FinBERT*, a next-generation extended language model tailored to the finance domain. FinBERT incorporates financial knowledge and can summarise contextual information in financial texts more effectively. The authors note that FinBERT's advantage is most pronounced when the training sample is small or when texts contain financial terminology not commonly found in general texts. FinBERT also outperforms other models in sentiment classification and in labelling discussions related to ESG issues. Angin et al. (2022) evaluate several machine learning models specialised in NLP-based text classification to determine their ability to classify sustainability reports by relevance to the Sustainable Development Goals (SDGs). Their findings show that the *RoBERTa* (Robustly Optimised BERT Pre-training Approach) model outperforms others, opening new opportunities for automatically processing large document collections to quickly assess SDG relevance. Anton et al. (2024) examine the implementation of AI-powered chatbots across more than 11,000 accounting and consulting firms in Romania between 2018 and 2022 within the framework of integrated reporting. Their analysis reveals that the adoption of such technologies is particularly prevalent among firms with strong financial performance. The study highlights the potential of chatbot integration to enhance financial reporting and management processes, particularly by improving reporting efficiency, ensuring greater accuracy, and increasing accessibility for a broader range of stakeholders. Boloş et al. (2024) explore the integration of AI in business, focusing on the usefulness of chatbots for analysing sustainability reports to enhance various aspects of business operations, including financial analysis, investor relations, and managerial decision-making. The study details the development and testing of chatbots based on ChatGPT technology, using the sustainability report of a company listed on the Romanian Stock Exchange as a case study. Dumitru et al. (2023) analyse the impact of evolving automation-based enterprise resource planning systems (ERPS) on sustainability accounting and reporting. Their research focuses on both the benefits and the challenges arising from the increased integration of robotic process automation and intelligent process automation solutions.

AI Transparency & Data Connectivity. Numerous authors (Domingo 2025; Lee et al. 2025; Chen 2024) propose various methodological frameworks and models for integrating ESG and AI. Domingo (2025) introduces a conceptual framework, the AI-ESG Integration Model, by mapping the dual impact of AI on ESG initiatives across three pillars: environmental (E), social (S), and governance (G). The environmental pillar addresses the high energy consumption of AI infrastructures and the optimisation of resource management. The social pillar examines AI's contribution to social responsibility, focusing on mitigating algorithmic biases, the transformative impact on the workforce, and the implementation of AI ethics. The governance pillar considers the implications of AI for compliance, transparency in AI-based decision-making processes, and the regulation of effective supervisory mechanisms. To promote responsible AI adoption, Domingo (2025) proposes concrete strategies, including the development of corporate AI transparency policies, the integration of

AI-based tools for fraud detection and enforcement, and the creation of AI ethics training programs for corporate leaders and decision-makers. Lee et al. (2025) introduce an ESG-AI analytical framework for investors, developed using data from 28 companies. This framework enables investors to assess the material impact, governance, and associated risks of artificial intelligence. It promotes digital sustainability and ethical AI investments by aligning AI innovation with ESG principles, thereby generating long-term benefits. The study makes a significant theoretical contribution by classifying AI-specific risks and governance challenges within the ESG framework. The paper emphasises that AI governance is a critical ESG concern beyond being merely a technical or ethical issue, and requires structured evaluation and disclosure mechanisms.

Chen (2024) proposes a hexa-dimensional framework for managing artificial intelligence in alignment with ESG principles to support sustainable and ethical development. The author examines the complex interactions between AI technologies and ESG criteria within the context of the twin transitions, sustainable and digital transformation. This analysis considers both opportunities and challenges. On the opportunity side, the study explores how AI can deliver ESG solutions, including: addressing critical environmental concerns, supporting the energy transition, reducing emissions, and improving waste management (E); optimising human resource management and personalising employee services (S); and enhancing governance and transparency by automating processes, detecting fraud, and ensuring compliance (G). The paper also identifies challenges that AI poses for ESG practices: the high energy consumption of large language models and e-waste issues (E); the risk of labour substitution, algorithmic discrimination, and the widening digital divide (S); and concerns related to data security, transparency, and the potential misuse of AI technology.

Alshi (2025) highlights that the convergence of AI and ESG presents significant opportunities for standardising and scaling reporting. AI can enhance transparency and comparability by uncovering data patterns, monitoring sustainability narratives, and supporting integrated reporting frameworks. However, risks related to lack of transparency and data confidentiality remain, particularly when ESG indicators lack clear definitions or verification mechanisms. Integrating AI with blockchain technology further strengthens transparency and comparability. By reducing human error and validating data against third-party sources, AI enhances accuracy and fosters stakeholder trust. Almadadha (2024) examines how blockchain's decentralised and tamper-resistant attributes can reinforce climate-related financial reporting, green financial instruments, and investment strategies. Using knowledge discovery in databases (KDD) methods, the research identifies patterns and rules that illustrate the fundamental role of blockchain in promoting transparency, accountability, and sustainability in the financial sector. Rerung et al. (2024) investigate the combined influence of innovations in financial technology (Fintech), ESG reporting, and blockchain technology on financial transparency and accountability through a qualitative literature review. Their findings suggest that the synergistic integration of

Fintech, ESG reporting, and blockchain technology can significantly optimise transparency and financial accountability. However, this transformation depends on overcoming systemic challenges, including regulatory barriers, the need for robust technological infrastructure, and concerns about data privacy and security. Rane et al. (2024) argue that advances in artificial intelligence offer increasing potential to enhance corporate sustainability. To fully realise these benefits, companies must adopt responsible and ethical AI implementation, ensuring transparency in decision-making, data protection, and management of algorithmic bias. By adopting an ethical and responsible approach, organisations can maximise the positive impact of AI while minimising potential negative consequences.

International examples demonstrate how artificial intelligence can fundamentally transform the integrated reporting process, extending from simple data automation to predictive analytics and more informed strategic decision-making. By adopting AI, companies can enhance the quality and transparency of their reporting, responding more effectively to the demands of investors, regulators, and civil society. Gosh (2025) examines how companies can successfully integrate AI technologies, emphasising the importance of organisational preparedness and effective change management for strategic and sustainable adoption. The success of AI integration depends on embracing a human-centric approach, where AI acts as a strategic partner that augments rather than replaces human cognitive capabilities. Gosh argues that successful implementation requires ongoing learning and the establishment of robust governance frameworks. A crucial aspect is maintaining a balance between technological advancement and ethical considerations, ensuring continuous human oversight. Companies that adopt adaptive AI models can better anticipate market disruptions, mitigate uncertainties, and achieve long-term growth, thereby gaining a sustainable competitive advantage in the digital economy. However, for these best practices to be widely implemented, it is essential to invest in technology, provide comprehensive training, and adapt regulatory frameworks accordingly. As Romania begins its journey in this field, it can learn from international models, tailoring them to local conditions to build a modern, efficient, and credible reporting system.

3 Data and Methodology

The research conducted in this study employs a hybrid methodology. In the first stage, the selection of listed companies focused on identifying a report that evaluates the transparency of disclosed information. The VEKTOR by ARIR tool was chosen for this purpose; it assesses transparency, proactivity, communication quality, and compliance with corporate governance standards (Romanian Investor Relations Association 2025). The VEKTOR by ARIR indicator measures the level of transparency in investor communications among listed companies using a set of objective criteria established through consultation with stakeholders in the Romanian capital market, including institutional investors, individual investors, analysts, and representatives of the Bucharest Stock Exchange (BVB) (Romanian Investor Relations

Association 2025). Within the VEKTOR by ARIR 2024 evaluation methodology, the criteria are grouped into four sections: A. Financial reporting; B. ESG; C. Corporate governance; and D. Other instruments. For this study, companies that achieved a maximum score of 100 for investor communication in the VEKTOR by ARIR 2024 assessment and included information on the use of artificial intelligence (AI) in their 2024 integrated annual reports were selected. At this stage, the sample consisted of 18 companies listed on the BVB.

To conduct a qualitative content analysis of integrated annual reports from the perspective of AI integration, the reports originally downloaded in PDF format were converted to CSV files and analysed using NVivo software. Information related to AI was extracted and examined in terms of both the extent of the data reported and the themes incorporated into the communication. This information was then coded to facilitate qualitative analysis. The qualitative textual analysis revealed that the overall quality of integrated corporate reporting on AI transparency is generally very low or even non-existent. Only a few companies explicitly mention artificial intelligence, and even then, the disclosures are sparse and lack comprehensive transparency regarding AI-specific practices, ethics, or governance. This suggests that AI transparency remains an emerging or underdeveloped area in these companies' integrated annual reports, highlighting the need for more structured frameworks and more detailed information, in line with evolving expectations for responsible AI use, reporting, and communication. Based on the textual analysis and the extracted AI disclosures, the selected companies were divided into three categories: (1) companies with moderate transparency but lacking disclosure of specific aspects; (2) companies aspiring to transparency, although it is not yet operational; and (3) most companies, which limit their communication to topics such as digitalization, automation, and cybersecurity. In the first category, only one company acknowledged the role of artificial intelligence in its business in its integrated annual report, yet provided little transparency regarding ethics, specific applications, or governance. The second category of companies offered very low transparency, referring primarily to industry trends rather than their own practices. The third category, while demonstrating good practices in general digital responsibility, provided no quality disclosure regarding specific AI transparency, as distinct aspects of artificial intelligence were not addressed. Following this analysis of the eighteen integrated annual reports, eight companies were removed from the sample due to insufficient information on AI transparency, which did not support further in-depth analysis.

In the next stage, a hybrid methodology was employed for the in-depth examination. First, quantitative scoring of disclosures was conducted on a 0–3 scale across multiple criteria, followed by qualitative extraction of relevant textual fragments. The analysis focused on two main topics. The first was *AI integration in corporate reporting*, which included assessing AI strategy, use cases, governance, risks, data governance, ethics, KPIs, targets, and investments, as well as workforce impact. The second topic was *AI transparency and data connectivity*, with an emphasis on AI transparency, financial–ESG data connectivity, data lineage, reconciliation, assurance, consistency, and restatements. Additionally, it covered data quality KPIs, standards alignment, AI for data quality, and traceability and access. In the final stage of the research, an *AI maturity index* was developed to measure the extent to which companies integrate Artificial Intelligence (AI) into their integrated reporting practices. This index combines two complementary dimensions: AI integration in corporate integrated reporting and AI transparency and data connectivity. The data sources consisted of the ten 2024 annual and integrated reports of Romanian listed companies. Data preprocessing involved extracting and normalising textual data. Analysis was performed in Python 3.11 using keyword-based regular expression mining and scoring algorithms, with visualisations generated using Matplotlib 3. Thematic qualitative analysis was carried out using NVivo 15. Each company received both an integration score and a connectivity score. The AI maturity index was calculated as the arithmetic mean of these two dimensions, normalised to a 0–100 scale.

4 Results and Discussion

4.1 Integration of AI issues in the Annual Reports

The data preprocessing analysis involved converting the CSV files into a unified text format, eliminating coding errors, and normalising the written content. Key phrases and words were then extracted based on predefined citations, followed by the application of a scoring algorithm (0 = absence of information; 1 = general mentions; 2 = details about specific processes and terms; 3 = presence of quantifications such as KPIs, percentage values, precise terms, or references to formal policies). Qualitative thematic content analysis involved extracting text fragments that mentioned AI integration and use, identifying examples of best practices, and highlighting areas where information was lacking. Ten criteria were used to score the AI-related text fragments: AI strategy, use cases, AI governance, risk, data governance/quality, ethics and compliance, KPIs, targets and deadlines, investments and resources, and workforce impact. The following weights were assigned to the qualitative assessment criteria for the AI text fragments: risk (0.20), KPIs (0.20), governance (0.15), ethics (0.10), data quality (0.10), strategy (0.06), targets (0.06), investments (0.05), resources used (0.05), and workforce (0.03). The final AI integration score was calculated using the formula: $\Sigma\ w_i \times (score_i/3) \times 100$ (range: 0–100). The resulting weighted score hierarchy reveals clear differences in maturity among companies (Fig. 2).

Scores increase when companies have (i) documented policies, defined roles, and risk management processes; (ii) measurable KPIs and time-bound targets; and (iii) explicit training budgets or programs. The integration AI analysis, shown in Fig. 3, highlights companies with stronger strategies, robust risk management, and quantified KPIs. In contrast, lower-ranked firms provide only generic mentions of AI.

The increased weighting on risk and KPIs enhances the ability to distinguish between companies that have formalised controls and explicitly measure the benefits of AI. Governance remains a cornerstone, supporting the consistency and auditability

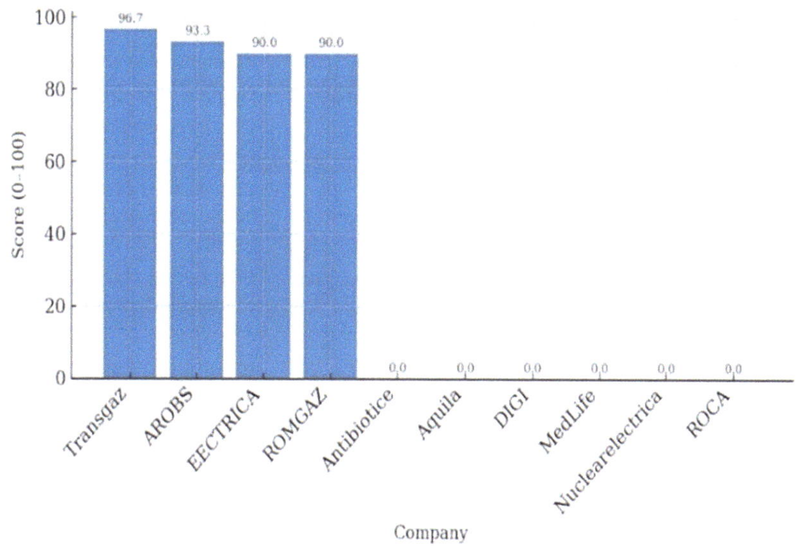

Fig. 2 Weighted AI Integration Score by company (0–100). *Source* Authors' projection

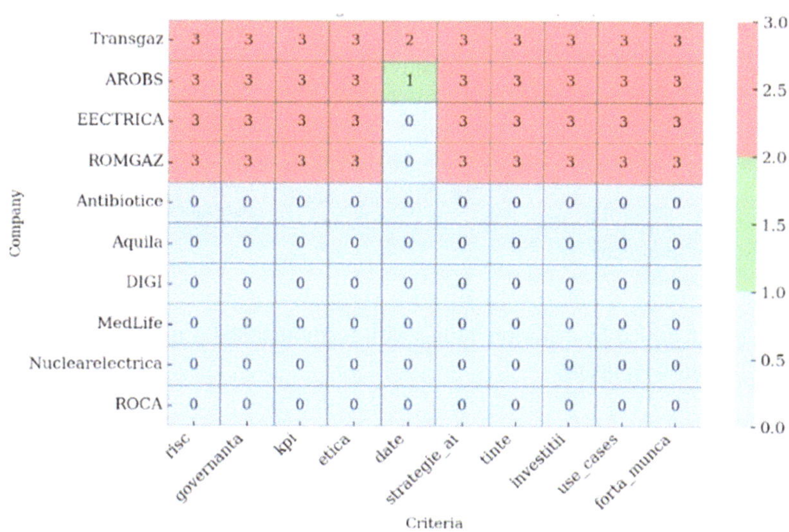

Fig. 3 AI integration matrix. *Source* Authors' projection

of reporting. The results show that simply listing initiatives (use cases) without accompanying KPIs, targets, and controls has limited impact on reporting quality. Recurring areas for improvement include data governance (ownership, lineage, policies), applied ethical assessments (impact assessments), and the systematic integration of indicators into non-financial performance sections. Table 1 summarises the

Table 1 The main AI integration gaps and recommended actions

Criterion	Gaps	Recommended actions
AI strategy	General mentions, without phased plans	Publishing an "*AI Roadmap*" with short, medium, long-term goals
Use cases	Enumerations without implementation details or results	Documenting case studies with performance and impact metrics
AI governance	AI policies rarely formalised; unclear roles	Establishing a board-level AI committee; appointing a Chief AI Officer
AI risks management	Vaguely mentioned risks, lack of methodology	Introducing AI risk assessment processes and annual reporting
Governance and data quality	Missing references to data catalogue, lineage, data owners	Implementing data governance policies and reporting on them
Ethics and compliance	General ethical statements, without oversight procedures	Publication of an "*AI Ethics Charter*" and ethical impact assessments
KPI and methodology	Rare KPIs, without definitions or core values	Defining and publishing specific KPIs per use case
Targets and deadlines	Vague deadlines, no clear milestones	Setting SMART goals with precise deadlines
Investments and resources	AI budgets poorly detailed; trainings only mentioned	Transparent budget allocations and training programs with indicators
Work force	Impact on jobs only generically described	Publishing upskilling/reskilling programs with clear indicators

Source Authors' projection

main gaps identified by criterion, along with recommended actions to improve the quality of future reporting.

4.2 AI Transparency and Data Connectivity

The qualitative analysis assesses how AI transparency facilitates the integration of financial and ESG data, thereby improving reporting accuracy. Ten criteria were used in the evaluation, each rated on a scale from 0 to 3 (0 = absence, 1 = generic presence, 2 = existence of details or processes, 3 = quantification or standardisation). Criteria were weighted according to their importance (totalling 0–100), with a focus on connectivity, reconciliation, assurance, and data quality KPIs. The evaluation criteria include: AI transparency (model description, boundaries, explainability);

Fin–ESG connectivity (cross-references, mappings, bridges); data lineage and governance (catalogues, data owners, standards); ESG–financial reconciliation (bridges, roll-forwards, IFRS/capex/opex links); accuracy and assurance (validations, audit/assurance); consistency and reviews (baselines, corrections, errata); data quality KPIs (accuracy, completeness, timeliness); alignment with standards (CSRD/ESRS, EU Taxonomy, XBRL/iXBRL/ESEF); use of AI for data quality (anomalies, automated reconciliation); and traceability and access to information (tables/annexes, machine-readable formats, APIs). The assigned weights (0–100) are as follows: connectivity = 0.18; reconciliation = 0.18; accuracy and assurance = 0.15; quality KPI = 0.12; lineage and governance = 0.10; traceability = 0.10; alignment to standards = 0.07; AI for data quality = 0.05; consistency = 0.03; and AI transparency = 0.02. The connectivity score was calculated using the formula: $\Sigma\ w_i \times (score_i/3) \times 100$. High scores (>70) indicate the use of explicit AI strategies, reconciliations, assurance, and alignment with standards. Medium scores (40–70) indicate partial maturity, where AI is mentioned but lacks measurable KPIs or assurance. Low scores (<40) correspond to generic mentions without structured integration.

The ranking reveals significant variations in Fin–ESG connectivity and accuracy assurance. Leading companies report reconciliation bridges between ESG indicators and financial impact, implement robust data governance processes, and include data quality KPIs (Fig. 4). The connectivity evaluation emphasises reconciliation between ESG and financial data, assurance processes, alignment with standards (CSRD, ESRS, XBRL), and the use of machine-readable formats. Top performers provide detailed reconciliations and assurance statements, while others lack explicit connections between these elements.

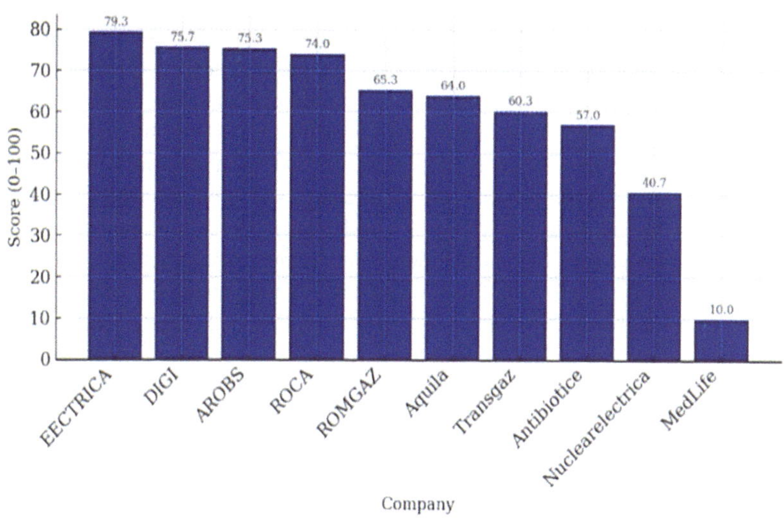

Fig. 4 Weighted connectivity and accuracy score by company (0–100). *Source* Authors' projection

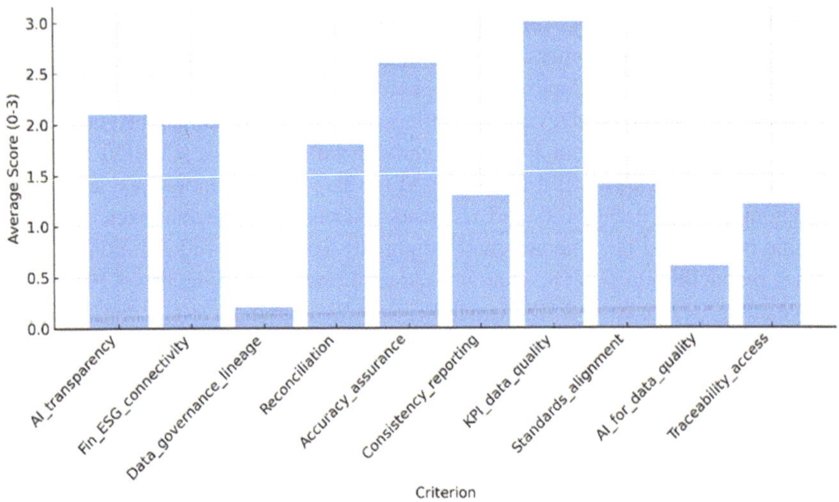

Fig. 5 Average connectivity score on criterion. *Source* Authors' projection

AI transparency can enhance data connectivity by documenting models, boundaries, and reconciliation processes. However, its impact on accuracy depends critically on robust data governance, assurance mechanisms, and quality KPIs (Fig. 5). Integrating tagging standards (XBRL/iXBRL) and publishing machine-readable tables reduces transcription errors and enables automated checks, such as consistency rules.

The analysis reveals that Fin–ESG connectivity and reporting accuracy are enhanced by explicit reconciliation processes, data governance with clear lineage and ownership, quality and assurance KPIs, machine-readable formats, and AI transparency that addresses limitations and provides explanations. Opportunities to improve data connectivity reporting through greater AI transparency include incorporating bridge diagrams between ESG and financial elements, publishing XBRL or CSV tables, and defining data quality indicators with annual targets. Additionally, placing greater emphasis on assurance underscores the importance of audit and verification processes for ESG and AI indicators, thereby strengthening investor and stakeholder trust. Increasing the focus on alignment with standards (CSRD/ESRS/XBRL) further demonstrates that compliance with European-recognised reporting frameworks and the use of machine-readable formats are essential for comparability and accuracy. In conclusion, integrating AI into corporate reporting delivers additional value when combined with strong connectivity between financial and ESG data and robust assurance mechanisms. Future reports should prioritise transparent reconciliation, alignment with digital standards (XBRL/iXBRL), and the definition of clear data quality KPIs. Together, these elements significantly enhance the accuracy and credibility of corporate integrated reporting.

4.3 AI Maturity Index (AMI)

The AI Maturity Index (AMI) combines Integration and Connectivity scores to provide a comprehensive assessment. The AMI (ranging from 0 to 100) is based on two complementary dimensions: AI integration in integrated reporting, which includes strategy, governance, risk, KPIs, and workforce impact, and AI transparency and data connectivity, which covers reconciliation, data lineage, assurance, standards alignment, and machine-readable formats. Each criterion within these dimensions is rated on a 0–3 scale and aggregated using weighted averages that reflect academic and regulatory priorities. Final weights place particular emphasis on assurance (0.20) and standards compliance (0.10), highlighting their essential roles in building trust and ensuring comparability. The AMI is calculated as the average of the two-dimension scores, standardised to a 0–100 scale. Companies excelling in both dimensions are expected to demonstrate more advanced AI-enabled reporting practices. Sectoral patterns are evident: IT firms outperform in integration, while energy companies are stronger in assurance and standards alignment. The analysis of AMI results reveals sectoral variation, IT and technology-driven firms achieve higher scores due to explicit AI strategies and detailed case studies, whereas energy and healthcare companies excel in standards alignment but lag in AI governance (Fig. 6). The index highlights a gap between adopting AI as a narrative and fully integrating AI into data assurance and reconciliation.

The AMI findings indicate that, although companies are increasingly mentioning AI in their reports, concrete applications for data quality, ESG–financial reconciliation, and assurance remain limited. AI is more frequently presented as a strategic

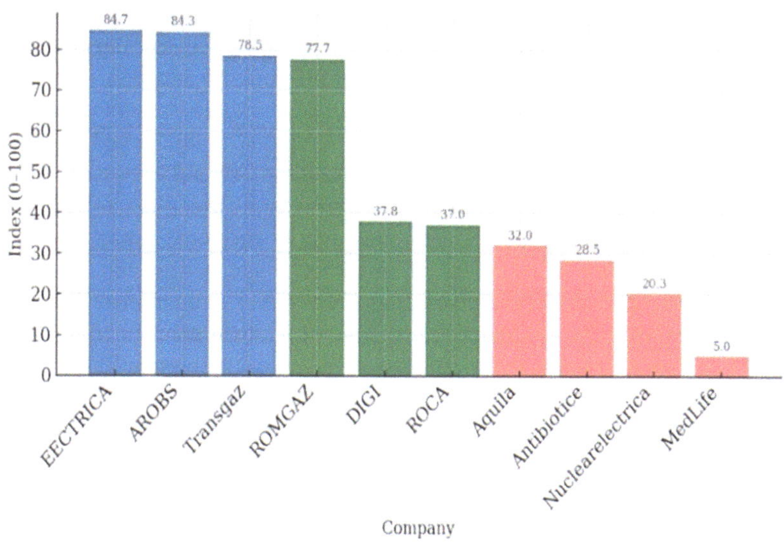

Fig. 6 AI maturity index (AMI). *Source* Authors' projection

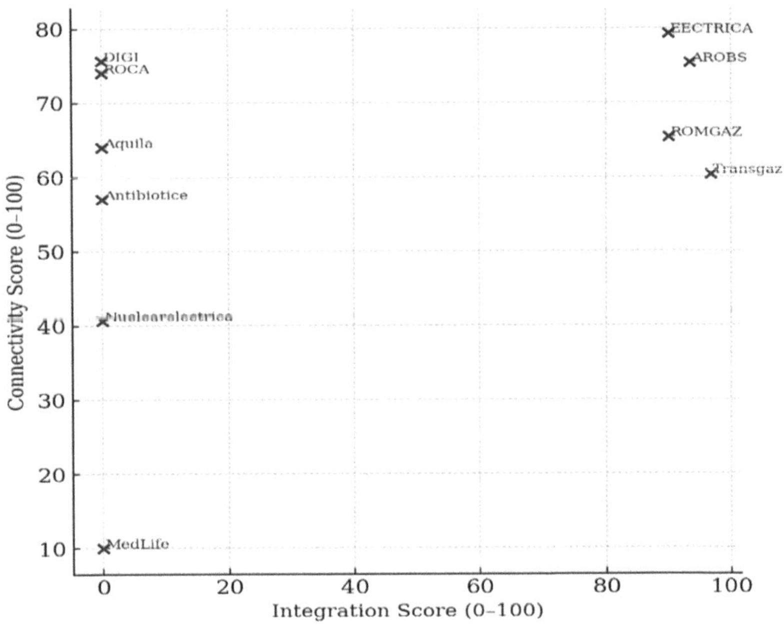

Fig. 7 Scatterplot of AI integration *vs.* AI transparency and connectivity. *Source* Authors' projection

innovation rather than as a governance tool. The scatterplot analysis reveals that companies may excel in AI integration without achieving strong transparency and connectivity, and vice versa (Fig. 7). The AMI analysis shows that balanced maturity requires progress in both dimensions; an imbalance between integration and connectivity reflects only partial maturity rather than holistic adoption.

Best practices observed include explicit reconciliations, assurance of non-financial KPIs, and XBRL-tagged disclosures. A key gap is the limited application of AI for data quality assurance and anomaly detection. Sectoral analysis shows that IT firms are early adopters of AI strategies, energy firms excel in standards alignment, and healthcare and pharmaceutical firms report workforce impacts. The main gaps identified are limited disclosure of data lineage and stewardship, insufficient use of AI for anomaly detection and assurance, and a lack of quantified KPIs linked to AI-enabled processes. To enhance the quality of AI integration and transparency in reporting, it is recommended to establish AI governance committees, publish AI ethics charters, align with ESRS datapoints and XBRL tagging, and adopt AI-based tools for assurance and reconciliation. In conclusion, the AMI reveals that Romanian companies are at an early to intermediate stage of integrating AI into their annual reporting. Future improvements should focus on embedding AI in data assurance, ensuring comparability through XBRL/iXBRL formats, and aligning AI disclosures with CSRD/ESRS requirements. These steps will enhance both transparency and stakeholder trust.

5 Conclusion, Identified Gaps and Recommendations

This study is predominantly qualitative and aims to assess the extent to which integrating AI into the annual integrated reporting process of listed companies contributes to enhancing the quality of external corporate reporting. The qualitative analysis focused on three dimensions: the degree of AI integration into annual integrated reports, the impact of AI transparency on financial and ESG data connectivity, and the evaluation of the AI Maturity Index (AMI). The results of the empirical analysis demonstrate that AI can improve integrated reporting quality when it is embedded in both strategic narratives and data assurance processes. Romanian companies are currently at an early to intermediate stage of maturity. Further progress depends on strengthening governance, improving assurance, and increasing alignment with CSRD/ESRS standards. The analysis of AI integration into the corporate reporting process shows that merely presenting AI initiatives or adoption cases has a limited effect on reporting quality. Presenting initiatives and AI use should be accompanied by key performance indicators (KPIs), achieved objectives, and methods of control. Opportunities for improvement exist in data management and governance, related ethical considerations, and the systematic inclusion of indicators in ESG performance sections. Increasing AI transparency can enhance the quality of Fin-ESG data connectivity reporting by integrating connectivity diagrams between financial and ESG data, presenting information in CSV or XBRL tabular formats, establishing indicators to assess data quality, and increasing the importance of ESG indicator auditing processes. These results are consistent with those of Cui (2025), Badmus et al. (2025), Majekodunmi (2025), Domingo (2025), and Khan et al. (2024).

The AI Maturity Index (AMI) provides a framework for benchmarking and guiding improvements in future reporting cycles. The results of the AMI analysis reveal that, although companies are increasing their maturity in adopting AI within the reporting process, concrete practical actions regarding data quality and assurance remain limited and poorly presented. AI is more frequently presented as a strategic innovation rather than as a genuine governance tool. Furthermore, the AMI analysis indicates that achieving true and balanced maturity requires progress in both integration and connectivity dimensions, and a holistic approach is recommended.

Identified gaps include limited governance of data lineage, absence of quantified AI KPIs, and lack of detailed assurance. The recommendations highlight the need to establish AI governance committees and assign chief AI officers, publish AI ethics charters and conduct impact assessments, define AI-related KPIs, set measurable targets, enhance assurance over AI-enabled metrics, and, last but not least, adopt machine-readable reporting (XBRL/iXBRL). The outcomes of the empirical thematic qualitative analysis on AI integration and transparency in Fin-ESG data connectivity within integrated annual reports have implications for company management, data governance, and report preparers, as well as for regulatory authorities. These findings highlight the need to periodically update and enhance provisions and ethical standards regarding the use and implementation of AI in operational business processes and corporate reporting. Like any study, this one has limitations due to the small sample size of companies and the single year of analysis. However, the analysis period was determined by the implementation of the CSRD and ESRS. Future research could expand the sample of companies and the period analysed, conduct cross-sectional industry analyses focusing the qualitative thematic investigation solely on AI and Fin-ESG data connectivity or the AMI, and further examine how CSRD implementation improves the quality of integrated reporting.

References

Aldabbous N, Riyath MIM (2024) Role of AI and digital transformation in corporate reporting: a bibliometric review. Int Bus Res 17(5):52. https://doi.org/10.5539/ibr.v17n5p52

Alhazmi AHJ, Islam SMN, Prokofieva M (2025) The impact of artificial intelligence adoption on the quality of financial reports on the Saudi stock exchange. Int J Financ Stud 13(1):21. https://doi.org/10.3390/ijfs13010021

Almadadha R (2024) Blockchain technology in financial accounting: enhancing transparency, security, and ESG reporting. Blockchains 2(3):312–333. https://doi.org/10.3390/blockchains2030015

Alshi S (2025) Artificial intelligence, ESG, and the future of financial reporting. J Mark Soc Res 2(5):442–446. https://doi.org/10.61336/jmsr/25-05-49

Angin M, Taşdemir B, Yılmaz CA, Demiralp G, Atay M, Angin P, Dikmener G (2022) A RoBERTa approach for automated processing of sustainability reports. Sustainability 14(23):16139. https://doi.org/10.3390/su142316139

Anton CE, Ciobanu E, Brătucu G, Bucs L (2024) Using chatbots to enhance integrated reporting: insights from accounting and consultancy companies from Romania. Electronics 13(23):4801. https://doi.org/10.3390/electronics13234801

Antwi BO, Adelakun B, Eziefule A (2024) Transforming financial reporting with AI: enhancing accuracy and timeliness. Int J Adv Econ 6(6):205–223. https://doi.org/10.51594/ijae.v6i6.1229

Badmus O, Toromade RO, Adebayo AS (2025) Embedding AI into ESG-financial reporting frameworks to advance trustworthy non-financial disclosures and data-driven investment decisions. Int J Res Publ Rev 6(7):3977–3994. https://doi.org/10.55248/gengpi.6.0725.25165

Bogdan V, Rus L, Gherai DS, Florea AG, Bugnar NG (2023) A streamline sustainable business performance reporting model by an integrated FinESG approach. Sustainability 15(24):16860. https://doi.org/10.3390/su152416860

Boloş MI, Rusu Ş, Sabău-Popa CD, Gherai DS, Negrea A, Crişan M-I (2024) AI chatbots: fast tracking sustainability report analysis for enhanced decision making. Amfiteatru Econ 26(Special Issue No. 18):1241–1255. https://doi.org/10.24818/EA/2024/S18/1241

Chen, Y. (2024). A panoramic overview of the opportunities and challenges artificial intelligence brings to ESG investing. In Walker T, Gramlich D, Sadati A (eds), Artificial intelligence, finance, and sustainability. Palgrave Macmillan, Cham. https://doi.org/10.1007/978-3-031-66205-8_2

Chia HS, Muhammad Hisham MH, Jan KSV (2025) Fostering transparency, driving value creation and advancing SDGs: a review of integrated reporting. Int J Serv Manag Sustain 10(1):121–135. https://doi.org/10.24191/ijsms.v10i1.24219

Cojocaru A-C, Mihăilă S, Grosu V, Frumusachi L (2024) Enhancing integrated reporting processes through the integration of artificial intelligence into management systems. In: Dyczkowska J (ed) Human versus machine: Accounting, auditing and education in the era of artificial intelligence. Publishing House of Wroclaw University of Economics and Business, pp 102–113

Cucari N, Nevi G, Laviola F, Barbagli L (2023) Artificial intelligence and environmental social governance: an exploratory landscape of AI toolkit. SSRN Electron J. https://doi.org/10.2139/ssrn.4629933

Cui B (2025) The transformative role of AI in financial reporting: Opportunities, risks, and regulatory implications. Account Financ Res 14(2):1–87. https://doi.org/10.5430/afr.v14n2p87
De Villiers C, Dimes R (2023) Will the formation of the international sustainability standards board result in the death of integrated reporting? J Account Organ Chang 19(2):279–295. https://doi.org/10.1108/jaoc-05-2022-0084
Deliu D, Olariu A (2024) The role of artificial intelligence and big data analytics in shaping the future of professions in industry 6.0: perspectives from an emerging market. Electronics 13(24):4983. https://doi.org/10.3390/electronics13244983
Domingo MMR (2025) The impact of artificial intelligence on ESG: a conceptual framework for practitioners and policymakers. J Manag Glob Sustain 13(1):Article 2. https://doi.org/10.13185/2244-6893.1269
Dumitru VF, Ionescu B-Ş, Rîndaşu S-M, Barna L-E-L, Crîjman A-M (2023) Implications for sustainability accounting and reporting in the context of the automation-driven evolution of ERP systems. Electronics 12(8):1819. https://doi.org/10.3390/electronics12081819
EFRAG (2023) European Sustainability Reporting Standards (ESRS). https://www.efrag.org/en/sustainability-reporting/esrs/
European Commission (2022) Corporate Sustainability Reporting Directive (CSRD). https://eur-lex.europa.eu/eli/dir/2022/2464/oj/eng
European Union (2024) EU Artificial Intelligence Act. https://artificialintelligenceact.eu/the-act/
Farayola OA, Adaga EM, Egieya ZE, Ewuga SK, Abdul AA, Abrahams TO (2024) Advancements in predictive analytics: a philosophical and practical overview. World J Adv Res Rev 21(3):240–252. https://doi.org/10.30574/wjarr.2024.21.3.2706
Farooq MB, Zaman R, Bahadar S, Rauf F (2024) Forward-looking information: does IIRC framework adoption matter? Sustain Account Manag Policy J. Advance online publication. https://doi.org/10.1108/sampj-11-2023-0857
Gosh UK (2025) Transformative AI applications in business decision-making: advancing data-driven strategies and organisational intelligence. In: Baez MD (ed), AI-powered leadership: transforming organizations in the digital age. IGI Global. https://doi.org/10.4018/979-8-3373-1687-1
Gutierrez-Bustamante M, Espinosa-Leal L (2022) Natural language processing methods for scoring sustainability reports—a study of Nordic listed companies. Sustainability 14(15):9165. https://doi.org/10.3390/su14159165
Hillebrand L, Pielka M, Leonhard D, Deußer T, Dilmaghani T, Kliem B, Loitz R, Morad M, Temath C, Bell T, Stenzel R, Sifa R (2023) Sustain.AI: a recommender system to analyze sustainability reports. In: ICAIL '23: Proceedings of the Nineteenth International Conference on Artificial Intelligence and Law. ACM, pp 412–416. https://doi.org/10.1145/3594536.3595131
Huang AH, Wang H, Yang Y (2023) FinBERT: a large language model for extracting information from financial text. Contemp Account Res 40:806–841. https://doi.org/10.1111/1911-3846.12832
International Integrated Reporting Council (2021) International <IR> framework. Available at https://assets.kpmg.com/content/dam/kpmg/my/pdf/tl-irframework.pdf
Jejeniwa TO, Mhlongo NZ, Jejeniwa TO (2024) A comprehensive review of the impact of artificial intelligence on modern accounting practices and financial reporting. Comput Sci IT Res J 5(4):1031–1047. https://doi.org/10.51594/csitrj.v5i4.1086
Khan F, Jan SU, Zia-ul-haq HM (2024) Artificial intelligence adoption, audit quality and integrated financial reporting in GCC markets. Asian Rev Account 33(3):464–495. https://doi.org/10.1108/ARA-03-2024-0085
KPMG (2023) KPMG global tech report 2023. https://assets.kpmg.com/content/dam/kpmgsites/xx/pdf/2023/09/kpmg-global-tech-report.pdf.coredownload.inline.pdf
Kumar R, Khanna R (2023) RPA (Robotic Process Automation) in finance & accounting and future scope. In: 2023 Second International Conference on Augmented Intelligence and Sustainable Systems (ICAISS). IEEE, pp 1640–1645. https://doi.org/10.1109/ICAISS58487.2023.10250496

Lee SU, Perera H, Liu Y, Xia B, Lu Q, Zhu L, Cairns J, Nottage M (2025) Integrating ESG and AI: a comprehensive responsible AI assessment framework. AI Ethics 5:5121–5148. https://doi.org/10.1007/s43681-025-00741-5

Maama H, Mkhize M (2020) Integration of non-financial information into corporate reporting: a theoretical perspective. Acad Account Financ Stud J 24(2):1–15

Majekodunmi TG (2025) Embedding AI in ESG-financial reporting systems to enhance non-financial disclosure integrity, assurance, and investor decision relevance. Int J Adv Res Publ Rev 2(6):464–484. https://doi.org/10.55248/gengpi.6.0625.22101

Mayegun KO, Nwanevu C (2025) Harnessing big data and AI to revolutionize sustainability accounting and integrated corporate financial reporting. Int J Comput Appl Tech-Nology Res 14(6):111–128. https://doi.org/10.7753/IJCATR1406.1008

Mustafa F, Smolarski J, Elamer A (2025) The convergence of artificial intelligence and sustainability reporting: a systematic review of applications, challenges and future directions. Bus Strat Environ 1–24. https://doi.org/10.1002/bse.70090

Nazir S (2023) The role of integrated reporting in enhancing corporate accountability. Adv Soc Sci Arch J 1(1):47–55. https://assajournal.com/index.php/36/article/view/21

Ni J, Bingler JA, Colesanti-Senni C, Kraus M, Gostlow G, Schimanski T, Stammbach D, Vaghefi SA, Wang Q, Webersinke N, Wekhof T, Yu T, Leippold M (2023) Paradigm shift in sustainability disclosure analysis: empowering stakeholders with Chatreport, a language model-based tool. SSRN Electron J. https://doi.org/10.48550/arXiv.2306.15518

Rane N, Choudhary S, Rane J (2024) Artificial intelligence driven approaches to strengthening environmental, social, and governance (ESG) criteria in sustainable business practices: a review. J Acad Sci 1(2). https://doi.org/10.2139/ssrn.4843215

Rerung A, Paranita ES, Agung Ay RA, Salamah F, Tandililing EM (2024) The influence of fintech innovations, ESG reporting, and blockchain technology on financial transparency and accountability. J Acad Sci 1(2). https://doi.org/10.59613/fb73ds14

Romanian Investor Relations Association (2025, January) VEKTOR by ARIR 2024 aggregate report. https://ir-romania.ro/wp-content/uploads/2025/01/Raport-agregat-VEKTOR-by-ARIR-2024.pdf

Sarker I (2022) AI-based modeling: Techniques, applications and research issues towards automation, intelligent and smart systems. SN Comput Sci 3(2):158. https://doi.org/10.1007/s42979-022-01043-x

Tian H, Wang J, Cai Y (2025) Artificial intelligence adoption and corporate ESG performance. Bus Strat Environ. Advance online publication. https://doi.org/10.1002/bse.70032

Umair S (2023) Assessing the implementation of sustainable development goals: does integrated reporting matter? Soc Environ Account J 43(2):190–191. https://doi.org/10.1080/0969160x.2023.2242712

Vitolla F, Raimo N, Rubino M, Garzoni A (2019) How pressure from stakeholders affects integrated reporting quality. Corp Soc Responsib Environ Manag 26:1591–1606

Yu X, Fan L, Yu Y (2025) Artificial intelligence and corporate ESG performance: a mechanism analysis based on corporate efficiency and external environment. Sustainability 17(9):3819. https://doi.org/10.3390/su17093819

A Successful Romanian AI-Based FinTech Startup

Claudia-Diana Sabău-Popa, Alexandra-Maria Bele, and Corneliu Cristian Bențe

Abstract Digitalization of modern society in recent years has led to real changes in the economy. The financial sector is at the heart of the digital transformation, led by fintech, which is currently shaping a new segment of modern financial markets. Based on an analysis of international experience, this chapter formulates key approaches that, when implemented, allow states to stimulate the adoption and development of new financial technologies in the entrepreneurial sphere. Thus, the case study of a successful Romanian fintech start-up is focused on the characteristics of the business transformation process, associated with adaptive business processes, which allow FinTech's, using AI, to radically transform a business. The chapter also explores the challenges and opportunities that open up for users of artificial intelligence and financial institutions in the context of rapidly changing markets.

1 Introduction

The sphere of financial technology is not limited to clear interfaces. The fintech industry is, first of all, the infrastructure "under the hood": scoring, anti-fraud, Open Banking, as well as integrated finance. Digital financial technologies change not only the user experience, but also the very principles of financial systems - they automate processes, reduce costs and open access to data. This is why fintech has become a key driver of digital transformation in banking and related areas (Ignatyuk et al. 2020).

Traditional banks and fintech companies operate in the same field, but their perspectives are different. Traditional banks have processes that have been refined

C.-D. Sabău-Popa (✉) · A.-M. Bele · C. C. Bențe
Faculty of Economic Sciences, University of Oradea, Oradea, Romania
e-mail: dpopa@uoradea.ro

A.-M. Bele
e-mail: alexandra.bele@didactic.uoradea.ro

C. C. Bențe
e-mail: cbente@uoradea.ro

C. Sabău-Popa (ed.), *Artificial Intelligence in Finance, Accounting and Business Administration*, Contributions to Finance and Accounting,
https://doi.org/10.1007/978-3-032-22737-9_16

over the years, have strict regulations and a high level of stability. Fintech requires flexibility, technology and a focus on the user experience.

In practice, however, the differences between fintech and traditional banks are gradually blurring. More and more players are looking to combine innovative financial technologies with sustainability. Many banks are launching their digital products, developing IT departments, developing R&D labs or buying existing fintech startups. At the same time, fintech companies are entering the regulatory environment, obtaining banking licenses and adapting to compliance requirements. As a result, both are increasingly on the same ground, but with different levels of flexibility.

2 Literature Review

The term "fintech" has only begun to be actively used in the last 10–15 years, but the idea of using information technology in the financial sector is nothing new. The history of fintech can be divided into several stages, each of which is associated with certain technical changes in society (Setiawan and Maulisa 2020).

In simple terms, as noted by Anagnostopoulos et al. (2025) Fintech operates at the junction of three worlds:

- Finance. Compliance with laws, security of assets and transactions, accuracy is important here.
- Technologies. This includes application development, data analysis and working with big data.
- User experience. The customer will choose the fintech service that is faster, simpler and more convenient.

In the 1950s–1980s, the mass automation of banking infrastructure began. First, the first prototypes of banking software appeared, then electronic payment systems and ATMs. During this period, financial technologies operated inside banks; customers did not interact with them directly (Ratecka 2020).

The era of online banking began between the 1990s and 2000s. During this period, the first electronic wallets appeared, online payments and currency exchange platforms developed. Thanks to services such as PayPal, user habits began to change. People learned to interact with money not through the cash register, but through a browser. At this stage, fintech began to spread (Cavallero 2022).

In the years 2010–2020, with the spread of smartphones, various financial applications appeared like mushrooms after the rain: mobile banking, smart investment services, expense tracking systems, crowdfunding, P2P transfers and many others. Promising startups began to develop into full-fledged financial services, and traditional banks began to actively compete with them. Thus, fintech became an integral part of the digital experience of ordinary users (Packin 2023).

Modern fintech has become even more flexible and integrated into everyday life. This is a period of rapid development of open banking and neo-banks, DeFi projects, KYC/AML tools. Integrated finance literally surrounds us everywhere: financial services are integrated into e-commerce, logistics, travel platforms, educational projects. At this stage, fintech is not just an "alternative to banks", but a full-fledged market player and an integral part of modern life (Sak 2024).

The development of financial technologies is not happening for the sake of fashion for digitalisation, but because of the numerous limitations of the classical banking system: from complex processes to low accessibility. The main task of the fintech industry is to make financial services more convenient, faster, more transparent and scalable, using modern technologies (Amstad 2019).

Fintech products are developing in conditions of high competition, a complex technological environment and strict government regulations. Here it is important not only to boldly enter the market, but also to initially consider dozens of factors: from legal restrictions to the sustainability of the architecture. The characteristics of fintech compared to other IT projects are working with sensitive data, compliance as part of the architecture, dependence on legacy systems, the peculiarities of entering the market in different regions and difficulties in hiring (Khotinskay 2019).

Creating a fintech product requires deep interdisciplinary expertise, which distinguishes the industry from most other IT fields. Fintech means speed, flexibility and technology. But where money and personal data meet, the price of error is always high. Despite their apparent simplicity, fintech services operate in conditions where the slightest malfunction can cost a company millions, both in terms of reputation and in the literal sense of the word. Therefore, financial technologies and financial security should always go hand in hand.

The Fintech risks that most projects face are: technological, financial, security and legal risks.

a) Technological

Fintech products are often linked to a complex architecture: real-time transaction processing, API integrations, scoring and anti-fraud systems. Any vulnerability – from XSS to a logical error in the algorithm – can lead to calculation errors, data leaks or loss of funds. It is also worth considering the requirements for fault tolerance, loading and update speed – all of which indicate the need for a very high technical standard for projects (Sruthi et al. 2024).

b) Financial

Mistakes happen even with automated scoring and ML forecasting. Customers are not allowed to repay loans, use fraudulent schemes, or abuse the system through errors they find. Fintech companies are responsible for the quality of risk assessment and, therefore, for their algorithms and the data they are built on (Giudici 2018).

c) Security risks

Fintech works with sensitive information: money, personal documents, contracts. Any data leak, replacement of details or hacking of wallets is not just an unfortunate incident, but a real threat to the reputation and survival of the business (Tang et al. 2020).

d) Legal

A fintech project must comply with a wide range of regulations: from KYC/AML and GDPR to local requirements in each jurisdiction. At the same time, local legislation can change quickly and unpredictably. An error in interpreting the law or a late update of processes, and you can lose your license, be sanctioned or receive a fine of millions of dollars (Kandpal et al. 2025).

3 Fintech Industry in Romania

In recent years, fintech fields have covered almost the entire financial sector, from insurance and investments to accounting and gambling. One of the most developed and saturated fintech fields is payment solutions. This includes all kinds of payment methods, from contactless methods to QR codes and wallets integrated into applications. SelfPay, NETOPIA Payments, and PayU Romania facilitating secure and efficient online transactions.

Another category that has gained momentum is neobanking. These are fintech banks that offer completely online services, without paper contracts and branches. Convenient mobile interfaces, instant account opening, card personalisation, expense analysis and push notifications have become true standards in banking thanks to this type of fintech (Palos-Sanchez et al. 2025).

Investments and wealth management is another popular fintech industry that has fundamentally changed the attitude towards traditional financial instruments. Thanks to fintech projects, investments are no longer the prerogative of professional brokers; they are now available to anyone (Panda et al. 2023).

Stock and ETF trading apps provide simplified access to the stock market. For example, a user can buy stocks, bonds, or ETFs directly from a smartphone, often without commission (Cullen 2021).

Cryptocurrency investment services are an extremely attractive fintech area in terms of storing, exchanging, staking, and trading cryptocurrencies. Some platforms offer automated portfolios, diversification tools, and interest on asset storage (similar to a bank deposit, but only for cryptocurrencies). Here we can mention Elrond (MultiversX) and Tradesilvania, advancing cryptocurrency transactions and blockchain applications;

Startups and small businesses are increasingly abandoning traditional accounting in favour of this fintech industry. Everything is simple, convenient, and you don't need to be a professional accountant: automatic invoicing, integration with the bank, tax calculation, accessible financial analytics. Fintech works in conjunction with SaaS and takes over routine tasks that previously required a separate specialist (Wu and Pambudi 2025).

Fintech insurance is also actively developing, changing the realities of the traditional market. Flexible tariffs (depending on the individual parameters of the applicant), dynamic pricing, APIs, and integrated insurance products (for example, insurance automatically provided when buying a ticket or renting a car) appear. Life is

Hard, Amodo Romania, and Faragrija. ro are Romanian innovating digital insurance services.

The advantages of fintech services are quick registration (often it is enough to tick once), automatic payments and transparent conditions. Fintech lending is developed not only for individuals (buy now, pay later systems), but also for small and medium-sized enterprises. The key advantage is instant scoring, which is based on big data, user behaviour and open-source data analysis. This provides access to fintech loans even to those who do not meet classic banking criteria (Berg et al. 2022).

The trend towards sustainable development has also penetrated the fintech sector. ESG projects help users invest, taking into account environmental, social and governance criteria. These include analytical platforms and brokers with "green" portfolios (Puschmann and Khmarskyi 2024).

Modern Fintech is no longer a separate industry, but a technological layer integrated into the processes and services we are used to, becoming the basis of other businesses. An eloquent illustration can be found below with the distribution of the Fintech companies based on type of activity in Romania. The largest share is digital payments, followed by enterprise technology provisioning and enterprise technology provisioning (Table 1).

At the opposite pole, the lowest weights are given by Cybersecurity and Digital Identity, Digital capital raising and InsurTech.

Table 1 Distribution of the Fintech companies based on type of activity in Romania

Digital payments	29.76%
Enterprise Technology Provisioning	23.81%
Credit and Data Analytics	9.52%
RegTech	9.52%
Digital assets exchange	8.33%
Digital lending	8.33%
WealthTech	4.76%
Cybersecurity and Digital identity	2.38%
Digital capital raising	2.38%
InsurTech	1.19%

Source Own elaboration based on data collected from https://bbs.ase.ro/wp-content/uploads/2024/05/RoFin.Tech_Romania-Bulgaria_Report2023_ebook_1.pdf

4 Development of Fintech Companies in Europe and Romania

The development of FinTech has led to the active digitalisation of financial companies, including banks, and to the creation of FinTech companies. The Financial Stability Board, considering FinTech, highlights financial innovations directly related to the provision of financial services, the emergence of new products, all of which have a fundamental impact on financial organisations and markets and lead to the emergence of new business models (Financial Stability Board 2024).

Ernst and Young Global Limited (2019) provides the following definition of a FinTech company: a company that uses new business models based on the application of modern data processing technologies in the production and sale of financial services.

According to the audit company KPMG International (2025), for the first half of 2025, the fintech investment map is dominated globally by companies from the USA. However, the top 10 global fintech deals are led globally by Preqin from London, UK, with a $3.2 billion buyout. This is considered the year's largest fintech deal so far. In second place, we find Next Insurance from Palo Alto, US, which led by the $2.6 billion acquisition by Ergo Group. The ranking is followed by Binance from George Town, Cayman Islands, with a $2 billion raise.

At the European level, the top is made up of Preqin from London, UK, followed by Esker, Villeurbanne, France, with $1.7B and Rapyd Financial Network, Takeley, UK, with $500M. (KPMG International 2025).

In recent years, the Fintech phenomenon has gained momentum in Romania. Thus, in 2025, we can talk about approximately 393 companies operating in this sector. The latest data shows that 78 of these companies have invested $101 million in private equity and venture capital money, 20 being Series A+ Companies, and 16 being Series C+ Companies. However, starting with 2022, the trend of Romanian Fintech startups is downward. In the graph below, you can see the evolution of the funding of Fintech companies in Romania, with a maximum of 42 in 2021 and a minimum of 6 in 2024, as it can be seen in Fig. 1.

In Romania, the Fintech sector has had significant fluctuations in terms of total funding (Fig. 2).

Although the lowest values were reached in 2017 in the amount of 600k dollars, the peak was reached in 2018, with a maximum of 32.6 million dollars. However, the trend is decreasing, in 2024, less than half of the total funding of 2018 was recorded.

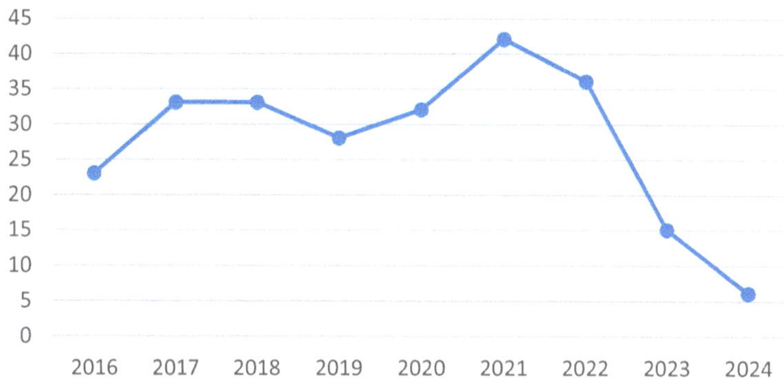

Fig. 1 Romanian Fintech start-up evolution from 2016 to 2024. *Source* Own elaboration based on data collected from https://tracxn.com/d/explore/fintech-startups-in-romania/__38FtfxfYPbd2pJZUtqxCh4HeNaJdaSn8b4pYkGvWuYI#top-companies

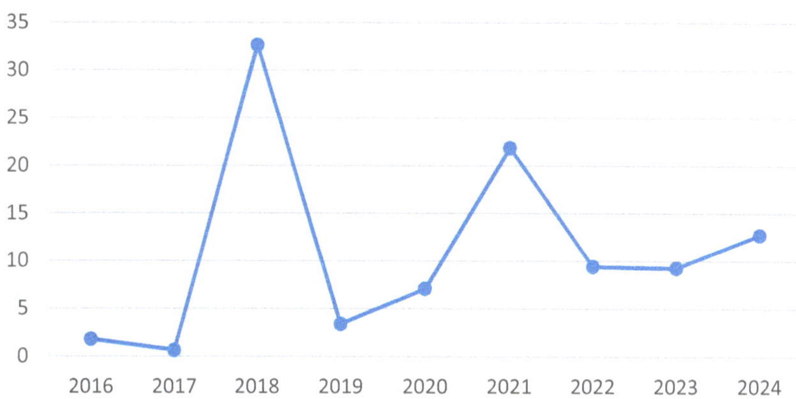

Fig. 2 Romanian Fintech total funding evolution from 2016 to 2024. *Source* Own elaboration based on data collected from https://tracxn.com/d/explore/fintech-startups-in-romania/__38FtfxfYPbd2pJZUtqxCh4HeNaJdaSn8b4pYkGvWuYI#top-companies

5 Market Impact and Scalability of AI Fintech Companies in Romania

In Romania, AI-based fintech companies began to appear timidly in 2015 and to gain momentum in 2018. The smallest total funding of approximately 100k euros belongs to Assista AI, followed by COGNISYNC TECH SRL with 1 million euros, Druid AI with 47 million euros and Doxory with 85 million euros. It can be noted that FintechOS leads this ranking by a wide margin, not only in terms of total funding but also in terms of the number of investors (Table 2).

In terms of FintechOS performance, significant changes have occurred in recent years, leading to prolific development. The FintechOS startup is on the rise, with 40%

Table 2 Top Romanian Fintech AI companies

	Country	Founded	Total Funding	Investors
Druid AI	RO	2018	47 mil.euro	Endeavor, GapMinder Venture Partners, Hoxton Ventures, Karma Ventures, Smedvig Capital, TQ Ventures, and Verve Ventures
Dexory	RO	2015	85 mil.euro	Atomico, Bootstrap Europe, Capnamic Ventures, DTCP, Lakestar, Latitude Ventures, and WaVe X
FintechOS	RO	2017	144 mil.euro	BlackRock, Cipio Partners, Earlybird Venture Capital, GapMinder Venture Partners, Molten Ventures, and OTB Ventures
Cognisync Tech SRL	RO	2024	1 mil.euro	Early Game Ventures
Assista AI	RO/USA	2023	100k euro	Gluon Syndicate

Source Own elaboration based on data collected from https://www.romaniajournal.ro/business/three-romanian-ai-startups-on-track-to-becoming-unicorns

revenue growth in 2023 compared to 2022, demonstrating profitability and attractiveness for investors. Even in the banking and insurance sector, notable progress can be seen, materialising by a 300% YOY growth in insurance and 70% overall.

New financial technologies are already competing with traditional systems, the time to market for FintechOS users is 3 times faster and could completely change the way we perceive money management, with 120% more profitability. An indicator of the rapid and successful implementation of technology in this area is not only the number of projects, but also their activity and success. This is felt primarily by customers who report a 70% reduction in product launch costs, while servicing costs have decreased by up to 80%.

6 Technologies Used by the Company FintechOS

FintechOS is a Bucharest-based IT start-up that initially launched with a leading end-to-end financial products management platform. The startup received a Series A investment of $14 million two years after its founding. In 2020, the Romanian company was named the best European financial technology (fintech) startup at The Europas Awards competition, held in London (Crăciun 2024).

A year later, FintechOS obtained a Series B investment of $60 million, led by Draper Esprit, one of the most active funds in Europe, investing in fast-growing technology companies with global ambitions. The company subsequently attracted another $10 million in financing (Crăciun 2024).

FintechOS is a complete financial product management platform that enables banks and insurance companies to quickly and efficiently integrate powerful, low-code functionalities to accelerate digital transformation without replacing existing core systems. The platform minimises the risks of adopting new technologies through an iterative approach to modernisation. Powered by Artificial Intelligence, the FintechOS platform provides financial institutions with the tools they need to create personalised and data-driven products, improving customer experience and optimising internal operations, while reducing the risks and costs associated with traditional digital transformation projects.

Among the most widely used technologies using artificial intelligence, FintechOS uses natural language processing (NLP). Thus, the company has approached innovative strategies for automating the interpretation of customer messages, in the most natural language possible, virtual assistants such as chatbots and the analysis of unstructured documents through automatic data selection (FintechOS 2025).

Regarding Machine Learning and Deep Learning, FintechOS presents new models for credit risk assessment. Image recognition and fraud prevention integrate OCR technologies. Fraud is prevented by identity verification, facial recognition and the KYC process. Financial services users can benefit from payment solutions with double identification on their phones, which helps secure payments through digital transactions (FintechOS 2025).

Credit risk assessment is based on information provided by FintechOS by integrated micro-services that have functions such as fraud detection, credit risk scoring methods, KYC/AML using AI (FintechOS 2025).

Table 3 presents the main services offered by FintechOS through the integrated platform.

7 Conclusions

FinTech has led not only to the emergence of companies of the same name, but also to the digitalisation of traditional banks and the emergence of neo-banks. As a result, the market for financial and banking services has fundamentally changed, and competition has increased sharply, which has created a threat to the existence of traditional banks.

In terms of development, domestic developments in the field of fintech have outpaced global ones over the past two decades. Fintech is now an integral part of all types of financial services: it is implemented in lending, payments and transfers, savings, investments, insurance, etc. However, the leaders are companies that work in several areas at once, using different tools and helping customers complete financial tasks to the maximum in a convenient interface.

In Romania, the issue of increased technologicalisation of banks and companies is a matter of time. Fintech startups rarely have technologies that are not available to them. Many startups rely on the inflexibility of existing banking systems and the general slowness of financial sector actors. But the process is inevitable, Romanian

Table 3 The main products and services offered by FintechOS

Personal Banking	Small Business Banking	Commercial Banking
Checking Saving and CD Borrowing Home Loans Credit Cards Personal Loans Auto Loans BNPL Split Payments	Checking Savings Credit Cards Lending Lines of Credit	Asset-Based Financing Lending Real Estate Equipment Financing
Personal Insurance	**Group Insurance**	**Business Insurance**
Home Holiday Home Motor Multicar Classic Car Pet Travel	Group Travel Group Healthcare Cash Plan Cover Private Health Cover	Private Landlord Employers Liability Motor Fleet Mini Fleet Specialist Vehicle Property Commercial Landlord

Source Own elaboration based on data collected from https://fintechos.com/fintechos-24/

companies have begun and will continue to change, and the further they go, the closer they will be to fintech.

In the coming years, in Romania the main emphasis will be on the development of artificial intelligence technologies that will allow choosing an optimal solution. With the development of artificial intelligence, there is potential for expanding the functions of digital assistants. They will massively anticipate the client's wishes based on the analysis of his data and offer him the most optimal solutions to his problems. In addition, the further development of blockchain, which can become the basis for creating new business models, such as decentralised payment systems or platforms for data exchange between financial market participants, will contribute to improving the security of transactions.

References

Amstad M (2019, October). Regulating fintech: objectives, principles, and practices (ADBI Working Paper No. 1016). Asian Development Bank Institute. https://www.econstor.eu/bitstream/10419/222783/1/1680064665.pdf

Anagnostopoulos I (Yiannis), Sails T, Alexandrou G (2025) FinTechs, BigTechs and diminishing bank franchise values: stakeholder perspectives on a disruptive emerging financial ecosystem. Technol Forecast Soc Chang 213. https://doi.org/10.1016/j.techfore.2024.123924

Berg T, Fuster A, Puri M (2022) FinTech lending. Annu Rev Financ Econ 14:187–207. https://doi.org/10.1146/annurev-financial-101521-112042

Cavallero F (2022) Literature review-fintech and social media: should PayPal acquire Pinterest? Rising stars by Sunshine 2022. Retrieved from https://rs.pubpub.org/pub/xrz85yys

Crăciun D (2024, 30 mai) Finanţare de 60 milioane dolari pentru startup-ul românesc FintechOS: “Obiectivul nostru nu este să fim un unicorn”. StartupCafe.ro. https://startupcafe.ro/finantare-startup-fintechosm-obiectiv-unicorn-organizatiem-globala-htm-27232
Cullen J (2021) Exchange-traded funds (ETFs) and FinTech: market efficiency and systemic risk. In: Routledge handbook of financial technology and law. Routledge, pp 227–244. https://www.taylorfrancis.com/chapters/edit/10.4324/9780429325670-13/exchange-traded-funds-etfs-fintech-jay-cullen
Ernst & Young Global Limited (2019) Global FinTech Adoption Index 2019: As FinTech becomes the norm, you need to stand out from the crowd. EY. Retrieved August 31, 2025, from https://www.ey.com/en_gl/ey-global-fintech-adoption-index
Financial Stability Board. (2024). Financial Innovation. In: Financial innovation and structural change. Retrieved from https://www.fsb.org/work-of-the-fsb/financial-innovation-and-structural-change/financial-innovation/
Financial Stability Implications from FinTech: Supervisory and regulatory issues that merit authorities' attention // FSB. Retrieved August 22, 2025, from https://www.fsb.org/wp-content/uploads/R270617.pdf
FintechOS (2025) FintechOS 24. FintechOS. Retrieved August 31, 2025, from https://fintechos.com/fintechos-24/
Giudici P (2018) Fintech risk management: a research challenge for artificial intelligence in finance. Front Artif Intell 1:Article 1. https://doi.org/10.3389/frai.2018.00001
Global FinTech Adoption Index 2019: as FinTech becomes the norm, you need to stand out from the crowd // EY. Retrieved August 22, 2025, from https://www.ey.com/en_gl/ey-global-fintech-adoption-index
Ignatyuk A, Liubkina OV, Murovana T, Magomedova A (2020) FinTech as an innovation challenge: from big data to sustainable development. E3S Web of Conferences 166:Article 13027. https://doi.org/10.1051/e3sconf/202016613027
Kandpal V, Ozili PK, Jeyanthi MP, Ranjan D, Chandra D (2025) Regulation of the fintech industry. In: Digital finance and metaverse in banking: decoding a virtual reality towards financial inclusion and sustainable development. Emerald Publishing Limited, Singapore, pp 181–198. https://doi.org/10.1108/978-1-83662-088-4_20251009
Khotinskay G (2019) FinTech: fundamental theory and empirical features. In: Mantulenko V (ed), Global challenges and prospects of the modern economic development, vol 57. European Proceedings of Social and Behavioural Sciences. Future Academy, pp 222–229. https://doi.org/10.15405/epsbs.2019.03.23
KPMG International (2025, August 1) Pulse of fintech H1 2025: global analysis of funding in fintech. KPMG International. https://assets.kpmg.com/content/dam/kpmgsites/xx/pdf/2025/08/pulse-of-fintech-h1-2025.pdf
Mordor Intelligence. (2025). Europe fintech market size, growth analysis (2025–2030). Mordor Intelligence. Retrieved from https://www.mordorintelligence.com/industry-reports/europe-fintech-market
Packin NG (2023) A history of financial technology from corporations to crowdfunding. J Int Comp L 10:133. https://www.jicl.org.uk/storage/journals/June2023/sbk409E8VQWEMWQunkZ7.pdf
Palos-Sanchez PR, Chang-Tam RJ, Folgado-Fernández JA (2025) The role of Neobanks and FinTech in sustainable finance and technology. The customer/user perspective for entrepreneurs. Sustain Technol Entrep 100109. https://www.sciencedirect.com/science/article/pii/S2773032825000148
Panda AC, Patnaik A, Pawar A, Birari A (2023) Adoption of Fintech towards asset and wealth management: understanding the recent scenario in India. In Mishra P, Sharma A, Khanra S, Kundu SK, Mishra SK (eds), Digital economy post COVID-19 era. Springer, pp 357–367. https://doi.org/10.1007/978-981-99-0197-5_23
Puschmann T, Khmarskyi V (2024) Green fintech: developing a research agenda. Corp Soc Responsib Environ Manag 31(4):2823–2837. https://doi.org/10.1002/csr.2675

Ratecka P (2020) FinTech—definition, taxonomy and historical approach. Zeszyty Naukowe Małopolskiej Wyższej Szkoły Ekonomicznej w Tarnowie 1(45):53–67.

Renduchintala T, Alfauri H, Yang Z, Di Pietro R, Jain R (2022). A survey of blockchain applications in the FinTech sector. J Open Innov: Technol Mark, Complex 8(4):Article 185. https://doi.org/10.3390/joitmc8040185

Sak MH (2024, April) KYC/AML technologies in decentralized finance (DeFi). Glucksman Institute, Stern School of Business. https://www.stern.nyu.edu/sites/default/files/2024-07/Glucksman_Sak_2024.pdf

Setiawan K, Maulisa N (2020) The evolution of fintech: a regulatory approach perspective. In: Proceedings of the 3rd International Conference on Law and Governance (ICLAVE 2019). Atlantis Press, pp 218–225. https://doi.org/10.2991/aebmr.k.200321.029

Sruthi S, Kumaran U, Oyyavuru PK, Emadaboina S, Machavarapu SP, Balasubramanian S (2024) Securing financial technology: mitigating vulnerabilities in fintech applications. In: Goar V, Kuri M, Kumar R, Senjyu T (eds), Advances in information communication technology and computing. lecture notes in networks and systems. Springer Singapore, Singapore, pp 205–214. https://doi.org/10.1007/978-981-97-6103-6_14

Tang KL, Ooi CK, Chong JB (2020) Perceived risk factors affect intention to use fintech. J Account Financ Emerg Econ 6(2). https://doi.org/10.26710/jafee.v6i2.1101

Wu CH, Pambudi PDL (2025) Digital transformation in fintech: choosing between application and Software as a Service (SaaS). Asia Pac Manag Rev 30(2):Article 100342. https://doi.org/10.1016/j.apmrv.2024.12.006

A Successful Hungarian AI-Based FinTech Startup

Péter Bajnai and János Szenderák

Abstract The authors explore the rise and impact of FinTech—financial technology—on the modern financial services landscape, with a particular focus on innovations in accounting and the transformative role of companies like Számlázz.hu in Hungary. The chapter discusses the varied definitions and scope of FinTech, highlighting its influence on efficiency, user experience, and business models globally. Számlázz.hu is a pioneering provider in online invoicing in Hungary. Initially struggling with low customer numbers, the company's fortunes improved dramatically following strategic consultancy, it reshaped the market, leaving competitors behind. The substantial growth in user base also drove significant improvements in its financial performance, which enables the company to revolutionize online invoicing further with IT automation, increasingly taking advantage of the opportunities offered by AI.

1 The FinTech Phenomenon

In the modern digital economy, consumers increasingly rely on online channels, and financial services are no exception. The Fourth Industrial Revolution has brought not only technological penetration but also a paradigm shifts in business models, forcing traditional financial institutions to adapt to a digital environment (Póta and Becsky-Nagy 2022). Advances in information technology have enabled new market niches to emerge, giving rise to FinTechs: financial technology entities that aim to reduce transaction costs and offer more personalised services (Puschmann 2017).

FinTech (financial technology) is the intersection of modern financial services and digital innovation. FinTech solutions and the companies that develop them aim to make financial processes more efficient, faster and more user-friendly, whether it's

P. Bajnai (✉) · J. Szenderák
Faculty of Economics and Business, University of Debrecen, Debrecen, Hungary
e-mail: bajnai.peter@econ.unideb.hu

J. Szenderák
e-mail: szenderak.janos@econ.unideb.hu

C. Sabău-Popa (ed.), *Artificial Intelligence in Finance, Accounting and Business Administration*, Contributions to Finance and Accounting,
https://doi.org/10.1007/978-3-032-22737-9_17

payments, investments or even accounting. In the field of accounting, FinTech solutions—such as automated invoicing, online banking or real-time financial analytics—have revolutionised administrative work, reducing errors and manual intervention, speeding up processes and increasing customer satisfaction through simpler operation and lower costs. Számlázz.hu is an outstanding example of this phenomenon in Hungary: a successful Hungarian startup that has made the everyday lives of hundreds of thousands of businesses simpler and more transparent with its innovative, cloud-based invoicing and accounting solutions.

Defining the exact concept of FinTech is neither simple nor obvious, as it depends on the perspective from which the topic is examined. Among researchers in the field, some interpret the term as referring to the companies or service providers, such as Muthukannan et al. (2020): "… agents that interact with each other to provide a wide array of financial products and services to end customers", or Milian et al. (2019): "innovative companies active in the financial industry making use of the availability of communication, the ubiquity of the internet, and the automated processing of information." In other cases, the term FinTech refers to the specific technological developments: "financial services and innovations, dealing with issues of financial industry regulation and local legislation or the financial system globally," as described by Milian et al. (2019), or, according to Nakashima (2018): "FinTech therefore refers to new technological solutions that will even initiate a revolutionary transformation in the world of finance."

However, it is certain that the global growth of FinTechs has deeply altered the international financial system, reshaping institutional roles and enabling innovative solutions such as crowdfunding, mobile transfers, and electronic contract signing (Tello-Gamarra et al. 2022). Fintech represents not only a fancy new trend, but an entire reform process within finance, making services more efficient, accessible, and often cheaper through the use of advanced technologies (Póta and Becsky-Nagy 2022).

Just as its definition is simple, the phenomenon itself cannot be treated as a uniform process. Expansion patterns of FinTechs vary regionally: Asia shows rapid adoption, North America is driven by strong investor interest, and Europe advances mainly through bank partnerships or niche markets (MNB 2017). Different categories can also be identified in terms of target groups: FinTechs represent financial innovations for users of different economic levels, consumers or institutional actors (Senyo et al. 2021). Moreover, their corporate nature also differs: while some are innovative startups, others are large established financial companies introducing technology-driven solutions (OECD 2018).

The spread of FinTech solutions and companies also comes with a number of risks. Financial markets are fundamentally highly regulated—and with good reason—and are particularly sensitive, so the chance that decentralised financial services that imitate traditional financial services without adequate regulatory control and the experience of incumbent actors could cause problems for the entire sector increases. In addition to the risks arising from day-to-day operations, serious cybersecurity issues may also arise, which are only amplified by the increasing popularity of AI. The uncritical use of data processed by AI techniques and information generated by them can lead to distortions in the market; in addition, it is very important to properly establish liability relationships in the regulation of AI (Becsky-Nagy et al. 2022).

The Hungarian National Bank (MNB) presents a report each year about the FinTech sector (MNB 2024). According to this report, in 2022 there were 212 companies registered in Hungary that are specifically engaged in FinTech activities, in addition to the dominant incumbents of the local financial market. The growth rate of FinTech companies appears to be slowing down globally, but the number of these innovative companies has continued to expand in America and Europe. While the total value of global FinTech investments has declined, interest in smaller investments and new technological solutions has remained strong. Digital payment and lending solutions remain the most popular within the sector, and a significant proportion of FinTech companies continue to be B2B-focused micro and small enterprises. The report also highlights that 2024 was a significant year for the regulation of the technology and FinTech sectors in the European Union: the world's first comprehensive regulatory framework for AI has been developed, which aims to harness the transformative power of AI in a responsible and safe manner.

2 Fintech Solutions in the Field of Accounting

The rapid expansion of FinTech, driven by AI, machine learning, big data, blockchain, cybersecurity, and cloud technologies, is inevitably transforming the accounting profession (Salin et al. 2024). Techniques of AI and machine learning enable the automation of manual bookkeeping processes, improving accuracy and efficiency (Pelau et al. 2021; Fülöp et al. 2022). Robotic Process Automation (RPA) enhances efficiency by using software robots to perform repetitive tasks such as data extraction and invoice processing, while AI-based optical character recognition (OCR) identifies key invoice details like amounts and due dates (Jain 2023). Cloud-based accounting systems provide flexibility and accessibility through internet-based platforms (Fülöp et al. 2022). Blockchain technology offers significant potential for finance, accounting, and auditing by enhancing transparency and data security (Fullana and Ruiz 2021). Routine accounting activities such as preparing offers, issuing invoices, and recording transactions can now be automated, reducing human workload (Fülöp et al. 2022). Overall, the integration of AI and big data has a significant positive effect on accounting practices, supporting improved financial reporting, auditing and fraud management (Osei-Assibey Bonsu et al. 2023).

However, the above-mentioned FinTech solutions were preceded by much more traditional, now seemingly every day technological innovations, the most important of which are related to digitisation, i.e. the conversion of paper-based documents into electronic ones. Such was the emergence of electronic invoices, a highly disruptive element (Gavrila and de Lucas Ancillo 2021), which made invoicing and accounting processes faster, more cost-effective and greener. A Hungarian startup was ahead of its time: the Számlázz.hu website made its online invoicing public in 2005, a decade before the FinTech revolution.

3 Számlázz.hu—A Hungarian Fintech Success Story

An online invoicing system is a system that provides invoicing services via the internet. In Hungary, the first such system was created by the team of Számlázz.hu—the Hungarian expression can be roughly translated into English as "Bill!", "Make invoice!" or "Do invoicing!". According to an interview with their CEO in 2023, after 4–5 years of operation, they had only about 700 customers, 70 of whom paid for the service, meaning that for years, the business was not particularly successful. Then, with the help of a strategic consultant, they ramped up their activities, and by 2023, they had 680,000 businesses as customers. Since then, the state has also embraced online invoicing, with the National Tax and Customs Administration (NAV) becoming the largest player in the "market" with its free online invoicing program. The largest of their market-based competitors is significantly behind them, with roughly 160,000 customers in 2023. According to the Számlázz.hu website, they currently (at the end of 2025) work with more than 850,000 customers and have issued more than 727 million invoices so far. Many of its users only use the free features, while nearly half of its customers pay for the service on a regular or occasional basis (Rácz 2023).

The growth in the customer base was, of course, accompanied by an increase in the company's financial performance, as shown in Table 1.

Since 2016, the company that operates Számlázz. hu has seen its revenue increase 20-fold, its profits almost 40-fold, and the value of its total assets more than 60-fold. In addition, the number of employees has grown from 6 to 55 persons—based on this data, the startup founded in 2005 is now considered a stable medium-sized enterprise. It is also important to note that the company became a member of the Visma

Table 1 The financial performance of the company behind Számlázz.hu (KBOSS.hu Kft.) over the past 10 years (EUR Thousands)

Year	Net sales revenue	Net Profit	Total assets	Average employee number
2016	659.66	159.09	227.25	6
2017	1058.02	330.05	485.38	10
2018	1354.64	114.73	918.62	13
2019	2752.61	1281.77	2495.72	15
2020	4452.32	1314.06	4652.43	20
2021	7332.39	4077.14	9426.44	29
2022	8631.62	5005.32	14,909.72	39
2023	10,474.96	6518.1	12,639.03	44
2024	13,209.12	6269.31	14,054.15	55
Change from 2016 to 2024	**2002.41%**	**3940.73%**	**6184.44%**	**916.67%**

Source Own editing based on the databases of the Hungarian Ministry of Justice and EMIS Next

Group in 2018, when the leading provider of business software and e-commerce IT developments in the Scandinavian region acquired a 50% stake in the company.

The company's main innovation was making online invoicing widely available, but over the past two decades, the range of services it offers has become much broader. The startup was not satisfied with the short-term success of its initial novelty; its leaders knew that the only way to achieve long-term prosperity in this rapidly changing sector was through continuous innovation. Their main services are still related to invoicing and administration: with their online, automated system, they essentially take over the basic administrative tasks of businesses, making their operations faster and cheaper. In addition to electronic invoicing, these activities include receipt issuance, mass invoice generation, incoming invoice management, invoice archiving, and postal services. The company's excellent marketing activities are reflected in the particularly effective names they give to their services. Their service, called "Számlaverzum" ("Invoice-verse"), promises that everything can be done in one place: outgoing and incoming invoices can be managed on a single interface, supplier invoices are received automatically, and accountants can access the necessary invoice data directly from there. Their "Invoice Agent" interface promises the total automation of a company's invoice management. In addition to the above, they have expanded their focus to include financial and tax services. They provide their customers with an online payment interface, assist them with cost accounting and receivables management, and offer digital factoring services. Of course, all these services are also available on a mobile application (Számlázz.hu 2025).

Another key to their success is that they have entered into numerous partnerships with other businesses, including innovative startups similar to their own. Companies operating webshops have integrated Számlázz. hu into their systems, they have data connections with the largest Hungarian banks and are in contact with accounting software and offices (Számlázz.hu 2025). It is worth noting that they have recently made a strategic partnership with the Hungarian FinTech neobank Binx, which specifically targets entrepreneurs and companies with a relatively cheap digital payment service—in 2025, they had 5000 customers and processed more than 100,000 transactions. The basis for the cooperation between Számlázz. hu and BinX were the integration goal of enabling customers to manage their company finances within a single administrative ecosystem (Turzó 2025).

In an interview, the CEO of Számlázz. hu emphasised the importance of AI, stating that innovation in this area is "absolutely typical" of the company. The automation and integration solutions described above are clearly related to some form of artificial intelligence. The managing director classifies AI as "how to do things even better": in business terms, they use AI to improve functions in such a way that the customer does not notice that AI is working in the background. However, he does not believe that humans can or should be replaced (Rácz 2023). "It may come as a surprise, but artificial intelligence has not taken over customer service at our company. And as long as we have such great customer service staff as we do now, it will stay that way." said the CEO (Adó Online 2025). Looking to the future, he added that humans are too valuable to do things that a machine can do. "Ideally, machines will do this kind of documentation in the future, and entrepreneurs won't have to spend a single second on it, nor will they even know how the invoicing process works (DigitalHungary 2025)."

It is clear that FinTech solutions and businesses are of outstanding importance, not only in the most developed countries, but also in an emerging economy like Hungary. FinTechs appear in many areas beyond the banking sector, including accounting, where the country's most successful FinTech company, which has now become a stable medium-sized company, operates: Számlázz. hu, which revolutionised online invoicing with IT automation, and which is increasingly taking advantage of the opportunities offered by AI.

References

Adó Online (2025) Háromszorosára bővült a 20 éves Számlázz.hu csapata. https://ado.hu/cegvilag/haromszorosara-bovult-a-20-eves-szamlazz-hu-csapata/

Becsky-Nagy P, Póta CP, Fazekas B (2022) FinTech cégek rendszerkockázati szempontú értékelése [The impact of FinTech on systemic risks]. Conference: Magyar Nemzeti Bank—Debreceni Egyetem kutatási konferencia Fenntartható gazdaság Versenyképesség és digitalizáció

DigitalHungary (2025) Számlázz.hu: Ideális esetben a számlázást a gépek végzik a jövőben [Számlázz.hu: Ideally, invoicing will be done by machines in the future]. https://www.digitalhungary.hu/e-volution/Szamlazz-hu-Idealis-esetben-a-szamlazast-a-gepek-vegzik-a-jovoben/27319/

Fullana O, Ruiz J (2021) Accounting information systems in the blockchain era. Int J Intellect Prop Manag 11(1):63–80. https://doi.org/10.1504/IJIPM.2021.113357

Fülöp MT, Topor DI, Ionescu CA, Căpuşneanu S, Breaz TO, Stanescu SG (2022) Fintech accounting and Industry 4.0: future-proofing or threats to the accounting profession? J Bus Econ Manag (JBEM) 23(5):997–1015. https://doi.org/10.3846/jbem.2022.17695

Gavrila SG, de Lucas Ancillo A (2021) Spanish SMEs' digitalisation enablers: e-receipt applications to the offline retail market. Technol Forecast Soc Chang 162:120381. https://doi.org/10.1016/j.techfore.2020.120381

Jain VCA (2023) Innovative processes in finance and accounting. Strat Financ 105(4):45–54. https://www.proquest.com/scholarly-journals/innovative-processes-finance-accounting/docview/2881894461/se-2

Milian EZ, Spinola MDM, De Carvalho MM (2019) Fintechs: a literature review and research agenda. Electron Commer Res Appl 34:100833. https://doi.org/10.1016/j.elerap.2019.100833

MNB (2017) Innováció és stabilitás: Fintech körkép Magyarországon [Innovation and stability: Fintech overview in Hungary]. Consultation document, Magyar Nemzeti Bank [Hungarian National Bank]. Budapest. Available: http://www.mnb.hu/letoltes/konzultacios-dokumentum.pdf

MNB (2024) FinTech és Digitalizációs jelentés 2024. https://www.mnb.hu/letoltes/fintech-e-s-digitaliza-cio-s-jelente-s-2024-hun-0719-2.pdf

Muthukannan P, Tan B, Gozman D, Johnson L (2020) The emergence of a Fintech Ecosystem: a case study of the Vizag Fintech Valley in India. Information & Management 57(8):103385. https://doi.org/10.1016/j.im.2020.103385

Nakashima T (2018) Creating credit by making use of mobility with FinTech and IoT. IATSS Research 42(2):61–66. https://doi.org/10.1016/j.iatssr.2018.06.001

OECD (2018) Financial markets, insurance and private pensions: digitalisation and finance

Osei-Assibey Bonsu M, Wang Y, Guo Y (2023) Does fintech lead to better accounting practices? Empirical evidence. Account Res J 36(2–3):129–147. https://doi.org/10.1108/ARJ-07-2022-0178

Pelau C, Ene I, Pop MI (2021) The impact of artificial intelligence on consumers' identity and human skills. Amfiteatru Econ 23(56):33–45. https://doi.org/10.24818/EA/2021/56/33

Póta CP, Becsky-Nagy P (2022) The impact of digitalisation on the financial sector. Competitio 21:1–14. https://doi.org/10.21845/comp/2022/1-2/6

Puschmann T (2017) Fintech. Bus Inf Syst Eng 59(1):69–76. https://doi.org/10.1007/s12599-017-0464-6

Salin ASAP, Hasan HC, Kamarudin NNAN, Mad S (2024) Formulating a competency framework for accountants on environment, social and governance (ESG) standards and finance digitalization. Inf Manag Bus Rev 16(3 (I)):309–317. https://doi.org/10.22610/imbr.v16i3(I).3857

Rácz G (2023) Számlázz.hu: Hol tarthatna az ország, ha nem a számlagyárba menne a kreativitás? [Számlázz.hu: Where would the country be if creativity didn't go to the invoice factories?]. https://hvg.hu/gazdasag/20230808_Szamlazzhu_interju_angyan_balazs_szamlazas_digitalizacio_vallalkozas

Senyo PK, Effah J, Osabutey EL (2021) Digital platformisation as public sector transformation strategy: a case of Ghana's paperless port. Technol Forecast Soc Chang 162:120387. https://doi.org/10.1016/j.techfore.2020.120387

Számlázz.hu (2025) The company's website. https://www.szamlazz.hu/szamla/main

Tello-Gamarra J, Campos-Teixeira D, Longaray AA, Reis J, Hernani-Merino M (2022) Fintechs and institutions: a systematic literature review and future research agenda. J Theor Appl Electron Commer Res 17(2):722–750. https://doi.org/10.3390/jtaer17020038

Turzó ÁP (2025) Nagyon beindult egy új magyar fintech startup, elhalássza a bankok ügyfeleit? [A new Hungarian fintech startup is really taking off, will it steal banks' customers?]. https://www.portfolio.hu/bank/20250210/nagyon-beindult-egy-uj-magyar-fintech-startup-elhalassza-a-bankok-ugyfeleit-739919

Research Perspectives and Future Directions in Romania and Hungary

Opportunities for Applied Research in Collaboration with Romanian Universities

Alexandru Constăngioara

Abstract This chapter undertakes an investigation of the opportunities for applied research into finance, accounting, and business administration in collaborations with Romanian University. The analysis commences with an examination of the current state of research, which reveals a pattern for the adoption of AI that can be described as diverse, yet at the same time it is uneven across the different sectors. In Romania, the studies have shown a concentration on areas including managerial accounting, the management of risk in banking, and the digital transformation affecting small and medium-sized enterprises. Despite the benefits which have been documented, including an enhancement of efficiency and an improvement in the making of decisions, significant barriers continue to persist.

1 Introduction

The penetration of artificial intelligence (AI) into the domains of finance, accounting and business administration represents a process of transformation that is of significant importance, which acts to reshape workflows within organizations, the roles played by professionals, and the making of strategic decisions. Across the economies of the contemporary world, one can observe that AI technologies are becoming embedded in an increasingly manner within processes related to the analysis of finances, reporting, auditing, forecasting, and also the support for decisions at managerial level. However, it is to be noted that the pace together with the form taken by this transformation are showing considerable variation from one region to another, being dependent upon factors such as the readiness of institutions, the availability of human capital, and the maturity found within academic and professional ecosystems.

Within the specific context belonging to Romania and Hungary, the diffusion of AI unfolds under particular conditions of economic, institutional and also cultural nature

A. Constăngioara (✉)
Faculty of Economic Sciences, University of Oradea, Oradea, Romania
e-mail: alexandru.co@gmail.com

C. Sabău-Popa (ed.), *Artificial Intelligence in Finance, Accounting and Business Administration*, Contributions to Finance and Accounting,
https://doi.org/10.1007/978-3-032-22737-9_18

which are characteristic for the region of Central and Eastern Europe. These countries are facing simultaneous pressures related to the modernization of digital capacities, the upskilling of the workforce, and the integration into broader frameworks for European innovation, while they must still address structural constraints which have been inherited from stages of development belonging to earlier times. The existing research from academic circles demonstrates that a successful implementation of AI technologies is not something guaranteed merely by their availability; instead, it depends in a fundamental way on factors such as the readiness of human capital, the culture within organizations, the awareness of ethical matters, and the capacity for innovation within academic and institutional spheres (Vărzaru 2022a; Zaharia 2024).

This chapter undertakes an examination of the current perspectives within research and outlines the directions for future applied research concerning AI in finance, accounting and business administration, with a focus that is particular on Romania and Hungary. The emphasis is being placed upon opportunities for applied research which can serve to bridge the inquiry from academic sources and the implementation in practical terms. A special attention is given to the frameworks of cross-border institutions, notably the collaboration existing between the University of Oradea, Faculty of Economic Studies, and the University of Debrecen, Faculty of Economics and Business, which has engaged in projects of a joint nature and provides a platform that is stable for investigative work of a long-term character.

2 Current State of Research and AI Implementation

2.1 Sectoral Applications and Focus of Research

The landscape of contemporary research shows that the applications of AI across various sectors in both countries present a picture that is diverse but also uneven. In Romania, a considerable part of the research focuses its attention on managerial accounting, examining the use of AI for purposes such as the detection of fraud, the automation of reporting activities, and systems for the support of decisions (Vărzaru 2022a; Banţa et al. 2022). These studies bring to light both the gains achieved in efficiency and the changes occurring in professional judgment, especially in environments where the tasks of routine nature are becoming automated.

Research also explores the integration of AI within the banking sector and the management of financial risk, with an emphasis placed on predictive analytics and the monitoring in real-time of financial exposures (Ţîrcovnicu and Haţegan 2023). At the level of the organization, small and medium-sized enterprises (SMEs) have been studied in a primary way through case studies of exploratory character, such as the one concerning the Exonia Group, which illustrates in what manner AI tools can give support to operational efficiency, marketing activities, and internal processes, even under conditions where resources are constrained (Călinescu 2024).

The research originating from Hungary, while it is less represented within the specific domains of accounting and finance in this set of literature, contributes with perspectives related to digital transformation, smart development, and ecosystems for regional innovation (Gyulai et al. 2022). When these studies are taken together, they suggest an expansion of AI use that is gradual, though it is often fragmented and shows an uneven distribution across different sectors and regions.

2.2 *Benefits and Persisting Barriers*

The benefits coming from the adoption of AI are substantial in nature. Studies report improvements in operational efficiency, a reduction in the time required for processing, an enhancement in the quality of decisions, and a better utilization of data belonging to organizations. Within accounting and finance, AI enables a detection of fraud that is faster, a greater level of accuracy, and reporting capabilities in real-time (Vărzaru 2022a). For SMEs, the applications of AI show a potential to support competitiveness and innovation, particularly in cases where the traditional processes are intensive in their use of labor (Călinescu 2024).

However, barriers that persist remain in place. Constraints of a financial nature and a limited access to personnel possessing the necessary skills are cited frequently as obstacles, especially among SMEs. Concerns of ethical character regarding the security of data, bias within algorithms, and accountability in decision-making supported by AI are particularly pronounced within accounting and finance, where processes that are opaque or errors can carry consequences of significant weight (Vărzaru 2022b). Furthermore, the concentration in geographic terms of infrastructure for support, such as Digital Innovation Hubs, found mostly in capital cities, acts to limit access in regions that are peripheral (Gyulai et al. 2022).

Another limitation present within the literature is its focus which is predominantly national. The majority of studies examine either Romania or Hungary in an isolated manner, with few providing perspectives that are comparative in a systematic way. This imbalance highlights an opportunity that is clear for applied research of a cross-border nature, which is capable of capturing the differences in context and the challenges that are regional.

3 Cross-Border Collaboration as a Foundation for Research

The collaboration between the University of Oradea and the University of Debrecen, developed through programs for cross-border cooperation, represents an asset of institutional importance. This partnership has already facilitated activities of academic nature that are joint, outputs from research that are collaborative, and demonstrates the feasibility of a cooperation that is sustained across boundaries that are administrative and national.

Beyond this collaboration which is bilateral, the broader context of European nature provides additional structures for support. The network of European Digital Innovation Hubs (EDIHs) offers an infrastructure suitable for experimentation, training, and engagement with industry. Together with the instruments for funding from the EU such as Horizon Europe, these mechanisms allow for applied research to be embedded within settings that are organizational, ensuring relevance and an impact of practical character.

These frameworks enable applied research to move beyond an inquiry from academic sources that is isolated, supporting instead a continuous interaction taking place between universities, businesses, and institutions of public nature. For universities located in border regions, this positioning offers an advantage of strategic character in the coordination of studies that are comparative and in the piloting of initiatives that are joint.

4 Opportunities for Applied Research

4.1 Comparative Studies on AI Adoption Patterns

An avenue for applied research that shows promise involves the systematic comparison of organizations in Romania and Hungary, particularly SMEs operating within accounting, finance, and related services for business. Studies of comparative nature could examine in what way differences present in regulatory frameworks, professional norms, cultural attitudes toward technology, and access to networks of support act to shape the trajectories for adoption of AI.

Through the coordination of surveys, interviews, and case studies on both sides belonging to the border, researchers can isolate the variables of contextual nature which influence the speed, the depth, and the sustainability of adoption. Such research provides insights that are actionable for policymakers and institutions of support which aim to tailor the strategies for digital transformation to the conditions specific to the region.

4.2 Development of SME Digitalization Frameworks

The repeated identification of barriers related to cost and skills highlights the necessity for applied research that is oriented toward solutions and which targets SMEs. Teams for research of a joint nature could develop and test frameworks or toolkits of practical character to support the adoption of AI, including programs for training of modular design, diagnostic tools for assessing the readiness of organizations, and models for analysis of cost–benefit that are simplified and adapted to the realities of small business.

The piloting of these frameworks and the systematic evaluation of outcomes would contribute both to knowledge from academic sources and to tangible support for enterprises. The dissemination through networks already existing could act to amplify their impact.

4.3 Ethical and Responsible AI Implementation

Concerns of ethical character are especially salient within accounting and finance, where decisions supported by AI affect the reporting of financial information, the allocation of credit, and the accountability of organizations. Applied research could examine the professional and regulatory environments present in Romania and Hungary, identifying gaps and inconsistencies within the ethical guidance for the use of AI (Vărzaru 2022b).

Teams for research of interdisciplinary nature could develop frameworks specific to the region for the implementation of AI in a responsible manner, including guidelines of practical character to manage bias in algorithms, ensure transparency, and maintain oversight from human actors. These outputs would be applicable in a direct way to professional bodies and organizations which are in the process of adopting tools based on AI.

4.4 Longitudinal Research on Educational Integration

The use of AI within higher education remains at a stage that is early, often limited to experimentation and studies focused on perception. Applied research of longitudinal design could provide insights that are deeper into how the integration of AI affects the outcomes of learning, the practices of teaching, and the roles within academia across time. Pilot courses that are coordinated and delivered in Oradea and Debrecen could track the performance of students, the confidence of teachers, and the adaptation in pedagogy across multiple semesters.

This approach would give support to the reform of curriculum based on evidence and the development of education oriented toward competences, which is aligned with the needs of the labor market as driven by AI (Zaharia 2024).

4.5 Towards a Regional Research Hub

As an objective of long-term nature, the formalization of a hub for research of joint character focused on AI in Business and Economics represents an opportunity of strategic importance. Such a hub could provide a platform of collaborative nature for datasets that are shared, environments for experimentation, engagement with practitioners, and applications for grants that are coordinated. A movement from cooperation based on projects to collaboration that is institutionalized would enhance the sustainability, the visibility, and the impact of the research.

Applied research concerning AI also requires a reflection on matters of methodology. The dominance belonging to designs of cross-sectional type acts to limit the understanding of AI adoption as a process that is dynamic. Designs of mixed-method and longitudinal character capture in a better manner the learning, adaptation, and resistance of organizations across time.

The development of human capital must extend itself beyond the skills that are technical in nature. Confidence, professional identity, awareness of ethics, and the willingness to engage with systems that are intelligent are critical for a successful adoption of AI. These dimensions which are softer, though they are harder to measure, are essential for an integration that is sustainable and merit applied research that is focused.

5 Conclusions

The integration of AI into finance, accounting, and business administration in Romania and Hungary presents a landscape that is complex, composed of opportunities and constraints. While the potential offered by technology is evident, an implementation that is successful depends in a heavy way on human capital, the maturity of institutions, frameworks of ethical nature, and the strength of collaboration between academia and industry.

The existing partnerships of cross-border nature, particularly the one between the University of Oradea and the University of Debrecen, provide a foundation that is solid for the advancement of applied research. By focusing on studies of comparative type, solutions oriented toward SMEs, the implementation of AI in an ethical manner, integration within education, and collaboration that is institutionalized, these institutions can contribute in a meaningful way to the digital transformation of the region.

In the end, the future of AI within these domains will be shaped less by the sophistication of technology alone and more by the capacity of organizations and academic systems to learn, to adapt, and to govern in an intelligent manner. Applied research plays a role that is central in this process, translating the insight from theory into pathways of practical nature for an adoption of AI that is sustainable and responsible.

References

Banţa V, Rîndaşu S-M, Tănasie A, Cojocaru D (2022) Artificial intelligence in the accounting of international businesses: a perception-based approach. Sustainability 14(11):1–12

Călinescu G (2024) Artificial intelligence–opportunities and challenges for small and medium enterprises in Romania. A case study on the Exonia Group. In: Proceedings of the International Conference on Business Excellence, vol 18, no 1. Sciendo, pp 1363–1371

Gyulai T, Nagy M, Cibu-Buzac R (2022) Smart development with digital intelligent cities in cross-border regions. Pandémia—Fenntartható Gazdálkodás—Környezettudatosság 1:45–58

Ţîrcovnicu GI, Haţegan CD (2023) Integration of artificial intelligence in the risk management process: an analysis of opportunities and challenges. J Financ Stud 8(15):198–214

Vărzaru AA (2022a) Assessing artificial intelligence technology acceptance in managerial accounting. Electronics 11(14):2256

Vărzaru AA (2022b) Assessing the impact of AI solutions' ethical issues on performance in managerial accounting. Electronics 11(14)

Zaharia R (2024) Challenges for competence-oriented education in the context of the development of artificial intelligence systems. Amfiteatru Economic 26(65):153–170

Opportunities for Applied Research in Collaboration with Hungarian Universities

Peter Lengyel

Abstract This chapter examines how cooperation between Hungarian higher education institutions strengthens applied research performance, with a particular focus on the business, financial, and accounting applications of artificial intelligence. The analysis presents the domestic higher education and research management environment, the organizational forms of cooperation, and the role of infrastructure and human resource sharing. The chapter explores AI-driven research opportunities, the importance of joint doctoral programs and industrial partnerships, and highlights the challenges of financing, management, and intellectual property management. Based on the results, the study formulates strategic recommendations for the development of institutionalized, long-term sustainable university collaborations to strengthen applied research and national innovation performance.

1 Introduction

Higher education institutions (HEIs) have become key players in national innovation systems. Today, universities are expected to do more than educate, they're also seen as drivers of research commercialisation, regional development, and digital transformation. In Hungary, this shift is particularly significant due to the increasing complexity of scientific challenges, the emergence of artificial intelligence (AI), and recent reforms in the governance of higher education. As a result, effective collaboration among universities is now considered essential for enhancing applied research and supporting Hungary's transition to a knowledge-based economy (OECD 2023a).

In Hungary, collaboration on applied research among universities extends beyond administrative or organisational concerns, reflecting broader changes in European science policy. EU programs, such as Horizon Europe and the European Research Area, encourage collaborative research models that bridge institutional and disciplinary divides (European Commission 2023). Given the diversity among Hungarian

P. Lengyel (✉)
Faculty of Economics and Business, University of Debrecen, Debrecen, Hungary
e-mail: lengyel.peter@econ.unideb.hu

C. Sabău-Popa (ed.), *Artificial Intelligence in Finance, Accounting and Business Administration*, Contributions to Finance and Accounting,
https://doi.org/10.1007/978-3-032-22737-9_19

universities in terms of size, funding, and academic focus, collaboration enables them to leverage their strengths, share resources, and utilise public funding more effectively. The growing role of AI in fields such as economics and management adds even more urgency: successful AI applications depend on access to large datasets, high-performance computing, and interdisciplinary teams' capabilities that no single institution can manage alone.

This chapter provides a detailed examination of how Hungarian universities can capitalise on new opportunities in applied research by collaborating, particularly in AI-driven fields such as finance, accounting, and business administration. Drawing on recent policy documents, university initiatives, and academic research from 2018 to 2025, this study examines the national context, collaboration strategies, governance challenges, and long-term development goals, all grounded in a thorough review of the current literature.

2 The Hungarian Higher Education Context

Hungary's higher education system comprises 65 accredited institutions, including public, private, and church-run institutions, which serve around 260,000 students (Hungarian Central Statistical Office [HCSO] 2024). The system features strong regional diversity, with major universities concentrated in Budapest (e.g., Eötvös Loránd University, Corvinus University of Budapest, and Budapest University of Technology and Economics), and others forming regional innovation centres in Debrecen, Szeged, Pécs, and Győr.

Since 2021, a major reform known as the *foundation model* has restructured many Hungarian universities into privately managed foundations. These entities enjoy greater financial and administrative autonomy, theoretically enabling more flexible collaboration (OECD 2023b). However, critics note that increased autonomy without clear accountability frameworks may fragment the system further (Kováts and Temesi 2022). The National Research, Development and Innovation Office (NKFIH) remain the main public funding agency supporting research and development. Its programmes, such as *Thematic Excellence Programmes* and *Cooperative Doctoral Programmes,* encourage consortium-based projects across institutions. Meanwhile, the *Hungarian Accreditation Committee (MAB)* continues to oversee quality assurance, including the evaluation of collaborative doctoral training and research excellence clusters.

Hungary's *National Smart Specialisation Strategy (S3)* emphasises cross-institutional research collaboration in priority areas, such as advanced manufacturing, ICT, and health. Complementing this, the *Digital Education Strategy (DES)* encourages joint development of digital curricula and research infrastructure (OECD 2023c). These policy frameworks highlight a national consensus: innovation thrives through collaboration. However, funding fragmentation persists. Most NKFIH programmes run for three years, which is too short to institutionalise cooperation. Long-term, performance-based schemes could stabilise partnerships. Similarly, the data-driven evaluation of collaboration outcomes, such as joint patents, co-authored papers, and shared doctoral supervision, remains underdeveloped (HCSO 2024).

3 Forms and Mechanisms of Collaboration

Joint research centres form the backbone of inter-university collaboration. Examples include the *Artificial Intelligence National Laboratory (MILAB)*, involving Eötvös Loránd University (ELTE), the University of Szeged, and the University of Debrecen. MILAB focuses on AI in natural language processing, autonomous systems, and data analytics (MILAB 2023). Similarly, the *Industry 4.0 National Technology Platform* connects universities and corporations for research in robotics, automation, and digital manufacturing (Oraveczné Kiss and Varga 2022). These centres demonstrate that collaborative governance can succeed when goals are shared and funding is secure. Yet, sustainability remains a challenge once project cycles come to an end. A unified national framework for joint research governance could prevent duplication and ensure continuity.

Access to costly infrastructure, supercomputers, laboratories, and digital platforms is a critical driver for cooperation. The *National Laboratory Programme,* launched in 2019, pools high-value equipment across institutions (OECD 2023c). Universities such as Szeged and Debrecen now share facilities for biotechnological and AI research. However, administrative barriers, including ownership disputes and accounting practices, still hinder joint use.

To address this, several universities have proposed creating inter-institutional service consortia that operate shared infrastructures independently of individual accounting systems. Such models, already tested in Germany and Finland, could enhance efficiency and access (European University Association [EUA] 2022). Collaborative doctoral schools promote interdisciplinary research and capacity building. In Hungary, the *Cooperative Doctoral Programme* (CDP) supports joint supervision between universities and companies. The University of Debrecen and Corvinus University, for instance, co-supervise doctoral projects on AI-driven logistics and financial forecasting (NKFIH 2023). Joint PhD frameworks encourage student mobility, cross-fertilisation of ideas, and shared publication efforts.

Industry collaboration remains central to applied research. Universities partner with multinational and domestic firms through R&D consortia and dual education models. However, as Inzelt (2019) argues, the dominance of foreign companies can misalign university research with national interests. Building strong ties with domestic SMEs could create a more balanced innovation ecosystem. The Hungarian government's *Higher Education and Industrial Cooperation Centres (FIEK)* initiative represents a step forward in this regard.

4 AI-Driven Applied Research Opportunities

AI provides fertile ground for applied research collaboration because of its complexity, interdisciplinarity, and strategic significance. Universities can pool resources and expertise to generate high-impact outcomes across sectors. AI technologies enable automation in auditing and accounting. Algorithms can detect anomalies, assess risk, and process massive datasets faster than traditional manual methods (Heye 2021). Hungarian universities are experimenting with audit simulation tools and predictive models tailored to local accounting standards (Simon 2020). Collaborations between universities with strong informatics faculties (e.g., Budapest University of Technology) and business schools (e.g., Corvinus) create a natural synergy for these projects.

AI also transforms financial services. Collaborative research between the University of Pécs and Corvinus University is exploring AI-driven investment modelling and risk prediction. These studies contribute to national FinTech innovation ecosystems while providing students with hands-on experience in algorithmic trading and financial data science. The establishment of joint FinTech labs could formalise these activities. For example, Poland's SGH Warsaw School of Economics has successfully established a consortium-based FinTech research hub; Hungarian universities could emulate this model (Pleśniarska 2019).

The integration of AI into accounting and business curricula requires a joint development of digital resources. Shared online platforms and virtual classrooms enable cost-effective course delivery. The University of Debrecen and the Budapest Business School have co-developed a *Digital Finance* course using AI-based case studies, demonstrating that curricular collaboration can extend beyond research into pedagogy. Developing shared AI data repositories would strengthen research efficiency. Current fragmentation means datasets remain locked within individual institutions. Establishing a *National Research Data Infrastructure for AI* could ensure accessibility and standardisation, facilitating large-scale projects on finance, sustainability, or public policy. Similar models operate in the Netherlands (SURF) and Denmark (DeiC) (EUA 2022).

AI research also holds potential for addressing regional economic disparities. In the Eastern regions, where universities like Debrecen and Nyíregyháza play vital economic roles, AI-based agricultural analytics and logistics optimisation could spur local development. Collaboration among regional institutions could thus serve dual purposes: promoting academic excellence and fostering territorial cohesion.

5 Policy and Governance Challenges

While opportunities abound, structural barriers still constrain collaboration. Universities' new foundation status has increased autonomy but also competition. Without coordination mechanisms, institutions risk duplicating research areas or competing for the same grants. A national *Council for University Collaboration* could provide strategic oversight, aligning projects with national priorities (Kováts and Temesi 2022). Short-term project cycles undermine sustainability. Transitioning from project-based to mission-oriented funding, similar to the EU's "flagship missions", could stabilise collaboration. Longer-term programmes would enable infrastructure investment, career pathways for researchers, and measurable impact assessment.

Hungarian universities often lack harmonised IP frameworks. Joint projects raise questions about ownership of AI algorithms and datasets. Model contracts developed by the Hungarian Intellectual Property Office and shared technology transfer offices could resolve these issues (Korányi and Fülöp 2025). Academic performance metrics focus on individual output (publications, grants) rather than collaborative impact. Introducing indicators that measure joint publications, shared PhD supervision, or collaborative patents would encourage cooperation. International best practice, such as Norway's *Performance-Based Research Funding System*, illustrates how funding formulas can reward collaboration.

Collaboration requires trained managers, legal experts, and communication specialists. Many Hungarian universities lack sufficient administrative staff to coordinate large consortia. Developing shared professional training, possibly through the Hungarian Rectors' Conference, would strengthen the system's managerial backbone.

6 Strategic Directions and Best Practices

To transform cooperation from sporadic partnerships into a sustainable system, Hungarian universities need long-term strategies that combine academic, industrial, and governmental efforts. Strategic coordination should move beyond project-based collaboration toward institutionalised networks capable of addressing national innovation challenges.

Creating thematic university alliances can align institutional strengths around common research goals. For instance, a *Hungarian Network for AI and Digital Business Research* could unite universities specialising in informatics, economics, and management. Such networks should operate under shared governance structures, allowing coordinated grant applications and unified communication with policymakers. The *European University Initiative* (EUI) offers a relevant model: transnational consortia have demonstrated that joint governance and shared infrastructure can enhance visibility and attract competitive funding (European Commission 2023). Applying similar principles domestically would help Hungarian institutions pool expertise while retaining autonomy.

AI research demands enormous data and computational resources. Establishing a National AI Supercomputing Centre jointly managed by leading universities would enable shared access to GPUs, cloud services, and big-data analytics tools. This could complement existing structures, such as MILAB, but extend them to business-oriented applications. The platform could also host a repository of anonymised financial, environmental, and educational datasets, resources essential for applied AI studies. Governance should ensure data ethics, compliance with GDPR, and transparent access rules. Strengthening the human capital base requires doctoral schools that transcend institutional boundaries. Joint programmes focusing on *AI and Business Analytics*, co-supervised by professors from different universities, would foster a new generation of interdisciplinary researchers. Doctoral students could rotate between institutions and industrial partners, building networks and applying research to real-world challenges.

The University of Debrecen's cooperation with Corvinus University and Budapest Business School already demonstrates the feasibility of such arrangements through their *Cooperative Doctoral Programme* (NKFIH 2023). Scaling this model nationally would multiply its impact. Technology transfer offices (TTOs) remain unevenly distributed across Hungary's universities. Collaborative TTO networks could share expertise in patenting, licensing, and spin-off creation. Korányi and Fülöp (2025) found that coordinated IP management significantly increases innovation efficiency in Central Europe.

Joint innovation funds and incubators would also help commercialise AI-based research. The *Budapest Innovation Group*, a proposed consortium of universities and local investors, could catalyse startup ecosystems focusing on AI in accounting, agriculture, or healthcare. International partnerships can reinforce domestic cooperation. Participation in Horizon Europe consortia, Erasmus + mobility, and Interreg projects exposes Hungarian universities to global standards and practices. The E2U-AI project exemplifies how cross-border experiences foster internal capacity building. Its workshops and curriculum development activities have also strengthened institutional collaboration within Hungary. To maximise impact, universities should adopt a "dual-layer collaboration" approach: domestic alliances for resource sharing and international engagement for benchmarking and visibility. This layered model could integrate Hungarian research more firmly into the European Research Area.

Collaboration among Hungarian universities has become an integral part of the national research and innovation strategy. The evidence presented in this chapter shows that effective cooperation enhances applied research capacity, facilitates digital transformation, and contributes to economic resilience. The integration of AI into finance, accounting, and business administration illustrates the tangible benefits of shared expertise and infrastructure.

Nevertheless, systemic challenges persist: fragmented governance, short funding cycles, inconsistent IP frameworks, and limited incentives for collaborative outputs. Addressing these requires a holistic policy approach grounded in transparency, inclusivity, and long-term commitment. Hungary's future competitiveness depends on transforming its higher-education institutions into a connected ecosystem rather than isolated entities. Building national research networks, expanding shared infrastructures, and integrating collaboration into evaluation systems are crucial steps toward achieving this goal. By embracing collaboration as a guiding principle, Hungarian universities can move beyond incremental improvements and become regional leaders in applied AI research.

Ultimately, fostering applied research collaboration is not merely an academic exercise; it is a strategic necessity for sustainable economic development, talent retention, and technological sovereignty. As OECD (2023a) aptly notes, „The universities of the future will be those that collaborate best." For Hungary, the time to act on this insight is now.

References

European Commission (2023) Horizon Europe: the European research and innovation programme 2021–2027. Publications Office of the EU. https://doi.org/10.2777/0608

European University Association (EUA) (2022) University collaboration for research infrastructure: Policy and practice report. Brussels

Heye AM (2021) The future of auditing: an analysis of AI implementation in the Big Four accounting firms. University of Colorado Boulder

Hungarian Central Statistical Office (HCSO) (2024) Education, research and innovation indicators 2023. HCSO Press, Budapest

Inzelt A (2019) Business–university collaboration in Hungary. In: University–industry collaboration strategies in the digital era. Springer, pp 149–170. https://doi.org/10.1007/978-981-32-9350-2_7

Korányi G, Fülöp Z (2025) Technology transfer efficiency in Central European universities: A comparative analysis. J Open Innov: Technol, Mark, Complex 11(1):100527. https://doi.org/10.1016/j.joitmc.2025.100527

Kováts G, Temesi J (2022) Governance reforms in Hungarian higher education: between autonomy and accountability. Hung Educ Res J 12(3):155–171. https://doi.org/10.1556/063.2022.00125

MILAB (2023) Artificial Intelligence National Laboratory Annual Report 2022–2023. Budapest: ELKH

NKFIH (2023) Cooperative Doctoral Programme for supporting industry-linked research. National Research, Development and Innovation Office

OECD (2023a) Higher education in Hungary: Review of the higher education system. OECD Publishing. https://doi.org/10.1787/98a5f1e0-en

OECD (2023b) Assessment frameworks for external quality assurance in Hungary. OECD Publishing. https://doi.org/10.1787/7d644534-en

OECD (2023c) Supporting institutions to enhance the quality of digital higher education in Hungary. OECD Publishing. https://doi.org/10.1787/2d003a2e-en

Oravecznè Kiss É, Varga G (2022) Hazai felsőoktatási és vállalati együttműködések az Ipar 4.0 szempontjából. Educatio 31(1):124–139. https://doi.org/10.1556/2063.30.2021.3.12

Pleśniarska A (2019) The intensity of university–business collaboration in the EU. Acta Universitatis Lodziensis. Folia Oeconomica 1(339):139–155. https://doi.org/10.18778/0208-6018.339.09

Simon J (2020) Public accounting in Hungary: Situation and challenges. J Educ Cult Soc 11(2):124–133

Regional Collaboration: AI Initiatives in Central and Eastern Europe

Dana-Simona Gherai and Luminița Rus

Abstract This paper explores the rapid evolution of Central and Eastern Europe from a post-communist transitional region into a dynamic global hub for Artificial Intelligence innovation. By analysing the unique trajectories of leading nations—Poland, the Czech Republic, Hungary, and Romania—the study identifies how the region leverages strong technical education, foreign direct investment, and strategic EU integration to foster specialized AI ecosystems. Key findings highlight Poland's dominance in natural language processing and enterprise solutions, the Czech Republic's focus on Industry 4.0 and automotive AI, Hungary's advancements in precision agriculture, and Romania's integration of AI within healthcare and education. The study concludes that regional collaboration and the transition toward a "critical mass" of talent and computing infrastructure are essential for CEE to sustain its competitive edge in the global digital economy.

1 Introduction

Central and Eastern Europe (CEE) has emerged as a dynamic hub for artificial intelligence development and innovation in recent years. The region, comprising countries such as Poland, the Czech Republic, Hungary, Slovakia, Slovenia, Croatia, Romania, Bulgaria, and the Baltic states, has leveraged its strong technical education systems, growing tech ecosystems, and strategic geographic position to become a significant player in the global AI landscape.

This transformation represents a remarkable evolution from the region's post-communist transition to its current status as a competitive force in digital innovation. The combination of skilled workforce, government support, EU funding, and increasing private investment has created fertile ground for AI development and cross-border collaboration.

D.-S. Gherai (✉) · L. Rus
Faculty of Economic Sciences, University of Oradea, Oradea, Romania
e-mail: dana.gherai@gmail.com

C. Sabău-Popa (ed.), *Artificial Intelligence in Finance, Accounting and Business Administration*, Contributions to Finance and Accounting,
https://doi.org/10.1007/978-3-032-22737-9_20

Academic discourse surrounding this transformation highlights the significant strides made by various regional nations, particularly in fostering environments conducive to digital innovation.

The literature reveals that the post-communist transition in CEE has facilitated distinct economic restructuring characterised by market-oriented reforms. Jasiecki discusses how the region's transition has transformed its capital structures, which are now better integrated into the global economy (Jasiecki 2018). This integration has facilitated the rise of digital economies, allowing nations like Poland, Hungary, and the Czech Republic to emerge as competitive players in technology and digital innovation. Jasiecki further asserts that the post-transition framework has encouraged a search for new economic languages to articulate the distinct characteristics of CEE's evolving market dynamics (Jasiecki 2018).

Nedučin and Krklješ (2017) explore the effects of urban restructuring on the technological landscape throughout CEE, arguing that urbanisation's trajectories post-communism have provided both challenges and opportunities for innovation. The authors state that various urban changes following the fall of the Berlin Wall have stimulated not only economic revivals but also technological advancements, further enhancing CEE's status as an emerging region in digital innovation.

Moreover, Brouthers et al. (2023) illustrate Romania's economic transformation through privatisation as a critical element that enabled it to embrace international markets and, subsequently, digital innovation practices. They discuss how the transition from communism to a market-oriented system has encouraged countries in the region, including Romania, to adopt technology-driven approaches to bolster their economies, demonstrating how external pressures can catalyse internal innovation.

Sýkora and Bouzarovski (2011) discuss the broader societal transformations accompanying economic restructuring in CEE, emphasising that these transitions are not merely economic but also involve profound social changes that contribute to a conducive environment for digital innovation. Their exploration into political restructuring offers insights into how societal engagement in transformation plays a crucial role in sustaining competitive advantages in technological fields.

Overall, the transition of CEE from post-communist states to competitive forces in digital innovation illustrates significant progress over the last three decades. Factors such as market integration, urban restructuring, and societal transformation have collectively created an environment ripe for technological advancement and innovation, positioning the region favourably within the global digital economy.

2 Data and Methodology Research

In order to identify regional collaborations on artificial intelligence, the design of the research methodology is the one shown in Fig. 1 and starts from the establishment of the proposed objectives for the study of the topic.

The establishment of research questions is the pillar of the proposed scientific approach. The next step is the study and sorting of information on the countries of

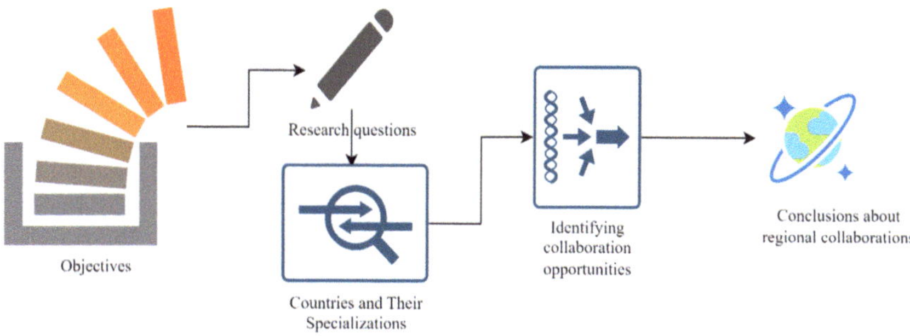

Fig. 1 The Conceptual research plan

Central and Eastern Europe on the specialisations of each, followed by the identification of opportunities for collaboration between these countries in the use of artificial intelligence. The research findings will be formulated in response to the proposed research questions.

3 Historical Context and Foundation

3.1 Post-Communist Transformation

The post-communist transformation of Central and Eastern Europe (CEE) towards artificial intelligence (AI) leadership reflects a unique and multifaceted journey. Several key factors contribute to this trajectory, including the region's historical context, economic reforms, integration into global markets, and a growing focus on technological innovation.

Firstly, the historical background of CEE countries, which transitioned from centrally planned economies to market-driven systems post-1989, plays a critical role in shaping the region's path toward AI leadership. During this transformation, countries such as Poland, Hungary, and the Czech Republic adopted neoliberal policies, resulting in significant regulatory and economic shifts that nurtured entrepreneurial ecosystems conducive to technological advancement (Hrinko 2023; Bugarič 2016). The neoliberal framework facilitated foreign direct investment (FDI), which has been essential for economic growth in CEE. Hrinko highlights that FDI has been pivotal for the economic transformation of these countries, enabling access to capital and technology crucial for advancing AI capabilities (Hrinko 2023).

Moreover, the rapid globalisation and integration into the European Union (EU) framework have opened new avenues for collaboration and investment in AI. The EU's emphasis on digital transformation and technological readiness encourages CEE countries to develop AI technologies. While Zhang's article discusses the EU's integration strategies, it is primarily focused on the Western Balkans and may not directly apply to general CEE integration regarding AI (Zhang 2024). This integration has not only yielded economic advantages but also fostered innovation through the creation of incubators and partnerships that enhance AI research and development. Additionally, the region possesses unique capabilities in fields such as mathematics, computer science, and engineering, resulting in a skilled workforce contributing to AI advancements.

Sekliuckienė's research specifies that emerging CEE economies are characterised by early internationalisation of their new ventures that often involve AI technologies (Sekliuckienė 2017). This trend reflects a growing understanding of the significance of technological entrepreneurship for securing competitive advantages in a global market increasingly reliant on AI solutions.

However, challenges exist in balancing rapid technological growth with sustainable economic policies. External economic pressures, particularly related to debt and investment security, add complexity to the transition toward a robust AI framework (Chentukov et al. 2021). Furthermore, Kadzierski and Lewandowski emphasise how internal limitations within CEE countries can hinder the presentation of a cohesive strategy for leading in AI (Kedziora and Lewandowski 2020).

3.2 EU Integration Benefits

The integration of Central and Eastern European (CEE) countries into the European Union (EU) has generated significant benefits, particularly in the context of artificial intelligence (AI) initiatives. As these countries navigate their post-communist transformation, EU membership has provided vital economic, regulatory, and funding mechanisms that facilitate the development of AI technologies and enhance regional competitiveness.

One key benefit of EU integration is the substantial increase in Foreign Direct Investment (FDI) directed towards CEE countries. Research indicates that EU membership has accelerated economic growth and convergence, particularly through the influx of FDI and trade liberalisation, which improves labour productivity and fosters innovation Zaman and Meunier (2017). This financial inflow is crucial for AI development as it finances startups and research initiatives focused on technological innovation. Furthermore, the EU's commitment to boosting the economies of poorer regions serves as a platform to enhance CEE countries' capacities to leverage innovative technologies like AI. Promoting economic growth in these regions is essential to unlocking untapped potential, as recognised in various studies (Kley 2024).

Another significant advantage stems from the regulatory framework provided by EU membership. CEE states are encouraged to adopt pro-competitive policies aligned with the EU's digital strategy, which enhances the quality of regulation in these countries (Böheim and Friesenbichler 2015). This regulatory alignment facilitates smoother integration into the single market and creates a consistent environment for AI initiatives, enabling businesses to operate across borders with minimal friction.

The EU's emphasis on digital capabilities provides a political impetus for member states to advance their AI sectors in alignment with broader European goals.

Additionally, the EU's funding mechanisms, such as the European Structural and Investment Funds, offer substantial financial support for AI development projects in the CEE region (Vaqif et al. 2023). These funds improve infrastructure and foster an innovation-driven environment, crucial for the growth of AI initiatives. Accession to the EU has led to heightened investments in research and development, advancing technological initiatives that align with the European strategy toward AI leadership (Jiroudková et al. 2015). Such funding opportunities enable CEE countries to establish research centres and collaborations, positioning them to remain competitive in the global AI landscape.

Furthermore, the potential for knowledge exchange through EU programs contributes to the region's technological advancement. Educational initiatives and exchange programs offered by the EU help build a skilled workforce adept in AI technologies. The integration of CEE countries into the EU framework creates networks for collaboration that incentivise knowledge sharing in AI research and implementation, enhancing their ability to develop innovative solutions (Papadimitriou et al. 2017).

The convergence of socio-economic dynamics highlights the importance of unified efforts towards common goals in sustainability and AI advancement, ultimately aiming for a competitive edge at the global level. This collective movement reinforces the potential for CEE countries to emerge as critical players in the AI field, supported by a well-established ecosystem provided through EU integration.

3.3 *Current AI Landscape in CEE*

The current landscape of artificial intelligence (AI) in Central and Eastern Europe (CEE) reflects a dynamic interplay of historical evolution, economic transformation, and technological advancement, facilitated largely by European integration. As these countries strive to carve out a space in the global AI ecosystem, they leverage their unique socio-economic contexts, human capital, and strategic partnerships within the EU framework.

One foundational aspect of AI development in the CEE region stems from significant foreign direct investment (FDI) that has flowed into these countries post-EU accession. FDI has played a critical role in the economic transformation since the early 1990s, creating an environment conducive to technological innovation and infrastructure development. This investment boost has been essential for establishing research facilities, tech startups, and collaborative platforms focused on AI. The Visegrád Group (V4), comprising Poland, Hungary, the Czech Republic, and Slovakia, serves as a primary example of how CEE nations band together to strengthen their capabilities and attract investment, resulting in faster economic growth and technological advancement. The recognition of AI's potential as a driver for economic growth has prompted governments in the region to prioritise policies that support AI research and innovation.

The EU's regulatory framework has also played a pivotal role in shaping the AI landscape in CEE. The adoption of EU-wide digital strategies has encouraged compliance with high standards of governance while fostering an environment that promotes innovation. This alignment with EU norms not only enhances the credibility of CEE nations in the international market but also ensures that they are part of larger EU projects focused on AI development. As CEE countries work to navigate the balance between innovation and regulation, the supportive policies of the EU are critical in promoting responsible AI development that adheres to ethical considerations.

In terms of human capital, CEE countries possess a rich pool of skilled labour in fields such as mathematics, computer science, and engineering, which are fundamental to AI development. The region's education systems have begun to adapt to the evolving demands of the AI sector, with many universities developing specialised programs to prepare students for careers in AI and related fields. Additionally, partnerships between academia and industry foster environments where research can be effectively translated into practical applications.

However, despite these advancements, several challenges remain. Issues surrounding data privacy, infrastructure readiness, and the digital divide among different CEE countries can hinder progress. Moreover, some nations struggle with bureaucratic obstacles that slow down the implementation of effective AI strategies. Ensuring equitable access to technology and digital literacy across populations is vital for maximising the benefits of AI and preventing further socio-economic disparities.

Overall, the current AI landscape in CEE is marked by significant progress supported by EU integration and a conducive investment climate. The emphasis on strategic partnerships, human capital development, and adherence to regulatory standards positions CEE countries for enhanced roles in the global AI ecosystem. Moving forward, addressing the existing challenges will be crucial for sustaining growth and advancing CEE's competitiveness in the rapidly evolving field of artificial intelligence.

4 Leading Countries and Their Specialisations

Poland has firmly established itself as the AI powerhouse of the region, with its major tech hubs in Warsaw and Krakow excelling across several specialised domains, most notably natural language processing and machine translation, Fintech AI applications, AI for the gaming and entertainment sectors, and comprehensive enterprise AI solutions.

Key initiatives include the Polish AI Strategy 2020–2027 and significant investments in AI research centres at universities like the University of Warsaw and AGH University of Science and Technology.

The impact of foreign direct investment (FDI) on Poland's technological landscape has been profound, particularly in the context of its economic transformation post-1989. Hrinko highlights that the inflow of FDI into Poland has facilitated a substantial restructuring of its economy, enabling it to embrace advanced technologies, including AI Hrinko (2023). The availability of capital from foreign entities has accelerated the establishment of tech firms and stimulated local innovation capacities, thus positioning Poland as a competitive player in the AI domain. Warsaw, as the capital, has been at the forefront of this transformation, drawing significant investments that contribute to its growing reputation as a tech hub.

Krakow has also emerged as a pivotal city in Poland's AI ecosystem. The city is home to numerous universities and research institutions that foster collaborations between academia and industry. This is particularly important for AI, where research and practical applications must often work in concert. While the reference provided by Chen and Zhang (2025) discusses the impact of AI technology on urban public health resilience, it does not directly support the claim regarding Krakow's academic infrastructure and its role in AI development. Therefore, this citation should be removed from this context.

Polish governmental policies have been instrumental in shaping the AI landscape. The introduction of national strategies aimed at fostering innovation, particularly in the technology sector, reflects a commitment to making Poland a leader in AI development. The reference Bartoszkiewicz et al. (2021) is irrelevant as it pertains to clinical trials rather than policies related to AI. Thus, it should be omitted from this discussion.

Furthermore, the role of collaborative governance regimes in Central and Eastern Europe has been significant in fostering an environment of innovation. As highlighted by Hajnal and Jeziorska, collaborative efforts among various stakeholders—governmental, non-governmental, and private sectors—are crucial in addressing the challenges posed by rapidly evolving technological landscapes (Hajnal and Jeziorska 2021). This emphasis on collaboration extends to AI initiatives, facilitating the sharing of knowledge and resources, which is pivotal in a field that is inherently interdisciplinary.

In summary, Poland's assertion as a regional AI powerhouse is well-founded. The combination of robust foreign investment, strong educational institutions, supportive government policies, and collaborative frameworks positions Warsaw and Krakow at the forefront of AI development in Central and Eastern Europe. This environment not only encourages the growth of local firms but also attracts international talent and capital, ensuring Poland's continued advancement in the global AI arena.

The Czech Republic has channelled its efforts toward highly practical AI applications in its traditional sectors, with a strong focus on advanced solutions for Manufacturing and Industry 4.0, Healthcare AI, including medical imaging, Smart City initiatives, and leveraging its robust automotive sector for specialised Automotive AI solutions.

Prague has become a regional centre for AI startups, supported by government initiatives and EU funding.

One of the primary drivers for AI adoption in traditional industries is the Czech Republic's robust manufacturing sector. As an industrialised nation, the country has a significant share of its economy dedicated to manufacturing, especially in the automotive and machinery sectors. Markaki et al. discuss how this industrial landscape has been shaped by a modern industrial policy aimed at optimising production structures, arguing that enhancing productivity through innovation is paramount, positioning AI as a critical tool to rejuvenate traditional industries by making processes more efficient and responsive to market demands Markaki et al. (2021).

AI's integration into the manufacturing sector is evident in the context of "Industry 4.0," which emphasises smart manufacturing systems that leverage AI technologies. Povolná and Švarcová examine the macroeconomic context surrounding investments in machine tools, highlighting the sector's innovative capacity and the role of AI technologies in enhancing production efficiency. Their study underscores how traditional sectors like machine tool manufacturing are pivotal to the Czech economy and show strong potential for AI applications to meet contemporary challenges (Povolná and Švarcová 2017).

In agriculture, AI is being harnessed to improve productivity and sustainability practices, marking a significant application of technology in traditional sectors. Perunová emphasises that traditional industries, particularly in the bioeconomy, are being revitalised through enhanced technologies and AI applications. This shift reflects a broader trend towards integrating precision agriculture practices, employing AI for tasks such as crop yield prediction and resource management, thus contributing to enhanced operational efficiency (Perunová 2022).

Furthermore, the ethical implications of AI deployment in traditional sectors cannot be overlooked. Sýkorová et al. discuss integrating AI into human resource processes, highlighting broader systemic transformations across various sectors, including those with traditional roots. As organisations in the Czech Republic adopt AI for recruitment and management, the ethical implications of such technology become increasingly pertinent, influencing business practices within traditional industries (Sýkorová et al. 2024).

In summary, the Czech Republic's focus on practical AI applications within traditional industries reflects an adaptive approach toward modernising these sectors. Through strategic investments and policy frameworks supporting technology integration, traditional industries such as manufacturing and agriculture can leverage AI to address contemporary challenges, enhance efficiency, and foster sustainable practices.

Hungary has strategically carved out specialised niches in the AI landscape, focusing primarily on key areas such as Automotive AI and autonomous systems, Agricultural technology and precision farming, advanced Healthcare diagnostics, and efficient automation solutions for financial services.

The Hungarian government's Digital Success Program includes substantial AI components and research funding. The development of artificial intelligence (AI) in Hungary reflects the country's efforts to integrate advanced technologies into various sectors, alongside its unique socio-economic context following the post-communist transition. The literature reveals multiple facets of this evolution, from national strategies and economic implications to sector-specific applications.

One significant area of focus is the Hungarian government's strategic commitment to advancing AI. Szalavetz discusses the development of an AI-based strategy in Hungary's market economy, emphasising the potential of AI to contribute to economic growth and the necessity of navigating global power dynamics (Szalavetz 2019). This strategic framework is vital for fostering an environment conducive to AI advancements, particularly in a region with intense external competition where localised adaptation is essential.

A central theme in understanding AI's role in Hungary's economic landscape is the relationship between AI and the labour market. Horváth and Vicsek highlight insights from Hungarian AI specialists regarding the future of work, emphasising optimism about AI's potential to enhance productivity while also raising concerns about job displacement and the need for a workforce equipped with new skills (Horváth and Vicsek 2023). This dynamic illustrates the need for a balanced approach to AI deployment, ensuring that economic benefits are accompanied by adequate support for worker retraining and adaptation.

Furthermore, economic studies emphasise the quantifiable benefits of AI to Hungary's overall growth. Xian's analysis reveals that AI may significantly stimulate economic growth through productivity improvements, although specific contributions in terms of labour and capital should be carefully assessed to understand the broader impact (Xian 2023). This aligns with Liu's findings, which underscore AI's potential to enhance economic performance when thoughtfully integrated into existing structures (Liu 2024).

Additionally, agriculture stands out as a sector where AI applications are gaining traction. Bai et al. indicate that while agriculture's contribution to Hungary's GDP is relatively modest, the adoption of precision farming technologies powered by AI presents substantial opportunities for innovation within this traditional industry (Bai et al. 2022). This not only enhances productivity but also addresses sustainability challenges, positioning Hungarian agriculture competitively in the global marketplace.

Regulatory frameworks significantly shape the landscape for AI development. The Hungarian AI Strategy 2020–2030 aims to foster innovation while ensuring that ethical considerations are integrated into AI systems. Saputra et al. analyse this strategy, emphasising its comprehensive approach to balancing technological advancement with governance and regulation, which reflects Hungary's proactive stance in the international AI discourse (Saputra et al. 2024).

In conclusion, the development of artificial intelligence in Hungary is characterised by a strategic commitment to fostering innovation, enhancing productivity across sectors, and ensuring that ethical considerations guide technology deployment. The interconnection of government policies, economic implications, and sectoral applications creates a robust framework for Hungary's ongoing evolution as an emergent player in the global AI landscape.

The development of artificial intelligence (AI) in *Romania* has gained momentum over recent years, driven by a combination of strategic policies, investments, and sector-specific initiatives. The literature illustrates different facets of how AI is being integrated into various sectors in Romania, particularly healthcare, education, and technology.

One pertinent area of focus is the integration of AI into the healthcare system. Wolff et al. provide insights into the successful implementation of AI technologies within Romanian healthcare, highlighting the development of GDPR-compliant AI applications aimed at enhancing data protection and privacy in health insurance systems (Wolff et al. 2021). Their findings emphasise the importance of designing AI solutions that align with local regulations while also enhancing operational efficiency.

Fitzek and Choi further assess the potential impact of AI on the Romanian healthcare infrastructure, discussing its promise to improve diagnostic processes, treatment protocols, and health management (Fitzek and Choi 2023). They note that while AI can enhance healthcare delivery significantly, it also presents challenges, including ethical concerns and the need for comprehensive training for healthcare professionals to effectively utilise AI technologies. This framework underscores the dual nature of progress and challenges accompanying technological integration in a critical sector.

The implications of AI extend beyond healthcare into education and higher learning. Bucea-Manea-Ţoniş et al. explore how AI can enhance educational environments in Romanian higher education institutions (Bucea-Manea-Ţoniş et al. 2022). Their study suggests that AI technologies can aid in developing new curricula, creating adaptive learning environments, and promoting interdisciplinary skills, which are vital as education systems increasingly incorporate digital methodologies.

Moreover, in a broader economic context, the integration of AI technologies is essential for supporting sustainable development goals. Firoiu et al. discuss the role of AI in addressing sustainability challenges in Romania, indicating that intelligent systems can optimise resource use and contribute to achieving environmental objectives (Firoiu et al. 2019). This perspective reinforces the idea that AI can serve not only as a tool for economic growth but also as an enabler of sustainable practices across various sectors.

Collaboration across sectors is also highlighted as a crucial factor in AI development in Romania. The engagement between governmental bodies, industry stakeholders, and academic institutions fosters a robust ecosystem for AI innovation. The collaboration emphasises the need for strategic investments and infrastructure development that support AI initiatives, ensuring they align with both local and EU goals.

In conclusion, the development of artificial intelligence in Romania is shaped by multifaceted initiatives across healthcare, education, and sustainability sectors. By integrating ethical considerations, fostering collaborative environments, and strategically investing in technology, Romania is advancing its capabilities in AI, positioning itself to meet both national and regional challenges effectively.

5 Lines of Action for European States

At the European Union level, April 2025 brought Member States an action plan focused on the development of artificial intelligence technologies with the aim of boosting Europe's competitiveness in introducing the benefits of AI into various economic sectors.

The action plan contains measures concerning Computing Infrastructure, increasing access to high-quality Data for companies, strengthening AI skills, development strategies and AI adoption in strategic sectors, as well as facilitating the implementation of the AI Act.

The Computing Infrastructure comprises actions in three directions: AI Factories, AI Gigafactories, and Cloud and AI development. With a budget of ten billion euros for the 2021–2027 period, the first direction aims to establish at least 13 operational AI Factories by 2026 (Fig. 2).

These factories are created through collaborations between Member States via consortia and are focused on different sectors of activity, noting three inter-state consortia and ten intra-state consortia (Fig. 3).

Regarding the sectors of activity for which these AI Factories were created, major interest is observed in health, manufacturing, finance, life science, energy, climate, and the public sector.

Romania is part of the Barcelona Supercomputing Centre AI Factory, which aims to develop computing services specifically designed for AI-driven workflows, such as Large Language Models. It also aims to create a single, AI-optimised platform for testing new technologies.

The other two lines of action of the computing infrastructure have as their objectives the training and development of complex AI models and the stimulation of

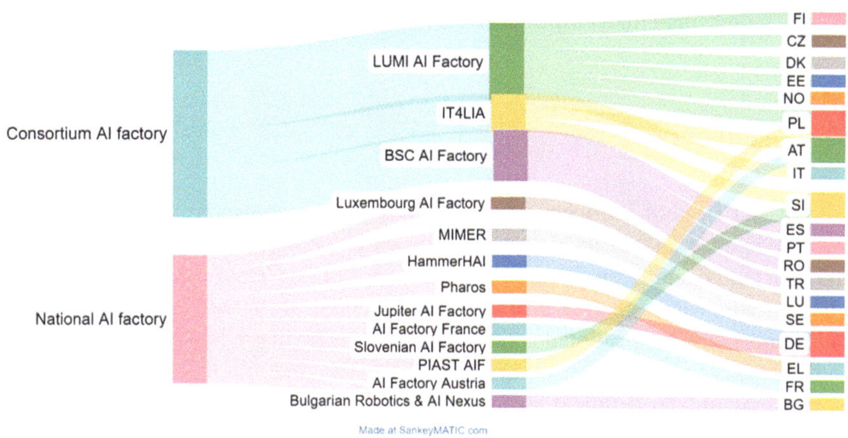

Fig. 2 Artificial intelligence factories' location

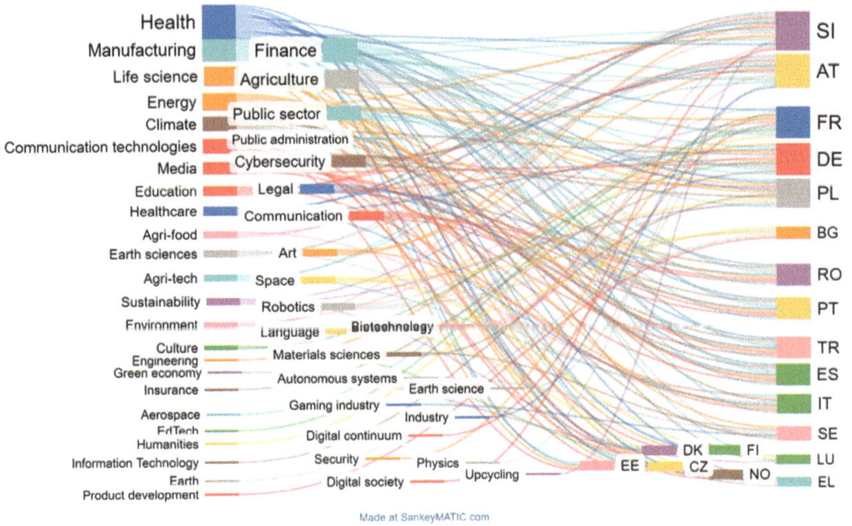

Fig. 3 AI factories and their sectors

sustainable research by encouraging investments, as well as, in the medium term, tripling the capacity of the European Union's data centres.

Objectives of the AI Action Plan also aim at improving companies' access to data, the qualitative collection and selection of data from different sources, and forming international partnerships through scholarships granted to students and researchers in the field of artificial intelligence.

Improving AI skills, as a professional retraining support measure, will assist companies and public administrations in implementing digital innovation solutions, thereby increasing citizen trust.

6 Conclusions

Central and Eastern European (CEE) countries are increasingly turning to Artificial Intelligence (AI) as an essential driver for boosting economic competitiveness and efficiently addressing societal challenges, ranging from healthcare to public administration. Recognising the disruptive potential of this technology, the region is moving away from isolated action. On the contrary, there is a growing emphasis on regional collaboration as a vital strategy to overcome fragmented resources and limited individual investment levels.

This trend toward strategic cooperation is primarily motivated by the necessity of creating a critical mass of talent and infrastructure. By joining forces, CEE countries can more effectively compete with established global technological powers.

References

Bai A, Kovách I, Czibere I, Megyesi B, Balogh P (2022) Examining the adoption of drones and categorisation of precision elements among Hungarian precision farmers using a trans-theoretical model. Drones 6(8):200. https://doi.org/10.3390/drones6080200

Bartoszkiewicz M, Kufel-Grabowska J, Litwiniuk M (2021) Number of clinical trials of new therapeutic agents in the European Union countries of Central and Eastern Europe, 2000–2019. Pol Ann Med. https://doi.org/10.29089/2020.20.00146

Böheim M, Friesenbichler K (2015) Exporting the competition policy regime of the European Union: success or failure? empirical evidence for acceding countries. JCMS: J Common Mark Stud 54(3):569–582. https://doi.org/10.1111/jcms.12321

Brouthers L, Văduva S, Tiron-Tudor A, Burtic D (2023) The transformation of the Romanian economy through privatization and internationalization. J East Eur Manag Stud 28(2):265–292. https://doi.org/10.5771/0949-6181-2023-2-265

Bucea-Manea-Ţoniş R, Kuleto V, Gudei S, Lianu C, Lianu C, Ilić M, Păun D (2022) Artificial intelligence potential in higher education institutions enhanced learning environment in Romania and Serbia. Sustainability 14(10):5842. https://doi.org/10.3390/su14105842

Bugarič B (2016) Neoliberalism, post-communism, and the law. Annu Rev Law Soc Sci 12(1):313–329. https://doi.org/10.1146/annurev-lawsocsci-110615-084545

Chen E, Zhang H (2025) Research on the impact of artificial intelligence technology on urban public health resilience. Front Public Health 12. https://doi.org/10.3389/fpubh.2024.1506930

Chentukov Y, Marena T, Zakharova O (2021) Challenges and threats to the debt security of Central and Eastern European countries. Środkowoeuropejskie Studia Polityczne (2):135–152. https://doi.org/10.14746/ssp.2021.2.8

Firoiu D, Ionescu G, Băndoi A, Doran N, Jianu E (2019) Achieving sustainable development goals (SDG): implementation of the 2030 agenda in Romania. Sustainability 11(7):2156. https://doi.org/10.3390/su11072156

Fitzek S, Choi K (2023) Potential impact and challenges of implementing artificial intelligence in the Romanian healthcare system. PostmodIsm Probl 13(2):148–192. https://doi.org/10.46324/pmp2302148

Hajnal G, Jeziorska I (2021) Collaborative governance regimes in illiberal democracies: a comparative case of drug harm reduction policy in Central and Eastern Europe. Transylv Rev Adm Sci (62 E):60–80. https://doi.org/10.24193/tras.62e.4

Horváth Á, Vicsek L (2023) Visions of Hungarian artificial intelligence specialists about the future of work and their roles. Sci Technol Soc 28(4):603–620. https://doi.org/10.1177/09717218231186105

Hrinko J (2023) Examining the relationship between foreign direct investment and export in the region of selected Central and Eastern European countries. University of Economics in Bratislava, pp 149–162. https://doi.org/10.53465/edamba.2022.9788022550420.149-162

Jasiecki K (2018) The strengths and weaknesses of the varieties of capitalism approach: the case of Central and Eastern Europe. Int J Manag Econ 54(4):328–342. https://doi.org/10.2478/ijme-2018-0030

Jiroudková A, Rovná L, Striełkowski W, Šlosarčík I (2015) EU accession, transition and further integration for the countries of Central and Eastern Europe. Econ Sociol 8(2):11–14. https://doi.org/10.14254/2071-789x.2015/8-2/1

Kedziora D, Lewandowski J (2020) Transitional challenges cycle of service offshoring delivery centres in Central and Eastern Europe. Int J Technol Policy Manage 20(1):35. https://doi.org/10.1504/ijtpm.2020.104865

Kley F (2024) The regional economic foundations of European identity. Polit Cent Eur 20(1):9–73. https://doi.org/10.2478/pce-2024-0002

Liu D (2024) The impact of artificial intelligence on economic growth—an industrial structure based perspective. Adv Econ Manag Polit Sci 123(1):192–199. https://doi.org/10.54254/2754-1169/123/2024mur0143

Markaki M, Papadakis S, Putnová A (2021) A modern industrial policy for the Czech Republic: optimizing the structure of production. Mathematics 9(23):3095. https://doi.org/10.3390/math9233095

Nedučin D, Krklješ M (2017) Post-socialism and urban transition: transforming the socialist city. Facta Universitatis—Series Architecture and Civil Engineering 15(3):347–357. https://doi.org/10.2298/fuace160817023n

Papadimitriou D, Baltag D, Surubaru N (2017) Assessing the performance of the European Union in Central and Eastern Europe and in its neighbourhood. East European Politics 33(1):1–16. https://doi.org/10.1080/21599165.2017.1279608

Perunová M (2022) Employment in the agriculture and forestry in the European Union, v4, and the Czech Republic in the period 2000–2019. https://doi.org/10.36689/uhk/hed/2022-01-063

Povolná L, Švarcová J (2017) The macroeconomic context of investments in the field of machine tools in the Czech Republic. J Compet 9(2):110–122. https://doi.org/10.7441/joc.2017.02.08

Saputra B, Hartati H, Bene O (2024) Hungary's AI strategy: lessons for Indonesia's AI legal framework enhancement. Jambe Law J 7(1):25–58. https://doi.org/10.22437/home.v7i1.325

Sekliuckienė J (2017) Factors leading to early internationalization in emerging Central and Eastern European economies. Eur Bus Rev 29(2):219–242. https://doi.org/10.1108/ebr-12-2015-0158

Sýkora L, Bouzarovski S (2011) Multiple transformations. Urban Stud 49(1):43–60. https://doi.org/10.1177/0042098010397402

Sýkorová Z, Hague D, Dvouletý O, Procházka D (2024) Incorporating artificial intelligence (AI) into recruitment processes: ethical considerations. Vilakshan—Ximb J Manag 21(2):293–307. https://doi.org/10.1108/xjm-02-2024-0039

Szalavetz A (2019) Artificial intelligence-based development strategy in dependent market economies—any room amidst big power rivalry? Cent Eur Bus Rev 8(4):40–54. https://doi.org/10.18267/j.cebr.219

Vaqif S, Dadashov K, Dadashova K, Egorov I (2023) European integration processes in EECCA: dependencies and drivers. J Ethn Cult Stud 10(2):41–74. https://doi.org/10.29333/ejecs/1484

Wolff J, Pauling J, Keck A, Baumbach J (2021) Success factors of artificial intelligence implementation in healthcare. Front Digit Health 3:594971. https://doi.org/10.3389/fdgth.2021.594971

Xian F (2023) Quantifying the economic benefits of artificial intelligence technology. https://doi.org/10.4108/eai.9-12-2022.2327579

Zaman C, Meunier B (2017) How much has Romania benefited from ten years of EU membership? AIJES 10:44–53. https://doi.org/10.15837/aijes.v10i0.2866

Zhang L (2024) Advancing European integration in central and Eastern Europe: a comprehensive examination of reconciliation and Collaborative Progress in the Western Balkans. Stud Soc Sci Humlties 3(2):54–65. https://doi.org/10.56397/sssh.2024.02.09

Human Capital Development: Academic Programs and Doctoral Research in AI

István Füzesi

Abstract The chapter examines the transformation of human capital development in the age of artificial intelligence, with a particular focus on higher education programs and the role of doctoral research. The analysis presented highlights that in a digital and data-driven economy, the integrated development of technological competencies, interdisciplinary knowledge, and ethical and social responsibility will become crucial. The chapter discusses in detail the importance of education and research ecosystems, industrial collaborations, and government strategies in renewing human capital. Special attention is given to trends in higher education and doctoral training in Europe and Central and Eastern Europe, particularly in Hungary and Romania, and their contribution to strengthening AI-based innovation and sustainable competitiveness.

1 The Role of Human Capital in the Age of AI

Artificial intelligence (AI) is one of the most defining technological factors of our time, fundamentally transforming economies, labour markets, and education systems (Georgieva 2024). AI is not just a new tool for increasing productivity, but a comprehensive innovation that requires a reassessment of human knowledge, skills, and creativity. The "human capital "development—that is, the development of human capital—is a key response to the challenges of the era of artificial intelligence, as it determines the adaptability and competitiveness of society in the long term.

The concept of human capital has traditionally been identified with the economic value of knowledge, skills and experience (Schultz 1961; Becker 1964). Today, however, this concept has taken on new dimensions: in the digital age, cognitive flexibility, technological literacy, and interdisciplinary thinking are at least as important as formal qualifications. In the age of artificial intelligence, human capital is not just an input to the labour market, but also a driver of technological progress (Brey

I. Füzesi (✉)
Faculty of Economics and Business, University of Debrecen, Debrecen, Hungary
e-mail: fuzesi.istvan@econ.unideb.hu

C. Sabău-Popa (ed.), *Artificial Intelligence in Finance, Accounting and Business Administration*, Contributions to Finance and Accounting,
https://doi.org/10.1007/978-3-032-22737-9_21

and van der Marel 2024; Samek 2021). The rapid rise of AI is redefining the relationship between education and the labour market. According to the OECD (2021), the demand for professionals with AI skills has tripled in the past decade, while the supply of skills has not grown at the same rate. The "skills" bundle phenomenon—that is, the combination of complementary digital, analytical, and interpersonal skills—has become a fundamental element of successful human capital in the AI era. This is especially true for countries and companies that actively invest in education and knowledge reuse (Brey and van der Marel 2024). The labour market effects of AI are twofold: some occupations disappear, but new ones emerge that require higher levels of cognitive and technological competencies (Drydakis 2025; Hampole et al. 2025). Experience shows that AI not only replaces but complements human work, especially in sectors where decision-making, creativity, and ethical sense remain a human monopoly. All this means that the development of human capital has become not only an economic but also a social issue.

More and more countries around the world are recognising that modernising education and research systems is the most important prerequisite for harnessing the potential of AI. In the European Union, for example, AI strategies have focused on lifelong learning and strengthening STEM (Science, Technology, Engineering and Mathematics) education, as regions with the highest human capital account for more than 50% of AI adoption (Brey and van der Marel 2024). Improving education systems and strengthening academia are, therefore, not only a social goal but also an economic necessity. However, in the AI-driven economy of the twenty-first century, human capital remains the most valuable resource. The combined development of human knowledge, values, and creativity ensures that AI technologies do not displace, but rather strengthen, the central role of humans in the world of work and innovation (World Economic Forum 2025).

Human capital theory is a fundamental pillar of modern economics, emphasising the economic value of human capabilities, skills, and knowledge. According to this approach, education, training, and health are investments that increase individual productivity and thereby contribute to economic growth (Becker 1964; Schultz 1961). The classical theory was further developed by Gary S. Becker and Theodore Schultz, who demonstrated that investment in human capital, such as education, is a key factor in the competitiveness of nations and companies (Almendarez 2016; CIPD 2024). The basic idea of the theory is that people make rational decisions to develop their own knowledge in order to increase their future income potential (Aghion and Howitt 2008; Acemoglu and Autor 2012). Modern economic models have further expanded this to include aspects of human behaviour, motivation, and creativity, as the ability to innovate and adaptive thinking has become the new engine of economic growth (Tian and Tóth 2024). Knowledge, creativity, and social capital together form the "cumulative knowledge stock" that fuels innovation and value creation (OECD 2021).

In the twenty-first century, the concept of the knowledge society has become a central concept of digital transformation. The essence of the knowledge society is that economic and social development is no longer based on physical resources, but on knowledge, technology and the flow of information (da Silva 2023; Gifford et al.

2023). Innovation ecosystems, such as the "Quadruple Helix model—based on collaboration between government, industry, academia and civil society—play a key role in knowledge sharing and collective learning (da Silva 2023). Such ecosystems are vital for AI and technological innovations, as they enable multidisciplinary collaboration and rapid adaptation of knowledge. The emergence of artificial intelligence has intensified the demand for new types of skills and competencies, which are essential for the "lifelong learning" paradigm. In an AI-driven labour market, the rate of skills obsolescence is faster than ever, requiring new forms of training and institutional flexibility (OECD 2024; UNESCO 2024). According to OECD (2024), AI will also force the reform of education and vocational training, as technological literacy, digital ethics and creative problem-solving will be the most valued competencies.

UNESCO (2024) emphasises that lifelong learning is not merely an educational goal, but the foundation of social resilience. AI competency frameworks are being integrated into higher education and vocational training, enabling human capital to adapt and evolve in response to technological advancements. In this context, human capital development is not only a fundamental pillar of economic growth but also of social cohesion and democratic development policies (OECD 2024; UNESCO 2024).

2 The Ecosystem of Human Capital Development

Human capital development in the age of artificial intelligence (AI) is not just a matter of university programs and individual training, but is the result of a complex, multi-actor ecosystem. This ecosystem includes educational institutions, research institutes, industry players, government agencies and civil society groups, which collaborate to create an innovation environment for the development of AI-related knowledge and skills (da Silva 2023; OECD 2024). Universities and research centres play a key role in this system, as they train talent and conduct basic and applied research. Interdisciplinary research groups and innovation laboratories allow PhD students and young researchers to work together on the development of the latest technologies, while involving industrial partners to quickly and effectively apply research results (Gyulai 2025; PTE 2025). However, the role of industry goes beyond funding: technology companies are active partners in the design of training programs, providing practical mentoring, internships and joint development projects for students. This synergy helps to develop the "skills" gap" and supports the development of an adaptable workforce (HolonIQ 2025; Deloitte Hungary 2025). At the government level, as part of the artificial intelligence strategy, states are increasingly encouraging the creation of innovation clusters that operate as sustainable ecosystems, integrating education, research, industry and innovation (European Commission 2025c). Hungary has also created such clusters, which provide professional networks, funding and infrastructure for researchers and businesses working on artificial intelligence (Kormány.hu 2025).

Startup incubators and technology labs are key elements of hands-on learning. These platforms offer opportunities for young people to participate in real-world development projects while receiving mentoring and market feedback. This process accelerates the integration of innovation into education and promotes practice-oriented development of human capital (StudyCare 2025). Mentoring and professional networking are critical elements of the human capital development ecosystem. Conferences, workshops, and professional meetings organised for PhD students, postdocs, and young professionals provide opportunities for knowledge sharing and collaboration, which are essential for progress in the complex discipline of AI (ELTE BTK 2025).

3 Competencies, Soft Skills, and Ethical Dimensions

In the age of artificial intelligence (AI), human capital development cannot be limited to the mere transfer of technical knowledge. Development is based on complex, multidimensional capabilities and soft skills. It is the integrated development of skills (social and emotional competencies). These—such as critical thinking, creativity, problem-solving skills, communication and empathy—are essential for human agents to be able to make meaningful, ethical and practical decisions alongside AI systems (Artificial Intelligence Strategy of Hungary 2025).

Technical skills such as programming, machine learning and data analysis are now essential in the field of AI, but the OECD and other international organisations emphasise that ethical awareness, social responsibility and digital literacy are equally important. These skills will help prepare workers for the new professions generated by AI and to deal responsibly with the consequences of automation (OECD 2024; UNESCO 2024).

The treatment of AI, complemented by cognitive and emotional skills, brings with it a fundamentally new concept of "AI literacy", which goes beyond mere technical knowledge. This includes a critical attitude towards data, an understanding of how algorithms work, and attention to the transparency and fairness of decision-making processes (UNESCO 2025). Ethical issues arising in the application of artificial intelligence—such as data protection, discrimination or social inequalities—are becoming increasingly prominent; therefore, the development of ethical sensitivity is an essential part of education (Hungarian Government 2025).

Multifaceted competence development supports the preservation of "human superiority" in tasks that automated systems cannot or only to a limited extent perform, such as empathy-based human relations, value-based decision-making or creative innovation. Issues of diversity and inclusivity also receive special attention in order to ensure that the development and use of AI does not further reinforce social inequalities, but contributes to their reduction (OECD 2025).

4 The AI Education System—University Programs and Training Trends

Artificial intelligence (AI) education has become one of the fastest-growing sectors of higher education in recent years. According to the 2025 Stanford AI Index Report, the number of AI-related university programs worldwide has grown to more than 1,200, more than double the number in 2020 (Stanford HAI 2025). AI-related programs are expanding significantly on all continents, especially in the United States, the European Union, and Asia, where technology-driven economic policy programs are fostering partnerships between educational institutions and industry (QS World University Rankings 2025). Three main characteristics of AI-based higher education programs can be observed: interdisciplinarity, a practice-oriented approach, and ethical embeddedness. Modern AI curricula not only include technical courses such as machine learning, algorithm theory, or data mining, but also complement them with social science and philosophy modules that prepare students for ethical AI development and understanding of societal impacts (UNESCO 2025; Zam 2025). Institutions such as MIT, Stanford, Oxford and the National University of Singapore have introduced integrated training models where theoretical foundations are complemented by experimental research, startup incubation and industry cooperation (StudyCare 2025). One of the key trends in curriculum development is adaptive and personalised learning. AI is increasingly being used not only as an educational subject but also as an educational tool—that is, artificial intelligence helps to design learning paths, assess student performance and customise content. AI-Powered A study titled Educational Technologies (2024) showed that AI-based adaptive systems can improve student satisfaction and learning efficiency by 35%, especially in STEM fields (Kovács and Zhao 2024). The rapid development of educational programs is also supported by the OECD and UNESCO guidelines, which have set the standard for "human-centred" and "inclusive" technology education (UNESCO 2025; OECD 2024). The UNESCO 2025 Digital Learning, for example, a prominent topic at the Week event was how to ensure the equity of AI-supported education and how to protect human agency against algorithmic pedagogies (UNESCO 2025).

Global trends show that the focus of AI education is on the "education-to-employment" logic: university programs are increasingly linked to the needs of the labour market. HolonIQ Education Trends According to Snapshot (2025), education systems worldwide are facing the so-called "skill" crisis. They are moving towards an "economy" model that emphasises practical knowledge, work-based learning, and corporate partnerships (HolonIQ 2025). This is especially important in the artificial intelligence and data-driven economy sectors, where skill needs are changing rapidly.

Finally, it is important to mention the moral and regulatory aspects of the digitalisation of education. The emergence of generative AI (e.g., ChatGPT, Claude, Gemini) has raised dilemmas in the areas of educational integrity, knowledge assessment, and intellectual property. Leading universities are therefore developing new codes of ethics and guidelines for data use, while digital literacy, AI ethics, and critical thinking about data are becoming mandatory elements of curricula (Zam 2025; Giannini 2025).

5 Doctoral Research in the Field of AI

Artificial Intelligence (AI) has become one of the fastest-growing and most influential areas of science research today. AI can be understood as the "new language" of modern science, fundamentally changing research methodology, data processing procedures and the logic of scientific thinking (European Commission 2025a; Ludovika Blog 2025). In the scientific community, AI is no longer seen solely as a technological tool, but as a driver of innovation capable of creating new forms of knowledge and promoting interdisciplinary research. In 2025, the European Commission launched the European Strategy for Artificial Intelligence in Science (RAISE) programme, which aims to make Europe a global hub for AI-driven science (European Commission 2025b). The strategy treats the development of doctoral and postdoctoral training as a key pillar. In this context, separate resources are allocated to the RAISE Doctoral Networks that engage the most talented young researchers in ethical and responsible AI research. The program allocates €58 million to support doctoral training focused on AI, integrating not only technical but also ethical and social science dimensions (European Commission 2025b).

The topics of doctoral research related to artificial intelligence encompass a broad spectrum, ranging from theoretical machine learning models (such as deep learning and reinforcement learning) to applied areas, including medical diagnostics, natural language processing, and autonomous systems. However, an interdisciplinary approach is increasingly important, where AI techniques interact with other disciplines—such as psychology, biology, ethics or social sciences (Gyulai 2025; HUN-REN 2025). Such research aims to use AI not only as a technical tool, but also as a complex analytical and predictive system to expand human knowledge.

The Hungarian academic community is also actively involved in the development of the AI doctoral research ecosystem. The Hungarian Artificial Intelligence Strategy (2025–2030) sets a specific goal of involving at least 300 PhD students in AI-related research by 2030 (Kormány.hu 2025). Eötvös Loránd University (ELTE), Budapest University of Technology and Economics (BME), University of Debrecen (DE), and University of Pécs (PTE) have all established dedicated AI workshops and doctoral programs that work with industrial partners, such as research institutes and technology startups (PTE 2025; ELTE BTK 2025). The rapid development of the Hungarian research infrastructure is facilitated by the HUN-REN Science Cloud, which provides high-performance computing capacity for doctoral and postdoctoral research (HUN-REN 2025). With this system, PhD students can run complex model learning experiments—for example, U-Net-based image processing or time-series data analysis—in fields such as medicine, agriculture, or economics. The research typically uses adaptive pipelines built from multiple data sources, as the goal is no longer to increase the performance of the models, but also to develop ethical, transparent, and interpretable AI models (Gyulai 2025).

Doctoral research is therefore key to developing human capital, as these programs combine deep technological knowledge with ethical, legal, and social considerations. The new paradigm of AI-driven science means that future researchers need not only to be good at programming—they must also be able to understand how technology impacts human life, decision-making and values.

6 Regional Perspectives—Situation in Europe, Hungary and Romania

The European Union's AI strategy places a strong emphasis on developing artificial intelligence and increasing human capital in education and research (European Commission 2025b). The EU's 2030 objectives include transforming Member States' education systems to support the development of AI skills, and encouraging researcher mobility and interdisciplinary collaborations. Lifelong learning and strengthening STEM fields are given high priority, as they are essential to maintaining competitiveness in the global AI race (OECD 2024).

Hungary is an active player in the AI development and research ecosystem. The Hungarian Artificial Intelligence Strategy 2025–2030 supports the strengthening of university research groups, especially at ELTE, BME, DE and PTE, where an increasing number of doctoral programs and research projects integrate AI-supported solutions (Kormány.hu 2025). The country aims to develop a significant AI research base by 2030 and strengthen its international cooperation. At the same time, the brain drain phenomenon is also present as a challenge: the most talented young people are looking for new opportunities abroad, so the continuous development of the research environment and the maintenance of competitive jobs are key (HUN-REN 2025).

Romania faces similar challenges and opportunities in the field of AI research and education. Although the country currently has a smaller AI research capacity, significant progress has been made in the development of university programs in recent years, especially at the Technical University of Bucharest, Babes-Bolyai University of Cluj-Napoca, and Alexandru Iași University of Iași. John through the AI centres of Cuza University (European AI Observatory 2025). Through strengthening industrial collaborations and support from European Union funds, Romania is actively seeking to expand its research network and international mobility.

A comparison of AI developments in the Central and Eastern European region shows that both Hungary and Romania are striving to modernise educational programs and expand research infrastructure, but mobilising resources and aligning industrial needs with scientific training remains a challenge. While Hungary has a stable research base and a more developed innovation ecosystem, Romania is on a rapid growth trajectory, the key to which is regional cooperation and the efficient use of EU financial support (Central European AI Forum 2025).

It is important to mention the possibility of regional cooperation, which, in addition to sharing knowledge and innovation, increases the region's competitiveness on the European and global AI map through joint projects and researcher mobility. Central and Eastern European countries, including Hungary, Romania, the Czech Republic and Poland, are increasingly launching joint research programs aimed at strengthening and harmonising AI education and research (European Commission 2025b).

7 Future Trends and Challenges in AI Human Capital Development

The rapid development of artificial intelligence brings both new opportunities and significant challenges for the development of human capital, especially in education and research. In Europe, AI-driven education transformation has become part of everyday practice, but issues of regulation, ethics and social justice remain unresolved. According to the EU AI Act, AI systems used in education are considered high-risk, which imposes strict requirements on security, transparency and human oversight on users. Maintaining a balance between the effective implementation of this framework and the rapid development of technology is a challenge (European Commission 2024). Ethical issues such as algorithmic bias, data protection and liability are common issues in AI education. For example, algorithms can reflect past social inequalities, which can lead to further reductions in educational opportunities for disadvantaged groups, such as rural or Roma students (European Union Agency for Fundamental Rights 2025). In addition, the GDPR and the increasingly valid European data protection guidelines ensure the protection of educational data, although the regulation needs continuous refinement due to the intensive development of technology (UNESCO 2025).

Reducing the digital divide is one of the biggest challenges, as many students in rural and disadvantaged areas do not have reliable internet access or modern devices. This situation threatens equal access to AI-based learning opportunities and requires increased support from government and EU programs in this area (World Bank 2025; UNESCO 2025). Although Hungary has better infrastructure than the EU average, the situation in digital skills is still unbalanced, especially among vulnerable groups (European Commission 2024).

Another challenge is to prepare teachers and educators to use AI tools effectively and ethically. Teachers in different European countries support the integration of AI in education to varying degrees, but many are still sceptical about improving academic outcomes, although they acknowledge the potential of AI to increase efficiency in administrative and repetitive tasks (Sanoma Learning 2025). Teachers' pedagogical expertise and critical understanding of AI applications are key to the successful adoption of AI (DigiEduHack 2025). In the future, the key to developing human capital will be comprehensive, ethical and inclusive education in AI competencies, combining technical knowledge with social responsibility and respect for human values. The systematic development of AI literacy enables students to become not just users, but also conscious and responsible critics who are able to evaluate and shape the impacts of AI in society (AILiteracyFramework 2025).

References

Acemoglu D, Autor D (2012) The basic theory of human capital. London School of Economics Discussion Paper. Retrieved from https://econ.lse.ac.uk/staff/spischke/ec533/Acemoglu%20Autor%20chapter%201.pdf

Aghion P, Howitt P (2008) Human capital theory: overview. ScienceDirect. https://www.sciencedirect.com/topics/social-sciences/human-capital-theory

Almendarez L (2016) Human capital theory: implications for educational development. University of the West Indies

AILiteracyFramework (2025) Empowering learners for the age of AI: draft framework. Retrieved from https://ailiteracyframework.org/wp-content/uploads/2025/05/AILitFramework_ReviewDraft.pdf

Becker GS (1964) Human capital: a theoretical and empirical analysis, with special reference to education. University of Chicago Press

Brey B, van der Marel E (2024) The role of human capital in artificial intelligence adoption. J Econ Behav Organ. https://doi.org/10.1016/j.econlet.2024.111949

Central European AI Forum (2025) Regional cooperation and challenges in AI research and education. Budapest

CIPD (2024) Human capital theory: assessing the evidence for the value of people in organisations. Chartered Institute of Personnel and Development

da Silva GS (2023) Towards effective innovation ecosystems: a framework for mapping knowledge governance. Scitepress. https://doi.org/10.5220/0012251900003654

Deloitte Magyarország (2025) Magyar MI Körkép 2025. Retrieved from https://www.deloitte.com/hu/hu/what-we-do/deloitte-magyar-mi-korkep-2025.html

DigiEduHack. (2025). The reality of AI-driven learning in European classrooms. Retrieved from https://digieduhack.com/news/the-reality-of-ai-driven-learning-in-european-classrooms

Drydakis N (2025) Artificial intelligence and labour market outcomes. IZA World of Labour

European AI Observatory (2025) Artificial intelligence development in Romania: educational and research context

European Commission (2024) Digital decade monitoring and EU AI Act. Retrieved from https://digital-strategy.ec.europa.eu/en/policies/2024-state-digital-decade-package

European Commission (2025a) Can we get AI in education right? Ludovika Blog. Retrieved from https://www.ludovika.hu/en/blogs/the-daily-european/2025/10/02/can-we-get-ai-in-education-right

European Commission (2025b) European strategy for artificial intelligence in science (RAISE)

European Commission (2025c). European strategy for ai innovation ecosystems. COM(2025) 732 final

European Union Agency for Fundamental Rights, *Fundamental rights report 2025*, N/A (2025).

ELTE BTK (2025) DH Budapest 2025: young researchers conference.

Georgieva K (2024) AI will transform the global economy: let's make sure it benefits humanity. IMF Blog

Giannini S (2025) Artificial intelligence in education: challenges and opportunities. UNESCO Digital Education Initiative

Gifford E, et al (2021). The evolution of knowledge-intensive innovation ecosystems: Co-evolving entrepreneurial activity and innovation policy in the West Swedish maritime system. Ind Innov 28(5):651–676
Gyulai T (2025) Mesterséges intelligencia felelősségteljes innovációval kombinálva. HUN-REN Regional Science Institute
Hampole M, et al (2025) Artificial intelligence and the labour market. NBER Working Paper No. 33509. https://doi.org/10.3386/w33509
HolonIQ (2025) Education trends snapshot 2025: AI, skills, and workforce pathways. Retrieved from https://www.holonIQ.com
Hungarian Government (2025). Magyarország Mesterséges Intelligencia Stratégiája (2025–2030) Hungary's Artificial Intelligence Strategy 2025–2030, N/A (2025).
HUN-REN (2025) Science cloud projects and the PhD research pathways
Kormány.hu (2025) Magyarország Mesterséges Intelligencia Stratégiája (2025–2030). Retrieved from https://cdn.kormany.hu/uploads/document/...pdf
Kovács D, Zhao L (2024) AI-Powered educational technologies: impacts on curriculum design. Southeast European Journal of Public Health. https://doi.org/10.3389/bjbs.2024.14048
Ludovika University (2025) A mesterséges intelligencia a tudomány új nyelve. Öt Perc Európa Blog. Retrieved from https://www.ludovika.hu/blogok/ot-perc-europa-blog/2025/10/20/a-mesterseges-intelligencia-a-tudomany-uj-nyelve
Magyarország Mesterséges Intelligencia Stratégiája (2025) Kormányzati dokumentum a digitális és AI-korszak kompetenciáiról
OECD (2021) The human capital behind AI. OECD Publishing. https://doi.org/10.1787/2e278150-en
OECD (2024) Reskilling and lifelong learning: adapting to the AI-driven job market. Retrieved from https://www.oecd.org/education/
OECD (2025) Trends shaping education 2025
Pécsi Tudományegyetem (2025) AI-hírek és doktori kutatási programok
QS World University Rankings (2025) Data science and artificial intelligence subject rankings. Retrieved from https://www.topuniversities.com/university-subject-rankings/data-science-artificial-intelligence
Samek L (2021) The human capital behind AI. OECD Report
Sanoma Learning (2025) European Teacher Survey 2025 on AI in education. Retrieved from https://www.sanomalearning.com/en/news-container/20252/ets-2025-ai-in-education/
Schultz TW (1961) Investment in human capital. Am Econ Rev 51(1):1–17
Stanford Human-Centered Artificial Intelligence Institute (2025) AI Index Report 2025. Retrieved from https://hai.stanford.edu/ai-index/2025-ai-index-report
StudyCare (2025) Top universities for studying AI and technology. Retrieved from https://studycare.ma/blogs/top-universities-ai-technology-2025
Tian X, Tóth A (2024) New human capital theory from the perspective of time allocation: evolution and prospects. Prosperitas, 11(2), Article 4
UNESCO (2024) The challenges of AI in higher education and institutional leadership
UNESCO (2025) Artificial intelligence in education. UNESCO digital education initiative. Retrieved from https://www.unesco.org/en/digital-education/artificial-intelligence
World Bank (2025) AI in schools: opportunities and challenges in Europe and Central Asia. Retrieved from https://www.worldbank.org/en/programs/vienna-development-knowledge-center/brief/ai-in-schools-opportunities-challenges-realities-for-the-future-of-learning
World Economic Forum (2025) Fortifying human capital against artificial intelligence
Zam X (2025) AI in education: global trends and insights. LinkedIn Pulse. https://www.linkedin.com/pulse/ai-education-global-trends-insights-from-mayjune-2025-dr-zam-yr5mc/

AI's Future Directions in Human Capital Development, Academic Progress and Doctoral Research

Alexandru Constăngioara

Abstract This chapter examines the role that is critical of human capital development, progress in academic spheres, and doctoral research in the shaping of a sustainable integration for artificial intelligence (AI) within the sectors of finance, accounting, and business administration in Romania and Hungary. A theme that is central is the gap which has been identified between the potential offered by AI and the current state of competencies at a professional level and structures within education. The chapter identifies further inefficiencies of a structural nature within the ecosystems for academic research in both countries: Romania and Hungary, including disparities in the output of publications, a concentration of resources in geographic terms, and limitations in the funding for doctoral studies, which collectively act to restrict the scale and the impact of inquiry that is scholarly.

1 Introduction

The embedding of artificial intelligence into finance, accounting, and business administration happens increasingly, reshaping the professional roles, the processes for decision-making, and the organizational strategies. In Romania and Hungary, this transformation is taking place under specific institutional, cultural, and economic constraints characteristic for the Central and Eastern Europe.

While both of the countries demonstrate growing engagement with AI research and policy initiatives, the pace together with the depth of adoption are varying significantly across the sectors and regions. Existing scholarship underlines that the technological capability alone is not enough; rather, the success of AI implementation depends in primary way on human capital, institutional readiness, and academic capacity (Vărzaru 2022a; Zaharia 2024).

A. Constăngioara (✉)
Faculty of Economic Sciences, University of Oradea, Oradea, Romania
e-mail: alexandru.co@gmail.com

C. Sabău-Popa (ed.), *Artificial Intelligence in Finance, Accounting and Business Administration*, Contributions to Finance and Accounting,
https://doi.org/10.1007/978-3-032-22737-9_22

Consequently, the research perspectives and future directions must give priority to development of skills, reform in education, and doctoral research as the foundational pillars for a sustainable AI integration.

2 AI Implementation and Institutional Context

Empirical studies from Romania and Hungary reveal that AI applications are the most advanced in the domains of accounting, finance, and selected business operations, meanwhile education and public administration stay at exploratory or pilot stages (Banţa et al. 2022; Bucea-Manea-Ţoniş et al. 2022). In Romania, the research activity concentrates in major academic centers like for example Bucharest University of Economic Studies, having strong links to multinational firms and also the IT&C sector. Hungarian AI research is similarly centralized, being located predominantly in Budapest through such institutions like Eötvös Loránd Research Network and SZTAKI, what limits the diffusion of innovation toward peripheral regions (Gyulai et al. 2022).

Across both countries, the AI technologies find use for fraud detection, robotic process automation, decision support, and predictive analytics in accounting and finance, often integrating with enterprise systems as for example SAP (Vărzaru 2022a; Banţa et al. 2022). In business administration, AI gives support for marketing personalization, optimization of processes, and smart industry applications, while the educational uses focus on personalized learning, automation of administration, and analysis of student performance (Pisică et al. 2023; Dietz 2020). These uneven levels of implementation underline the importance of institutional maturity and readiness of workforce as main determinants for the success of adoption.

3 Human Capital Development and Skills Transformation

The development of human capital is consistently identified like the primary challenge and also the opportunity associated to AI implementation. In accounting and finance, AI automates the routine tasks, shifting the professional roles towards analytical judgement, strategic decision-making, and interpretation of data (Vărzaru 2022a). This transformation demands hybrid competencies that combine accounting expertise with digital skills, cognitive skills, and skills for systems-thinking (Banţa et al. 2022). Instead of eliminating the employment, AI restructures the profiles of jobs, reducing the demand for roles with low skills while increases the demand for professionals having advanced analytical and technological capabilities.

In the education, the confidence of teachers and the perceived usefulness of AI are stronger predictors for adoption than the technical proficiency alone (Pisică et al. 2023; Bucea-Manea-Ţoniş et al. 2022). Educators from Romania and Hungary report frequently insufficient training in AI and digital pedagogy, what constrains an effective integration despite recognition of the potential benefits. These findings suggest that the programs for professional development must prioritize the building of confidence, adaptation of pedagogy, and awareness of ethics, not only the technical instruction.

In the IT&C and business sectors, the neuroleadership has emerged as a relevant framework for managing the organizational change driven by AI. The research indicates that the leadership styles which emphasize learning, adaptability, and psychological safety are facilitating the acceptance of AI systems by employees and also enhance the capacity for innovation (Stăneiu et al. 2024). This intersection between AI, leadership, and human capital development represents a promising avenue for the advanced academic research.

4 Educational Reform and Academic Progress

The reform in education is a critical mechanism for sustaining the human capital development enabled by AI. Studies are emphasizing the need to integrate the AI literacy, ethics, and skills for problem-solving into the curricula starting from early educational stages until higher education and professional training (Zaharia 2024; Dietz 2020). Universities are encouraged to introduce interdisciplinary courses which combine technical knowledge with communication, analysis of systems, and strategic thinking, aligning in this way the academic output with the demands from labor market.

The output of academic research in AI knows an expansion, as evidenced by bibliometric analyses examining over one thousand publications about AI and education based on competencies (Zaharia 2024). However, the structural inefficiencies are persisting. Romania exhibits a gap between the number of researchers and the output of publications, while the research productivity of Hungary is constrained by geographic concentration and limited capacity in provinces. Although exists institutional co-financing of doctoral programs, many studies report a reliance on internal funding instead of competitive research grants, limiting the scale and the ambition of doctoral projects.

5 Benefits, Barriers, and Ethical Considerations

The benefits from AI implementation include gains in efficiency, improved quality of decisions, enhanced outcomes in learning, and support for innovation. In education, AI reduces the burdens of administration, enables the personalized learning, and improves the engagement of students (Bucea-Manea-Ţoniş et al. 2022). In accounting and finance, AI enhances the detection of fraud, reporting in real-time, and the accuracy of analytics (Vărzaru 2022b).

Despite these advantages, the barriers remain substantial. The financial constraints are affecting approximately one-third of Romanian SMEs, while shortages of skills, resistance to change, and limited strategic vision are hindering adoption across sectors (Călinescu 2024). Ethical concerns related to privacy of data, bias in algorithms, and displacement of jobs are pervasive and are influencing significantly the trust and acceptance (Vărzaru 2022b). Addressing these challenges demands clear regulatory frameworks, guidelines for ethics, and responsible practices for management of human resources.

6 Doctoral Research Opportunities and Future Directions

The doctoral research plays a central role for advancing the knowledge about AI implementation in finance, accounting, and business administration. Promising directions for research include the development of maturity models for organizational AI adoption, longitudinal studies which track the trajectories of implementation, and comparative research examining the cross-cultural influences on acceptance and effectiveness. Neuroleadership and the human capital development enabled by AI represent particularly fertile areas for doctoral inquiry, making a bridge between management, psychology, and research in information systems (Stăneiu et al. 2024).

In education, the doctoral studies should move beyond the analysis of adoption towards a rigorous evaluation of learning outcomes, examining how the infrastructure, the design of curriculum, the preparation of teachers, and the assessment are interacting to shape the effectiveness of AI. In accounting and finance, the research is needed on decision-making assisted by AI, mitigation of bias, and impacts on performance across different institutional contexts.

7 Long-Term Research Agenda and Conclusion

A coherent agenda for long-term research requires a sustained investment in academic capacity, expanded funding for doctoral studies, and strengthened international collaboration. European initiatives like Digital Innovation Hubs and research networks cross-border provide valuable platforms, but their integration into the training for doctoral students stays underdeveloped. Dedicated doctoral programs, competitive fellowships, and partnerships between industry and academy are essential for to translate the AI research into value for society and economy.

In conclusion, the integration of AI in Romanian and Hungarian finance, accounting, and business administration depends in fundamental way on human capital development more than on technological capability alone. The reform in education, the academic progress, and the doctoral research are not concerns of peripheral nature but central determinants for sustainable AI adoption. The future research must prioritize, therefore, the interdisciplinary inquiry, the ethical responsibility, and the guidance for policy based on evidence for to ensure that AI gives contribution to organizational effectiveness and flourishing of humans.

References

Banţa V, Rîndaşu S-M, Tănasie A, Cojocaru D (2022) Artificial intelligence in the accounting of international businesses: A perception-based approach. Sustainability 14(11):1–12

Bucea-Manea-Ţoniş R, Kuleto V, Gudei SCD, Lianu C, Lianu C, Ilić MP, Păun D (2022) Artificial intelligence potential in higher education institutions enhanced learning environment in Romania and Serbia. Sustainability 14(10):5842

Călinescu G (2024) Artificial intelligence–opportunities and challenges for small and medium enterprises in Romania. A case study on the Exonia Group. In: Proceedings of the International Conference on Business Excellence, vol 18, no 1. Sciendo, pp 1363–1371

Dietz F (2020) A mesterséges intelligencia az oktatásban: Kihívások és lehetőségek. Scientia Et Securitas 1(2):151–162

Gyulai T, Nagy M, Cibu-Buzac R (2022) Smart development with digital intelligent cities in cross-border regions. Pandémia—Fenntartható gazdálkodás—Környezettudatosság 1:45–58

Pisică AI, Edu T, Zaharia RM, Zaharia R (2023) Implementing artificial intelligence in higher education: pros and cons from the perspectives of academics. Societies 13(5):118. https://doi.org/10.3390/soc13050118

Stăneiu RM, Stratone ME, Dabija DC, Mititean P (2024) Leveraging neuroleadership and adopting AI to improve human capital development in IT&C business organisations. Amfiteatru Economic 26(67):721–740

Vărzaru AA (2022a) Assessing artificial intelligence technology acceptance in managerial accounting. Electronics 11(14):2256

Vărzaru AA (2022b) Assessing the impact of AI solutions' ethical issues on performance in managerial accounting. Electronics 11(14):2221

Zaharia R (2024) Challenges for competence-oriented education in the context of the development of artificial intelligence systems. Amfiteatru Economic 26(65):6–11

Glossary

Project title: *Exchange of Experience for research and usage of Artificial Intelligence' Advanced Techniques in finance, accounting and business administration in Bihor-Hajdu Bihar Region, JEMS code: ROHU00120*
Lead partner: *University of Oradea, Faculty of Economic Sciences*
Publishing date: *February 2026*
The project is funded by the European Union un- der the Interreg fund and co-financed by Romania and Hungary.
The responsibility for the content of this material is that of the author(s).
The content of this material does not necessarily represent the official position of the European Union.

C. Sabău-Popa (ed.), *Artificial Intelligence in Finance, Accounting and Business Administration*, Contributions to Finance and Accounting,
https://doi.org/10.1007/978-3-032-22737-9

MIX
Papier aus verantwortungsvollen Quellen
Paper from responsible sources
FSC® C105338

If you have any concerns about our products,
you can contact us on
ProductSafety@springernature.com

In case Publisher is established outside the EU,
the EU authorized representative is:
Springer Nature Customer Service Center GmbH
Europaplatz 3, 69115 Heidelberg, Germany

Printed by Libri Plureos GmbH
in Hamburg, Germany